A Quick Index to Twenty Essential Questions

BUILDING TYPE BASICS FOR

College and University Facilities

BUILDING TYPE BASICS

Books are available for each of the following:

BANKS AND FINANCIAL INSTITUTIONS
By Homer Williams

ELEMENTARY AND SECONDARY SCHOOLS, SECOND EDITION
By Bradford Perkins

HEALTHCARE FACILITIES, SECOND EDITION
By Richard L. Kobus, Ronald L. Skaggs, Michael Bobrow, Julia Thomas, Thomas M. Payette, Stephen A. Kliment

HOUSING, SECOND EDITION
By Joan Goody, Robert Chandler, John Clancy, David Dixon, and Geoffrey Wooding

PLACES OF WORSHIP
By Nicholas W. Roberts

RECREATIONAL FACILITIES
By Richard J. Diedrich

RESEARCH LABORATORIES, SECOND EDITION
By Daniel D. Watch, Stephen A. Kliment, Perkins & Will

SENIOR LIVING, SECOND EDITION
By Perkins Eastman

TRANSIT FACILITIES
By Kenneth W. Griffin

BUILDING TYPE BASICS FOR

College and University Facilities

Second Edition

DAVID J. NEUMAN FAIA, LEED AP

WILEY

Cover image: Medical Education Building at the University of Virginia
Building: Claude Moore Medical Education Building
Architect: CO Architects
Photograph: © Robert Canfield
Cover design: Anne-Michele Abbott

This book is printed on acid-free paper. ♾

Published by John Wiley & Sons, Inc., Hoboken, New Jersey
Published simultaneously in Canada

Library of Congress Cataloging-in-Publication Data:
Neuman, David J.
Building type basics for college and university facilities / David J. Neuman.—Second Edition.
pages cm
Includes index.
ISBN 978-1-118-00802-7 (cloth); ISBN 978-1-118-33019-7 (ebk); ISBN 978-1-118-33120-0 (ebk);
ISBN 978-1-118-33291-7 (ebk); ISBN 978-1-118-44376-7 (ebk); ISBN 978-1-118-44380-4 (ebk)
1. College buildings. 2. Campus planning. 3. College facilities—Planning. I. Title.
NA6600.N48 2013
727'.3—dc23

2012017301

Printed in the United States of America
10 9 8 7 6 5 4 3 2 1

CONTENTS

ACKNOWLEDGMENTS

David Neuman thanks Erinn A. Scheibel for her expertise, enthusiasm, and just plain "hard work," not only on Chapter 1, but also on the entire book; Danielle MacGregor and Alexander Howle, student interns, who assisted me and the other chapter authors in the initiation of this book with equal levels of energy and diligence.

David Nelson would like to thank Sophie Izon, Rebecca Roke, and Matthew Foreman for their assistance.

Steve Farneth would like to thank Cora Palmer for her support and assistance.

Graham Wyatt thanks Mark Loeffler and Mark Holden for their insights related to lighting and AV/IT systems, and Delia Conache, who is responsible for Robert A.M. Stern Architects' ever-expanding collection of classroom diagrams, many of which are featured in this book.

John Ruble and Jeanne Chen wish to thank Willie Brown, Tom Hier, Larry Moneta, and Marty Redman for inspiring a discussion of housing issues, and Victoria Lam for constant creative input to our conception and organization of the chapter.

David Body acknowledges Roy Viklund AIA as author of content retained from the previous edition and also Cynthia Hilliers, Tina Pietrobon, Christopher Whitcomb, and Lavonia Allen for their advice and support.

Brenda Levin would like to thank Margaret Bach, Delyte Adams-Lawrence, Cameron Izuno, and Alice Valania for their assistance in the preparation of their chapter.

William Rawn and Cliff Gayley thank Mark Oldham for his advice on technical issues and Kate McCoubrey for her editorial assistance.

CHAPTER 1

CAMPUS PLANNING

David J. Neuman, FAIA, LEED BD + C

OVERVIEW

Campus planning, architecture, and landscape are critical topics at every university and college with a physical setting, for three important reasons:

- They create the *actual environment* that supports the mission and goals of the institution.
- They define the tangible *identity* that the institution portrays to its alumni, faculty, students (both current and future), and the general public.
- They assist in portraying the level of *sustainability* commitment made by the institution.

In short, an academic institution's campus is a critical component of its very existence and survival. This volume is dedicated to translating this important fact into practical terms at the levels of planning, design, and implementation. The chapter authors have each contributed to the phenomenon known as the *campus* through specific plans, buildings, and landscapes, each of which has in its own way contributed to the further development of this unique environment.

While designing the University of Virginia, Thomas Jefferson described his goal as the creation of an "Academical Village" (see Figure 1.1). This term expressed Jefferson's own views on education and planning, but it also summarizes a basic trait of American higher education from the colonial period to the twenty-first century: the conception of colleges and universities as communities in themselves—in effect, as cities in microcosm. This reflects educational patterns and ideals which, although derived principally from Europe, have developed in distinctively American ways.

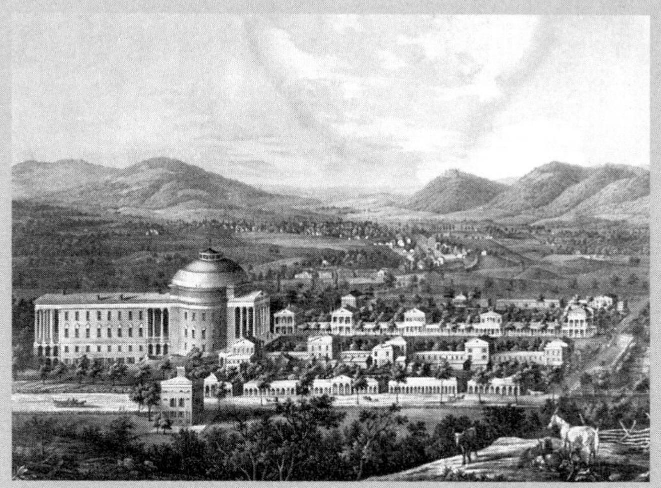

Figure 1.1 "View of the University of Virginia, Charlottesville, & Monticello," from the west. Edward Sachse, draftsman; Casimir Bohn, publisher, 1856. Courtesy of the Albert and Shirley Small Special Collections Library, University of Virginia.

Campuses have their origins in the Western tradition of the Greek *agora* and in the Socratic approach of open debate in the public realm. The term *campus* itself was derived from the Greek terminology for a "green" or open landscaped area, and later, the Roman military "camp" of well-planned order. At once, the concept represents a paradox of freedom and control that continues to this day. Although the Greeks may have viewed the campus as a setting to spur the commerce of ideas, the Romans saw its order in terms of colonization and a way to bring their brand of civilization to the conquered "barbarians." This approach is not unlike that of the early British colonists wanting to establish colleges in the fledgling communities in the American wilderness for instruction of not only their own children but also the native population after it had been "pacified" (see Figure 1.2).

▼ *Figure 1.2 Woodcut print depicting the teaching of Native Americans and American colonists.*

The new colleges symbolized both a continuation of cultural roots and a belief in the future of the pioneering spirit. The campus itself became the symbol or icon of the college and, later, the university.

Although the overall character of a university's physical plant can be simply a result of growth and change, a well-functioning and icon-laden campus results only when it is carefully planned and keenly managed. The qualities of such a place may be described as follows:

- Enduring planning framework
- Compelling landscape character
- Context-sensitive architecture
- Consistent perimeter treatment
- Carefully managed interface among all of these elements

The key is to incorporate these principles rigorously in every decision related to campus planning, from small to large. It is this "sense of place" in its entirety that makes for a campus's intelligibility, functionality, and overall aesthetic. Thus, relatively simple matters, such as maintaining a consistent sign system or a standard exterior light fixture, are important components to the appearance and sense of order of the campus. Some have argued that the campus itself has transcended into the realm of art. "Unlike the two-dimensional art of painting, the three-dimensional art of sculpture, and architecture, in which the fourth dimension is function, a campus has a fifth dimension: planning. The well-planned campus belongs among the most idyllic of man-made environments and deserves to be evaluated by the same criteria applied to these other works of art," wrote Thomas Gaines in 1991.

The campus is not just leftover spaces between buildings. It is, in fact, a series of designed places that reflect the values of an institution's wishes to be known for. It is a culturally dynamic, complex landscape setting. The campus must be a place that feels safe, encourages participation, enhances social interaction and appeals to students, faculty, staff and visitors on many levels [see Figure 1.3].

—Dayton Reuter, State University of New York

Those who carry on the mundane daily activities of operating and (re)developing the typical campus may balk at this statement; however, others have for years asserted the campus's role as *utopia.* This role carries with it not only the expectation of striving for physical perfection but also the spiritual

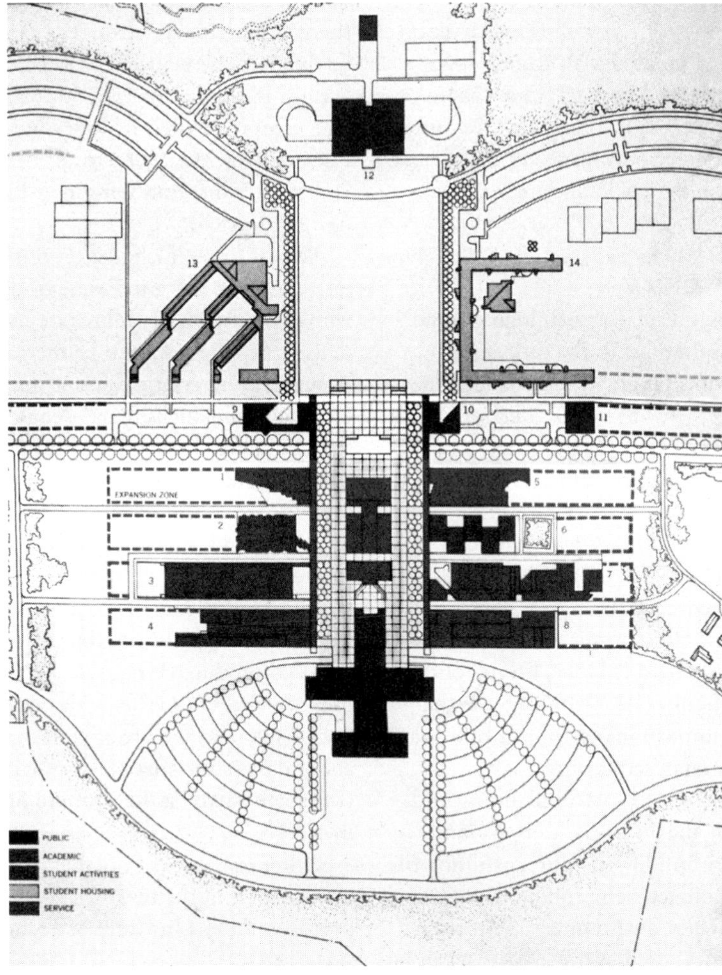

Figure 1.3 State University of New York, Purchase. Master plan by Edward Larrabee Barnes.

sense of enduring faith in human "improvement." This serious responsibility was once shouldered by our cities, but seemingly has now been lost in the postmodern era of globalization and exurban development.

A public or private institution such as a college or university, occupying its own tract of land . . . is peculiarly well situated to reap the inestimable fruits of forethought and skill in planning. Nowhere is it more essential to have the physical plant beautiful and well-knit together; nowhere should it be more feasible to enlist the careful thought of well-trained minds, to weigh and reconcile all component parts, to profit by the past, to measure accurately the present, to forecast the future as well as it can be forecast. . . . [We] have called this kind of planning an art; it is also a science.

—Charles Z. Klauder and Herbert C. Wise, 1929

Can campuses reach for such high ground? Certainly, aspirations to the utopian can be read into works ranging from Klauder and Wise's *College Architecture in America* (1929) to *Architectural Planning of the American College* by Larson and Palmer (1933) to Paul V. Turner's seminal work, *Campus: An American Planning Tradition* (1984), to *American Place* by M. Perry Chapman (2006). Moreover, Robert A. M. Stern's *Pride of Place: Building the American Dream* (1986) and Richard P. Dober's series of campus-related books (1962–2000) place the American campus squarely in this role as a model for human settlement.

The result of this careful planning and execution by means of the campus landscape and its buildings is often assumed to be at best a didactic environment. In 1923, the Commission on Architecture of the Association of American Colleges asserted that "a grouping of buildings, on a properly designed campus, constructed in accordance with simple and chaste architectural standards, has an art and a life value which the students . . . will assimilate unconsciously. . . . [Therefore,] it is possible for every college, even with limited means at its disposal, to contribute to the elevation of life by careful attention to its campus program."

Although Jefferson, his confidants Benjamin Latrobe and William Thornton, and many others have shared this concept, there is perhaps no stronger example than in the development of the Frank Lloyd Wright–designed Florida Southern College campus, which its longtime president, Ludd Spivey, described in part in 2001 as "[a] great education temple in Florida" (see Figure 1.4).

Wright himself labored on this project for more than 20 years, some of the time without compensation, because he believed that a truly site-responsive American architecture was necessary to foster the American ideals of individualism and democracy. Although he was never able to complete his goal of "Broadacre City," he came to believe that "When Florida Southern College as now planned becomes a reality—the great future will have begun in earnest." In fact, not only was the physical campus to work well as a college and be economical to build, it would produce, Wright believed, ". . . new clarity, the chord between Florida character and beauty and the life of your many boys and girls—as they have it day by day with you down there," as he wrote to Spivey in 1941.

Other examples of notable newer campuses begun in the twentieth century range from the Illinois Institute of Technology

Figure 1.4 Florida Southern College, Lakeland. Rendering of master plan for the campus begun in 1938 by Frank Lloyd Wright. Copyright © 1942, 1988, 1994, 2001 The Frank Lloyd Wright Foundation, Scottsdale, Arizona.

(1938–1940) by Ludwig Mies van der Rohe to the U.S. Air Force Academy (1954) by Walter Netsch of Skidmore Owings and Merrill, Philip Johnson's neo-Jeffersonian University of St. Thomas (1956), and William L. Pereira's circular plan, derived from the Garden City concept of Ebenezer Howard, for the University of California, Irvine (1963). Each of these examples underscores the belief that a well-ordered campus environment is critical to its educational mission and the well-being of its users; it is modernism's version of utopia (see Figures 1.5–1.7).

These plans, as well as a host of other new campus plans created in the last several decades, have their critics, especially among those who regard them as too rigorous in their order and/or too monolithic in scale. In many instances, these may be valid criticisms, but they should not lead to an opposite belief—that disorder and haphazard physical development are better. One needs only to look at the many originally well-planned campuses of the nineteenth and early twentieth centuries that have been victimized subsequently by lack of planning to see the general chaos, poor image, and inefficient land use that resulted. A balance between a commitment to order and an ability to adapt to changing needs is the better option to pursue.

▸ *Figure 1.5 Aerial view of the U.S. Air Force Academy, Colorado Springs, Colorado, 1962, by Skidmore Owings and Merrill.*

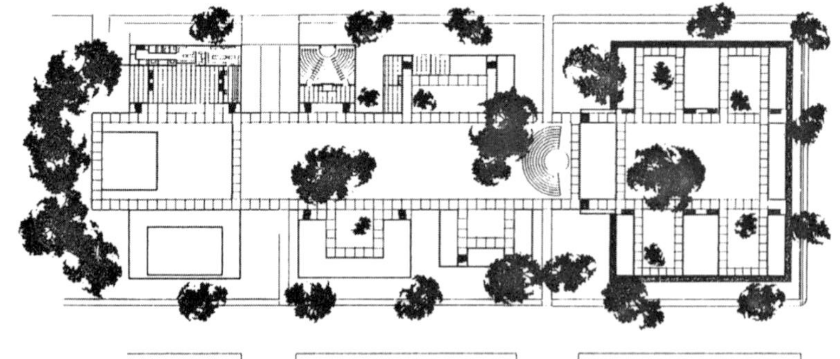

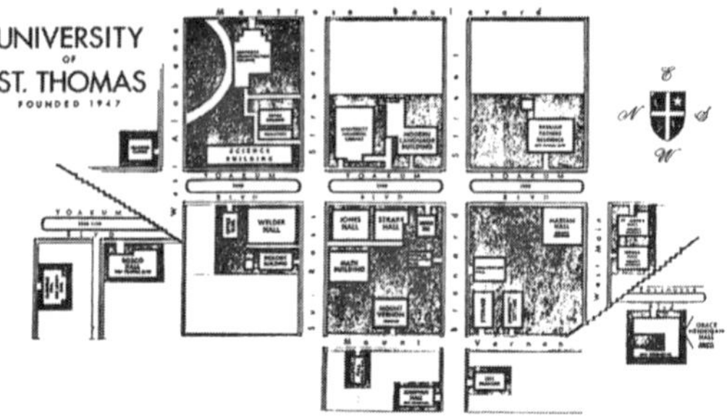

▸ *Figure 1.6 University of St. Thomas, Houston, Texas. Site drawings of the campus plan by Philip Johnson.* Courtesy of the University of St. Thomas.

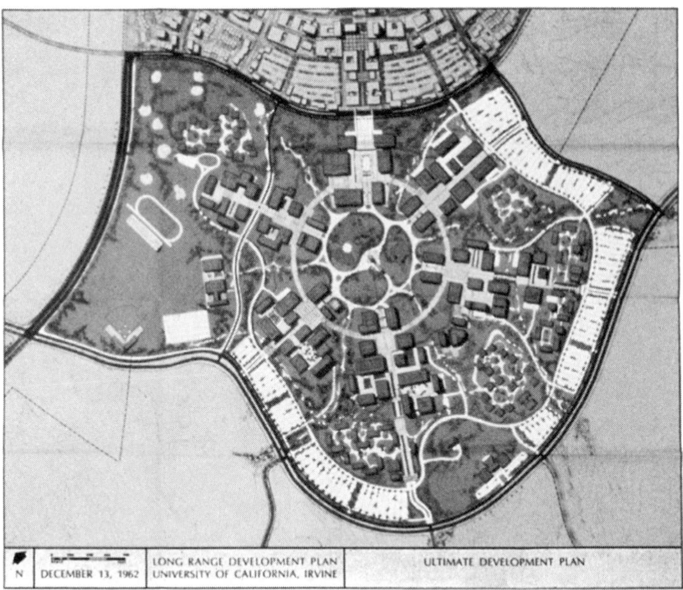

◀ *Figure 1.7 Long-range development plan, University of California, Irvine, 1963, by William L. Pereira Associates.* Courtesy of the University of California, Irvine.

CAMPUS PLANNING **CASE STUDY 1**

LONG RANGE DEVELOPMENT PLAN
University of California, Merced

Planner: Office of Physical Planning, Design and Construction, University of California, Merced
Consultant planner: RACESTUDIO
Distinction: 2011 Honor Award: Planning for an Established Campus, Society for College and University Planning
(See Figure 1.8)

> *UC Merced is committed to developing a physical presence that will model a healthier future for the region and the world . . . this approach will produce a campus whose urban planning, architecture, infrastructure, and landscape are uniquely regional in character and responses, while modeling sustainable design excellence on a global scale.*
>
> —Richard Cummings, University of California, Merced, principal planner

Project Objectives

1. Meet anticipated increases in enrollment demand for the University of California.
2. Serve historically underrepresented populations and regions.
3. Model environmental stewardship.
4. Avoid unnecessary costs.
5. Maximize academic distinction.
6. Create an efficient and vital teaching and learning environment.
7. Attract high-quality faculty.
8. Provide a high-quality campus setting.
9. Accommodate student housing needs.
10. Provide student support facilities.
11. Provide athletic and recreational opportunities.
12. Ensure community integration.

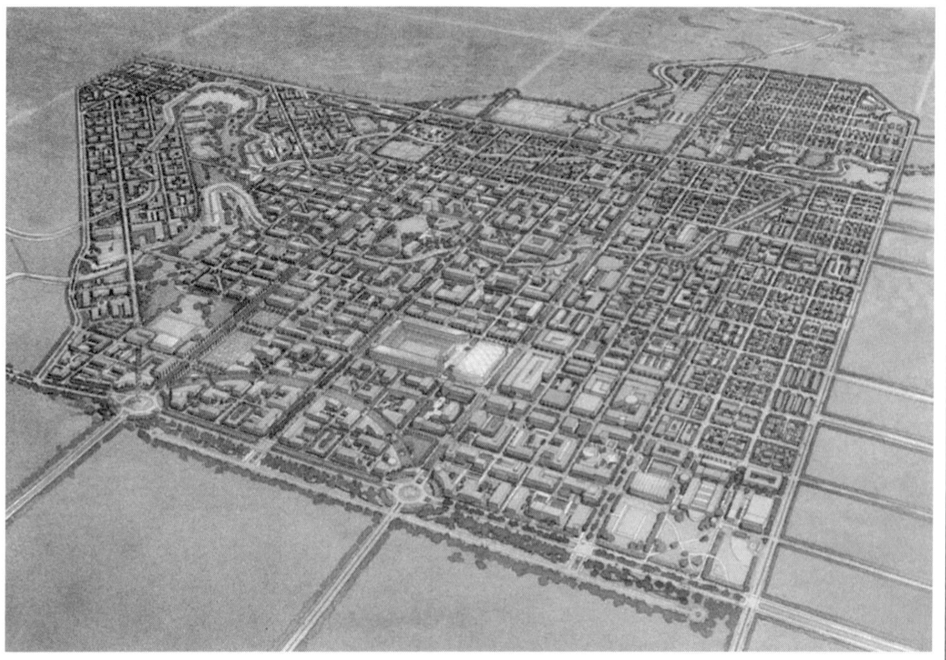

Figure 1.8 UC Merced plan. Bruce A. Race, FAIA, AICP, RACESTUDIO.

13. Provide regional harmony and reflect the San Joaquin Valley's heritage and landscape.

Areas of Focus

- A compact, pedestrian-oriented campus
- Distinct academic, residential, and research communities
- Natural, low-water environments
- Multimodal circulation
- Distributed services and utilities

(See Figure 1.9)

Figure 1.9 Town and gown district. Bruce A. Race, FAIA, AICP, RACESTUDIO.

PROGRAMS AND PLANS

Although this book emphasizes buildings, addressing both their specific planning and design requirements, overall planning for the campus environs, accomplished in four tiers, must occur to ensure success.

Four Tiers of Planning

The broadest tier is overall *land use planning*. As government agencies or specially appointed authorities, at the federal, state, and/or local levels, generally control land use patterns at most campuses, this is the critical basis for all physical planning. Increasingly, this level of planning is called "framework planning," in which the various elements of land qualities, infrastructure, existing development, and so on are outlined into a "framework" for use in future strategic planning efforts.

CAMPUS PLANNING
CASE STUDY 2

ONE OHIO STATE FRAMEWORK PLAN THE OHIO STATE UNIVERSITY, COLUMBUS

Consultant planners: Sasaki Associates
Distinction: 2011 Institutional Innovation and Integration Award, Society for College and University Planning, 2010

Fundamental Strategies

- Empower agile decision making.
- Concentrate academic activity.
- Regenerate the core.
- Invest in civic infrastructure.
- Transform the River and Green reserve.
- Strengthen connections and identity.
- Enhance residential life, neighborhoods, and recreation.
- Promote partnerships.

Civil Infrastructure

- Invest in infrastructure, transportation, transit, and open space.
- Develop a pedestrian core.
- Make the campus navigable with a restored street network and dynamic wayfinding.
- Park once (or not at all) using remote high-density parking areas.

One University

- Be transinstitutional.
- Ensure academic mission drives the physical environment.
- Integrate strategic, physical, and financial activity.
- Concentrate activity.

Space

- Build no net new academic space.
- Prioritize adaptive reuse and renovation.
- Link space allocation to utilization.

Practice

- Enable agile, data-informed decision making.
- Require that projects meet multiple goals.
- Develop partnerships that complement the academic mission.
- Decrease energy use and identify alternate energy sources, promote transportation options, enhance water resources, champion natural habitats, and manage material use.

Campus Life

- Create 24/7 campus.
- Improve existing on-campus residential districts; do not create new ones.
- Recognize the whole campus as part of the learning environment.
- Enhance neighborhoods in support of live/work philosophy.

(See Figure 1.10)

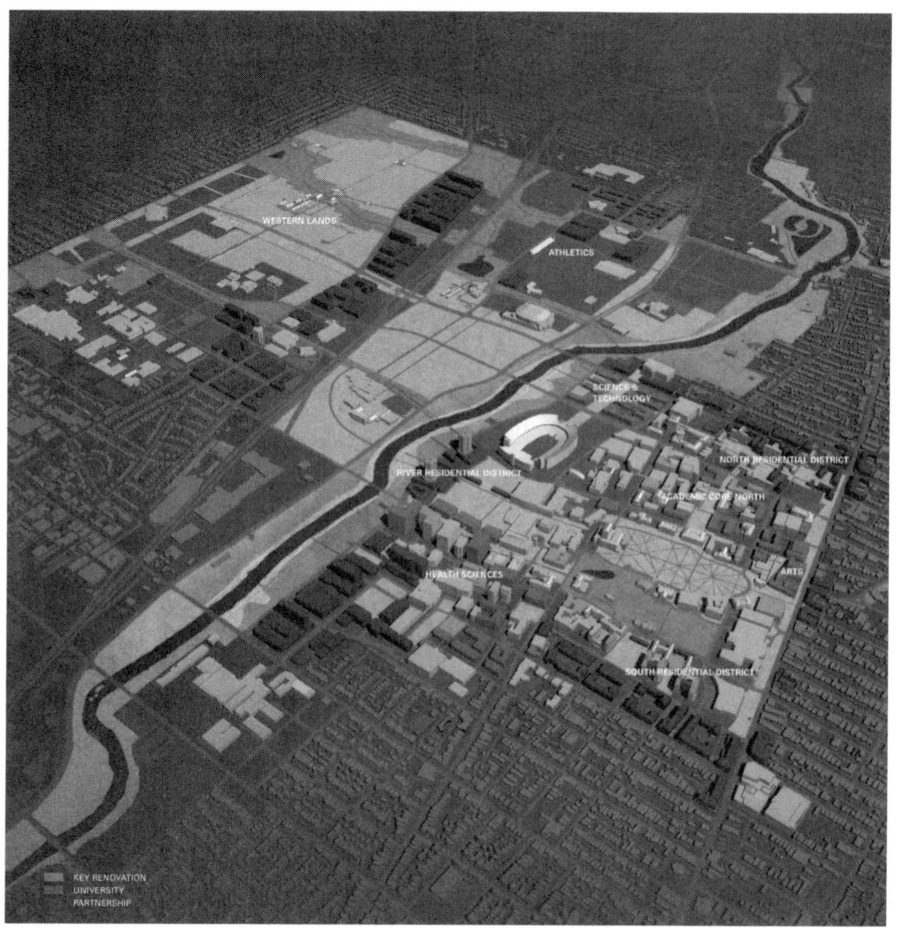

▸ *Figure 1.10 Long-term vision.* The Ohio State University and Sasaki Associates.

Land use planning must be distinguished from *campus planning*, which reflects specific urban design intentions. Within the campus plan is *district/precinct planning*, which views the campus at the scale of the neighborhood or specific program affinity level (e.g., sciences or engineering; residential or athletics; etc.). Next comes *site planning* designed to fit each individual facility into the overall fabric. All of these lead to the point where every new (and renewal) project contributes to building a campus that is greater than the sum of its individual parts.

Underpinning these levels of physical planning are the core academic and support programs themselves as well as the specialized plans linked to the campus infrastructure, ranging from utilities to food service to transportation. (See Figure 1.11) Plans as diverse as Frederick Law Olmsted's for Stanford University in 1888, which appears to borrow from Arturo Soria y Mata's concept

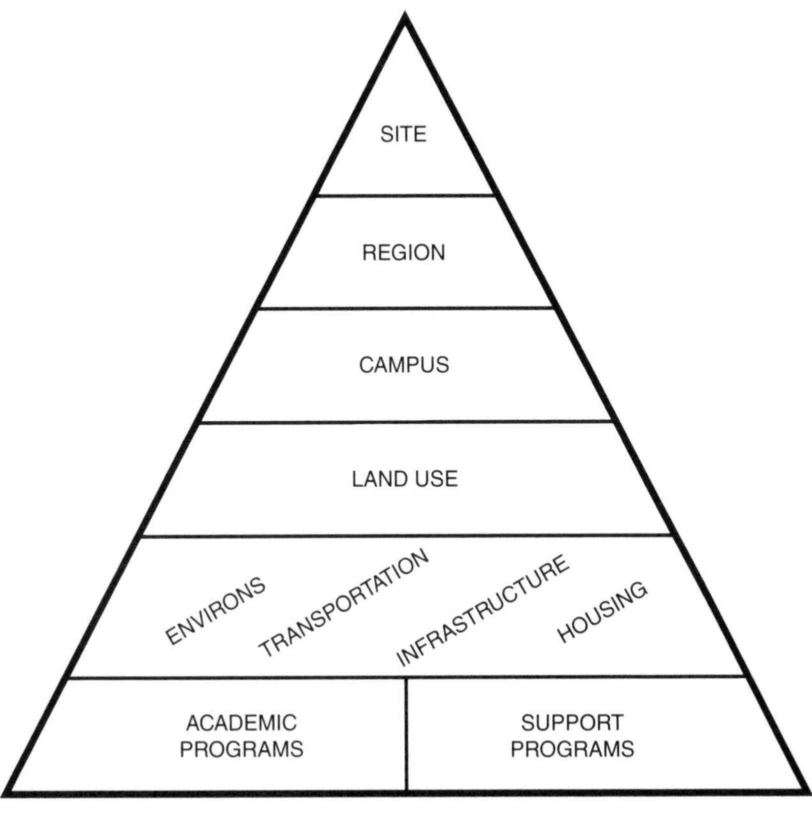

◀ *Figure 1.11 Integration of planning levels.* David J. Neuman, FAIA.

of the ordered "linear city" along a planned transportation mall (see Figure 1.12), to Edward Durrell Stone's plan for the State University of New York at Albany in 1962, with its well-distanced sea of parking lots, illustrate the inherent order that supporting infrastructure of various types can demand of a campus, especially in an era of fast-evolving technologies (see Figure 1.13).

Program Areas

Every educational campus has at minimum two core program areas: *academic* and *administrative.* Each has its own requirements determined by the size and complexity of its mission—from small college to major research university. A small college may be as basic in its mission as to have only a few hundred students engaged in learning traditional liberal arts; while a major public research university may have tens of thousands of full- and part-time students at all levels of study and research, in hundreds of specific and customized programs at several distinct campus locations. This academic diversity, in turn, drives the level of administrative and support needs. Basic services, such as admissions, registration, and facility operations, are augmented many times to meet the demands of increasingly diverse

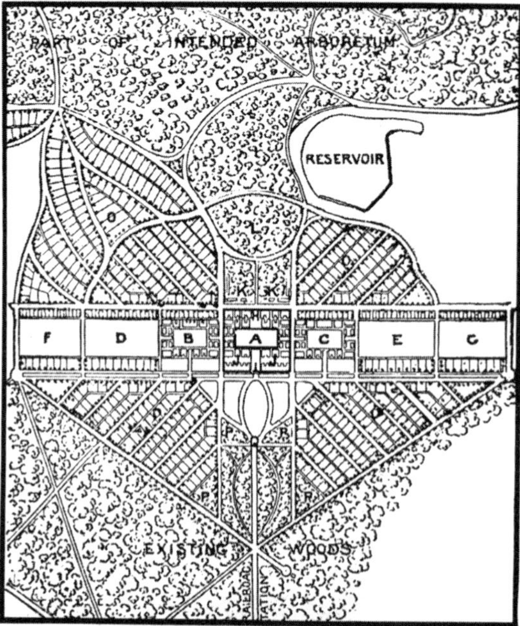

▶ *Figure 1.12 Stanford University, Stanford, California, Olmsted illustration, 1888.* Courtesy of Stanford University.

▶ *Figure 1.13 State University of New York, Albany, by Edward Durrell Stone. Aerial photograph of the campus, 1992.* Courtesy of the University Archives, University Libraries, University at Albany, State University of New York.

student bodies and very sophisticated academic programs.

Three additional program areas have grown to such a degree as to be considered separately in defining an institution's overall program: *housing, recreation/athletics,* and *student services.* Each has specific facility needs as well as specific land use relationships to the others and to the core academic and administrative programs. In developing (or reviewing) an institution's plans at any level, the fundamental programs in all five areas must be understood by the assigned planning team for the results to function in the near term and to be sustainable in the long term.

In the past, the decision to have a campus housing program was often voluntary. An academic institution could decide whether a resident population of students, faculty, and/or staff would enhance the core academic mission. Rural (and some suburban) institutions generally had little choice but to have student housing, if they were to attract students. Urban institutions could choose not to have a residential component because available rental housing existed nearby or might be developed by independent real estate interests. Economic conditions have changed to the point that nearly every institution, small or large, must now provide some form of housing services. This may range from rental subsidies and off-campus rental directories and placement assistance to on-campus accommodations, such as traditional dormitories, fraternity/sorority/co-op houses, and apartments for students, with even condominiums and single-family houses for faculty and staff.

The reasons for this shift from "voluntary" to "necessary" on-campus or campus-controlled residential programs are the conditions of the local real estate market, a desire to have residential learning programs, or both. Local housing markets must be gauged in relationship to student, faculty, and staff incomes. Residential education allows for a specific, often intensive, approach to an in-depth learning experience, particularly at the undergraduate level. Thus, from nearly every institution's perspective, land use planning now embraces three necessary program areas: academic, administrative, and residential.

For most institutions, the program list has also grown to include both recreation/athletics and student services. Increasingly, students, as well as faculty and staff, have insisted on recreational programs and related facilities to complement traditional collegiate athletic facilities for organized sports at both the intramural and varsity levels. The number of sports teams and their specialized facilities has burgeoned because of the diversity of interests and as a result of the legal requirements of Title IX, which mandates equality of opportunities for both men and women. In addition, in many students' minds, recreation has become synonymous with good health and attractive appearance. This has led to the expansion of traditional athletic venues, such as gymnasiums, sports fields, and aquatics facilities, as well as specialized recreation and exercise facilities for dance, aerobics, and strength training. In addition, faculty and staff have demanded (and received access to) recreational facilities to support their own interests and wellness.

An increase in returning and other nontraditional students has expanded the demand for student-related services such as child care, commuter student locker and study areas, career counseling, and financial aid assistance to the point where the planning and facilities development for these types of specialized programs are a major commitment on many campuses. Despite the advent of e-learning and the virtual campus, most colleges have not seen these approaches to learning replace traditional on-campus facility needs. Rather, colleges have had to provide additional services, often to nontraditional students, to satisfy the rising expectations created by the digital revolution and the World Wide Web. These new requirements range from providing convenient Wi-Fi access in many campus locations (e.g., classrooms, libraries, student centers, and student rooms) to creating more readily accessible student service programs—for example, specialized financial counseling. This new definition of student services has thus spawned a facility-oriented program of its own, which often overlays the core programs and increasingly commands its own specialized buildings, such as career development centers, particularly at community colleges (see Figure 1.14).

Infrastructure

No discussion of campus planning is complete without a mention of infrastructure. Infrastructure has become more than merely a support system for the core programs. It is a fundamental program of its own, with its own detailed planning and facility needs. It embraces myriad conventional utilities and specialized facilities, ranging from central plants to information technology centers to parking structures that hold a campus together, both literally and figuratively.

Although some infrastructure facilities are aboveground and visible in scale and presence, a significant amount of infrastructure is below ground, in tunnels, in duct banks, or directly buried. It is apparent only when being installed or under repair. Such facilities cannot be taken for granted. Indeed, they are becoming an

▸ *Figure 1.14 Campus Center, Foothill College, Los Altos Hills, California. Perkins + Will.* © 2008 New York Focus, LLC—www.newyorkcityfocus.com.

increasing concern because of their cost, their availability, and/or their environmental consequences. Rising energy costs, increasing demand for data service lines, global warming and sustainability, parking rates, bicycle facilities, and the like are all part of the daily milieu of a contemporary campus. Infrastructure has thus become a major concern to be debated and funded as well as balanced with the demands of other core programs.

Although these six programs (academic, administrative, housing, recreation and athletics, student services, and infrastructure) form the general basis for land use, campus, district, and site planning, many institutions add other programs that are outgrowths of their specific academic programs (e.g., a medical school has a need for a teaching hospital and related clinics). Another related development is the campus research park, where private corporations can buy or lease land and build facilities to avail themselves of the talent pool of faculty and graduate students at the host academic institution. In some cases, these facilities are made part of the overall land use plan for the institution itself.

Campuses of the future, like those in the past, must anticipate change and accommodate growth. Resultant campus planning issues are as likely to be driven by a larger student population as by rising expectations of the traditional campus community and its surrounding host community. Colleges and universities are increasingly called upon to serve "town," as well as "gown," for everything from extended learning opportunities to athletic events to performing arts and recreational facilities. Successful campuses will be those that plan accordingly and implement these public/private ventures in a spirit of openness and with an expectation of collaboration.

CAMPUS PLANNING
CASE STUDY 3

MASTER PLAN
Haverford College, Haverford, Pennsylvania

Architect/planners: VSBA, Inc.
Distinction: 2010 Honor Award, Planning for an Established Campus, Society for College and University Planning

> *The master plan will serve as a living document and decision making tool, providing guidance for the development of the college well into the future. The plan will balance our ambitions for academic and institutional development with our commitment to sustaining the physical beauty of the campus and its buildings. The plan aims to be comprehensive, historically responsive, and environmentally proactive, and to take into consideration what Haverford College has been in the past, where it is today, and where it sees itself going in the next quarter of a century.*
>
> —Haverford College Master Plan website

Key Spaces (see Figure 1.15)

College Walk

- Featherbed Orchard Walk
- Founders Green
- Green space

Campus Facts

- College founded: 1833

▸ *Figure 1.15 Plan, organizational axes.* Courtesy Venturi, Scott Brown and Associates, Inc.

- Plan completed: 2010
- Campus size: 216 acres
- Size of student body: 1,168
- Oldest planned college landscape in United States
- English gardener William Carvill laid out the grounds of the campus
- Tree to student ratio: approximately 3.25
- Arboretum campus
- Name derived from Welsh word for "goat crossing"

Key Concerns

- Preserving and maintaining historic buildings and landscape while updating them to serve evolving needs
- Providing greater degrees of accessibility, especially to those with impaired mobility
- Creating space for community activities at many different scales, campuswide
- Encouraging environmental stewardship

(See Figure 1.16)

Figure 1.16 Founders Green.

Areas of Emphasis

- Improved student residential space that includes better social space as well as needed beds
- Improved student social, activities, and performance and visual arts space; new facilities in fine arts, music, theater, exhibitions, collections; and digital media (film, photography, etc.) that serve to integrate the campus through a distributed model of arts facilities

- Improved and increased classroom, research, and academic departmental space around the Founders Green core

Founders Green is the symbolic heart and center of Haverford's campus. An important component of the plan is the realignment of the College's physical campus with its mission by returning more academic uses to buildings in and around the Green.

—Haverford College Master Plan

[W]e'll remain true to our legacy (and our promise) as we grow and adapt in ways that are informed by who and what we are, and value.

—College president Stephen Emerson, February 2008

CAMPUS PLANS, DISTRICT PLANS, AND SITE PLANS

Overall land use plans set the general direction for the development of the academic campus in much the same way as a general or comprehensive plan guides the overall development patterns and functional land use compatibilities of a city or county. For an academic institution's overall land use plan to work well, refinement and detail are required at several levels. These levels are the urban design level (*campus plan*), the neighborhood level (*district/precinct plan*), and the individual facility level (*site plan*).

Each of these physical plans and refinements is necessary to make the campus vision a reality at the individual user's level of experience and engagement. They cannot be replaced by one grand "master plan," as has been tried with very limited success in the past and, unfortunately, continues to be attempted at present. "The fixed master plan should be replaced by a physical framework that differentiates between the urban form of the campus as a whole and the opportunity for incremental, circumstantial design shifts within it." Regulating plans and sections should "define road, parking, utility, open space, and landscape configurations as the permanent physical order of a campus," as architect Stefanos Polyzoides remarked more than a decade ago; and those administering a campus must understand this over time as well.

Boards of outside experts and/or carefully structured campus/community-based committees can assist in implementing well-developed plans, but they cannot be expected to invent the plans on their own. Sound institutional planning and administrative commitment to such planning must be both long-term and dedicated.

Campus Plan and District Plans

The campus plan represents the pictorial medium for expressing the core programs and their future aspirations. It unites two-dimensional adjacencies as viewed in plan with the three-dimensional realities of topography, landscape, and building massing to bring about well-functioning and aesthetically pleasing environs. It is the urban design for a campus—*urban* as defined by a community's social welfare, and *design* as defined by creative and inspiring possibilities. It is not a "master" plan, because it must respond to change and be adaptive to new program developments and future

Figure 1.17 Campus plan, University of Wisconsin, Madison, 2005. University of Wisconsin–Madison, Ayers Saint Gross.

generations of faculty and students. Although rendered illustrations and models (traditional or digital) are needed to convey the intent of the campus plan and its urban design, these images must be more evocative than specific in content. This allows for a more strategic and creative response by subsequent campus planners and consultant-based design teams who carry out the various campus facility components over time.

The *district* or *precinct plan* becomes a more detailed vision of a particular area of the campus. It interprets the campus plan at the level of a specific campus neighborhood. This area can be defined by its use, such as a residential grouping or an academic cluster of interrelated studies and research. Plans of this type identify specific requirements to be addressed as the area grows and/or changes. Common requirements include service ways and loading docks, bicycle paths and disabled access routes, food services, shared landscape activity zones, and so forth. District plans should be used not only to verify common needs but also to execute them and to address their specificities, timing, and funding requirements. This level of planning is frequently overlooked when it is, in fact, critical to the overall implementation of the campus plan and the site planning for individual structures. (See Figure 1.18; Color Plate 1.) Because they are mid-range in concept, district plans must be updated frequently as growth occurs or programs change. These updates offer the opportunity to stage workshops in the different precincts of a campus to engage faculty, staff, and students in providing experiential feedback on the daily use of their facilities and landscapes as well as in planning the future aspects of their neighborhood.

Site Plan

Although it is a basic necessity for development of every new facility, a *site plan* is very often done in isolation from its role in campus planning. Realistically, the siting of a facility is one of the most important acts of campus planning, as it must take into account so many important criteria, such as the following:

- Conforming to existing land use, campus, and district plans

◀ *Figure 1.18 Arts Grounds plan, University of Virginia, Charlottesville. OLIN.*
Al Forrestor, Illustrator.

- Reinforcing physical relationships with relevant academic programs
- Respecting functional relationships to other programs and activities
- Meeting access requirements—pedestrian, bicycle, vehicular, service, and those of the Americans with Disabilities Act (ADA)
- Facilitating use of a site for the present purpose while allowing for future alternative uses
- Minimizing impact on natural and cultural resources
- Providing a developed site that is adequate, but not excessive, for the initial program, future expansion, and support uses
- Promoting site visibility and image as related to the overall campus and the specific program
- Creating an aesthetic character appropriate to the district in terms of architectural design, scale, landscape, setbacks, etc.
- Conforming to local agency requirements for zoning, density, etc. (as needed)

When these criteria, and others developed specifically for each project, are interpreted properly, the results will enhance not only the individual project but also the comprehensive and dynamic outcome of the campus itself.

SUSTAINABILITY

In planning parlance, the term *sustainability* has existed for many years. Its definition continues to evolve over time, a good sign that the concept is being discussed, debated, and used in making decisions about such diverse issues as energy use, local services, stormwater management, transportation, open space, resource conservation, air and water quality, and building design. But the term must incorporate a balanced concern for three interdependent areas: *equity, economy,* and *environment.* All of these "three Es" are part of campus planning.

Within the "three E" context, many campuses are developing guidelines for future planning and facility projects, both new and renewed. A sustainable building may be called "green," "high-performance," or "energy-efficient," but each of these terms inevitably refers to buildings that minimize the use of energy, water, and other natural resources and provide a healthy, productive indoor environment. To achieve these goals requires an integrated development process.

CAMPUS PLANNING
CASE STUDY 4

(See Figure 1.19.)

LONG-RANGE DEVELOPMENT PLAN

University of Hawaii, West O'ahu, Kapolei

Architect: John Hara Associates, Inc.
Campus planner: David J. Neuman, FAIA
Landscape architect: PBR Hawaii and William Johnson, FASLA
Distinction: 2006 Merit Award, Analysis and Planning, American Society of Landscape Architects

> *In addition to the development of state-of-the-art facilities, the UH West O'ahu Kapolei campus will be a model of sustainability, incorporating the latest green building technologies and design for the benefit of future generations. In Fall 2007, we enrolled our first-ever freshman class in the university's more than 30-year history. We are now poised to begin construction of a much-anticipated permanent campus (see Figure 1.21).*
>
> —Gene I. Awakuni, UH West O'ahu chancellor

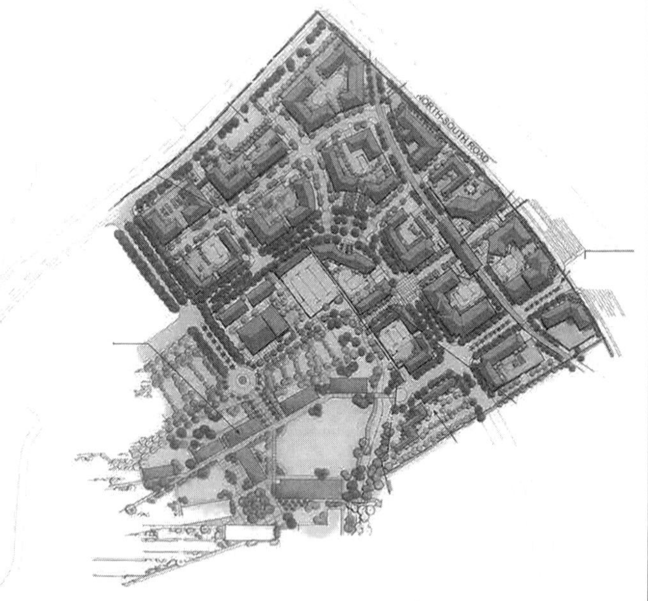

Figure 1.19 Mixed-use village conceptual plan. Photo courtesy of University of Hawai'i–West O'ahu.

Key Spaces

- Classroom
- Laboratory
- Maintenance
- Administration
- Library/resource center
- Student services/campus center
- The Great Lawn

A New Campus (see Figure 1.20)

- Ground blessing in January 2009 in anticipation of the new campus
- Incorporate LEED Standards for architectural sustainability
- Organized around a 3.9-acre open space called the "Great Lawn"
- Phase 1 completed for Fall 2012 semester

◀ *Figure 1.20 Aerial photograph, 2012.* Photo courtesy of University of Hawai'i–West O'ahu.

Development Plan

- Capitalizes on existing site features.
- Campus master plan will accommodate 7,600 students (742,845 GSF of buildings) with ample area for expansion.
- Initial 1,520 student campus concentrated at core to establish a physical presence for the campus.
- Design to be accessible to a possible lightrail transit stop and University Village.

Figure 1.21 The Great Lawn and obelisk. Photo courtesy of University of Hawai'i–West O'ahu.

In our every deliberation, we must consider the impact of our decisions on the next seven generations.

—Great Law of the Iroquois Confederacy

AASHE's mission is to empower higher education to lead the sustainability transformation. We do this by providing resources, professional development, and a network of support to enable institutions of higher education to model and advance sustainability in everything they do, from governance and operations to education and research.

—Mission Statement of the Association for the Advancement of Sustainability in Higher Education (AASHE), founded in 2005

An integrated development process combines design, construction, and maintenance practices that consider the environmental, economic, and social impacts of buildings and landscapes. This process must achieve the building program yet be cost effective. It expands and complements the classical building design concerns of the Roman author Vitruvius, of "firmness, commodity and delight," in a way that enhances both the interaction among building systems and the optimization of their energy and environmental performance.

Then no man can, by natural right, oblige the lands he occupied, or the persons who succeed him in that occupation, to the payment of debts contracted by him. For if he could, he might, during his own life, eat up the usufruct [utility] of the lands for several generations to come, and then the lands would belong to the dead, and not to the living, which would be the reverse of our principle.

—Thomas Jefferson to James Madison, September 6, 1789

All institutions must be concerned with such environmental issues as water conservation, land use, energy efficiency, and operational costs as well as providing healthful buildings for students, faculty, staff, and visitors. Moreover, the building industry has a great global impact on the environment. More than 30 percent of all energy in the United States is consumed by buildings, and 60 percent of all electricity in the country is consumed by building users. In addition, 12 percent of potable water in the United States is used in buildings. This topic is discussed further in Chapter 2 in a series of case studies of entire campuses as well as specialized buildings.

[Sustainability is] development that meets the needs of the present without compromising the ability of future generations to meet their needs.

—United Nations, Brundtland Commission on Environment and Development, 1987

LANDSCAPE

The term *academe* is based on the Greek expression for the fourth-century B.C. grove of olive trees planted for Plato's academy. Thus, the landscape is commemorated in its relationship to a "campus" long before buildings were built for academic pursuits as we know them today. Many articles, and several books, have been devoted to the landscape as an element in experiencing the campus. Prospective students are often attracted by the bucolic beauty of a campus as much as by the specific attributes of the campus buildings or even by the specific qualities of the academic programs themselves. Many campuses are in large measure defined by their siting (or setting) if they have not somehow managed to obfuscate it by poor planning, inappropriate landscape, and/or overscaled architecture. Some campuses are blessed with an unrivaled natural landscape setting, such as the University of Colorado, Boulder, with its magnificent Rocky Mountain backdrop; the Massachusetts Institute of Technology, with its Charles River frontage; and the University of California, Santa Cruz, with its redwood forest overlooking the Pacific Ocean. Other campuses must do with fewer natural attributes and have had to rely on their own best efforts at planning *and* planting to establish a sylvan character, as at University of Texas, Dallas (see Figure 1.23).

The following long-term goals set a positive framework of preservation, renewal, and management for the future vision of the campus landscape:

Educational Mission Develop the campus landscape in support of the educational mission of the University.

Campus Image Maintain the campus image of buildings in a park.

Historic Continuity Preserve and enhance the campus landscape features that provide continuity with the past.

Stewardship Provide stewardship to enhance the distinctive natural and physical attributes of the campus.

Landscape Character Provide and maintain sustainable, quality landscapes that enhance the use of campus open space.

Community Provide and maintain a welcome, safe and accessible campus environment.

University of California, Berkeley, Landscape Master Plan, January 2004.

Campus landscapes share many attributes; among them are scale, juxtaposition, climate responsiveness, and permanence.

Scale deals with the perception of objects (trees, buildings, etc.) in relationship to one another and to the person viewing them. Because this can be a relative perception, it can lead to misunderstanding. For example, to a person from a large city, many campuses seem "rural" in scale, whereas to a person from a suburb or a farm, the same campus may feel quite "urban." Two keys to the issue of correctly perceiving *scale* relate to consistency with the campus plan's original intent and commitment to maintaining a perceptible environmental quality over time.

Juxtaposition, in a campus landscape, relates to the tension among the layers of the observed environment (e.g., the ground plane in relationship to buildings or trees seen against the sky). This element creates a dramatic outcome essential to the memory of an overall environment.

Climate responsiveness entails sustainability and aesthetic appropriateness. Landscapes designed and maintained in response to local microclimates are not only more environmentally friendly to water use and plant longevity but also more economic to maintain.

Finally, *permanence* is a certain lasting quality that is sensed by alumni, as well as by current students, faculty, and staff, who want to believe they are a part of a place that endures, along with its values, beyond a normal lifetime. The campus landscape, when properly developed and maintained, can convey this quality more than the individual buildings themselves, which are frequently modified or even removed.

ARCHITECTURE

No campus development topic attracts more discussion (and controversy) than architecture, whether it is the design of a new building or the decision to renovate *or* to demolish an old one. A building's functionality and life-cycle cost warrant serious discussion, but too often these become lost in a debate over the appearance of the building. Few seek to be the engineer of a new building, but many want to be its architect, at least in its exterior design!

> Gothic architecture has added a thousand years to the history of the university, and has painted every man's imagination to the earliest traditions of learning in the English-speaking race.
>
> —*Woodrow Wilson, 1902*

> Every time a student walks past a really urgent, expressive piece of architecture that belongs to his college, it can help reassure him that he does have that mind, does have that soul.
>
> —*Louis Kahn, 1962*

Figure 1.22 Free University of Berlin. © Nigel Young/Foster + Partners.

Some claim that universal space is the cure for both current campus needs and future flexibility. Such proposals have been wide-ranging, from the original campus of the Illinois Institute of Technology to the expansion of the Free University of Berlin.

The Free University of Berlin development was viewed as extreme by many architects and campus planners, who decried its loss of sense of place (arguably not true). Others blasted its lack of landscape in the traditional sense (despite its urban setting). Many of these criticisms may have stemmed from fear of change, rather than any inherent flaws. In fact, the very design intent of universal space is filled with a commitment to the principles of an open university and a belief in an accessible physical setting for an educational utopia.

Despite criticisms, the facilities have served the Free University well and have been restored and renovated by Foster + Partners (see Figure 1.22). The Free University also demonstrates the benefits that universal space can bring to universities. Recent critiques of a university's failure to keep pace with current technologies often blame the excessive building constraints of many unduly specialized contemporary buildings as compared with the flexibility of the "old-fashioned" loft spaces in historic campus buildings. Prominent architects Robert Venturi and Denise Scott Brown have continued to stress the inherent benefits of flexible, high-ceilinged lofts both in their many campus buildings and in their prolific writing. From the University of Michigan to the University of California, Los Angeles, their concept of appropriate campus architecture has housed functions as diverse as student centers, business schools, and medical research labs, all in site-specific, flexible "decorated sheds" as opposed to overarticulated "ducks," in their vocabulary (see Figure 1.24).

We consider the university as a tool and as a place. Many of its functions and uses are known and many are not. We take as a working hypothesis that the principal function of the university (as distinct from the school or faculty) is to encourage exchange and intellectual regeneration between people in different disciplines, so as to enlarge the field of human knowledge and increase man's control over his collective and individual activities.

We are convinced that it was necessary to go beyond the analytic study of different faculties or activities in different buildings; we imagined a synthesis of functions and departments where all disciplines could be associated and where the psychological and administrative barriers which separate one from the other would not be reinforced through architectural articulation or the fragmentary identification of the parts at the expense of the whole.

—Shadrach Woods of Candilis, Josic and Woods, Architects for the Free University of Berlin, 1965

Figure 1.23 Landscaped entrance to the University of Texas, Dallas. Aerial Photography Inc. / PWP.

In 1997, author and critic Witold Rybczynski called for a campus architectural context in its broadest sense—that is, physical and cultural. The physical refers to scale, massing, window and roof treatments, materials, and colors. The cultural speaks to time; as Peter Rowe, former dean of Harvard's Graduate School of Design, stated, "We are in the twenty-first century. Why should we build in the style of the eighteenth?"; or, as former Harvard president Neil Rudenstine put it, "To think that all [our future buildings] should be stamped out in one particular form, would be, I think, a serious mistake" (see Figure 1.25).

There is, however, a distinct line between mimicry and honoring a strong architectural tradition. Many campuses have a robust architectural character, anchored by their original buildings and their own particular use of materials and details. A core campus architecture is an extension of the original plan, but it develops and changes over the years with new building technology, new codes, and new programs. To achieve a sense of continuity of character while also acknowledging change can be very difficult. The challenge is to be inspired by tradition without stifling innovation. This approach has recently led to various attempts at creating architectural guidelines for developed campuses.

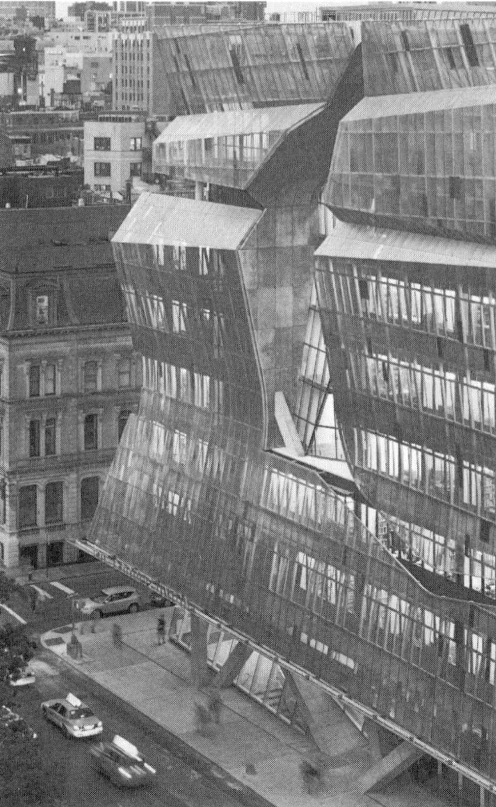

Figure 1.25 *41 Cooper Square, Cooper Union, New York, New York. Morphosis Architects.* Photo: Iwan Baan.

Figure 1.24 Life Sciences Institute, University of Michigan, Ann Arbor. Venturi, Scott Brown and Associates, Inc., in association with the Smith Group and Desman Associates. Photograph courtesy of VSBA, LLC.

CAMPUS PLANNING
CASE STUDY 5

CAMPUS MASTER PLAN
RICE UNIVERSITY, HOUSTON, TEXAS

Architect/planners: Michael Graves & Associates

The 50-year Master Plan locates infill buildings within the existing fabric to enhance outdoor spaces while providing covered paths. These paths increase comfort for students traversing in the Texas heat and rain. A new South axis is designed to link the university with the Texas Medical Center, promoting collaborative research and promoting larger footprint buildings which accommodate modern research labs. Upgraded sports, recreation and landscaping are also provided.

—Fifty-Year Master Plan

Campus Master Plan Facts

- Project type: master plan, mixed-use university: academic, recreational, residential, commercial/institutional, transportation
- Services provided: master planning, site analysis, general program verification, feasibility studies, design review
- Project size: 300 urban acres; 1.6 million sq ft academic and miscellaneous infill projects
- Project schedule: 11 years (ongoing)
- Principal-in-charge: Thomas Rowe, AIA, APA, CID

(See Figure 1.26.)

Campus Master Plan Goals

- Carefully build upon the principles in the historic campus plan.

Figure 1.26 Fifty-year master plan, 2004. Images courtesy of Michael Graves and Associates and Rice University.

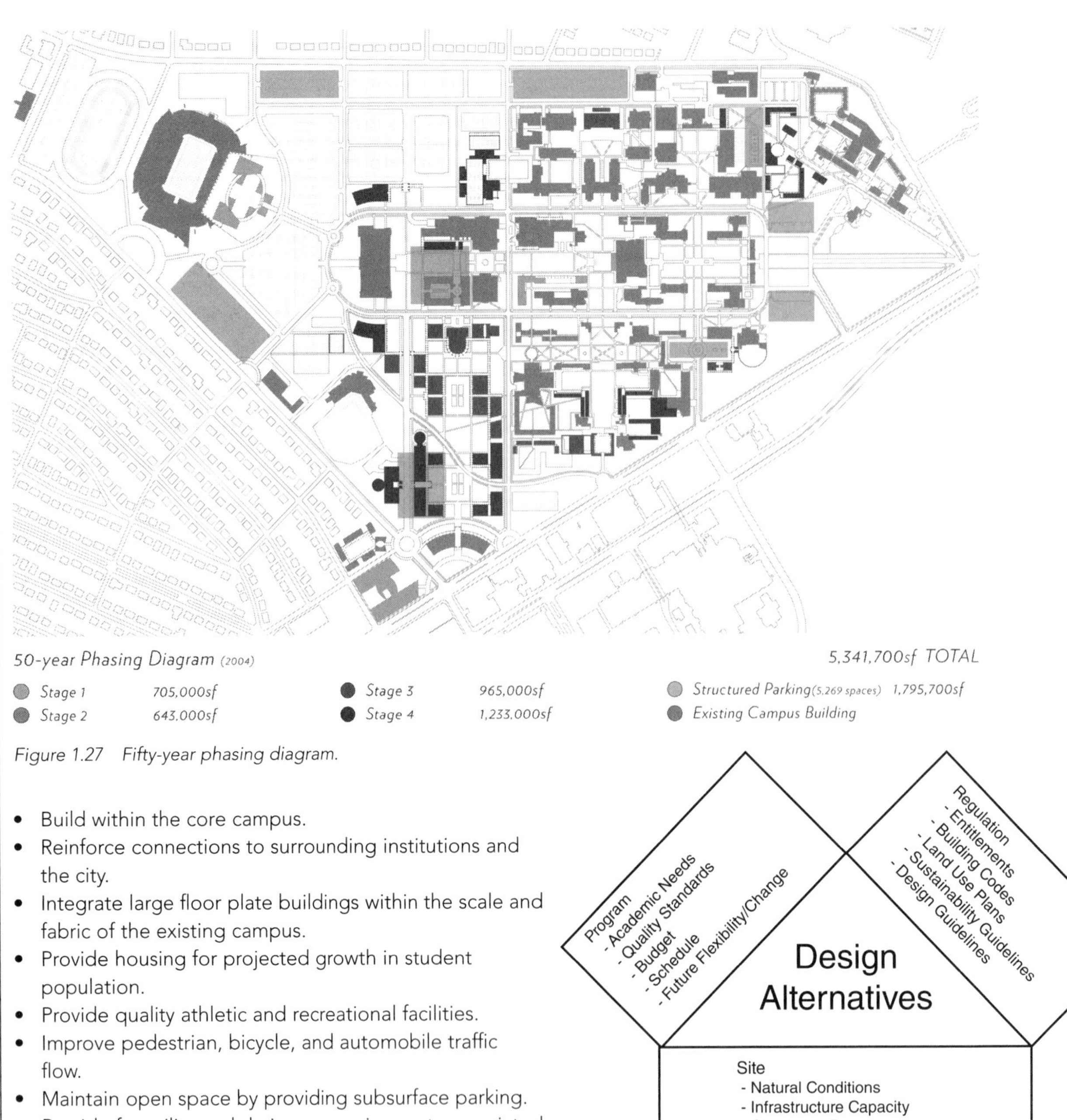

Figure 1.27 *Fifty-year phasing diagram.*

- Build within the core campus.
- Reinforce connections to surrounding institutions and the city.
- Integrate large floor plate buildings within the scale and fabric of the existing campus.
- Provide housing for projected growth in student population.
- Provide quality athletic and recreational facilities.
- Improve pedestrian, bicycle, and automobile traffic flow.
- Maintain open space by providing subsurface parking.
- Provide for utility and drainage requirements associated with growth.
- Reinforce axes and outdoor spaces with landscaping.

(See Figure 1.27.)

Figure 1.28 *Design alternatives graphic.* David J. Neuman, FAIA.

Guidelines

No written guidelines can fully detail all aspects of campus design criteria, nor should they imply direct imitation of any existing facilities. They do stress, however, that a new project should respond to its program, its immediate site, and context, and its cultural heritage. Guidelines should be intended to stimulate creativity based on a given campus, a specific site, and the facility program. The resultant designs will reflect a campus's commitment to its traditions and the relationship to its surrounding environs. This should be a matter of interpretation, not imitation; qualitative understanding, not merely quantitative proscription (see Figure 1.28).

The campus is a balance of physical planning, historical evolution, and technological progress. It also represents the physical responses to its varied users and must be a model of connectedness. It must inspire confidence in faculty, students, staff, and visitors through honest expression of the various functions and materials employed, the humanity of the overall scale, its sustainability, the detail and finish of its various spaces, its artistic creativity, and an overall physical harmony that reflects the institution's values.

Many a college has suffered architectural ruin through the practice of erecting individual buildings without regard to the total effect produced upon the campus, or to the larger purpose of the institution. Until comparatively recent years it was not unusual, when a new building was to be constructed, for a committee to walk over the ground and select whatever site might be available, without reference to the aesthetic whole or to the future progress of the college. The architect, in most instances commissioned for that building only, was

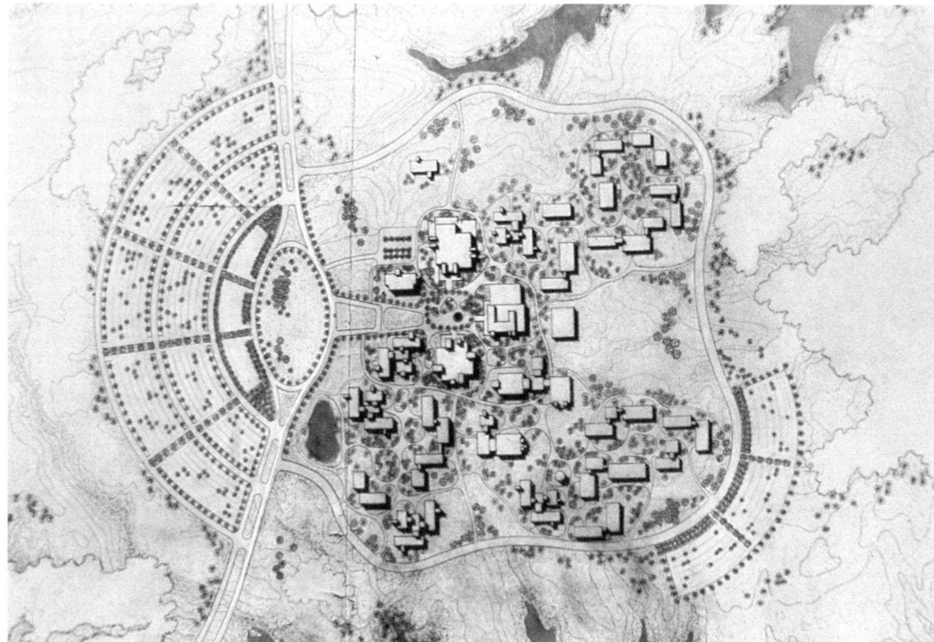

Figure 1.29 1962 master plan, Southern Illinois University, Edwardsville. Hellmuth, Obata + Kassabaum, Inc.

without opportunity to employ such vision as he might possess. Handicapped by the shortsighted policy of those in authority, he had no inspiration to produce work of outstanding character; and, even though the building might in itself be admirable, its relation to other structures on the campus would in all probability tend to obscure its excellence. The aesthetic disharmony and architectural mediocrity resulting from such a state of affairs is to be observed on too many college campuses to require specific illustration.

—*Jens Larson & Archie Palmer*, Architectural Planning of the American College, *1933*

Guidelines for campus architecture must acknowledge the history of the campus complex and imbue future planning and design with the best ideas of the past, yet inspire creativity in all future campus developments (see Figure 1.30). However, they constitute only one factor in determining the design response to program, site, and regulatory boundaries.

Although not intended to be prescriptive, design guidelines should define the parameters for a compatible design. Therefore, design guidelines provide *guidance* both for the project design team and for the university client team in understanding the appropriate

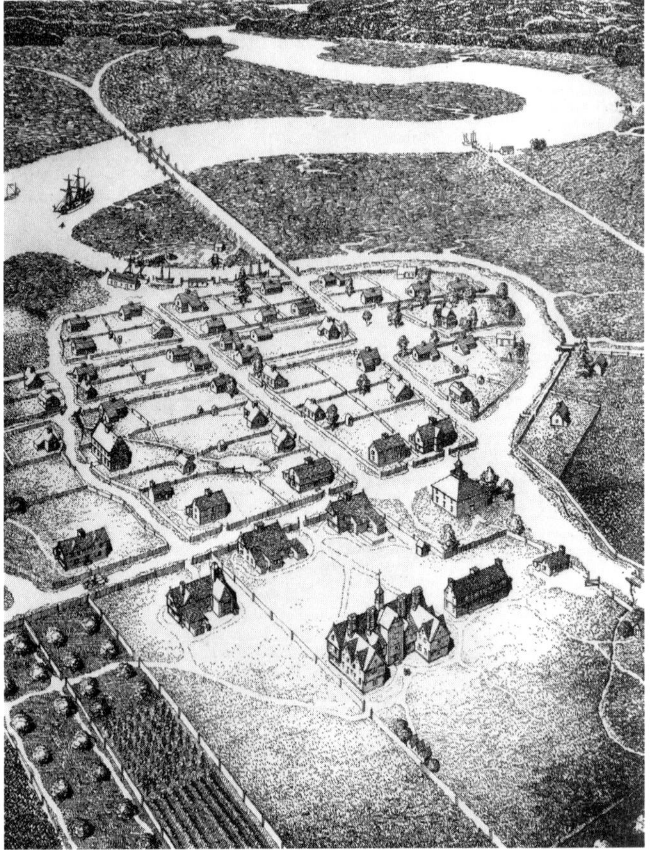

Figure 1.30 Illustration of the campus plan circa 1668, Harvard University, Cambridge, Massachusetts. Courtesy of the Harvard University Archives.

range of physical characteristics of a building and the associated landscape design that will be acceptable within the campus context.

The key principles to follow in regard to campus architecture and its design include the following:

- Develop a concise inventory of the similar high-quality characteristics among the major core campus structures.
- Define these compatibilities as design guidelines in generally understood terms of scale, massing, layering, materials, colors, etc.
- Apply these guidelines as "signposts" in evaluating building design proposals in the context of the overall campus and the specific building site.
- Incorporate consistent landscape treatment, both planting and hard surfaces, as an integral part of each design project.

"A university is, in part, defined by its architecture," stated Columbia University's president, Lee Bollinger, in 2001.

ENGINEERING AND OPERATIONS

Campuses have become increasingly dependent on their operating systems. Whereas early campuses needed minimal attention to utility planning and transportation, today's campuses rely on a support network that includes complex electrical/mechanical requirements, transportation options, emergency power, and constant information technology (IT) access.

Circulation Patterns

When many American campuses were first planned, the horse and carriage and, later, trains and trolleys were the vehicles of the day. Portions of these initial road networks remain, but current roadway patterns reflect changing circulation needs over the past century.

After decades of increasing automobile dependence, many campuses now advocate freeing the heart of the campus from private vehicles and commercial traffic, separating modes of traffic to increase pedestrian safety and transit access, and promoting general efficiency of land use. These proposals often include a plan for a peripheral circulation system.

These circulation patterns usually describe a system of *five* elements:

- Identifiable entryways that are connected directly to the accessible public circulation system
- Defined service/delivery routes and yards
- Networks of bicycle and pedestrian connectors
- Distinct "no vehicle" zones
- Internally managed and perimeter loop roadways

These concepts are supported by *five* circulation planning principles:

- Safe access for all legitimate campus users
- Efficiency of all travel modes
- Clarity and aesthetic character of the overall system
- Commodious respite areas for all users
- Environmental quality of the pedestrian experience

How well each principle succeeds is often as much a test of administrative will in the face of competing demands as it is proof of sound planning and economic investment. The notion of an individual's car near its destination is hard to change after years of sprawl and increased sensitivity to time allocation, especially for faculty.

Transportation Systems

The impact of the automobile culture on the pedestrian-oriented environment in the heart of a campus has been a significant drain on campus financial resources in terms of its management and accommodation. Patterns of development must provide for efficient movement of people, goods, and services to a campus while conserving land resources to best serve the academy. This functionality has been compromised significantly by the "invasion" of the private car into the general campus fabric.

Analyses of efficient utilization of parking facilities, environmental quality impacts, campus population distribution, and the proven concept of safe pedestrian campus encounters support the idea of establishing perimeter parking and eliminating most existing interior general parking.

As continued dependence on the single-occupancy vehicle (SOV) and population density have continued to grow in many areas of the United States, employers, government agencies, and the general public have become alarmed about clogged roadways, environmental impacts, and the cost of extending mass transit. Along with some capacity improvement and expansion, travel demand management (TDM) programs can lessen roadway congestion and parking needs, improve air and water quality, and promote alternatives to the SOV syndrome.

TDM programs offer a wide array of measures to reduce automobile dependency. They often include free on-campus and campus/community transit services, on-site sale of transit passes, programs that pay people not to drive, a "guaranteed ride home" for anyone stranded without a car, a computerized car pool matching service, preferred parking for car pools and van pools, clothes lockers and showers for bicyclists, car share and/or bike share programs, and an information web page on available travel modes and prospective ride share partners.

Parking demand can be managed, in part, by parking restrictions and parking fees. A TDM program can reduce the need for parking by reducing the number of people who drive to campus. To accomplish this, several planning principles must be followed:

- Focus new academic and residential development within the campus core and along designated transit corridors.
- Encourage walking and bicycling by maintaining and improving the internal campus circulation system and bicycle/pedestrian facilities.
- Continue to lessen the need to travel off campus by providing support services on campus, including child care.
- Continue to provide an efficient transit system and a safe and easily understood network of pedestrian pathways and bikeways that connect to destinations both on and off campus. (See Figure 1.31)
- Locate required parking structures on the edge of the campus to reduce internal roadway congestion, improve general air quality, accommodate various types of users, and encourage 24-hour use with shuttle and bicycle/pedestrian connectivity.

Utility Infrastructure

The link between infrastructure planning and facilities planning is often ignored, resulting in unwarranted issues for both users and administrators. Utilities constitute the vital support system for a college or university. A campus community depends on the utility system to move information, energy, water, and waste. This utility infrastructure must meet the demands of both campus residents and academic users, and accept/anticipate emerging technological advances. This system must plan for the following:

Figure 1.31 University Transit Service bus stop, University of Virginia, Charlottesville.

- Energy utilization and its related capacities
- Commitment to reduce carbon emissions
- Water source limitations
- Emission restrictions
- Stormwater limits on both quantity and quality
- Sewer discharge constraints

Some campuses in the United States provide nearly all their own utilities. These campuses may manage and provide the services for water; sewer; energy production through cogeneration, geothermal, or other local sources; recycling; and voice/data communications. Gas service is normally provided by a public utility, but many campuses have their own electrical substations, chillers/ice plants, and cogeneration facilities as well as miles of conduit, fiber-optic cable and utility lines. In addition, fuel cells, biomass fuel, solar thermal, solar electric, and geothermal wells are increasingly being considered as alternatives to traditional utilities.

Energy Production and Distribution Systems

While independent, renewable energy systems such as geothermal and solar/wind power are being explored on many campuses, central plants still provide heating and cooling through steam generation. The moderation of thermal conditions in buildings originated with traditional dense masonry structures that utilize the absorption of hot or cold outside temperature in an alternating "lead/lag" process. As the demand for greater cooling of equipment and space grew, artificial cooling became increasingly demanded by campus users. Initially, package units were located at individual buildings. In some cases, a decision was made to connect the buildings of the academic core campus to a central chiller system. With continued development, these chillers were linked to the central steam plant through an absorption-style design. Cogeneration systems (combined heat and power [CHP]) that generate multiple power supplies from one energy source—natural gas, coal, or biomass—are becoming more common. These facilities, with their associated plant apparatus and underground tank and thermal storage systems, demand a greater amount of space on the campus, and need to be anticipated. In addition, significant energy is needed to provide electricity and cooling and to control humidity for sensitive areas such as information technology centers, research laboratories, clinical areas, and museums.

As computing and controlled research environment needs have grown, so have codes and other regulations to minimize their energy demands. A centralized energy management and control system can monitor, adjust, and trigger alarm responses to conditions in most academic buildings. These have become a "standard requirement" for most campuses.

Although capital costs for new campus buildings are significant, more than 90 percent of the actual life-cycle cost of those buildings is in their operation, maintenance, and renovation. Therefore, it is vital to consider life-cycle costs at the initial facility planning and design stages of campus building projects.

Planning principles to consider include the following:

- Provide adequate sites for central and satellite plant facilities.
- Plan all new/renewed high-energy-consuming facilities so as to conserve energy and associated life-cycle costs.
- Locate utility corridors under vehicular or pedestrian pavement for easier access and maintenance.
- Plan utility rooms and associated spaces for flexibility, access, future equipment replacement, and expansion.

SPECIAL CONCERNS

Three added areas of special concern for campus planning are noted here: accessibility, safety and security, and public engagement.

Accessibility is regulated by the Americans with Disabilities Act (ADA), which replaced an era of prescriptive solutions to accessibility. ADA is a civil rights requirement that mandates accessibility for all. It is first a civil code giving all campuses the responsibility to review their physical barriers and to ensure that equal access to all services is available to all students, faculty, staff, and visitors. Rather than a one-time installation of ramps and elevators, it calls for continuous accommodation of those with disabilities, both temporary and permanent. Most campuses assign this responsibility to an administrator, who is available to assist in planning the campus and its facilities. Other campuses engage a specialized consultant. In either case, this is an ongoing responsibility under federal law, which has been significantly magnified by the recent enforcement of the 2010 ADA Facilities Code with its very specific requirements for both sites and buildings.

Safety and security have likewise become increasingly crucial components of campus planning. Included are not only the traditional security provided by campus police and fire personnel but also specialized equipment such as security cameras in parking garages, laboratories, and high-crime areas and card key locking systems for research labs, student residences, and, increasingly, all academic buildings as well as a "blue light" phone system throughout the campus. Crimes against persons, espionage related to research data, theft of personal property, and terrorist threats are, unfortunately, of increasing concern for students, faculty, and staff. Other safety issues include the concerns related to natural disasters (e.g., hurricanes, tornadoes, earthquakes, etc.) and how well the campus is prepared in the event of a disaster. Safety and security issues affect site planning and the design of campus buildings and landscape and must be considered in the early planning stages.

Public engagement covers a wide variety of functions for which the contemporary campus is host. Some, like intercollegiate athletic events, have a tradition on most campuses. Even these have multiplied over the years, as many additional competitive sports have been introduced. Sports like soccer, lacrosse, baseball, swimming, and tennis have added many more spectator venues.

Other public engagement activities include performing arts venues and museums. All have episodic peak demands on campus infrastructure depending on the size and season, including security and parking. Moreover, many activities, from continuing education to professional conferences, along with guided tours and informal public recreation, are now common. Use of the campus by the public brings both benefits and costs. Benefits include additional alumni (and nonalumni) financial contributions and community support for various development enterprises. Drawbacks include expenditures for energy use, security personnel, waste removal, and so on. These community-related uses are increasing for institutions of all types and in all locations. Generally, planning for campuses has ignored this issue; however, it is important to identify and to accept such engagement as reciprocity for being a part of the regional community, which craves extracurricular involvement.

GLOBALIZATION AND INFORMATION TECHNOLOGY

No discussion of campus planning today fails to note the impact on the "bricks and mortar" campus by information technology (IT) or the "digital revolution" and the globalization of culture. Some foresee the end of the physical campus as we know it, and others believe that IT will be additive to the physical setting by encouraging full use of the institution's buildings and grounds on a year-round, 24/7 basis.

Many colleges and universities have developed *multiple campuses* worldwide for a number of reasons—for example, to provide their students and faculty with a breadth of exposure to other cultures or to acquire more tuition-paying students. These campuses range from rented office spaces to actual campus grounds and specially designed buildings. All have the potential to provide an education to their host communities by offering courses and seminars to local residents. Their success rate has varied.

Higher education has also changed in the past fifty years. With the ability to quickly share ideas across time zones and datelines, today's universities are venues for global teaching and research—and global competitors for talent and prestige. At UC Merced, this means the physical form of the campus will be designed to facilitate the exchange of ideas, research and development, and the development of well-rounded graduates.

—*University of California, Merced, Long Range Development Plan, 2009*

Shared resources among colleges and universities that have been traditional competitors are on the rise, as are nonprofit and for-profit collaborations. These sorts of cooperative ventures will shortly bring about the need for new types of facilities such as learning centers, which offer access to multiple curricula and multimedia equipment. On one hand, demands for IT systems and their infrastructure will expand; on the other hand, the need for traditional facilities like classrooms and libraries will diminish and change markedly. The future of planning at campuses is therefore at the cutting edge of these global changes and IT innovations. Yet the key value of the place ("heart") of the institution appears to be ever more vital to the identity of both the institution and its users.

CONCLUSIONS

This book describes the characteristics of a series of seven discrete building types found on most campuses as well as the seminal issues of sustainability, historic preservation, and globalization. But it is critical to stress that the whole physical environment (campus) is greater than the sum of its parts (buildings and grounds). Each project, new or renewed, must contribute to *campus building*—that is, creating or renewing that memorable (utopian) place. In lieu of the traditional three Rs of American education—reading, (w)riting, and (a)rithmetic—we propose three Ps:

- *Programming* is more than a basic description of each facility type. It also includes the variety of campus systems that must interface with one another. For example, to be successful, a program for parking needs to incorporate campuswide objectives related to circulation, safety and security, site adjacencies, sustainability, lighting, and so on. A campus, although often described as a city, is actually quite different, because each program must anticipate and be sympathetic to all of those with which it shares links. The best campuses, therefore, are organic in the fullest sense of that term.
- *Planning*, as noted in this chapter, is more than simply the campus plan itself, although it and its renewal are essential. Planning entails variants—from long-term capital planning to strategic development planning to specific project planning. All levels of an integrated planning process are crucial to incubate and foster the sensitive environment known as the *campus*.
- *Perseverance* implies an institutional level of commitment to the guiding mission of the school, college, or university and to the campus setting developed to house this mission. And it must do so through many generations of faculty, students, and staff. Each campus has certain fundamental elements of plan, landscape, and architecture that have been proven to support the identity and the standing of the institution. These must be documented, passed on to each new generation of users, and maintained in good and not-so-good times (see Figure 1.32).

If the three Ps are followed, the campus can continue to serve its purpose in nurturing the expanding missions of academic institutions worldwide.

Campus sums up the distinctive physical qualities of the American College, but also its integrity as a self-contained community

◀ *Figure 1.32 View of Palm Drive, Stanford University, Stanford, California.*

and its architectural expression of educational and social ideals. As early as the 1870s the term was so evocative that an observer of one American College could write, "There is no spell more powerful to recall the memories of college life than the word *Campus*."

—*Paul Venable Turner,* Campus: An American Planning Tradition, *1984*

University campuses maintain a unique spot in our imagination. Linked to nostalgia for youth, they follow us in memory, and their physical aspects, particularly those that are most imageable, come to stand for the whole. Images of the campus stay with us on our life's journey and are thereby broadcast throughout the world.

—*Venturi, Scott Brown and Associates, 1998*

CHAPTER 2

SUSTAINABILITY, TECHNOLOGY, AND UNIVERSITIES

David Nelson, Foster + Partners

If we do not change our direction, we are likely to end up where we are headed.
—Chinese proverb

Higher education has never been more important than it is today, and its global nature is of paramount significance. If we are to solve many of the difficult political, scientific, financial, and medical issues that we currently face, we need to approach higher education from a broader platform that addresses the complexity of our time. It is becoming increasingly more difficult for isolated individuals in any field to achieve the kind of breakthroughs that are needed. The complexity of our time demands increased specialization into the constituent components of any problem, such as the cure for disease, a sustainable economic structure, or the resolution of political conflict or indifference. At the same time, this focused work must be seen as part of a broader pattern, and cross-disciplinary activity needs to be orchestrated to encourage solutions. This interrelated complexity is ably demonstrated by the challenges related to our ongoing survival on this planet. Therefore, the need for a widespread, highly educated population who can comprehend the challenges ahead has never been more pressing.

Our aesthetic culture has always made significant advances during periods of plenty. Our exploitation and ultimate dependency on oil and carbon fuels has created easier, more comfortable ways of living for those lucky enough to have been born in the West. This also has had a major impact on the subject matter of higher education, where it would seem that a greater emphasis is now placed on the arts and away from the academically more challenging field of the sciences. But as the fossil fuel energy source behind that abundance diminishes, without a refocus in education toward science and technology, we run the risk of failing to manage the planet's resources, on which we are wholly dependent.

This current situation calls to mind the first impetus for establishing universities in the Middle Ages—to provide the necessary broad skills to manage the emerging economies and cities of that time. We need the same sort of focus today to manage our planet and its resources, whether through a focus on real, significant issues such as governance, the creation of energy from new sources, or the integration of that supply from many unrelated sources; to the equally if not more complex issues concerning waste, recycling, and the ability to do more with less. This includes considering where our food comes from and what is required to produce it, to how water is retained, circulated, used, and recycled: all are complex subsystems for sustainability. The integration of all these issues will require great ingenuity in terms of solutions and systems for implementation, and that ingenuity needs to be fed by highly focused research. Creating the right conditions and facilities for such expectations becomes a prime activity when planning and designing what colleges and universities need to become. All of this is occurring at a significant time, when the advancement of computer technology has gone into overdrive, allowing for new challenges as well as new possibilities for what the future might be.

ECONOMIC GROWTH AND HIGHER EDUCATION

Growth underpins all of our economic, financial, and industrial endeavors, and, following the recent economic downturn in Europe and the United States, that growth is likely to remain at low levels for some time. Higher education becomes increasingly critical at this point, where meaningful economic growth is needed to replace the devalued speculative excesses of recent years. Consequently, the direct connection between higher education, innovation, and invention needs to drive the future of economic development much more directly than in the past.

SUSTAINABILITY, TECHNOLOGY, AND UNIVERSITIES CASE STUDY 1

TEST CASE

Bryant Park, New York, New York

Architect: Hardy Holzman Pfeiffer Associates
Landscape Architect: Hanna/Olin Ltd.
Client: Bryant Park Restoration Corporation (BPRC)

A model for environmental, social, and economic sustainability, Bryant Park was revitalized in the 1990s with the support of local businesses. The park now provides New Yorkers with a vibrant, well-maintained public space for leisure, work, and entertainment. Its large lawn, gardens, and established trees, as well as quality concessions for food and drink, are a foil for thousands of patrons who use the park throughout each day (see Figure 2.1). Investment by the BPRC has changed the park's previous use and reputation as a neglected, crime-ridden urban space to a dynamic, accessible, and safe meeting place. The park also acts as a large-scale green roof: it sits above two levels of book stacks housing volumes of the New York Public Library adjacent.

Figure 2.1 Bryant Park with laptops. © Alamy.

If we were searching for an example of how the newfound mobility given to us with computers then Bryant Park could be considered in some way a precedent (see Figure 2.2). Bryant Park has a higher concentration of wireless connectivity than many other locations in the city. In the summer months, you can see many people working on their laptops, reinforced with beverages from the pavilion café. At least one university, the City University of New York (CUNY), has one of its facilities located around the park. The New York Public Library is about to create a new public library within its internal boundaries. This mixture of potentially publicly accessible internal and external space could suggest an interesting prototype for how a more diffused university typology may evolve.

Date: 1986–1991
Park area: 39,000 sq m
Estimated number of visitors (annually): 4.2 million

The park serves an estimated 187,600 office workers within a two-block radius. This is set to increase with proposed building developments (see Figure 2.3).

Figure 2.2 Bryant Park offers higher concentration of wireless technology than many other areas of New York City. © Alamy.

Figure 2.3 Bryant Park is used by both students and area residents. © Alamy.

It is clear that economic growth is now highly dependent on technology-based innovation. The model for this remains innovation hot spots in the United States such as Stanford/Silicon Valley (see Figure 2.4) and Harvard/MIT/Route 128, which emerged with the Cold War and its military and technology races. These university-centric areas continue to make a disproportionately large contribution in terms of both patents filed and scientific papers cited as well as economically through the start-up companies they generate. MIT has estimated that the 28,500 companies founded by its alumni globally employ 3.3 million people and generate world sales of U.S.$2 trillion. If considered as an economy, MIT alumni firms would be the world's eleventh largest economy.

New locations based on these precedents are coming into existence. When the Øresund Bridge connecting Copenhagen, Denmark, with Malmö, Sweden, opened in 2000, both sides had much to gain (see Figure 2.5). Sweden benefited from a physical connection to the rest of mainland Europe; residents of Copenhagen had access to less expensive homes that were close to the city; and economic cooperation increased. In addition, Christian Matthiessen, a geographer at the University of Copenhagen, foresaw another benefit—the union of two burgeoning research areas. "Everyone was talking about the transport of goods and business connections," he says, "and we argued that another benefit would be to establish links between researchers."

Ten years later, those links seem strong. The bridge encouraged the establishment of the "Øresund Region," a loose confederation of nine universities, 165,000 students, and 12,000 researchers. According to Matthiessen,

Figure 2.4 Silicon Valley. Charles O'Rear/Corbis.

Figure 2.5 Øresund Bridge. © Hasse Schroder/Johner/Alamy.

co-authorship between Copenhagen and the southernmost province of Sweden has since doubled. The collaborations have attracted multinational funds from the European Union, and the European Spallation Source—a €1.4 billion (U.S.$2 billion) neutron facility—is scheduled to begin construction in Lund, Sweden, in 2013.

SUSTAINABILITY, TECHNOLOGY, AND UNIVERSITIES **CASE STUDY 2**

TEST CASE

Henning Larsen Tegnestue IT University, Øresund, Copenhagen, Denmark

The IT University of Copenhagen is one of the first construction projects completed as a result of the impact of the Øresund bridge. The café, restaurant, and library are an integral part of the city that surrounds them. With its atrium, which is 20 m wide, 60 m long, and 25 m high and linked with plazas to the north and south, it draws the adjacent city space into its heart (see Figure 2.6). The IT education offers a high degree of interactivity between students and researchers. The goal therefore is to create a structure that encourages social activities within the building. To make this happen, there is extensive use of portable computers and wireless networks, thereby increasing the possibilities of informal and spontaneous conversation. The building incorporates digital artwork to add to the dynamic nature of its internal spaces. The ground level is raised, which encourages recreation and performance (see Figure 2.7).

Figure 2.6 Map showing companies surrounding the Øresund Bridge area.

Figure 2.7 Tietgenkollegiet: halls of residence in the Øresund area.

Promoters of the region claim that the Øresund Region is emerging as the research hub of northern Europe, aided in part by construction of the bridge. For Matthiessen, the bridge also inspired the start of a unique research project—to catalogue the growth and connections of geographical clusters of scientific productivity all over the world. It appears that most research activities are concentrated around major metropolitan areas. By Matthiessen's count, the top seventy-five science-producing clusters in the world from 2006 to 2008 generated some 57 per cent of research—3.9 million papers in total.

—*Richard Van Noorden, "Building the Best Cities for Science," Nature, October 2010*

In other parts of the world, particularly India and China where dramatic population growth continues, demand for a higher number of educated people to administer and control the development of the country is especially profound. It is here that higher education will play an ever increasing and important role. China and India are currently the world's largest and third largest academic systems respectively, and will continue to grow rapidly. In the last decade alone, the annual number of graduates in China has risen from less than 2 million to 7 million. Of these graduates, around 25 percent registered for the Chinese Civil Service exams in 2009, even though only 16,000 jobs were on offer.

—Economist, *December 18, 2010*

Concurrent with the demand for well-educated individuals is the increasing commonality of the English language in scientific communication. In fact, the rise of English as a dominant language of scientific communication is unprecedented since Latin dominated the academy in medieval Europe. Its widespread use allows great mobility as shared and globally accessible information and communication technologies create a universal means of instantaneous contact and simplified scientific communication. This is also true for the arts and social sciences. It is estimated that by 2020 approximately 7 million international students will be moving around the globe freely, which will therefore create a pressing need for international cooperation. Linked to this mobility is the firmly established concept of knowledge itself being the basis for future economies. In postindustrial countries, the transformation to create service industries and knowledge economies is ever increasing; the pursuit of knowledge is also the basis of securing future funding. Countries that are rich in natural resources, such as oil, are now forced to envision a future in about 40 years' time when the supply of that resource will run out. This is reflected in current urban initiatives such as in Saudi Arabia, which has four knowledge cities under construction, while in Abu Dhabi, the Masdar Initiative and many other universities are under development.

The growth of private education internationally is also significant. Countries with over 70 percent of students in private enrollment include Indonesia, the Philippines, Japan, and South Korea. The private sector now educates more than half the student population in such countries as Mexico, Brazil, and Chile. A significant number of private schools (private in this instance meaning "for profit") are also found in China and India, and while private universities exist there, the mass clientele of private education serves secondary-level students and is therefore not directly focused on university-level standards. However, the balance between privatized tertiary and secondary levels already shows signs of changing, driven by population demand and reduced state funding, which, in turn, cause tuition costs to rise, all of which will increase demand for university education.

This relatively recent surge in global higher education is accompanied by its own problems. It is possible that up to half of the world's university teachers have only earned a bachelor's degree. In China, only 9 percent of the academic profession has doctoral qualifications, a percentage that rises to 35 in India. The production of professionals is quite phenomenal in India, where more than 300 universities and 15,600 colleges create 2.5 million graduates each year. In terms of the volume of production, India trails only the United States and, more recently, China. Each year, India produces 350,000 engineers—twice the number produced by the United States.

For India, the real infrastructural problem that has no solution in sight is not airports or electricity; it is the virtual absence of graduate education and research in information and other crucial technologies. The United States produces about 1,400 PhDs in computer science annually while China has around 3,000 graduates. In stark comparison, India's annual computer science PhD production languishes at roughly 40 (35 in 2010, according to P. Anandan, Managing Director of Microsoft Research India, who also offers five fellowships to students in India per year).

To gain perspective on this, the number of graduates from India is about the same as that for Israel, a nation with a population size roughly 5 percent of India's. Perhaps of even greater significance is the quality of graduate research in India, which lags significantly behind the USA and Europe with a few rare exceptions. This seems paradoxical in light of the fact that American academia and industry thrive on the research generated by Indian scientists. The reason for this discrepancy is that graduates from eminent Indian science and engineering schools prefer to complete their graduate work abroad, where they frequently excel and settle.

—*Prabhakar Raghavan, "India Has the Brains, but Where's the Beef?"* Forbes Magazine, *August 13, 2007*

CONSTRUCTING THE FUTURE UNIVERSITY

The fundamental reason for universities to exist is to equip students with the capability to learn and to understand how to continue to learn in the future. The skill of "learning how to learn" that is created during the period of higher education allows students continually to upgrade their knowledge throughout their careers. It could be said that conditions for the pursuit of excellence have never been better. Armed with the basic skills of how to learn, the necessity of a physical university is now arguable. Many study materials are now available for open access, so in order to reach a high standard of knowledge in almost any subject, an individual can go far with the will and determination to achieve, coupled with access to the Internet.

Turning knowledge into innovation and wealth requires a synthesis of advanced thinking, whether recognized through research, published papers, or other avenues such as Nobel Prize–winning projects. Crucially, these achievements depend on infrastructure that includes research and development grants, government investment, and inexpensive rental accommodation. Universities themselves play a part in this knowledge economy through structured coursework, which maintains a measurable set of standards and steadily progresses the student forward. Yet, as the world evolves, other skills such as entrepreneurship are also needed. It is interesting to note that the founders of Google, Microsoft, Apple, and Yahoo! are all yet to complete their degree programs! Individual entrepreneurs provide momentum and direction, but their achievements can only be accomplished if larger groups of individuals join with them to accomplish a common goal through combined effort. The nature and direction of university programs in the future will be influenced by a concentration of multiple knowledge bases that reflect the complexity of problems facing us today.

Concurrent with collaborative methods to evolve scientific research is the increasing amount of funding granted for interdisciplinary enterprise. Current fields favored by government for research funding include biomedical research and nanotechnology, both of which are interdisciplinary by their nature. This need for a collaborative education platform will force us to integrate physical and social connectivity between groups and individuals. There will be an emergence of cross-cultural nomadic groups, people from different parts of the world who will be drawn to integrate quickly, motivated by shared beliefs that form the basis for new understanding. To respond to this architecturally, we need to create a new approach to the planning of university infrastructures and perhaps consider approaches that are less about specific internal building configurations and more about the ability to change.

Architecturally, this can be expressed in the creation of flexible spaces—wireless labs and auditoriums, for example—that are equipped for a variety of media uses and are easily reconfigured. Social and leisure spaces that engender human interaction, and, in turn, create interdisciplinary cross-fertilization, have long been recognized as a key component of a learning environment. "Connectivity" is a popular buzzword, but the real importance of physical interaction must be fully recognized. We cannot afford to let the latest communication technology—social networking and the Internet—become a substitute for real social contact. It is a question of "face to face" as much as of Facebook.

"While change is inevitable and engenders necessary growth, change also brings its own challenges. The results of a recent study conducted among the most important management-oriented higher-education associations in the United States are telling. An increasing number of higher-education leaders identified the challenges associated with "aging and expanding facilities" as one of the top change drivers in the field. This concern was exceeded only by insufficient financial resources, technological change, and changing student demographics. In the same report, "insufficient facilities" were also considered among the top threats to the success of higher education. The study concluded with a call to action and the recognition that leadership is "a key ingredient that will ensure higher education's future success and help mitigate its threats." Two of these change drivers—resource scarcity and information technology—also figure in the top 10 critical issues that higher-education facilities professionals face, according to the Association of Higher Education Facilities Officers in the United States.[1]

1 Francesco Marmolejo, "Higher Education Facilities: Issues and Trends," OECD, 2007.

Confronted with the changing needs and means for delivering education, there is no question that institutional planners and managers need to reconsider the way higher education facilities are planned, designed and managed.

—Francesco Marmolejo, "Higher Education Facilities: Issues and Trends," OECD, 2007

GOVERNANCE

Any discussion of sustainability is inevitably overshadowed by the great cloud of environmental governance. This complex subject is much debated, and tertiary courses studying the subject have been established in universities around the world—from Manchester to Freiburg to Colorado. This subject tries to tackle the difficult and interrelated topics of overall sustainability—from the social and the political, to energy and waste. Through the integrated study of organizations, political instruments, financing mechanisms, rules, procedures, and norms that regulate the process of environmental performance, they seek to define issues. The political and practical resolution of such issues attempts to overcome the conflicting nature of negotiations between often diametrically opposed groups and individuals. It seems a daunting and almost impossible task: the resolution, or at best an "elegant balance," of these issues inevitably points toward radical reform. Environmental governance seeks to reform all of the systems that are in place that guide environmental design and to reform them simultaneously.

These objectives and mechanisms have so far failed on subjects such as the eradication of famine or placing a value on carbon use. Yet an optimistic belief remains: if we can deliver troops and Coca-Cola to any point on the planet, then there must be a mechanism to integrate the methodologies of environmental existence! We need to retain that optimism, as its counter approach could prove catastrophic. Inevitably, focusing on the big picture reinforces a top-down strategy. The creation and enforcement of policy, the establishment of rules and procedures, and the introduction of new approaches to financing must be established at the top in order to mitigate the opportunistic nature of our society and current preoccupations. However, this creates great frustration at the "middle" and "bottom" levels, where a strong desire for tangible results that can bring about change exists. When considering environmental performance, as with many related issues, governance is dramatically influenced by scale. The high ground and the big picture will remain and by necessity be the Holy Grail, yet results at a tactical level, derived from subassemblies of environmental thinking, allow us to move ahead. In this way, we can create jigsaw pieces of the puzzle without really knowing what that puzzle may ultimately look like.

If we develop this line of thought to the creation of urban environments, it is clear that what can be achieved at a city scale would be very different from what can be achieved by individual or small groups of buildings. Townships and villages can cover part of the remit for sustainability and at least some of the issues of technical integration can be studied and hopefully implemented. When considering the application of this at the scale of a university campus, which usually constitutes large groups of individual buildings, the possibilities for sustainable design are strong. The average size of a university allows for pressing issues, such as energy and water use, mobility, and waste management to be addressed. In addition to the design and technical approaches that will arise through any holistic examination of the needs of existing and new campuses, attention also needs to be focused on what may or may not be changeable at a local governance level. For example, if a decision is made to generate power within the confines of a university campus, one will inevitably face a degree of conflict with existing energy suppliers. On that topic alone, at a local level, discussion about environmental governance could highlight situations to be examined—and perhaps new agreements reached, creating significant new steps out of a bottom-up reappraisal. The energy providers and utility companies that any development such as a university campus will come into contact with are usually programmed to follow the status quo, making change harder to implement. But universities themselves are engines for change, and the creation and ongoing provision of environmental governance courses within them is testimony to that.

University planners need to acknowledge that they have a degree of responsibility to use the scale of a campus as a catalyst for change, implementing practical, as well as theoretical, techniques for improved environmental performance. Within the classroom, while the issues of population growth, equality, the poor, and women's rights are easily debated, the campus itself should focus on energy production. It ought to follow its own carbon count, including people, travel, goods shipped, energy, materials, and recycling, at a very hands-on level. As discussed previously, this requires simultaneous development and understanding of the big picture and detailed mechanisms. In this light, a localized, campus-scale approach to environmental governance should be implemented. The Association for the Advancement of Sustainability in Higher Education (AASHE) acknowledges the responsibility of universities in our long-term sustainability goals. AASHE works to provide leadership and knowledge for sustainability initiatives in higher education. It was the participation of the higher-education community that helped AASHE create the Sustainability Tracking, Assessment and Rating System, a self-reporting framework for colleges and universities to measure their sustainability performance. It is through programs like this that universities can realize their full potential as leaders in sustainable thinking.

DISTANCE LEARNING AND ITS EFFECTS

The concept of distance learning seems to be a relatively new phenomenon. However, as with many new ideas, often their origins lie in the past. The University of London was the first university to offer distance learning degrees when it established its external program in 1858. In 1969, the Open University was founded in the United Kingdom (see Figures 2.8 and 2.9). At the time, its primary delivery methodologies were television and radio, which placed it at the forefront of applying emerging technologies to learning. There are now many similar institutions internationally, often carrying the name "Open University." The Indira Gandhi National Open University (see Figures 2.10 and 2.11) is the largest in the world and currently has an enrollment of 3 million students. Virtually all of the largest colleges and universities in the United States now offer online courses in one form or another.

There are many benefits to this mode of learning. Flexibility is one; an online education allows study when "you" have time—any time of the day or night. It can reduce the long-term commute—the classroom is as close as a living room or home office. In many instances, it allows you to

Figure 2.8 The Open University broadcasting a lecture in the 1960s.

▶ *Figure 2.9 Open University premises.*

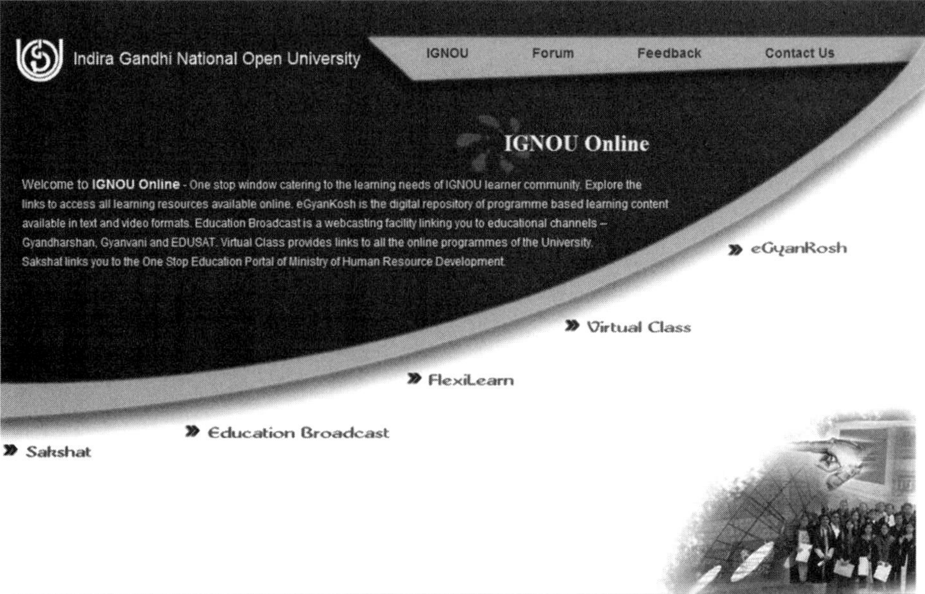

▶ *Figure 2.10 Indira Gandhi National Open University Online.*

◀ *Figure 2.11 Premises of Indira Gandhi National Open University.*

maintain your job, take care of your family, and genuinely create the possibility of balancing the needs and demands of education with those of family life. Another benefit is the expanded accessibility of education as information and communication technologies allow for the distribution of knowledge over tremendous distances. Primarily, the synchronous technologies that are used focus on group learning and include tools such as web-based voice-over, Internet protocol videoconferencing, web conferencing, direct broadcast satellites, Internet radio, and live streaming—even blogs can be harnessed for multiple sharing of information. These more recent technologies are available in addition to conventional asynchronous technologies of self-learning, such as e-mail, message board forums, printed materials, voice-mail, digital video disc (DVD), on-demand streaming, pocket PCs, and mobile learning—all different aspects by which distance learning can be achieved.

SUSTAINABILITY, TECHNOLOGY, AND UNIVERSITIES
CASE STUDY 3

OPEN UNIVERSITY
United Kingdom (Worldwide)

Originally known as the "University of the Air," the Open University was the first successful distance learning institution. Its inclusive intent was founded on a belief that communication technology could bring quality tertiary education to those who were unable to attend a traditional campus-based university. These progressive ideals about what remote learning could offer—and to whom—have continued in the 40 years since, with ongoing technological innovation in the way classes and information are delivered. Although the Open University has 13 national and regional student centers, it is most notable for its innovative pedagogical platforms, such as publications for free download from iTunes U and its OpenLearn site as well as its own virtual world island, Second Life.

The Open University commenced operation in 1969 using television and radio programs. Documentation was sent by mail to prospective students, and although many of the exams are still paper based, most of the coursework is now sent out electronically, reducing the two-warehouse storage capacity to one. The courses offer the possibility of face-to-face seminars and have created 13 regional bases to enable this to happen. For example, the Open University has a small office in Edinburgh, Scotland, and hires staff from other universities for the face-to-face seminar sessions. Only about 50 percent of the student population takes advantage of these sessions. Others carry out their process of course assessment using virtual rooms and seminars via e-rooms. Course assessment is carried out electronically. For practical subjects, residential periods are created, usually during the university holiday period, and laboratories are hired from other universities such as Nottingham. The Open University campus is primarily an office complex with some limited PhD facilities.

Open University, United Kingdom (Worldwide)

Opened: 1971

Original number of students: 25,000

Current number of students: 256,000

Average age of student: 32

Typical course fee: £15,000

The Milton Keynes campus, based around Walton Hall, acts as the Open University headquarters. This campus was designed by Maxwell Fry and Jane Drew (1969–1977).

More than 800 universities distribute information from their curriculum through Apple's iTunes U app on iTunes University. The total number of downloads from this source is now over 300 million. The Open University in the United Kingdom was the first to join the iTunes University, and its material is now downloaded more than 50,000 times each week, serving more than 250,000 students, more than 7,000 tutors, and more than 1,200 full-time academic staff, in addition to its 350,000 support and administrative staff (see Figure 2.12). The resulting potency of all this information dissemination and its open-ended nature is completely intertwined with new trends in social networking. The term "social networking" is also changing in people's minds. For many today, particularly the young, platforms such as Facebook and Twitter are to the fore and are challenging conventional forms of social interactivity.

The Open University has always maintained a balance between "private" study

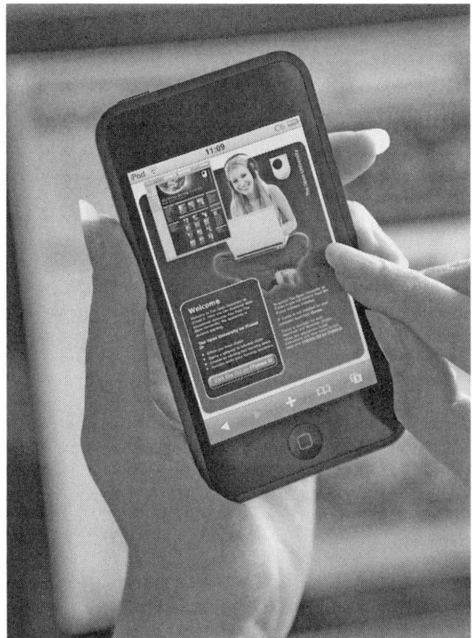

Figure 2.12 Open University iPhone app.

courses and the interaction of on-site tutorials. "Local" people are employed to assist students and, to a degree, provide mentoring. In complex areas of study, contributions made by human interaction remain invaluable. When people come together in a team or informal groups, the interchange of ideas is more spontaneous. Some of the greatest progress in science has been reached in a social gathering following periods of individual private study. Multifocus problem solving is particularly important for research programs. Research universities are at the pinnacle of the academic system, and although they directly involve global knowledge networks, they also require major expenditure to create laboratories, libraries, and information and technology infrastructures, all of which must be maintained to the highest international standards. Practical experimentation still forms a major part of technology development and to do that, state-of-the-art facilities must be provided, maintained, and upgraded at frequent intervals.

One could argue that these technical facilities could form the core identity of universities in the future—the expenditure being so significant that they automatically assume pride of place. In addition to providing prime locations for innovation, university buildings will need to create a sense of place and to link with residential and other social activities. Individual building typologies will be challenged by the technologies that currently enable distance learning. For example, we need to define the needs of the library—probably the university resource under the most extreme pressure. Some of the pertinent questions to consider include the following: What should a library store? How should it capture the latest developments and in what form? Does the "book" still have relevance? Should blogs and Twitter be recorded and retained? With rapidly changing scientific priorities and programs, other types of facilities, including laboratories, are also being challenged. An example is the growth of compositional fluid dynamics and its major impact on the design of aerodynamics.

THE JAMES H. CLARK CENTER

The James H. Clark Center at Stanford University was created to be the focal point of a scientific program originally called "Bio-X." The objective was to bring together the different aspects of biological science that until then had been contained in a series of separate subdisciplines, and the building location was chosen for its proximity to a number of existing buildings and courses that would also relate to the Bio-X program. The center itself was to unite different and diverse aspects of the biological and physical sciences with a common theme of imaging and simulation. Its creation coincided with the sequencing of the human genome, and the targets for its research outcomes were clearly aimed at the biotech industry. Because of the lack of support for stem cell research from the George W. Bush administration, James Clark was forced to remove funding from the program work, although construction of the building continued. When it opened in 2003, the scientific research being undertaken at the Clark Center had a major focus on biological sciences. Now, considering the course structure as it is presently configured within the larger footprint of Stanford University, one can begin to see a new emphasis that focuses on engineering. The "bigger picture" environmental sciences that focus on engineering facilities within Stanford now overlap with those of the biological sciences. As such, some of the programs currently undertaken at the Clark Center are now more closely associated with environmental engineering than they are with biology. Because the building was designed to be responsive to changing emphases, it appears to be coping well under such a transformation.

This mutability reflects how the timing and direction of multidisciplinary experimentation requires intensive flexibility in any university's building stock. Programs can shift and develop as new discoveries are made, and therefore the facilities have to respond at an ever-increasing rate. The obvious need for a physical location to house these activities must strike a balance between work and research activities that are site specific by nature, and those that are able to be achieved through distance learning.

Although less debated, distance learning also creates a huge potential to interconnect university-to-university activity. The mobility that technology allows us today creates greater freedom in where we live and work. Just as communication and information technologies allow us greater freedom in our personal lives, how we shape the physical world will affect the manner and the quality by which we progress academically. We clearly need a variety of spaces in which we can be fully private, totally concentrated in the nature of individual study; equally, we need other spaces that accommodate group activities and group learning. For those at the forefront of research, highly specific laboratories are particularly geared for the integration of new sciences.

The implications of these developments pivot on a fundamental balance between the human and the virtual experience of learning. The boundaries between these two possibilities are already being drawn: there are those who call for a greater level of human contact in the belief that practical curiosity-driven research manifests science and serendipity. Websites such as "The Human Factor Advocate" feature largely in such a debate. Ironically, the more academic pursuits of traditional Ivory Tower university subjects, which depend primarily on written material, will probably be the subject of greater change. With written and visual information more freely available in the forms described previously, the possibility of a more diffuse approach to university education has never been greater.

In terms of sustainability, the investigation of myriad interrelated subjects that need simultaneous consideration will require embracing the full extremes of these approaches to distance and home learning in university education. Breakthroughs achieved at a microscopic level will become as crucial as many of the other larger-scale planning issues. Practical experimentation leading to new, tangible technologies that can be fully integrated with design and production will need to harness a great wealth of information and focus it toward the end goal. This changing focus reflects one of the current mantras of sustainable thinking: "think global, act local."

INTERACTIONS BETWEEN SUSTAINABLE AND TECHNICAL THINKING

The problems we face in achieving a sustainable strategy existence are incredibly diverse, politically complex, and quite often shrouded in mystery, or are only partially understood due to misinformation. Many projects and institutions around the world have focused on specific aspects of sustainable thinking. The city of Curitiba in Brazil, for example, has gained worldwide acclaim for its strategic planning and execution of public transportation. Less well known are its achievements in the area of waste management. By working at a micro- and macroscale, the city has made tremendous inroads into this highly complex topic. The capacity for human comprehension about what is involved in difficult technical and management issues that form the bigger picture of sustainability is one of many challenges. Energy and its provision quite naturally form the centerpiece of any debate. In the end, it is what drives everything. At this point, there is no "silver bullet"—no new alternative that can replace a dependency on fossil fuels. After many years, the long quest for nuclear fusion has failed to provide the promised safe nuclear alternative. We therefore seem to be facing a future world that uses a cocktail of wind, wave, solar, thermal, and nuclear sources coupled with new technologies in the form of smart grids that collectively distribute power from these multiple sources. Even if there were a new source of energy on the horizon, other aspects of our world would still remain unsustainable.

Population growth in certain parts of the world is creating huge demands on everything from materials to food. The goal of these new populations is to create the same lifestyle that we have in the West. If all of the world's population lived as we do in Europe, we would require three planets in order to sustain that lifestyle; if the whole planet aspired to and achieved the standards in the United States, then we would need five planets.[2] Clearly, in all things we need to achieve a great deal more using much less: material, processes, water, energy use, food production as well as the endless list of everything that we touch and come into contact with in our world. To achieve all that is a fundamental technical goal, but in each of the subdisciplines involved is a myriad of complexity.

Take, for example, the concept of embodied energy. This is the amount of energy that is needed to produce anything that we make. For example, it takes about a gallon of oil to create a loaf of bread. To understand this cost, you have to start with the growing of the wheat—with the ground itself. Most food production areas today use fertilizer—fertilizer that is a by-product of the production of oil. The energy that is needed to refine that oil also has to be included within the overall energy count. The preparation and sowing of the seeds requires yet more energy, as does harvesting and transportation of the wheat to the mill. Often, the mill is a long way away from where the crop is grown. Further energy is needed to prepare it into dough and then to bake it into bread; still more energy is used in the production of the paper or plastic that it is wrapped in, and more again to transport it to the store where you will buy it—probably as part of a weekly shopping trip, and

2 One Living Planet, http://www.oneplanetliving.org/index.html.

transport it back to your home, probably in your car, thereby using more energy. Statistics would suggest that you would probably only eat half of it, thereby creating half of it as waste, along with the packaging, which of course begins the next cycle all to do with waste. Just this one example begins to indicate the technical sustainable challenges that face every move we make.

To address these challenges, we need more resources to focus on them, which is why higher education and universities, particularly research universities, need to focus to understand and then redesign many of our nonsustainable systems. We need to address creativity and ideas at all scales from the cellular to the global. Therefore, the current curricula of study need to be readdressed. Those who wish to take a broader approach to some of these issues may have to gain knowledge at a working level of subjects such as chemistry, architecture, finance, biology, or physics. Such is the complexity and scale of the task that they may then work as leaders of teams that focus on the sub-breakdowns of each of those topics. On an optimistic note, ingenuity has been proven to solve seemingly impossible tasks—quite often in relatively short timescales. For example, it is only 100 years ago that flight became a serious proposition. It took less than 60 years to progress from the first successful flight across the English Channel to landing on the moon. Less optimistically, it took less than 10 years from the development of the first atomic bomb to the creation of an arsenal large enough to destroy the entire planet.

Someone once said that you cannot look to the future without first having an understanding of the past. With the ever-increasing mobility around the world of students who are linked by the new information technologies, one is reminded of how the very first universities were established (see Figure 2.13). In 1088, in Bologna, Italy, lectures took place in houses rented by the

Figure 2.13 Padua: location of the very first university. © Jonathan Blair/ Corbis.

masters. Exams and assemblies were held in churches and convents. This created an indistinct community that was not focused on any particular building, but was located in the city itself—the city and university being one. We could be describing a new model now possible with the technology we have today. At that time, those attending lectures were drawn from the whole of Europe, and, as foreigners, they had little connection to any of the host cities.

University migration was a very common phenomenon—Cambridge University in England was created by people deciding to move en masse from Oxford (see Figures 2.14 and 2.15). Many from Bologna moved to Vicenza in 1205 and again from Bologna to Sienna in 1321. To counter this, Bologna built a chapel exclusively for scholars in 1322, which formed the first university building. As student numbers increased, more buildings were created as people moved less. The University of Paris built lecture halls, colleges, lodgings, and churches on the left bank of the Seine, called the *Quartier Latin*. The idea of the city and the university being unified in a particular area was also common to the previous examples. This idea can be seen even with the creation of the New World universities, such as Harvard, Colombia, Stanford, Virginia, and Johns Hopkins. Although these universities are more open and freely planned than their European counterparts, thereby creating the word "campus," they still have a relatively dense grain in plan that recalls a civic distribution of buildings and related public spaces.

Before universities came into being, knowledge was transferred from one of four

Figure 2.14 Cambridge city and university overlap. © Sandy Stockwell/Skycam/Corbis.

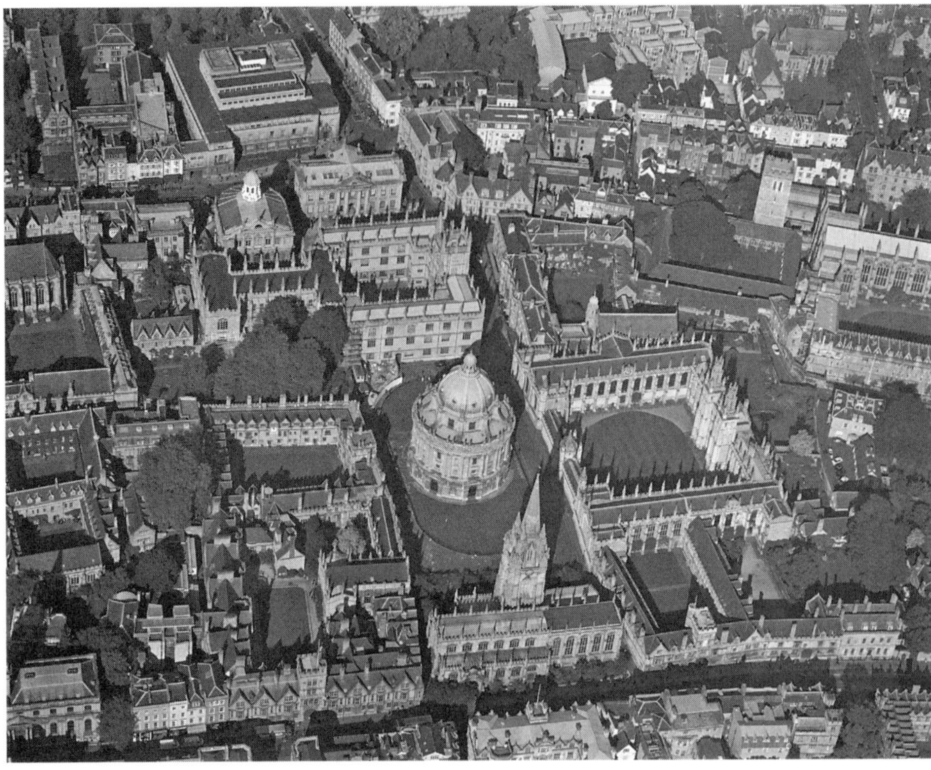

Figure 2.15 Oxford University and city interrelate. © Sandy Stockwell/Skycam/Corbis.

sources: the courts of the Holy Roman Empire, overseen by the monarch; the cathedrals, dominated by the Church; the monasteries, controlled by individual clerks; and apprenticeships, which included lawyers. The apprentice system was clearly integrated with a guild. The word *universitas* really means "guild." The process required masters to get pupils and students together in order to hire teachers and effectively create a corporation. The object was not to graduate, but to gain skill, the whole enterprise being grounded in the arts and conducted in Latin. The process allowed individuals to gain work as a scribe or a secretary and develop knowledge in Roman law and medicine. Some would continue to study to a higher level.

There were lectures and debates, thereby creating the skills to both defend and attack a proposition. Most formal study was focused on old texts: the geometry of Euclid, music with fifth-century melodies, and the philosophy of Aristotle. The situation was very open-ended and you could discuss anything, but there were implicit boundaries. The monasteries became critics of subject matter and although the Church was fragmented, with a pontiff a long way away, bishops tended to be local. The students paid for their existence and rented rooms, providing great mobility. Some, using their newfound skills, worked to generate finance. There were long summer breaks when it was possible to work at the Inns of Court during the holidays. The teacher became a moral tutor, a mentor. Some students were richer and their families paid for the process, though the Church provided a living for many. Later, regional universities were established to provide administrators for the state, and through this the university became recognized as the source of opinion. University scholars helped resolve the blend in politics and Christianity in the mid-fourteenth century. By this time, students were bored with the early texts. People were looking for new and fresh inspiration. New translations of the old texts were also beginning to appear.

Today, driven by the opportunities in the burgeoning worlds of India and China, there are demands for entirely new universities. Therefore, the concepts for their sustainable creation present a unique set of opportunities. While sustainable thinking is also very much about technical thinking, social needs and human desires play an integral part. The big issues of sustainability are best addressed at a scale larger than the individual building, and therefore the creation of a campus is an opportunity to embrace some of those bigger concerns. These could include how we use and produce our energy, how we manage and distribute water, how we control heating and cooling, how we control our waste, and how we manage mobility. All are crucial to consider when asking how a new campus should be created.

Each of these components of a sustainable design strategy has considerable technical challenges, which vary depending on location and climate and are wholly dependent on the scale with which they are to be undertaken. At present, there are few examples that pursue a holistic sustainable approach to planning on a campus scale. There are many examples where individual aspects of sustainability have been explored, but integration will require greater knowledge on how to achieve fully sustainable conditions. If we can reach this position by developing examples, then new university campuses will give us opportunities to make major advances in sustainable design. The knowledge gained from these projects will need to be applied to existing situations, as we also need to transform existing facilities, some dating back many hundreds of years, to achieve the higher performance standards that a sustainable future will demand.

There appear to be many affinities between the future of universities and the world that existed when universities were first established in medieval times. Concepts such as freedom of movement, decentralization of activity, overlapping of the university with another world, are all interesting when read in parallel with the global population migration into urban centers today. The need for education to be tailored in order to run and administer the urban environment of medieval Europe today matches the urgent need to focus on governance in order to change our efforts toward sustainability.

To dig deeper into the tangible aspects of sustainable technical thinking for the development of the university campus, it is worth examining the following topics in more detail.

Energy

The source of energy to power a campus is central to any discussion related to sustainability. The source of that power is probably the most complex problem. Though it is easy and desirable to suggest that energy should come from a renewable source, many technical and economic matters remain unresolved. There is conflicting dialogue between the centralists—those who believe that all power should be created and distributed from a central location—and the decentralists—those who believe that power should be generated from a number of different sources. Individual local circumstances need to be examined to determine the merit of each approach, and the scaling and phasing of any technology harnessed in the local production of energy also needs to be seen as part of a bigger picture. All energy providers are in business to make money, so great skill is needed when addressing governance of the relationship with energy providers.

Water

Water collection and distribution is another key concern that will increase in importance as time goes by. Again, the source of water is fundamental, but how it is managed through a campus needs to reflect the increasing scarcity of the resource. Water needs to be considered throughout its entire use cycle—from collection to levels of purification, use of graywater and blackwater, irrigation, appropriateness to climate and location, and again, scale: What issues work best at a building scale and what is better handled at a campus scale or larger?

Waste Management

Dry recyclable and compostable waste all have their own unique technical demands, and much of the processing equipment currently available is at its most economic at a scale even larger than most campuses could consider. Efforts to collect and sort waste into all its constituent components and to plan and implement recycling, waste to energy, composting, and so on will be needed to tackle many of the difficult problems of waste.

Mobility and Transport

How we move between short, medium, and long distances in a sustainable manner demands fundamental planning attitudes—shorter distances being the most fundamentally sustainable. Questions that concern transportation use include: How far can we walk from place to place in different climactic conditions? Where are we going to and from? At what point do we rely on a car or public transport? Planning density is critical here, but so, too, is the potential to live and work on campus.

Individual Buildings

The pursuit of sustainable design in buildings focuses on performance—trying to achieve much more with less material and less energy. The idea of increasing the amount of flexibility within our structures is clearly a valuable goal. Embodied energy—the energy used to create the materials from which we construct our buildings—should not be thrown away each time we make a significant change. Instead, creating adaptable structures that are more "loose-fitting" and easy to change by adding or removing systems over time can generate a longer building life. Planning a new building from a passive point of view—including orientation, shading, and so forth—is a fundamental cornerstone of any sustainable project.

The leading universities of the future will be defined by productivity and reputation. There is recognition that the academic profession will become more internationally oriented and mobile, but national circumstances will prevail at specific locations. The student population will become more varied—there will be greater numbers of international students, mature-age students, and part-time students, as well as those who are dependent on the university in distant places. The multinational nature of the student body and the need to be able to focus individually and work collectively will shape the planning of future campus design. The idea of returning to a living, working, and sustainably integrated university such as existed in the very first universities is now a distinct possibility.

Seeing a university in urban terms may be the direct consequence of sustainable strategies that focus on mobility and distribution. If this is to be the case, there will need to be an even greater focus on the nature of accommodation, as students from different parts of the world live together, and on how people in distance learning programs can feel a strong sense of association with a particular university. The physical environment of place, space, and social amenity linked with the educational standards and facilities will determine just where this nomadic, highly mobile group of eager students from around the world will decide on the best places to settle.

Never have these future new potentials been combined with a sustainable planning strategy more so than with the creation of Masdar City in the United Arab Emirates (UAE). The Masdar Initiative is an endeavor undertaken by the rulers of the oil-rich UAE to create an economic future beyond oil. The aim for the 640ha Masdar City project is to build a desert community at a small-city scale that is carbon neutral and zero waste and allows issues of sustainability to be addressed through real projects. In this regard, it is more of a test bed for future development, with research as a key catalyst. However, the mixed-use, low-rise, high-density development also has to be a livable and workable project that is achieved and occupied in phases.

Masdar City is strategically located to Abu Dhabi's transport infrastructure and links to neighboring communities and the international airport by existing road and rail routes. The city itself will be the first modern community in the world to operate without fossil-fueled vehicles at street level. With a maximum distance of 200m to the nearest rapid transport links and amenities, the city is designed to encourage walking, while its shaded streets and courts offer an attractive pedestrian environment, sheltered from climatic extremes. The surrounding land contains wind farms and photovoltaic panels, research fields, and plantations, allowing the community to be entirely energy self-sufficient.

SUSTAINABILITY, TECHNOLOGY, AND UNIVERSITIES

CASE STUDY 4

MASDAR UNIVERSITY

Masdar City, Abu Dhabi, United Arab Emirates

Architect: Foster + Partners

The Masdar Institute (MIST) is to be developed in a number of phases, the first of which was completed in December 2010. The development consists of the first phase of development for the larger Masdar complex and comprises mainly accommodations for students and staff and technical scientific and engineering and laboratory spaces (see Figure 2.16). The project satisfies the requirements of the overall master plan. In keeping with the architecture of the region, the buildings are placed very close together. Great emphasis is placed on the public spaces created between the two. This passive approach to the first phase of project planning allows greater reduction in temperature for these external public spaces. There are shops, cafés, and meeting

Figure 2.16 Masdar street view by night. © Nigel Young/Foster + Partners.

places where students, staff, and visitors can interact. The residential accommodations are naturally ventilated via their circulation spaces and in the completed first phase have very tall floor-to-ceiling heights to induce natural airflow within each of the rooms. The second phase will incorporate lower floor-to-ceiling heights in order to gain physical knowledge and confirmation of performance targeted at the design level. The student apartments are heavily shaded with external balconies and have protected views to the streets and spaces below. The laboratory buildings, which require full air conditioning in order to achieve consistent results during the course of certain experiments, have high levels of thermal insulation. Exterior cladding also incorporates ethylene tetrafluoroethylene (ETFE) cushions, which do not absorb heat, thereby reducing the external loading on the laboratories. This first phase has photovoltaic cells incorporated into the roof of both the residential and the laboratory spaces. In addition to this, a 10 MW solar farm is providing 40 percent of its power to the MIST project. The rest is being redirected into the grid. The transportation from the edge of the site to the MIST project is via 11 Personal Rapid Transport cars (driverless cars). With other measures being made in terms of waste and water management, this first phase can be considered zero carbon, zero waste.

Divided into two sectors, the development is bridged by a linear park, and is being built in phases, beginning with the larger sector, which contains the Masdar Institute (see Figure 2.17). The master plan is designed to be highly flexible, allowing it to incorporate emergent technologies and to respond to lessons learned during the implementation of the initial phases. Expansion has been anticipated from the outset, allowing for urban growth while avoiding the problem of sprawl that besets so many cities.

Knowledge gained during the process of designing and researching Masdar has already aided the development of Abu Dhabi's "Estidama" rating system for sustainable buildings. A range of pilot projects are under way, exploring alternative forms of transportation; cooling devices, such as wind

Figure 2.17 Aerial rendering of Masdar City. © Nigel Young/Foster + Partners.

towers; and new potential sources of power, including solar thermal cooling. It has already been possible to apply some of the region's wealth of expertise in oil exploitation to conduct further analysis into the use of bore holes for geothermal heating.

The Masdar Institute is the first completed phase, and in reference to examples of "standard" innovation hot spots, it forms the heart of Masdar. Operated in its first phase by MIT, the Institute focuses on renewable and environmental science, and its intent is to grow UAE Innovation, create new start-up companies, and attract other like-minded researchers to Masdar. Its residences and laboratories are oriented to shade both adjacent buildings and the pedestrian streets below, and the facades are self-shading. Over 5,000 sq m of roof-mounted photovoltaic installations provide power and further protection from the sun. A 10 MW solar field within the master plan site provides 60 percent more energy than is consumed by the Masdar Institute, all of which can be fed back to the Abu Dhabi grid.

The Institute laboratories, which have highly flexible, plug-and-play services to encourage interdisciplinary research, are shaded by horizontal and vertical fins and *brises-soleils*. The highly insulated facades are constructed from inflatable ETFE cushions, which remain cool to the touch under the intense desert sun. Cooling air currents are channeled through the public spaces using a contemporary interpretation of the region's traditional wind towers (see Figure 2.18), and green landscaping and water provide evaporative cooling.

The laboratories and residential accommodations are supported by a variety of social spaces, including a gymnasium, canteen, café, knowledge center, *majlis*—or meeting place—and landscaped areas that extend the civic realm. One-, two-, and three-bedroom apartments are housed in low-rise, high-density blocks, which act as a social counterpoint to the research environment. Windows in the residential buildings are protected by a contemporary reinterpretation of *mashrabiya*, a type of latticed projecting oriel window that is constructed with sustainably developed, glass-reinforced concrete and colored with local sand. This helps to integrate it with its desert context and to minimize maintenance. Perforations for light and shade are based on the patterns found in the traditional architecture of Islam (see Figures 2.17, 2.18, and 2.19).

FUTURE OPPORTUNITIES FOR SUSTAINABLE UNIVERSITIES

In light of all the challenges discussed above, future opportunities to develop universities have never been more relevant or important. The strategic thinking that took place in the 1950s, by people such as Vannevar Bush, helped to create a symbiotic and successful relationship between university research and the industrial machine in the United States. American universities have a greater awareness about how ideas that emerge from tertiary scientific research can be developed into the world of tangible applications. The development of start-up companies coupled with informed funding can lead directly to high-volume production. The connection

▸ *Figure 2.18 Masdar wind tower.* © Nigel Young/Foster + Partners.

◀ *Figure 2.19 View of Masdar City.* © Nigel Young/ Foster + Partners.

between the university, science, and technical research programs and their relationship with industrialized production is probably the only opportunity that we have to change the ways that we think, live, and work—and to do that with the knowledge that we only have one planet.

We have never faced a bigger task: the many routes leading to the identification of many solutions will require an unprecedented level of collaboration and integration between all actively involved individuals and groups. To achieve this, we must create better environments and better choices for people to isolate and combine in new ways and in new places and spaces. We need to maximize the benefits of freedom and mobility that new technology brings us, but in doing so also create new ways for social interaction. This changing approach needs to be linked with education as much as ideas.

The practical side of scientific and engineering exploration may well present itself in the fixed asset foundations around which future universities are planned. The cycle of ideas, hands-on experimenting, seeing and analyzing results, before again stepping back in the world of ideas, is the basis of scientific methodology and must be seen as a continuous loop.

With today's cautious view of health and safety, it is of concern that the practical aspects of science demonstrated ably by teachers at a school level in earlier times will now be viewed as being unacceptably risky. There are areas of development, particularly around subjects such as nuclear research, where these fears and concerns may well be justified. Against this position, MIT is inventing a concept of iLabs that will allow researchers to conduct online the difficult experiments that are not possible in ordinary laboratories.

The concept of iLabs, devised by MIT professors Jesus Del Alamo and Steve Lerman, treat the lab equipment as a resource. Once the investment has been made into the equipment, it can be used beyond the boundaries of one university. For example, MIT's iCampus is a joint development with Microsoft and already includes 19 universities on five continents, all of which are developing the iLab concept further. One example of the possibilities of this format lies in the Proscope HR, which is a handheld microscope with a touch view system that magnifies the view on a computer connected via a universal serial bus (USB) port. The possibility of this development is that much practical work may be controlled remotely; sensors can be manned by technicians who physically maneuver equipment for the digital instruction of different individuals located across the world.

ECONOMICS

In the United Kingdom, the rising costs of university education have been the cause of considerable concern. The British government, as part of a cost-cutting review, has created a situation where universities can charge increasingly higher fees. The effects of mortgage-sized debt on a student are highly likely to create a need for alternative ways to receive higher education. The concern is that the traditional residential university experience could become the preserve of the elite. Already in the United Kingdom about 80 percent of students work while they study, and about one-third of UK undergraduates study part-time. One in ten UK graduates will undertake distance learning courses of some form. A private market will provide all the material for distance learning technology at a fraction of the cost of a residential three-year degree course. This would mean such a degree course would cost somewhere between U.S.$7,500 and U.S.$11,000 compared to the U.S.$40,000 that a traditional "live-in" alternative would cost. Using the Open University's techniques, one-to-one contact with tutors can be far higher than is experienced in on-site postgraduate courses.

It is likely that the well-established, historic universities throughout the world will be able to maintain a "brand" based on their reputation (e.g., Harvard, Stanford, etc.) and therefore continue to provide the traditional experience. With a greater economic focus, this could well be reduced to a narrower band of institutions with more universities becoming closer to boarding schools. The concern about cost cutting on such a basis is that priorities will have to be clearly defined, and in the United Kingdom that will probably be carried out at a governmental level. In the United States, there are huge inequalities on campuses between those who have to work and study and those whose parents can afford the costs of tertiary education. The speed at which change is occurring can bring about dramatic reinterpretations of what a university might be. In addition to this, there are views that university education is, in its broadest sense, focused on providing a knowledge level that is far lower than the "white hot" demands of technology and the needs and skills of contemporary entrepreneurship.

Peter A. Thiel, a venture capitalist and macro hedge fund investor, is encouraging potential university students not to attend university. His thesis is that the entrepreneurial spirit is in many ways stifled by the university system. He quotes Bill Gates, Mark Zuckerberg, and Steve Jobs, who were either college dropouts or had very unorthodox connections to universities. His proposal is to grant a fellowship of $100,000 to 20 entrepreneurs under the age of 20, on the condition that they drop out of college for two years to pursue their venture full-time. Although this may prove to be a small-scale and one-off initiative, it has raised questions about where a university research program ends and where private industry should take the educational initiative. In the United States, technology research and development spending has hovered at around 2.5 percent of gross domestic product (GDP) for quite some time. In the 1960s, the federal government funded something like 1.5 percent of that figure. Today, the 2.5 percent remains fairly constant, but with private industry providing 2 percent of the total figure. This obviously blurs the relationship between university research and research realization; it potentially shifts the emphasis of high-end research, either moving it away from the university environment or causing the research to be more economically focused on the needs of the private sector.

One could argue that this blurring of boundaries is already under way given that California is always at the forefront of technical and scientific thinking in the United States. It is no accident that San Francisco has pioneered local coffee bars and cafés such as the Northstar Café, Ritual Coffee Roasters, the Summit, and Café Buon Giorno as unofficial creative incubators for the city's technology start-ups. It is reminiscent of London's coffeehouses of the eighteenth century where people met for business and to transfer information that fueled trade and colonial expansion.

In a speech about uncertainty and technological change, Nathan Rosenberg, the Fairleigh S. Dickinson, Jr. Professor Emeritus of Public Policy in the Department of Economics at Stanford University, said, "Many major breakthroughs included other innovation and their ultimate impact depends on identifying certain specific categories of human needs and catering to them in novel and more cost effective ways." New technologies need to pass an economic test just as much as a technological one. All this change is causing universities themselves to think. In Japan, the Future University Hakodate, known by its sobriquet "FUN," offers complex systems courses, intelligence systems courses, and courses on systems information science and media architecture. The university is looking at the complexities of the interaction between different disciplines and its effect on information and communication.

The belief that technological progress is becoming so rapid that the future will become almost impossible to predict inspired Vernor Vinge and Ray Kurzweil to create the Singularity University located at NASA's Moffett Field, part of the Ames Research Center, in the heart of Silicon Valley, where students gather during summer vacation for intensive coursework. A whole range of institutes and foundations now lie at the borders between conventional university pursuits and the demands of science. The Ford Foundation, the Bill and Melinda Gates Foundation, and the Kaufmann Institute Foundation all contribute billions of dollars to research and development. The Kaufmann, in particular, brings universities together with industry. The William and Flora Hewlett Foundation has also been in operation since 1967 and aims to solve social and environmental problems around the world.

The evolving needs of science and industry and the direction that technology takes in the future will therefore influence what courses will be offered at a university level. Not only does this require focus on subjects that have the potential for future economic growth but also on the pressing demands of health and environment that affect our everyday existence. The two may or may not be linked. For example, it is an established fact that environmental sciences in their broadest spectrum have great potential for technical and commercial growth. The desire to find the "newest" new thing already identifies sustainable research as a key area of future growth. Many of our universities now have a student population that is more familiar with issues of sustainability than ever before, with active university websites about sustainability that collect and distribute information for students and staff.

Cornell University, for example, has an online "roadmap" to achieve carbon neutrality by 2050; Bradford University in the United Kingdom outlines basic sustainability information such as transportation; and the University of Helsinki fully explores the reduction of energy and waste distribution. There is even a following for the University Leaders for a Sustainable Future (ULSF), and Harvard University has created a sustainable science program. Sustainability certainly forms one of the specific categories of human needs, and the diversity and complexity of the subject matter calls for the best minds to focus on solutions if our most pressing needs are to be conceptualized, developed, and brought to bear on practical issues that face us all.

If we accept therefore that the university as an institution has tremendous power and influence, then the notion of a national education policy that might guide university goals is clearly a possibility. If sustainability is truly an end game worthy of pursuit and if the condition of the world demands new and total action to be dedicated to the objectives of a longer-term sustainable future, the university as a source of knowledge and endeavor can truly play a dominant role in the future of sustainable thinking. Universities must focus on the real future of life on this planet. Historically and in pure capability terms, they have the power and authority to really transform our future. The institution of the university has always had this influence and ability, and right now the highest goal for humanity should be focused on our long-term survival. The ability to clinically analyze what we should focus on and what we should disregard has never been more pertinent in terms of the environmental position. Today, the universities of the world are at a major crossroads. If the institution of the university cannot be instrumental in bringing about change in the way we consider our lives on this planet, then I believe our hopes and endeavors for the future are futile. We need our best minds, our best abilities, and our strongest force to seriously engage with the environmental issues that face us. Personally, I am optimistic that the powerhouse of the university, if properly engaged, can seriously answer the clarion call for a new way of living.

CHAPTER 3

HISTORIC CAMPUS PRESERVATION

Stephen J. Farneth, FAIA, LEED AP

They [buildings of past times] are not ours. They belong, partly to those who built them, and partly to all the generations of mankind who are to follow us.

—John Ruskin

INTRODUCTION

College and university campuses are very special places, reflecting both the early ideals of the college's founders and designers and the embodied memory, intellectual development, and historical events that have occurred there over many generations. Buildings and landscape symbolize the campus experience for prospective, current, and former students. Preservation and careful redevelopment of buildings and landscapes are important not just for the physical quality of the campus but also for recruitment, the "student experience," and a continuing connection with alumni to the college. Preserving that essential character, while allowing the college to grow and change, is the primary objective of campus preservation planning.

The idea of the college campus as a separate place for education, a community of its own, is a distinctly American development. Thomas Jefferson's Academical Village at the University of Virginia serves as an early model. Because of this intention of creating a new or separate place, most college campuses developed in this country after the mid-nineteenth century began not in an incremental or vernacular manner but with a master plan, usually created by a highly distinguished architect or landscape architect. This plan set out the original concepts for the campus and often established its signature buildings. With that framework for the original campus, subsequent generations of designers, administrators, faculty, and students have added complex layers of physical change and institutional memory.

Campus design has attracted important architects and landscape architects from every generation. Consequently, almost all campuses today are mosaics of design ideas of several generations. These layers of change have sometimes been highly destructive of earlier work. More recent developments may have already achieved recognition and importance beyond the original plan. Understanding and making judgments about the relative significance of all of the layers of campus development is an important but very difficult and sometimes contentious task in campus preservation planning. The value of memory of shared historical events also affects these judgments.

One other element of preservation planning, which is often lost in looking at the glow of the past, is that every generation must create its own layers of new design. There must be room in the picture for new ideas that will be worthy of preservation in the future. This is particularly true for college and university design, where the advancement of human knowledge is a major principle.

Developments in Preservation Practice

Over recent years, the understanding of preservation has matured from simple preservation of the exterior features of a few selected monumental buildings to a much more broadly defined activity. Today, preservation practice recognizes the importance of the whole building, exterior and interior, and includes not just monumental structures but also more modestly designed buildings and vernacular structures. The activity of preservation expands beyond the consideration of single buildings to apply to districts of buildings, landscapes, and heritage areas, broad assemblages of natural and cultural development. It has also expanded beyond the built environment to include intangible values such as oral traditions, ritual, and memory. Of great importance to college campuses has been the development of the field of landscape preservation as a discipline in itself, establishing standards for the evaluation and treatment of cultural landscapes. The understanding of the relationship between sustainable design and preservation has also been an important development. Reuse and redevelopment of existing buildings is recognized as being inherently energy conserving, due to the energy already embodied in the existing structure. Understanding these potential efficiencies has led to a greater interest in preservation and building reuse.

An area of growing interest is in the buildings of the recent past. Beginning with the recognition of the importance of many midcentury modern buildings and landscapes, the discussion has expanded to consider buildings of even more recent vintage. While the great monuments of the modern movement are without question worthy of preservation, evaluation of the less renowned buildings of that generation has often sparked controversy. This is particularly true on college and university campuses, many of which experienced considerable (and sometimes highly destructive) growth to their original campus designs in the 1960s and 1970s. Attempting to recognize and evaluate the significance of buildings that have not yet stood the test of time has often resulted in the kind of disagreement that once occurred regarding preservation activities in general. This discussion of more recent layers of design on historic campuses has resulted in a rethinking of campus preservation plans to include a more comprehensive and layered valuing of the features of the campus, including the designs of the most recent generations.

HISTORIC BUILDINGS—PRESERVATION
CASE STUDY 1

DIANA CHAPMAN WALSH ALUMNAE HALL
Wellesley College, Wellesley, Massachusetts

Architect: Ann Beha Architects
Completion 2010

Figure 3.1 Auditorium after rehabilitation. © Peter Vanderwarker.

Building History
Designed by Cram and Ferguson, Alumnae Hall was constructed in 1922 and used for large gatherings, reunions, college convocations, and social events. By the time of the restoration and renovation, Alumnae Hall did not meet the needs for contemporary performance, teaching, or gathering. Its theater was compromised by poor acoustics and sight lines, and minimal lobby and rehearsal spaces. Access for the disabled was severely limited. The systems were outdated, and the building was not air-conditioned or code compliant. The interiors had seen many changes in finishes as well as the loss of original architectural detail and many special features (see Figure 3.1).

Project Priorities
The project budget, program, and the historic interiors were carefully considered in establishing priorities. The Secretary of the Interior's Standards and the college's own campus standards suggested that a period of research and study precede any final design. The project priorities included:

- Restoring exterior integrity through repairs and preservation of the building envelope
- Retrieving the original architectural expression of the building interior
- Offering new opportunities for patrons and performers
- Achieving building code compliance and providing accessibility for all
- Creating functional rehearsal and events spaces
- Providing improved acoustic quality
- Integrating new systems and technology into the historic building
- Including sustainable principles in all aspects of the design
- Establishing Alumnae Hall as a renewed magnet for the community and the college
- Completing the commitment to the campus land reclamation initiative

Rehabilitation and Restoration
Predesign Phase
- Historical research included archival review, photographic inventories, oral histories, and review of other Cram buildings.
- Preservation design philosophy was established to make new interventions explicit, but subservient to the overall building assemblage.

Exterior Envelope
- Replace and restore roofing systems.
- Clean, repoint, and repair exterior masonry.

Codes and Accessibility
- Enclose original exterior arcade to create lobby and accessible entrance.
- Remove barriers throughout the building and regrade floor slopes to create universal access.

Auditorium
- Revise concrete floor rake to improve sight lines and improve acoustical separation.
- Re-open and restore exterior windows to rediscover views and provide daylight.
- Revise seating layout to improve circulation, sightlines and accessibility, and replace seating.
- Install new theatrical lighting, rigging systems, and equipment.
- Restore and refurbish original chandeliers.
- Create new stage extension to provide greater flexibility for performance.

Lower Level Rehearsal Space
- Reconfigure ballroom space into multifunctional rehearsal areas.

Finishes
- Research, expose, and document original color palette and murals.
- Establish new color palette to enliven spaces and provide warmth.
- Restore and recreate original wall and ceiling murals.

Systems Integration
- Install all new heating and cooling systems, integrated with original supply registers throughout the building.
- Create new mechanical area provided as an acoustically isolated new addition.

Sustainability
- The completed project achieved a LEED Gold level of sustainability.

▸ *Figure 3.2 Entrance after rehabilitation.* Peter Vanderwarker.

PRESERVATION, RESTORATION, REHABILITATION, AND ADAPTIVE USE

Under the overall umbrella of preservation, design activities for existing buildings may involve a number of approaches, usually dictated by the historical significance and remaining integrity of the existing building. The scope and philosophy of each of these design activities are often mislabeled or misunderstood. The following are definitions provided by the Secretary of the Interior's Standards for the Treatment of Historic Properties, 1995.

Preservation is defined as the act or process of applying measures necessary to sustain the existing form, integrity, and materials of a historic property. Work, including preliminary measures to protect and stabilize the property, generally focuses on the ongoing maintenance and repair of historic materials and features rather than extensive replacement and new construction. New exterior additions are not within the scope of this treatment; however, the limited and sensitive upgrading of mechanical, electrical, and plumbing systems and other code-required work to make properties functional is appropriate within a preservation project.

The Hoover Tower, designed by Arthur Brown Jr., is one of the most prominent buildings on the Stanford University campus. This preservation project included the cleaning of all exterior surfaces, repair and repointing of cast stone masonry, and repair and limited replacement of damaged clay roofing tiles at the dome. Detailed survey and exploration determined the causes of staining on the building's surfaces (see Figures 3.3 and 3.4).

Rehabilitation is defined as the act or process of making possible a compatible use for a property through repair, alterations, and additions while preserving those portions or features that convey its historical, cultural, or architectural values.

The Leland Stanford Jr. Museum at Stanford University was established by Leland and Jane Stanford in 1891. At the time, it was one of the first reinforced concrete structures in the country. The building was heavily damaged in the great 1906 earthquake, partially rebuilt, and again heavily damaged in the 1989 Loma Prieta earthquake. This complete rehabilitation of the building to become the Cantor Center for the Visual Arts included seismic strengthening and upgrade of all building systems as well as programmatic changes to the use and operation of the building to serve a wide range of programmatic functions within the Department of Art. In addition to the rehabilitation of the historic building, a new 42,000 sq ft addition was included in the project (see Figures 3.5 and 3.6).

Adaptive use is not formally recognized in the Secretary of the Interior's Standards as a treatment separate from rehabilitation. However, as it is applied as well to nonhistoric buildings, it is the process of converting a building to a use other than that for which it was designed (e.g., changing a factory into housing). Such a conversion may be accomplished with varying degrees of alteration to the building.

Restoration is defined as the act or process of accurately depicting the form, features, and character of a property as it appeared at a particular period of time by means of the removal of features from other

▸ *Figure 3.3 Hoover Tower, Stanford University, Stanford, California.* Architectural Resources Group.

periods in its history and reconstruction of missing features from the restoration period. The limited and sensitive upgrading of mechanical, electrical, and plumbing systems and other code-required work to make properties functional is appropriate within a restoration project. The Secretary of the Interior's Standards for Restoration require that there be clear documentation in the form of historic photographs or drawings to guide the accuracy of the restoration work.

Although the pavilions of Thomas Jefferson's Academical Village at the University of Virginia are remarkably intact for their age, many changes have occurred over time. After extensive documentary and on-site research, the university embarked on a project to restore missing features, including major roof parapets on Pavilion X. Plaster finish materials and colors were also restored. The discoveries about original colors and forms and their resulting restoration has begun an active discussion about the most appropriate preservation treatments for the Academical Village (see Figures 3.7 and 3.8).

◀ *Figure 3.4 Hoover Tower, Stanford University, Stanford, California.* Architectural Resources Group.

◀ *Figure 3.5 Cantor Center for the Visual Arts, exterior, Stanford University.* Architectural Resources Group.

▸ *Figure 3.6 Cantor Center for the Visual Arts, interior, Stanford University.* Architectural Resources Group.

▸ *Figure 3.7 Pavilion X, before restoration, University of Virginia, Charlottesville. University of Virginia.*

◀ *Figure 3.8 Pavilion X, after restoration, University of Virginia, Charlottesville.* Mesick Cohen Wilson Baker Architects.

Most projects for existing buildings will incorporate elements of each activity in varying proportions. This is especially true for projects on college campuses, where upgrading the function of a structure to meet present-day standards is often the motivating factor (rehabilitation and adaptive use). Projects may adapt and improve functions; rehabilitate structure and building systems; preserve historic spaces, materials, and features; and sometimes restore missing historical features that have been lost in previous remodeling. The key question relating to the balancing of these various actions is how to treat the historic features of the building in the course of the work; what and how much of the building's original materials and features should be preserved?

The answer is unique to every project. It is a function of the building's historical, architectural, and institutional significance and of the integrity of its current condition. Buildings of high significance and integrity demand the highest level of preservation, while those buildings with less significance or which have been heavily altered allow for a greater level of change through rehabilitation and more invasive adaptation.

The determination of the exact boundaries between preservation and adaptation will be open to debate throughout the course of the project. However, the most critical task at the inception of the project will be to create a description of its overall objectives that clearly articulates the relative significance of the building and the general expectations of the project in terms of preservation and building performance. This description will serve to direct the design team and will become the basis for achieving an alignment of the expectations of fund-raisers, administrators, building users, and agency reviewers. Early agreement among all of these parties on the project's goals, especially those related to the extent of preservation, will greatly enhance the likelihood of a successful project.

PRESERVATION AND SUSTAINABLE DESIGN

The preservation and reuse of existing buildings is the most basic and effective form of sustainable design. While construction of new high-performance green buildings may create a higher public profile, rehabilitation of existing buildings with a focus on sustainability can achieve many of the same objectives, without the waste of demolition and without the energy consumed in making new materials and in the construction process. While measuring metrics vary, all sources agree that the energy embodied in the materials and construction of an existing building can represent a significant percentage of the energy consumed in operations and maintenance over the life of the building. Essentially, rehabilitated existing buildings have a very large head start over newly constructed buildings in their long-term energy use profile.

Through the process of rehabilitation, the performance of the existing building can be further enhanced. Preservation standards for historic buildings create some limits to the range of potential sustainability alterations that might be appropriate. However, historic structures also frequently reflect climate-sensitive design features for their era, which can be enhanced and maximized. In addition, most materials used in historic structures have longer life expectancies and are more maintainable over the long term than many modern materials.

Preservation and sustainable design are completely compatible and mutually beneficial. Sustainability objectives should be carefully integrated into all rehabilitation projects for both historic and nonhistoric buildings.

HISTORIC BUILDINGS—REHABILITATION
CASE STUDY 2

LINDE + ROBINSON LABORATORY FOR GLOBAL ENVIRONMENTAL SCIENCE

California Institute of Technology, Pasadena

Architect: Architectural Resources Group
Completion: 2012

Building History

The Henry M. Robinson Laboratory of Astrophysics was designed as part of a complex of three buildings for the Department of Astrophysics in the 1930s by the architectural firm of Mayers Murray & Phillip, formerly known as Goodhue Associates, in accordance with the Moorish and Spanish Churrigueresque style established by the 1916 campus master plan of Bertram Goodhue. The function of the laboratory was reflected in its cast stone ornamentation, light fixtures, and other decorative details which abound in celestial and solar motifs. The building construction is a reinforced concrete structure with cement plaster finish. The original laboratory featured a coelostat, a roof-mounted solar telescope that collected the sun's rays and transmitted them through a vertical solar shaft into the various below grade laboratories.

For decades, the lab housed Caltech's astrophysicists and astronomers. In 2009, they relocated across California Boulevard to the Cahill Center for Astronomy and Astrophysics, creating the opportunity for the building's rehabilitation and reuse.

◀ *Figure 3.9 Linde + Robinson Lab for Global Environmental Science exterior after rehabilitation.* Archives, California Institute of Technology.

The Linde + Robinson Lab for Global Environmental Science is a ground-breaking prototype Laboratory that brings together an amalgam of scientists to study the complex interactions between earth, its oceans, atmospheres, and biospheres, and the effects that humans have upon it. The project grounds this new center of science in one of the oldest buildings on Caltech's campus. It is an extraordinary example of how historic structures can be re-imagined to accommodate state-of-the-art scientific research in an extremely sustainable way, while retaining the historic character and significance of the structure (see Figures 3.9–3.11).

◀ *Figure 3.10 Linde + Robinson Lab for Global Environmental Science interior lounge area after rehabilitation.* Archives, California Institute of Technology.

Figure 3.11 Linde + Robinson Lab for Global Environmental Science interior main corridor after rehabilitation. Archives, California Institute of Technology.

Project Priorities

The concepts and priorities for the project were established through a series of meetings and workshops with the design team, scientists, and a wide range of user groups. The priorities included:

- Create a new and permanent home for the Linde + Robinson Laboratory for Global Environmental Science and bring together students and faculty from multiple Caltech divisions.
- Give the laboratory program an identity and center in a building that is centrally located for the Division of Geological and Planetary Sciences.
- Preserve the historical character and features of the building.
- Complete the project in the most sustainable and energy efficient manner possible, with the goal of achieving a LEED Platinum rating. Use the project to create a ground-breaking model of sustainability in a historic structure.
- Transform the building into a contemporary laboratory while maintaining its historic integrity.
- Provide code compliant egress and fire safety systems and disabled accessibility to and throughout the building.
- Perform a complete exterior envelope restoration.
- Meet the technical and performance requirements of the laboratories.
- Provide spaces that promote and foster interdisciplinary interaction and collaboration.

Rehabilitation and Restoration

Predesign Phase

- The programming phase included extensive multidisciplinary workshops, including the design team, consultants, scientists, and users, to explore reuse, preservation, and sustainability strategies.
- Detailed programming provided for identification of technical equipment needs, functional requirements, and systems adjacencies for shared use of facilities and equipment, and for coordination in limited existing spaces.
- The building's unique configuration, with three floors below grade, all connected by a solar tower light shaft, provided both opportunities and constraints that were explored during the predesign phase.

Site and Landscape

- Landscape areas adjacent to the building were replanned to accommodate outdoor activities, and planting and irrigation were detailed to collect, conserve, and reuse rainwater.

Exterior Envelope

- Roofing systems were replaced and roof areas were redesigned to accommodate roof-mounted equipment.
- Steel sash window systems were preserved and restored.
- Exterior stucco and cast stone ornamental elements were cleaned and restored.

Codes and Accessibility

- A new addition was created to the west to house a new second egress stair and elevator.
- The historic central stair was restored and upgraded with compliant handrails and guardrails.
- Accessibility to the building and throughout all levels was provided.

Above Grade Classrooms and Public Spaces

- Significant historic spaces on the upper two levels were preserved and reused for gathering spaces, including classrooms, lecture room, and lounge.
- Special decorative wall and ceiling finishes in the upper spaces were conserved and restored.
- Historic light fixtures were restored and relamped.

Below Grade Laboratory Spaces

- Below grade laboratories were completely remodeled to become state-of-the-art laboratory spaces.

Daylighting

- Historic steel sash was reglazed with high-performance glazing.
- Automated shades and daylight harvesting electric lighting control systems were installed in all daylit spaces.

Repurposing of the Coelostat

- The coelostat was repurposed to serve as a source of daylight to the below grade laboratories, connecting the sunlight beam into specially designed fiber-optic light fixtures.
- The coelostat continues to provide light beams to the labs for experimental use and projects a real-time solar image into the upper shaft lobby area.
- The lower pit area of the solar shaft serves as a storage area for chilled water, greatly reducing the size of cooling tower needed for the building.

Structural System

- Only limited seismic strengthening of existing concrete structural system was required.

Mechanical and Electrical Systems

- Use of radiant heating and cooling panels reduced duct sizes in tight-ceilinged lower levels.
- An air ventilation system was developed with a monitoring system that measures air quality for contaminants, increasing air exchange when needed.
- Recommendations were made to replace outdated lab equipment and to change operating parameters for existing equipment, resulting in a 50 percent reduction in plug load energy use.
- Rooftop-mounted photovoltaic panels and fuel cells produce electric power sent to the main distribution panel for use by all campus buildings.
- Night cooling of water, stored in the lower coelostat pit, provides chilled water to the building and is pumped to other campus buildings via the central plant.

Sustainability

- The completed project achieved a LEED Platinum level of sustainability and is the first renovated historic laboratory to achieve such distinction.

The LEED (Leadership in Energy and Environmental Design) program of the United States Green Building Council has become the most prominent program for evaluating and measuring sustainability in design and construction. As a consistent means for measuring and comparing design decisions against a standard of sustainability, the LEED program has been very effective in inspiring not just design professionals but also administrators and politicians to move toward more sustainable design. The program does not as yet recognize historic buildings as a separate design category and in some ways may not adequately measure the various values of preserving existing structures. However, as a consistent measuring device for evaluating the relative sustainability merits of a project, it is a very important program. Historic buildings, carefully rehabilitated, can achieve Silver, and often Gold, levels of certification.

PROGRAMMING/PREDESIGN PHASE

The predesign phase of preservation/reuse projects is critical to the success of the project. It involves not only programming for the building but also developing a detailed understanding and analysis of the building on which all subsequent phases will rely. Investment of time and money in the predesign phase will pay dividends throughout the course of the project.

Predesign begins with the preparation of a historic structure report (HSR). The HSR may vary in detail, depending on the significance of the building and the amount of existing information or analyses that already exist. An HSR may be prepared for buildings independent of whether they are planned for upgrading or rehabilitation, as these reports provide a basis for overall decision making on campus planning as well as for ongoing priorities such as maintenance and operations. The scope of work for an HSR may include the following:

1. *Historical research and analysis.* Research and summarize the building's history and development and evaluate the building's significance in the context of the campus, or on a broader community, statewide, or national level. Collect historic photographs and other documents that supply information about the early periods of the building's design, construction, and use.
2. *Identification of significant spaces and features.* Identify and categorize the building's most significant spaces and character-defining features (see Figure 3.12). Identify areas of the building that are less sensitive to change, where alterations for building upgrades can more easily be accommodated.
3. *Documentation of the construction chronology of the building.* Identify layers of remodeling and changes over time. In some cases, remodeling campaigns are of important historical value. Evaluate which, if any, layers of change are worthy of preservation.
4. *Exploration of the building's physical fabric.* Develop an understanding of how the building was originally constructed; categorize existing materials and assemblies; assess the current condition of the building; and document its needs for maintenance, repair, and potential upgrading of building systems. As part of the exploration, outline testing and/or further exploration of concealed conditions will need to occur as the project moves forward. These further explorations may occur as a part of the predesign phase, as in many cases unknown conditions must be understood adequately in order to make appropriate informed decisions as the project moves forward. This phase of exploration and analysis should involve a

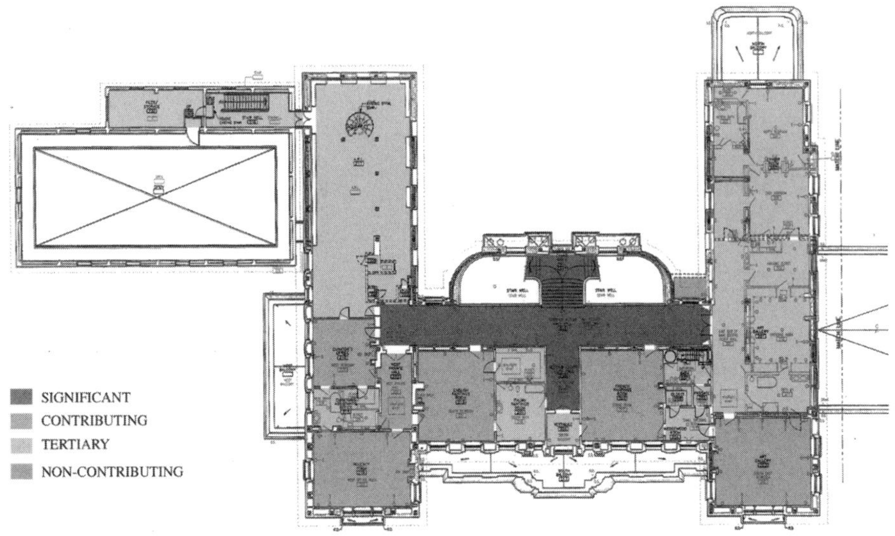

◀ *Figure 3.12 Significance diagram, The Huntington Library, Art Collections, and Botanical Gardens, San Marino, California.* Architectural Resources Group.

range of team members, in addition to the architects and materials conservators, including structural, mechanical, and electrical engineers.

5. *Preparation of accurately measured drawings of existing conditions.* These measured drawings will serve as base drawings to be used throughout the project.

Concurrent with the development of an understanding of the existing building is the programming for its adapted or upgraded use. Appropriate programming for the building is equally critical in determining the ultimate success of the project. One of the most common mistakes in this process is to overprogram the historic building, placing demands for changes to spaces and configurations that will result in destruction of historic character and create a muddled architectural result.

The process for programming for a historic building is not simply to identify proposed square footages, uses, and relationships, but to do this in an iterative process that coordinates the program requirements with the existing building's capacity to support that program. It starts with a proposed use profile, which is generally compatible with the existing building both in terms of its overall functional/spatial requirements and its historic/symbolic fit. Then the program develops to work hand-in-hand with the identification of significant spaces for the building and with the framework of spatial hierarchy and circulation that are the core of the building's original integrity. Frequently, historic circulation spaces, lobbies, hallways, and vestibules to primary spaces are more spacious than those found in current standards for modern construction, resulting in less efficiency of use. However, this graciousness is often the essential quality of a historic building, which, if lost, greatly alters the character of the building. Recognition of this attribute of the building as part of the programming phase is essential. Frequently, it is necessary to reduce the original program expectations, in order to preserve the building's primary spaces and essential character.

The programming process also provides an opportunity to consider removal of later layers of remodeling to expose and restore important lost elements of a building's character. The HSR will have identified these areas and outlined opportunities for restoration or remodeling in ways that may be considered in the programming for the building.

Test fitting the proposed program on the building floor plate also will involve evaluation of a number of program requirements. Common needs for historic buildings in their adaptation to new functions are enhanced fire egress and disabled accessibility. Understanding the general expectations in these areas is an essential part of the programming phase. In addition, expected acoustical performance and/or separation of spaces identified in the program should be evaluated in this phase for changes that might be required in the building.

Where program needs exceed the building's capacity, and there is no ability or desire to reduce the program requirements, consideration of an addition to the building may be a preferred approach to extensive interior remodeling of the existing building. A new addition can often conveniently provide additional circulation elements, including elevators, as well as specially configured spaces that may not be easily achievable in the historic areas of the building.

Project Process and Management

Project Team

In addition to the normal design team for an architectural project, a preservation/reuse project may include a number of additional members in the project team. Some of the following roles may be filled by the same consultant if he or she has the appropriate range of training:

1. *Architectural historian.* This consultant conducts research into the history of the building and assists the design team in evaluating the significance of the building and its primary spaces and features, establishing a context for making decisions.
2. *Preservation architect.* An architect with training and experience in working on historic buildings, this consultant may be the primary architect on the project, leading the entire design team, or he or she may be a consulting architect to the lead firm. This decision is often made based on the scale of the proposed project. Either model can be successful; however, the preservation architect must have a strong enough voice, authority, and skills to guide major project decisions, whether he or she is in charge of the overall project team or is a consultant.
3. *Materials conservator.* This consultant should have training and experience in the appropriate treatment of historic materials. He or she evaluates the condition and constituent parts of historic materials and assemblies, develops diagnoses of their deterioration processes, and prepares appropriate plans and specifications for repair and restoration.
4. *Materials testing engineer.* Working in conjunction with the structural engineer, this consultant samples and tests existing and/or historic structural materials for their condition and capacity, forming a basis for structural design.
5. *Nondestructive exploratory engineer.* Using a range of nondestructive survey and analytical equipment, this consultant evaluates and documents materials conditions in unexposed structural assemblies.
6. *Fire safety engineer.* This consultant assists the design team in working with fire safety codes, the building's existing construction, and the proposed occupancy of the building, to create a life safety strategy.

The work may entail sophisticated analyses such as fire and egress modeling.

7. *Hazardous materials engineer.* Often under direct contract to the owner, this engineer conducts sampling and analysis of the building to identify potential hazardous materials, such as lead or asbestos, existing in the building and develops an appropriate remediation plan.

Special Review Processes

Historic buildings can be subject to a number of special review processes. These vary and are dependent on local jurisdictions. However, there are many consistent elements which are described here. It is generally not necessary for a building to be officially listed on the National Register of Historic Places or on a local or state listing of historic buildings to be considered historic and therefore subject to review. Being considered eligible to be listed on these registers is generally the threshold to require review.

1. *Local-level review.* The local community planning department and/or historic landmarks advisory board may have jurisdiction to review the project at a planning level. In the past, local landmarks reviews were largely focused on exterior changes and impacts; however, in many locations, these reviews are now more comprehensive, evaluating impacts and changes planned for the entire building and site.
2. *State-level review.* Every state government has a State Historic Preservation Office and Officer (SHPO); which is the lead agency for review of impacts on historic resources. These reviews may vary somewhat depending on the overall environmental review process mandated by the state; however, the SHPO will review the proposed project for impacts and issues (this review may entail cultural resource impacts, in addition to the building itself, such as archeological issues or Native American concerns).
3. *Federal-level review.* The potential for a federal level of review depends largely on whether the project will use any federal funding. If federal funds are involved, the project will be subject to review under Section 106 of the National Historic Preservation Act to determine the project's effect on historic resources. The Section 106 review process is led by the State Historic Preservation Officer, reporting to the federal Advisory Council on Historic Preservation (ACHP).

The basis for all of the reviews is compliance with the Secretary of the Interior's Standards for the Treatment of Historic Properties. This set of documents (discussed later) provides the relatively flexible framework for all preservation-related decisions on a project. Interpretation of the standards, however, can vary depending on the sophistication and general approach of the reviewing agency and particularly the reviewer. Because of this variability, it is very important to meet early with the responsible agencies, to review the direction of the project and document early decisions of approval of approach. This conceptual approval should serve as the basis for future, more detailed reviews.

Budget and Cost Controls

Preservation/reuse projects have developed a reputation for being difficult to control from a budgeting point of view. It is true that there are many examples of preservation/reuse projects where cost control has been a major failure. But with careful attention in the early planning stages, budgeting and cost controls for preservation/reuse projects can be as manageable as those for new construction.

The most important difference between budgeting for existing buildings and budgeting for new buildings is the element of unknown conditions in existing construction. Understanding and estimating these unknown areas is crucial to budget control and must be attended to throughout the course of the project. The first efforts at budgeting for the project should identify where these areas of uncertainty exist. They may be geotechnical conditions, potential for hazardous materials, structural conditions, unknown deterioration conditions for special materials, or any number of others. In the predesign phase, these unknown elements should be identified, as much as possible, and targeted with a budgeting contingency. Rather than one large contingency on the overall project, targeted contingencies should be developed for every named uncertainty. The targeted contingencies should not necessarily present the worst case conditions, since the incremental result of multiple contingencies can create so much fear that the project becomes infeasible. Rather, unknowns should be presented as a realistic range of possible costs yet to be identified.

Early in the predesign phase, exploration of existing conditions should be conducted in order to begin to reduce the reliance on contingencies and establish a better understanding of the realities of the conditions and the range of alternative options and costs involved in dealing with them. At the end of the predesign phase, a budget should be able to be developed that both estimates the known scope of the project and attaches a range of costs to those areas that are still unknown or unquantifiable. As the project moves forward through design, areas of unknown scope should become reduced as more detail is developed about the requirements of the rehabilitation, allowing the gradual reduction of contingencies in the estimate.

In some cases, there may remain areas that are unsurveyed and unquantified. Common examples include areas of wood rot or termite damage or areas of mortar repointing on a masonry wall. Bidding of these unquantified areas will either result in a bid that is overly high (covering the contractor's risk) or unrealistically low (assuming the least scope to win the bid, then adding on through change orders later). The preferred approach would be to bid a given area of the work at a fixed price (allowance) with a bid unit cost for the work over or below the contracted amount. This is both the fairest and the most accurate means of estimating and contracting the work. It does require careful oversight during construction in order to document the actual areas of work completed.

UNIQUE DESIGN CONCERNS

There are a number of special design considerations that are specific to working on historic buildings.

Design Standards

The Secretary of the Interior's Standards for the Treatment of Historic Properties are a collection of documents that provide criteria to guide decision making on historic projects. Originally written in 1976 and revised in 1981, 1986, and 1995, the standards have become accepted over 35 years of use. There are different sets of standards for preservation, rehabilitation, restoration, reconstruction, and archeology—and for both historic buildings and landscapes. The standards most applicable to preservation/reuse projects are the Secretary of the Interior's Standards for Rehabilitation.

The Standards for Rehabilitation consist of 10 broadly worded criteria describing the preferred approach to different actions to be taken in the course of rehabilitation. Over time and use, the understanding and application of the standards has developed and matured. Guidelines for Rehabilitating Buildings, which have been written by the National Park Service as a companion document, add further detail to the interpretation of the standards.

These 10 standards form the basis for the decision making of the design team and for evaluation of the design by outside reviewing agencies. They are written in an open-ended manner to have broad applicability across the range of potential project types. This breadth, while allowing for applicability to many different conditions, also allows for differing interpretations of the standards, often leading to disagreements between the project team and reviewing agencies regarding whether the proposed project design complies with the standards. Therefore, the project team should seek consultation and review of all project proposals as early in the design process as possible.

Design Life

One of the most important concepts related to preservation/reuse projects has to do with the intended design life of the project. By choosing to preserve a building, one is deciding to extend the planned life of the building as far into the future as possible. The life of the proposed program is much shorter than the design life of the historic building; therefore, all of the interventions required to support the current program must be considered as short term. Over the future life of the building, the building's use program will probably change many times. Current design interventions must be detailed in such a way that in the future their removal or alteration will not entail demolition of historic materials. This concept of *reversibility* is a basic tenet of the art conservation world and applies in most cases to preservation/reuse projects. In making decisions for the current project, it is important to consider what the next generation of design professionals will face in remodeling or repairing the current work. This consideration not only affects major design interventions, such as whether to remove a wall or not, but also has an impact on the level of detail: How will coatings and preservation repair systems be maintained over time? Are they maintainable? Selecting appropriate repair and replacement materials must be done with an eye to a longer life cycle.

New/Old Interface

Consideration must be given to how new materials will relate to original materials, both visually and physically. There is not one standard answer philosophically to questions of new/old interface, but a range of solutions and approaches. In some cases, historical materials must be conserved with the least possible intrusion of new material; in other cases, it is appropriate and necessary to replace historical materials that have reached the end of their life with new materials to match the original being replaced; and in a third category, it is often necessary to install new elements and features that are not in any way historical. How these new materials are detailed to relate to and meet the historic materials of the building is a defining design question.

New Additions

The question of new/old interface also exists at the scale of the building itself. If new additions to the building are necessary, how will they be treated? The Secretary of the Interior's Standards states that new additions shall be compatible with the original building, but shall also be clearly contemporary so that there is no confusion about what is new and what is original. In practice, this general standard has been interpreted in many ways to suit the architect or design review committee's preferences. It leaves a great deal of room for interpretation. Each building has its own set of sensitivities and each new addition also has its own set of requirements. There is not one approach, but a range of approaches to the building that attempt to achieve a level of appropriateness. Design for new additions must begin with consideration for the special features, both exterior and interior, of the existing building (see Figure 3.13).

SITE ISSUES

Any discussion of changes to the site around the building involves coordination with the overall campus landscape and circulation plan. Most university campuses began with a clear master plan creating the original context for the buildings. As the campus grew and developed over time, layers of change were added to this original base.

Just as it is necessary to understand the history, significance, and layers of change for a historic building before undertaking work on it, so, too, is it necessary to understand these issues for the site. Undertaking a campus-wide cultural landscape report (CLR), or campus preservation plan, is an important task in developing an understanding of the significant layers of development of the campus and identifying those features that should be preserved.

Similar to an HSR, the CLR researches and documents the early history and design concepts of the site and then identifies remaining significant features for preservation. It creates a framework for new development, rehabilitation, or restoration of areas of the campus (see Figure 3.14).

▸ *Figure 3.13 Bowdoin College Museum, Bowdoin College, Brunswick, Maine.* © Facundo de Zuviria.

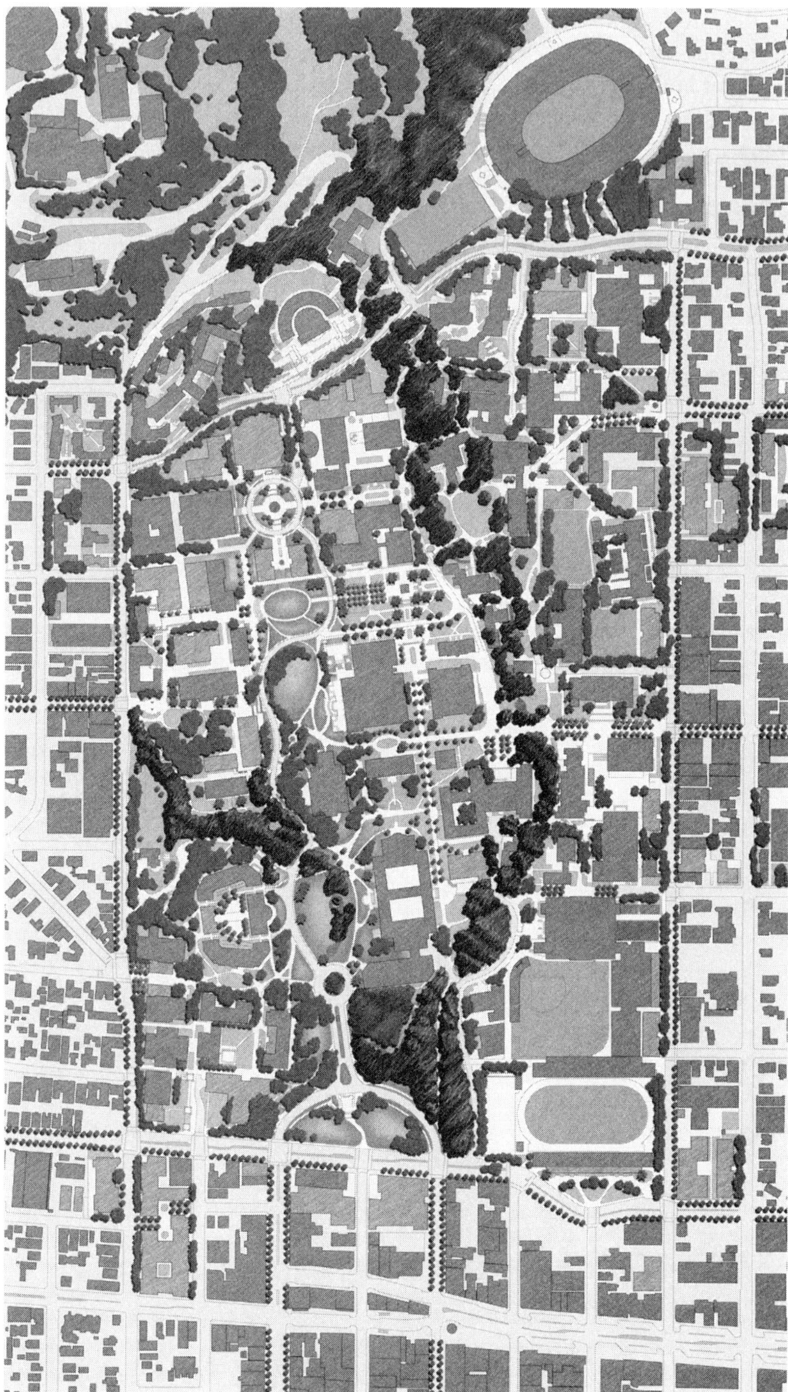

◀ *Figure 3.14 Landscape heritage plan, University of California, Berkeley.* Regents of the University of California.

Once this work is completed on a campus-wide basis, development, rehabilitation, or restoration of individual building sites can be accomplished in a coherent and consistent manner.

ACCESSIBILITY

Making historic structures and sites accessible to people with disabilities is a requirement of the Americans with Disabilities Act as well as national and international building codes. While most building codes provide for a limited amount of flexibility in meeting access requirements, the overall goal should be to provide universal access to historic buildings and sites. Meeting these requirements for access, without destroying the primary historic features of a building or site, can be very difficult.

An overall campus plan for accessibility defines the paths of travel throughout the campus and establishes the path to the building. The front entrance to most historic and many more recent buildings often has many barriers to accessibility, including a monumental front stairway, inadequately sized landings, lack of handrails, monumental doors, and thresholds. In almost all cases, modifications to the site, front stairway, and doors are required. If these modifications cannot be achieved without major alterations to the main entry, other solutions might be considered, including utilizing a second entrance that is adjacent to the main entrance and could provide equivalent access to the main lobby.

Development of a second entrance with an interior two-sided elevator, directly adjacent to the main entrance, provides complete access to the building while preserving the complex character of the main facade and entry hall (see Figures 3.15 and 3.16).

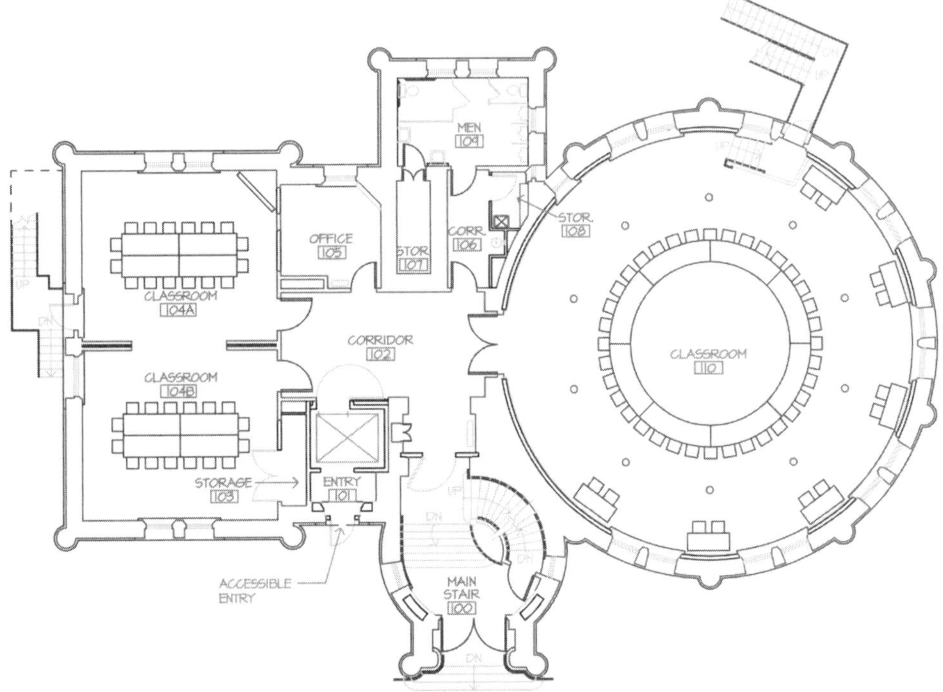

▸ *Figure 3.15 Scott Hall, San Francisco Theological Seminary, San Anselmo, California. Floor plan showing new elevator and entrance.* Architectural Resources Group.

◀ *Figure 3.16 Scott Hall, San Francisco Theological Seminary, San Anselmo, California. Front elevation new accessible entrance is directly adjacent to the main entry.* Architectural Resources Group.

Once inside the building, a path of travel must be established to all primary spaces. An elevator within the building to provide access to all floors is, in almost all cases, a necessity, involving alterations to the building. Ideally, the elevator would be located in service spaces adjacent to the main circulation path. In special cases where occupancy and available space are minimal, a limited use/limited access (LULA) elevator may be permitted. These elevators are smaller in all dimensions and provide space for one wheelchair and one person only. In the case of very small, or very historically sensitive buildings, access to the second floor may not be required, provided that all of the program activities or services provided on the second floor are available at grade.

Making historic restrooms accessible can involve extensive changes to historic finishes and features as well as greatly reducing the plumbing fixture count. An often acceptable alternative to remodeling historic restrooms is to add new accessible restrooms (gender-neutral or family restrooms), appropriately located on the path of travel.

Accessibility requirements can have impacts on a variety of other elements of historic fabric, particularly at doors: knobs, door widths, swings, and thresholds. Alternatives to replacing these features include specially constructed lever attachments for doorknobs, projecting hinges to increase door openings, and special ramps at thresholds.

Most historical building codes will recognize all of these alternative solutions, provided an equal level of access is achieved. An essential part of the design process involves presenting these potential alternatives to the appropriate access review body for their review and approval, prior to proceeding with the design.

BUILDING CODES

The code compliance process for preservation/reuse projects begins with establishing what the appropriate applicable code standards will be. This list of standards begins with the applicable national, state, or international model codes that govern construction in the jurisdiction of the project, such as the International Building Code (IBC) or the National Fire Protection Association (NFPA) Life Safety Code (NFPA 101). These primary building codes are augmented with additional codes and standards that are tailored to consider the special circumstances of existing construction and historic materials. Augmenting codes, such as the International Existing Buildings Code (IEBC) and NPFA 914 (Code for Fire Protection of Historic Structures), serve to give a level of performance flexibility to the interpretation of the model codes. In addition, some states, such as California, have written special codes for historic buildings into the framework of the overall state building code. Use of these alternative performance codes is intended to protect the life safety of the building occupants while allowing for solutions that preserve the historic features of the building.

The design team must be familiar with the structure and use of all of the alternative codes that may be applicable to the project. Early in the project, the architect will identify those areas of the building that either will not comply with the code or will require extensive demolition and alteration of historic materials for code compliance. A few common examples of code problems on historic buildings where historic building codes may apply include:

- *Egress path issues.* Adequate means of egress, separation of exits, existing exit door widths and swings, level changes at door thresholds
- *Stairway issues.* Number and location of stairways, rise and run, guardrail and handrail sizes and configurations, stairway enclosure
- *Fire separation issues.* Fire-rated corridors, walls, and occupancy separations

Once code issues are identified, the design team will develop proposed alternative solutions to achieve the intended level of safety with limited change to historic features and spaces.

In support of these solutions, it is sometimes necessary to develop sophisticated analyses such as fire modeling and egress modeling.

ENERGY/ENVIRONMENTAL IMPROVEMENTS

Creating a preservation-sensitive energy conservation strategy for the building begins with the development of an understanding of the original environmental concepts for the building. Most buildings built before World War II were designed with considerable attention to concerns for natural climate control and daylighting and are very amenable to changes to improve their energy performance.

Design concepts for this era of structures include many ideas that have recently returned to favor such as careful building orientation, thermal mass, courtyards, porches and outdoor shading, configuration of a narrow floor plate to assure daylighting and cross ventilation, skylighting with operable ventilation, operable windows, internal chases for ventilation and wall thermal breaks, and operable seasonal features such as awnings and storm windows. Although the building may have originally been conceived with these features, frequently many of them have been altered over time.

Rehabilitation planning to coordinate sustainability and preservation must begin by designing the energy strategy around the building's original basic forms and inherent energy-conserving features. Once these basic strategies are in place, additional ideas for sustainability may be developed to enhance them.

By today's standards, the exterior envelope assemblies of historic buildings are deficient in their thermal performance. Adding insulation to the wall assembly is always desirable, but must be achieved with a minimum amount of removal of historic finishes. Care must be taken to avoid creating areas of condensation from trapped vapor within the wall assembly. Window performance is a major component of a building's exterior envelope profile. Especially in severe climates, window replacement can make the building more energy efficient. However, replacement is not always necessary. Considerable improvement can be made to existing window performance simply through the repair of the existing sashes and frames and by the addition of high-quality weatherstripping. Some historic sash configurations will also accept reglazing with insulated glass. Every effort should be made to preserve existing windows, as they are very important features of the original building. Where windows must be replaced, new sashes should be carefully detailed to match the original as closely as possible. Upgrading the performance of existing historic windows is often possible, even in severe climate settings.

In contrast to earlier generations of buildings, those erected after World War II often ignored the most basic principles of ecological design. They often relied on the brute force of mechanical systems and artificial lighting to overcome climatic or lighting imbalances in the building. It is harder to make these buildings energy efficient, while still preserving their original design features. Upgrading the performance of modernist buildings often involves replacement of large areas of original material (e.g., window walls) with new materials detailed to match the original as closely as possible. The extent of replacement that might be considered may depend on the architectural importance of the building and the seriousness of its energy loss as well as other code-related defects such as the requirement for tempered or laminated glass.

A common example of this need for replacement involves early curtain wall systems, which were detailed with single-pane glazing and without thermal breaks in the mullion systems. These assemblies are impossible to both preserve and upgrade substantially. In practice, they have generally been replaced with new higher-performance curtain wall systems, detailed as closely as possible to match the original. Rehabilitation of the exterior skin of the S. R. Crown Hall building, a modernist icon located on the campus of the Illinois Institute of Technology, required complete replacement of glass and mullion systems due to corrosion and code compliance issues. Great care was required in detailing to ensure that the details of the new glazing systems matched Mies van der Rohe's original concepts (see Figures 3.17 and 3.18).

▸ *Figure 3.17 S. R. Crown Hall, Illinois Institute of Technology, Chicago. Front facade after rehabilitation.* William Zbaren.

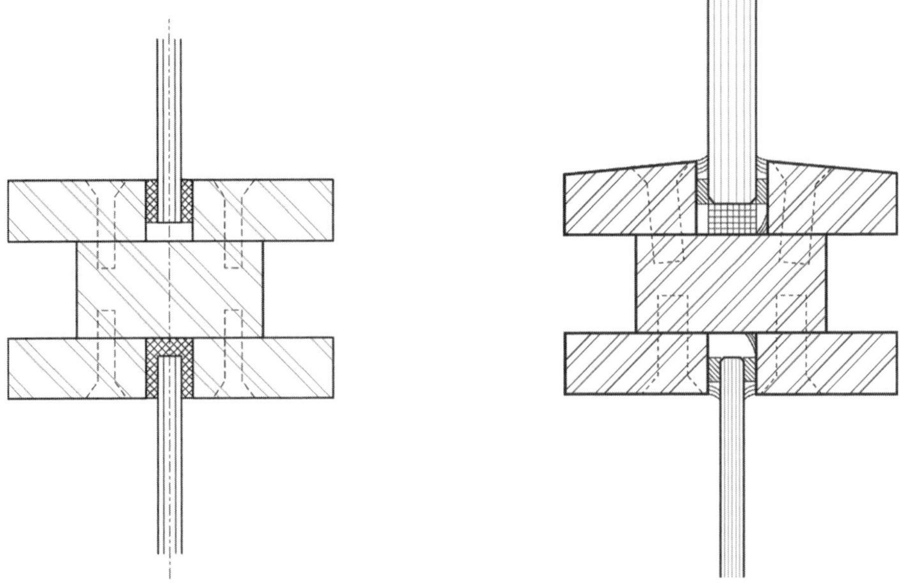

▸ *Figure 3.18 Window details, S. R. Crown Hall, Illinois Institute of Technology, Chicago: original (left); restoration (right).* Kreuk & Sexton.

Similarly, modernist buildings often feature structural systems exposed on the interior and exterior faces, without any insulation and without any concealed areas in which to install it. In these cases, a decision has to be made concerning which side of the assembly to alter in order to improve performance or which features are critical pieces of the design and should not be altered. Large areas of unshaded glass walls also are a common problem for modernist buildings, creating uncontrolled heat gain and glare. New shading systems, either interior or exterior, can be developed to fit the character of the original design. Often, these relatively invasive actions do not comply with the Secretary of the Interior's Standards but are generally justifiable because of the special details and extensive performance problems of many modernist buildings.

STRUCTURAL SYSTEMS

The structural design process for a preservation/reuse project begins with a comparative analysis between the structural requirements of the proposed function for the building and the capacity of the existing structure to meet those requirements. Establishing the functional requirements for the structure begins by first establishing the appropriate design standards for the project. This is not as simple as it might appear, as structural codes and performance standards vary with respect to existing and historic structures. The structural engineer must be familiar with current structural design standards for historic structures. This is particularly important in establishing an appropriate performance level for seismic resistance. While most historic structures have fairly well conceived structural systems to resist gravity and wind forces, in most cases, seismic design was not very well considered. The determination of an appropriate design standard for seismic performance will have a major impact on the overall design of the project.

A comprehensive understanding of the building's existing structural system and its condition is necessary in order to evaluate the extent of new structural strengthening that will be required. In the past, structural capacities of existing historic structural assemblies were ignored or underestimated due to the difficulties in analyzing them. This process often resulted in wholesale structural replacement and extensive demolition of interior features of buildings.

The development of more sophisticated diagnostic and evaluation tools has led to the current approach, which involves much more exploration, evaluation, and testing to more completely understand the actual capacities of members and their connections. This level of sophistication on the part of the structural engineer is essential. The predesign phase of the project may entail considerable structural testing and exploration, including geotechnical studies, coring and testing of concrete, nondestructive explorations of reinforcing steel, probes of masonry wall assemblies, sampling and grading of wood members, and, in some cases, test loading of suspect or unquantifiable elements to prove their capacity.

MECHANICAL SYSTEMS

New mechanical systems generally form an important part of the scope of work for preservation/reuse projects and can have a major impact on the historical features of a building. Selection of appropriate heating, ventilation, and air conditioning (HVAC) systems is largely a function of the building's programmatic requirements, sustainability concepts, and the campus infrastructure. However, building preservation issues must be considered as well.

System selection criteria should be based on access and visual conditions as much as on cost and efficiency. This is particularly true in considering the location and visual and acoustical screening of new HVAC equipment. HVAC equipment should be sized early in the project and carefully shown to scale on plans and elevations. In addition to locating primary equipment, distribution systems must be carefully laid out in concert with the building's historic features. Utilization of concealed spaces of the existing structure for ducts and distribution is an obvious objective. In some buildings, chases and concealed spaces can be repurposed as distribution access ways. Frequently, new soffits or other interventions are necessary to conceal ducts. Location of these new elements needs to be considered carefully. A frequent oversight in the development of the design and construction documents is in the coordination between structural and mechanical requirements in constrained existing spaces. Examples abound of projects that encountered near-insurmountable, very costly, or highly invasive changes during construction for equipment or ducting that did not fit. Recent development of 3D documentation systems for construction documents (e.g., building information modeling [BIM]) improves the design team's ability to review and coordinate tight conditions.

New HVAC systems inserted into a historic building will have a shorter design life than that of the building itself. These systems should be designed as replaceable elements within the building fabric. Ideally, they would be installed with minimal effect on historic features, so that, at the end of their useful life, they could be removed and replaced with minimal damage.

In some situations, original or historic heating systems or equipment such as steam radiators may be considered as important features to retain. Radiators can be flushed, rehabilitated, and converted to serve modern hot water heating systems.

Installing new heating and cooling systems, particularly in buildings that may not have originally had cooling, requires that careful consideration be given to existing and proposed roof and wall assemblies to assure control of vapor transmission and the potential for internal condensation.

New or improved fire suppression systems are almost always a part of preservation/reuse projects. They are a primary element in the fire and life safety program for the building, and are usually essential for mitigating inherent code and fire safety limitations of the existing building. While steel pipe sprinkler systems remain the most common and economical system, other piping materials can be used in areas where access is limited. Copper, stainless steel, and polyvinyl chloride (PVC) piping systems can often be installed in sensitive historic spaces with much less damage to historic materials. In addition, mist systems have developed as an alternative method for achieving fire suppression in areas where pipe size is an issue or where a high volume of water may create damage to the building or its contents, such as an adobe building or a room with highly water sensitive finishes or artifacts.

New fire suppression systems generally require a large backflow preventer on the site, adjacent to the water supply to the building, and may also require a post indicator valve and fire department connections. These elements are often not considered carefully in the design phase. They have major visual impacts and need to be carefully considered in the landscape plan. Similarly, the building main riser, often shown diagrammatically on drawings, needs to be placed carefully.

ELECTRICAL/COMMUNICATION SYSTEMS

In almost all cases, electrical and telecommunication upgrades will be a part of preservation/reuse projects. New electrical service capacity, main panels, and distribution systems per current code are usually involved. Location of main panels and electrical closets throughout the building are often a new program requirement that can be difficult to locate in historic spaces.

Particularly with telecommunication and audiovisual systems, design must be considered with the understanding that they will be changed out again in the near future and that it should be possible to accomplish this without damaging historic material.

Fire alarm systems are sometimes not carefully considered for their impact on the visual qualities of historic spaces. Locations of speakers, strobes, annunciator panels, and other communication hardware need to be coordinated in special historic spaces.

MATERIALS

Historic Materials

The original materials of the building comprise its historic fabric. Providing for the proper care and preservation of those materials is an important piece of all preservation projects. This effort involves a number of tasks:

- *Condition survey and documentation.* Describe, inspect, and document the types of materials, their connections to the building, their current condition, and the types of deterioration affecting them. This survey may initially be done visually, but as the project proceeds, closer evaluations, including sampling and testing, will be necessary. Survey techniques such as infrared thermography provide nondestructive information about the existing conditions of the exterior envelope.
- *Diagnosis of deterioration processes.* Identify the causes and specific processes of deterioration affecting the different materials. In some cases, this may be an obvious process of damage due to interaction with the environment. In other cases, the deterioration may be caused by other forces such as irrigation systems or building alterations, or there may be a chemical reaction occurring between neighboring materials such as dissimilar metals corrosion. Understanding the exact causes of the deterioration is necessary in order to propose appropriate treatments.
- *Treatment recommendations.* Develop treatment recommendations specific to each material. The treatments proposed will vary depending on each condition and could include any of the following: no action, maintenance, conservation (limited repair), replacement with material to match, or removal and replacement with a substitute material.
- *Documentation and treatment testing.* Prepare drawings and specifications for the treatments and, where possible, create mock-ups, samples, and on-site testing of proposed treatments. Mock-ups and treatment testing can be very helpful during the design phase for evaluating the constructability of the treatments, their visual effect, and their potential cost. Mock-ups of proposed conservation treatments are essential in developing final treatment specifications.
- *Construction administration.* Oversight by trained professionals of the treatments and workmanship throughout construction is critical.

New Materials

New materials must be selected with consideration of their relationship to the historic materials. Their physical and chemical properties must be compatible with those of the historic materials where they are in contact or close proximity. Frequent issues in this regard include specifying new metals such as aluminum or galvanized steel in contact with historic copper or lead, setting up a galvanic corrosion process, or installing new timber adjacent to old timber in ways that do not allow for shrinkage. Also, the maintenance cycles of new and existing materials must be coordinated. For instance, a historic clay tile roof that is being removed and reset should be coordinated with new copper or similar long-lived flashing systems.

Reversibility

Both in the treatment of historic materials and in the installation of new materials, care should be given to thinking about the next conservator's efforts. All treatments should consider the long-term maintenance and potential reversibility of the treatments.

ACOUSTICAL CONTROL

Acoustical considerations often play a role in preservation/reuse projects, as most older buildings were designed without great consideration for acoustical issues. Proposed new uses or upgraded performance expectations may require changes to support both improved room acoustics and improved acoustical separation between spaces. These changes can be both costly and destructive to historic wall and floor/ceiling finishes. Consultation with the acoustical consultant during the programming phase will be important to understand the limitations of the existing building in supporting the acoustical and/or vibration requirements of the proposed program and the scope of changes that may be required.

Improving room acoustics in historic spaces will involve adding either absorptive or reflective material to the space in order to alter its basic acoustical performance. These changes can generally be accomplished in a reversible manner (since the proposed program will change over time). It is generally not necessary or desirable to permanently alter the physical configuration of historic spaces in order to achieve the required level of performance. If permanent alteration is necessary, consideration should be given to changing the program requirements.

Improving acoustical separations generally involves adding mass, in the form of gypsum board, plaster, or concrete, to the existing wall or floor/ceiling assembly. This will affect finishes on at least one side of the assembly, possibly requiring removal and reinstallation of the finishes. Finishes removed may be installed over the assembly on isolating channels to further enhance the separation. Prior to committing to these treatments, measure the actual acoustical performance of the existing assembly by physically testing it in the building, creating mock-ups of alternative assemblies and testing them to ensure that the proposed treatment will achieve the desired separation.

LIGHTING DESIGN

Lighting design may involve both treatment of historic light fixtures and design of new lighting systems. Light fixtures were a prominent design feature of most historic buildings. They provided not just light, but scale, ornament, and texture to historic spaces. Where original light fixtures still exist, their proposed treatment may depend on the level of preservation being considered for the project. While no longer meeting current standards for illumination, they nonetheless can provide a basic level of lighting and, at the same time, strengthen the historic quality of primary spaces. Rehabilitation and reuse of historic light fixtures involves inspection; possible rewiring, repair, and conservation of glass and metal elements; and relamping. Most historic light fixtures were incandescent and of a fairly low wattage. Relamping to higher levels of brightness or adding more replica fixtures than originally existed in order to achieve higher levels of illumination is not generally recommended.

A preferred approach is to allow historical fixtures to provide one level of illumination, augmented by contemporary lighting to achieve the illumination requirements of the program. Controls can be arranged to allow for different levels of lighting: historic only or historic and new.

Where no historic light fixtures exist, new lighting systems should be contemporary, energy efficient, and compatible with the historic spaces. These systems should be designed with the understanding that they will be replaced during the future life of the building, as more efficient lighting systems are developed.

HISTORIC BUILDINGS—REHABILITATION
CASE STUDY 3

FRANK BATTEN SCHOOL OF LEADERSHIP AND PUBLIC POLICY
University of Virginia, Charlottesville

Architect: Architectural Resources Group
Completion: 2011

Figure 3.19 Garrett Hall. Exterior view with Annex, after rehabilitation. University of Virginia.

Building History and Description

The Frank Batten School of Leadership and Public Policy is the first academic school added at the University of Virginia in over fifty years (see Figures 3.19 and 3.20). The new school is located in historic Garrett Hall, which was designed by Stanford White of McKim, Mead & White and constructed in 1908. The building is situated at the southern end of Thomas Jefferson's Academical Village, a World Heritage Site. One of the first buildings added near the Jeffersonian core of the grounds, Garrett Hall was known as The Commons and was the first large refectory, or dining hall, for students and faculty at the University. The refectory was a large, central, double-height space that dominated the plan. Secondary spaces, such as the lobby, locker rooms, and a faculty dining space, bordered the student dining room. In 1959, after dining was relocated to the newly constructed Newcomb Hall, Garrett Hall was converted to office use and underwent major renovations. In 1970, a below-grade addition to the east, known as the Annex, was constructed. Many original features and spaces were lost or altered over time, including the original double-height lobby and open stair; the second floor was infilled, the open stair was removed and replaced by an

▸ *Figure 3.20 Garrett Hall, Front facade after rehabilitation.* Architectural Resources Group.

enclosed stair, and a glazed entry vestibule was added. The faculty dining room and a portion of the refectory were subdivided into smaller spaces, and most interior woodwork outside of the refectory was replaced with modern finishes.

Project Priorities

The project had two related priorities: create a special place to serve as the home for the Frank Batten School of Leadership, and in the process, rediscover and restore the original qualities of Garrett Hall. Working with leaders from the Batten School, a programming document was developed for the rehabilitation that outlined the more detailed priorities for the project, including:

- Rehabilitation of the exterior envelope
- Repair of structural deficiencies in the north wall
- Restoring three primary historic spaces: the refectory, the main lobby and stair, and the faculty dining room
- Use the refectory space to serve as a multifunctional center for the school and Integrate the other spaces to suit the other functional requirements of the school
- Providing code compliant egress and accessibility for all
- Integrating new systems and technology into the historic building
- Incorporating sustainable design improvements into the historic structure
- Improving the functionality and quality of the Annex

Rehabilitation and Restoration

Predesign

- Historic structure report and investigations into structural failures at the north wall and plaster ceiling system were conducted prior to beginning the project.
- Conceptual alternatives were developed to explore Batten School functional requirements and fit with existing Garrett Hall spaces.

- Compliance with the Secretary of the Interior's Standards for Rehabilitation required, review by University staff and Virginia SHPO.

Site and Landscape

- New sloped walkway for disabled access was created to the main entrance portico. Front portico steps were reconfigured and replaced to allow adequate dimensional clearances.
- North side service areas were reconfigured to incorporate new building egress paths and to improve garbage and service access.
- Annex roof areas were redeveloped to create social spaces for students and faculty, green roof areas, and new skylights into Annex spaces below.
- East and south areas adjacent to the building were relandscaped to improve appearance and to coordinate with campus planting guidelines for this area of campus.

Exterior Envelope

- Original windows were rehabilitated, and missing iron window grillwork restored in first floor window areas; original operable canvas awnings were restored.
- Exterior masonry was cleaned and repointed.

Codes and Accessibility

- Restoration of the two-story lobby and open stairway necessitated the development of new exits from the Great Room (refectory) and from the Faculty Conference Room (Faculty Dining Room).
- Fire separation requirements between the Great Room and adjacent faculty offices were mitigated through the provision for a new fire suppression system.
- A new elevator to all levels provides accessibility to all areas of the building.

Interior Spaces Reuse

- *Great Room:* The old refectory space was restored to its original dimensions and converted to serve a range of uses for the school, including student gatherings, receptions and banquets, and lectures. Range of uses required a careful balancing of acoustics, lighting, furniture flexibility, and service issues.
- *Faculty Conference Room:* The original Faculty Dining Room, a mezzanine space above the Great Room, was converted to function as the Faculty Conference Room. A new glazed wall was created along the mezzanine edge to maintain visual connection, but allow for acoustical separation from the Great Room.
- *Lobby and Main Stair Level Restoration:* The original two-story lobby space and open stairway were restored based on the original drawings and remaining site condition documentation.

Finishes

- The plaster ceiling in the Great Room was conserved and strengthened by improving hanger connections from the attic.
- Oak paneling and flooring in the Great Room were restored.

Acoustics

- Acoustical plaster panels were added in selected areas of the Great Room to improve acoustical legibility.

Structural System

- The failing north retaining wall was excavated, and a system of concrete buttresses, grade beams, and waterproofing was installed. Excavation also allowed for the installation of a new egress stair from the refectory.

MEP Systems

- All new heating and cooling systems were installed, connected to the University central plant.
- Original light fixtures in the Great Room were restored and reinstalled.
- Fire suppression system in the Great Room was specified as a mist system, to allow the system to have minimal impact on the plaster ceiling and to reduce visual impact.

Sustainability

- The completed project achieved a LEED Gold level of sustainability (see Figures 3.21 – 3.23.)

▸ *Figure 3.21 Garrett Hall Annex roof after rehabilitation.* University of Virginia.

▸ *Figure 3.22 Garrett Hall main entry after restoration.* University of Virginia.

◀ *Figure 3.23 Garrett Hall Great Room after rehabilitation.* University of Virginia. © Philip Beaurline Photography.

INTERIORS

Preservation treatment of interior spaces can vary greatly depending on their architectural significance and the amount of original material and design integrity that remains. Preservation of interior spaces, particularly important public or ceremonial spaces, can be of equal importance to preservation of the exterior. Where these spaces still exist, every effort should be made to preserve them in their original form and to design new interventions for program needs to be as reversible as possible. Many university buildings have been heavily remodeled in earlier building campaigns and are amenable to a much freer hand in designing new interior spaces, both in terms of new spatial configurations and design aesthetic. As discussed previously, evaluating the importance and integrity of the interior spaces, coordinating the program so that it does not require drastic changes to the sizes and configurations of the primary spaces, and establishing the amount of freedom for change to the interior with which the design team will operate are the most important steps in the project's design process and will determine the appropriate treatment of the interior spaces.

Even in buildings whose primary spaces, materials, and finishes have been preserved over time, finish colors and furnishings often have been altered drastically from their original design. It may be desirable to return these spaces to their original concepts for color and finish, offering dramatic, often surprising, and occasionally controversial results. Even if these restoration campaigns are limited to a few primary spaces of the building, they may have a major impact on the overall colors and finishes program for the entire building.

Interior finish and color restoration planning must be carefully conceived and developed. It begins with a careful sampling, documentation, and evaluation of the layers of finishes and the periods of the building's life to which these finishes relate. Depending on the complexity of the space, there may be a large number of samples necessary in order to understand the entire color scheme. Samples are analyzed microscopically and chemically to identify all of the layers of finishes applied over time. Interpretation of the microscopic samples involves considerable judgment and requires conservators who are specialists in the field of historic coatings analysis. Historic photographs and other related historical documents will help highlight design intentions and chronology of finishes.

Coordinating the finishes' chronology with the design periods of the building's history guides the discussion with respect to which era and/or color scheme is the most appropriate for the building's restoration. This process must evaluate and answer the question: What is the period of significance for purposes of finish restoration? This may not be simply the earliest, but may be the period that relates to the construction era of historic materials and features that currently remain in the space. The discussion of period of significance for restoration can become complicated where spaces have been changed over time and where those changes are also very important to preserve.

OPERATIONS AND MAINTENANCE

Preservation and reuse projects provide a number of opportunities for improved operations and maintenance. The research phase of the project, collection of original documents, and development of an HSR provide information that can be organized and utilized for ongoing operations and maintenance. These documents are not one-time-only reports but form the beginnings of an active, developing database of information about the building to guide operations and maintenance staff as well as be available to the next design team. A consistent system of organizing information for each building on campus should be developed and available for ongoing reference.

As the project moves forward through construction, as-built documentation should be added to the building database. Construction photographs of normally concealed areas that were exposed during construction should be organized and retrievable, as they will provide important information for future work. Likewise, as-built documentation that describes how newly installed systems were inserted into the building will be important in the future when they are removed and updated. As-built documentation of procedures applied to the conservation of special materials, as well as specifications for their ongoing maintenance, should be required elements in the contractor's project close-out procedures.

Frequently, building rehabilitation projects are considered as unique projects on campus, both by the design team and the operations and maintenance staff. In fact, many of the original materials on both the interior and the exterior are often typical of the buildings of that particular development era on campus. Developing standard campus preservation specifications and techniques that can be applied to multiple buildings with the same materials is a simple way to achieve consistent quality control from one project to another. It is also much more cost effective as materials and techniques become well understood by designers and artisans, leading to more consistent estimating and lower construction costs.

This approach to creating consistent preservation standards for historic materials campus-wide has the added benefit of standardizing maintenance procedures. It allows maintenance staff to be better trained and more efficient in maintaining campus buildings.

CHAPTER 4

LIBRARIES AND LEARNING CENTERS

Shirley Dugdale, AIA, Dugdale Strategy

Over the last two decades the design of libraries and places for informal study outside of the classroom has changed radically. The nature of the library as a building type is now richer, encompassing more functions and a wider range of services. As the library becomes more engaged in education, boundaries between academic building types are blurring. Today, many libraries are becoming learning centers in their own right.

Technological change has had a profound impact on the library as a building type since the 1980s. Historically, libraries were repositories of knowledge in the form of books and other print materials developed and organized by librarians. Libraries first served as intellectual sanctuaries where scholars could advance research through independent study and reflection. Today databases, the Internet, and electronic resources expedite rapid information searching and sharing. Remote access to online networks, aided by the proliferation of wireless systems and mobile devices, makes library resources ubiquitous. All users—students, teaching faculty, researchers—now work wherever they wish, forcing libraries to reconsider the best use of their space and resources.

Traditionally located at the center of campus, the library served as the symbolic heart of an intellectual community and safeguarded extensive print collections, valued by their size. Since Thomas Jefferson's library was built in 1828 at the head of his Academical Village at the University of Virginia, libraries have been built on American campuses in a variety of architectural styles from classical and Gothic to modernist. Many now need renovation, particularly the severe "brutalist" buildings of the 1960s notable for their concrete waffle slabs and slit windows.

The preservation of academic research collections will continue to be an important aspect of the college and university library mission. However, acquiring an ever-larger print collection—and the implications that has for planning—is no longer the primary driver for space. Libraries are now seeking ways to reallocate collections storage space at the heart of the campus into more effective user space, and that is transforming the nature of the library and its role in the institution.

THE CHANGING LEARNING EXPERIENCE IN THE TWENTY-FIRST CENTURY

Technological advances foster richer and more complex learning experiences. Educators' adoption of a "learner-centered" paradigm[1] refocused institutional planning from a faculty-centric to a learner-centric perspective. Trends in pedagogical approaches explore ways to move away from didactic teaching dependent on lectures to more active modalities with team-based learning, collaborative work, and multimedia integration. This creates greater demand for informal settings outside the classroom, where

1 Robert B. Barr and John Tagg, "From Teaching to Learning: A New Paradigm for Undergraduate Education," *Change Magazine* 27, no. 6 (1995): 12–25.

small student groups can study together and work on projects.

Traditional libraries served predominantly as quiet environments without much space for collaborative activity except for a few group study rooms. Now the balance of activity in libraries is reversing, with most open space dedicated to collaborative work and enclosed conversation-free rooms available for quiet reading.

Technology is generating new ways of learning and tools to support them. Most high school graduates today are digitally literate and expect media-rich material. Seeking more collaborative or immersive experiences, they rely on social networks to stay in constant communication with peers. Learning is just as likely to happen in virtual space as in physical space. Simulations of dynamic systems and "serious gaming" exemplify the new ways of learning that libraries have started to embrace.

New Scholarship and Research Trends

While the amount of research being generated and published grows, so does the cost of scholarly resources. With squeezed budgets, librarians are forced to choose between purchasing electronic journals or books. Data-driven research has also transformed the publishing industry, particularly in the sciences. The National Science Foundation, National Institutes of Health, and other U.S. agencies now require that findings from their funded research studies be made publically available, with more published electronically together with data sets. As the pressure for discovery accelerates, scientists are collaborating earlier, well before the traditional cycle of peer review and journal publishing. In response, many universities are exploring alternative methods for publishing scholarly work and developing institutional digital repositories. Librarians are responding by developing new skills in knowledge management, scholarly communications, and data curation.

Libraries are responsible for providing the electronic resources that academic communities have come to expect. However, users often do not recognize the role the library plays in purchasing and negotiating licenses for those resources as well as covering the expenditures for equipment, network infrastructure, and technology upgrades required to make knowledge accessible anywhere on demand. Helping scholars and researchers navigate the nuances of copyright issues and digital scholarship is a new frontier, prompting the formation of a growing specialization in scholarly communications. Library planning needs to anticipate growth in these staff work groups and associated user service areas.

Over the last decade faculty members have become more comfortable with digital resources. Electronic browsing is easier, and, together with "delivery to the desktop," significantly reduces faculty visits to the library building itself. The model of the traditional scholar working independently is now complemented by collaborative inquiry. As the demands of interdisciplinary research prompt faculty to form new academic relationships and collaborations between universities, librarians must provide remote support services such as creating portals, wikis, and other tools for special communities.

To respond to these trends, academic library designers must conceive of libraries as learning centers, very flexible environments able to accommodate evolving roles and services. Research libraries hosting developments in digital humanities and e-science need to have facilities that support evolving research partnerships. On some campuses libraries may actually become mixed-use facilities. For all types of campuses they offer value as a neutral ground for collaborative centers where the entire academic community can work together with digital information in new ways.

The following sections address essential phases of planning: from predesign planning through programming, to building and systems design.

LIBRARIES AND LEARNING CENTERS CASE STUDY 1

JAMES B. HUNT JR. LIBRARY

North Carolina State University, Raleigh, North Carolina

Design architect: Snøhetta Architects
Executive architect: Pearce, Brinkley, Cease & Lee
Programming consultant: DEGW
Completion date: 2012
Size: 220,000 GSF (139,000 NSF, of which library functions are approximately 87,000 NSF [20,439 sq m])
Project budget: $115 million
Capacity: 1,700 seats
LEED Silver certification

Key Features

Library

- Faculty Research Commons, Graduate Student Commons
- Immersion Theater
- Skyline Reading Room and Terrace
- Creativity Studio
- Teaching and Visualization Lab
- Media Production Studios
- Group study rooms (100)
- Makerspace
- Snack bar
- Usability Lab
- 100- and 400-person auditoriums

Institute for Emerging Issues

- Gallery and exhibit about North Carolina issues
- IEI Forums meeting spaces
- Offices for Institute staff

Automated Book Delivery System (ABDS)

- 2 million volume capacity
- Engineering, biotechnology, textiles, fragile collections

We seek nothing less than to create the best learning and collaborative space in the country.

—Susan Nutter, Vice Provost and Director of the NCSU Libraries

The NCSU Hunt Library will be a sophisticated blend of elegant architecture, innovative planning, and the latest in thinking about the academic library of the future. North Carolina State University is expanding onto its new Centennial Campus and developing a library building as a focus for this research community of engineering disciplines. Named the top research park in the United States in 2007, the Centennial Campus brings together students, faculty, and researchers with corporate, governmental, and institutional partners. The James B. Hunt Jr. Library will be an iconic signature building, designed by the Norwegian architectural firm Snøhetta, which has been conceived as an intellectual and social forum to showcase the research achievements of the university and the leadership of the NCSU Libraries.

The elegant architectural design for the Hunt Library building responds to the site, providing a multistory space along the main frontage to the green Oval and special rooms and the Skyline Reading Room Terrace oriented toward the view of Lake Raleigh (see Figure 4.1). The treatment of the facade was inspired by the weaving of textiles, evocative of the interweaving role the library plays in integrating so much of the campus community. The entry zone and library commons above will run along the facade to the Oval, flooded with filtered daylight (see Figures 4.2 and 4.3). The design will provide a landscape of collaborative spaces, reading rooms, and meeting rooms, all with technology-enabled settings and display capabilities (see views in Figure 4.4).

The mixed-use building will have several occupants, primarily the Library and the Institute for Emerging Issues.

Figure 4.1 West elevation. SNØHETTA/NCSU.

Figure 4.2 Hunt Library entry. SNØHETTA/NCSU.

Figure 4.3 Looking down from the fourth level. SNØHETTA/NCSU.

Figure 4.4 Institute for Emerging Issues exhibit lobby. SNØHETTA/NCSU.

The Institute for Emerging Issues is a public policy "think-and-do tank" that convenes leaders in business, government, and education to address issues of importance to North Carolina's development. It hosts annual forums and events and will maintain a gallery of displays about key issues.

The NCSU Libraries are renowned as a leader in defining the research library of the future and being an incubator of new information technology initiatives. The building design will offer a wide range of user facilities and technology-enhanced work areas. Special spaces will include a Creativity Lab, which can be easily reconfigured for any teaching, learning, and collaborative activities in support of innovation, and a Teaching and Visualization Lab, which will enable three-dimensional (3D) immersive experiences. Staff and user work areas have been planned to maximize collaborative work and allow flexibility for future change.

An important early decision was to integrate a high-density storage facility into the building, which will use an automated book delivery system (ABDS). This allowed a much greater storage capacity than open stacks would have for the same cost, and the ABDS will allow speed of retrieval and reduced operational costs over time. Four robotic retrievers will service the 53 ft high storage units. Moving to a high-density collection storage solution will not only put fragile materials into more stable environmental conditions but also allow the crowded main Hill Library to transfer infrequently used materials to the new ABDS facility, freeing up space there that can be converted to badly needed additional user work space.

PREDESIGN PLANNING: SETTING THE CONTEXT

The Need for a Learning Landscape Perspective

The global information environment in which learners and scholars are immersed requires a new perspective and fresh approach to learning space design. It is helpful to conceive of this as a "Learning Landscape,"[2] the total context for learners' experiences, made up of a diverse landscape of learning settings available today—from formal to informal, from specialized to multipurpose, and from physical to virtual. The Learning Landscape perspective acknowledges this richness and designs to maximize encounters among people and ideas, just as a vibrant urban environment does. Using this learner-centered approach, campuses can be conceived as "networks" of places for learning, discovery, and discourse between students, faculty, staff, and the wider community.

The Learning Landscape approach is about leveraging the power of planning for interaction at the campus level. It emphasizes planning learners' experiences rather than buildings. It envisions a future campus as overlapping networks of compelling places which offer choice and generate synergies through adjacencies and the clustering of facilities. Libraries and other informal learning centers can become rich hubs in this network supporting learning (see Table 4.1).

2 For further explanation see article by the author, "Space Strategy for the New Learning Landscape," *EDUCAUSE Review*, vol. 44, no. 2 (March/April 2009). http://net.educause.edu/ir/library/pdf/ERM0925.pdf

A Spectrum of Formal and Informal Learning Spaces

The nature of generic space types on campuses is changing, too. Technology trends are influencing space in several important ways:

- Traditional categories of space are becoming less meaningful as activities blend, space becomes less specialized, boundaries between disciplines blur, and operating hours extend toward 24/7 access.
- In the future, space types are more likely to be designed around patterns of human interaction than around the specific needs of particular departments, disciplines, or technologies.
- With greater mobility, students have a choice as to where they can work, and they tend to gravitate to spaces they enjoy—so quality of design matters more. New space models for educational institutions therefore need to focus on enhancing quality of life as well as supporting the learning experience.

Table 4.1 Characteristics of the Learning Landscape Approach to Campus Planning

Conventional Campus Planning	Learning Landscape Planning
Campus fabric focused	Learning Landscape context aware
Looks backward, relying on planning standards and benchmarks	Forecasts changing needs of users, based on research and engagement with special tools and methods to envision future models
Linear process, from analysis to conception to implementation	Nonlinear process, emphasizing co-creation of concepts with users, pilot projects, ongoing refinements, and incremental implementation
Produces a "plan" to be implemented	Produces a set of strategies and concepts, to be applied, tested, refined, refreshed, and reapplied
Based on needs assessment by school and department	Engages hybrid groups to complement needs assessment process and build consensus around solutions
Conceived spaces are more important than the activities within them	Activities drive the planning process: space is conceived to support them
Prioritizes formal instructional space	Focuses on planning informal as well as formal learning environments
Focuses on classroom experience	Plans networks of physical and virtual learning spaces for distributed, hybrid, and social learning experiences
Single-use space types	Mix of specialized and flexible, multipurpose spaces supporting blended activities
Specialized spaces assigned by semester	Specialized spaces booked on demand
Single-owner model	Layered ownership model, from public to invited to private space

Source: © S.Dugdale, 2009.

A key challenge for campus planners is to define the right balance between formal and informal study space. Formal learning spaces accommodate scheduled instruction, whereas informal learning spaces host a full spectrum of places where knowledge sharing and study occur—from libraries and computer centers to cafes, lounges, or residences—the "spaces between" diagrammed in Figure 4.5 that make up so much of the campus experience. As teamwork is encouraged by curriculum change, more collaboration takes place outside of the classroom. This trend, combined with students' desire to study in groups, is driving more demand for informal study spaces, not only in libraries

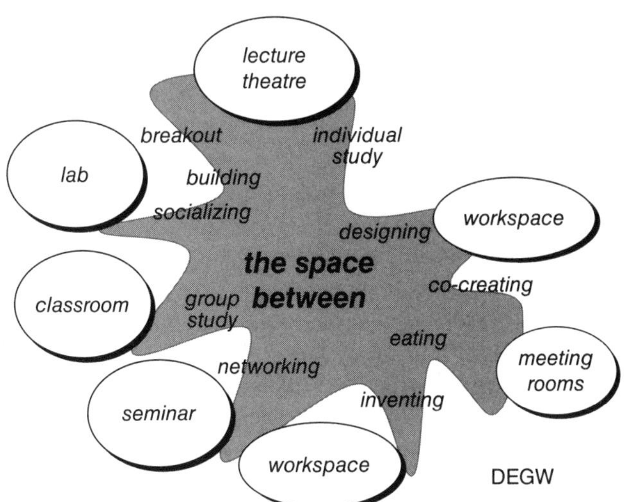

◀ *Figure 4.5 The Informal Learning Landscape.* DEGW.

but also at other campus locations, including food facilities reconceived as social learning spaces. The matrix in Figure 4.6 is a framework for analyzing these shifts, considering spaces in terms of formality (scheduled or unscheduled activities) and specificity (single use or multipurpose). The planning process maps the campus context of existing and planned informal learning spaces, so the design of the new facilities can respond to and complement the overall fabric.

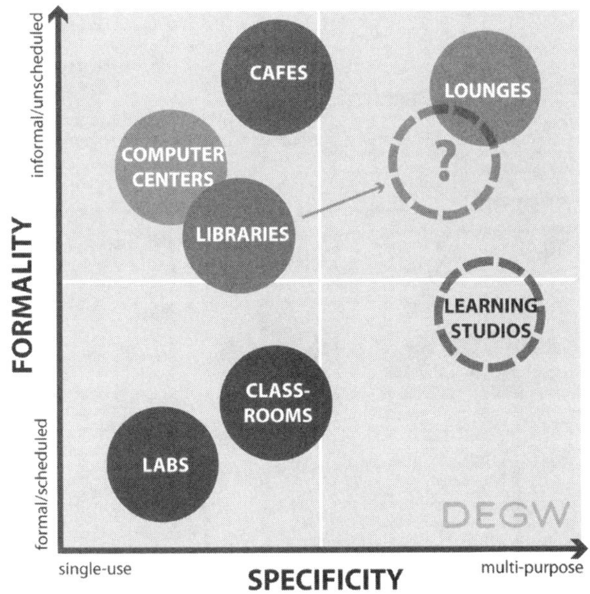

◀ *Figure 4.6 A workshop tool for exploring the shifting character of learning space.* DEGW.

MANAGING THE PLANNING PROCESS

Engagement of Stakeholders and User Needs Research

As rapid technological change drives new ways of learning and working, it is more critical than ever for the planner, at both the campus and the building scale, to study user behavior and engage stakeholders from the beginning of the process.

The planning team must understand the changing needs of students, staff, and faculty. Although surveys provide useful feedback on campus space performance, facilitated interactive workshops often draw out more nuanced information about campus culture, user experiences, and perceptions (Figure 4.7). Workshops also engage stakeholders in co-creating their vision for a building or campus of the future. By compiling information from interviews, workshops, focus groups on key topics, data from space performance surveys, and other sources, combined with findings from observational studies, planners can build study or work profiles, identify needs, and provide insights about the unique aspects of campus culture to inform the design process.

Stakeholder engagement ideally happens throughout the planning process. Their feedback is useful from the initial planning and programming stages right through schematic and design development stages as well as during post-occupancy evaluations after the project is completed.

Considering Alternative Futures

Library organizations have been subjected to such rapid technological change that they are going through fundamental transformations without a clear sense of the future. During programming, a scenario-planning exercise offers a useful way to explore alternative futures and reflect on their implications for planning. Ideally, a building design

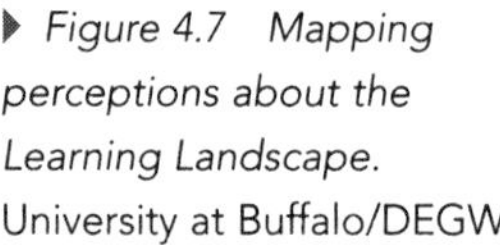

▸ *Figure 4.7 Mapping perceptions about the Learning Landscape.* University at Buffalo/DEGW.

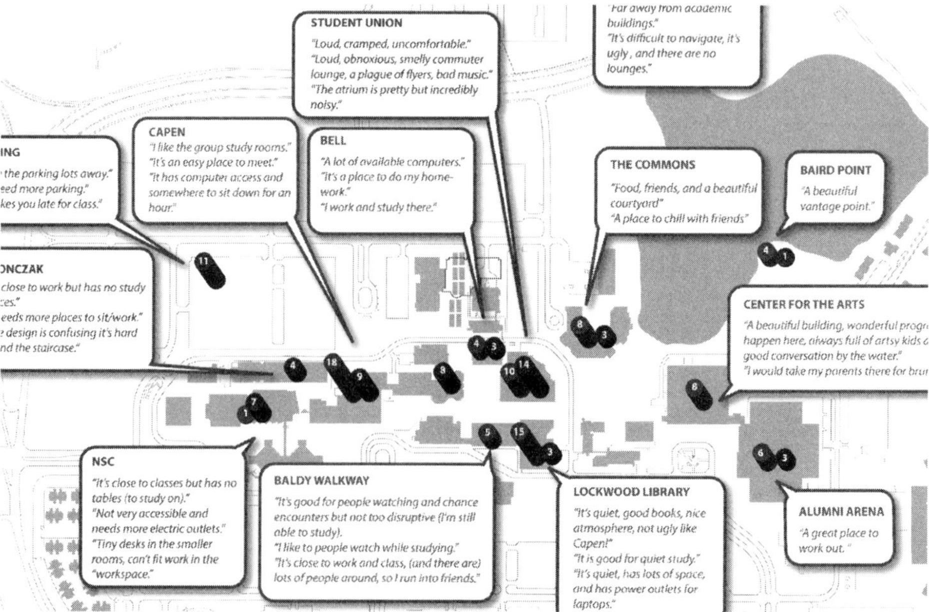

should be flexible enough to adapt to alternative futures over time, whether in response to continually evolving technologies or to behavioral change.

Expanding the Traditional Design Team

As libraries include more functions and partner with other service providers, the design process needs to embrace these partners as well as librarians. Groups that support learning should be involved in planning a learning commons or work space within a library building. These might include representatives from curriculum design teams, teaching and learning centers, academic technology, and audiovisual experts. As campuses recognize the need to manage informal learning spaces, groups responsible for their planning, management, and maintenance should be involved, and libraries offer a great deal of experience with this.

An Iterative Cycle to Stimulate Experimentation and Innovation

Given the rapidity of technological change and new experiments in teaching methods, a prudent planning process will include pilot projects that allow staff, faculty, and students to provide input that will inform the design of future spaces.[3] An iterative cycle testing pilot projects can stimulate experimentation and foster innovative planning. After construction, a process of postoccupancy evaluation should be organized to evaluate the performance of the facilities and inform subsequent campus developments.

3 One such process was the planning of the Georgia Tech Library East Commons, which included extensive user input before and during design, and ongoing assessment afterwards. See Robert Fox and Crit Stuart, "Creating Learning Spaces through Collaboration: How One Library Refined Its Approach," *EDUCAUSE Quarterly* 32, no. 1 (2009).

PROGRAMMING

Learning Centers of the New Learning Landscape

Although much learning will still occur in teaching spaces, an increasing proportion will take place outside the classroom in informal settings. Teaching today happens in many places: library classrooms, offices, group meeting areas, labs, online community spaces, and, increasingly, virtual worlds. Experiential learning in off-campus locations is growing, as is peer learning in skills centers. Distance collaboration with cohorts in other institutions is becoming more common, and now consortiums provide online use of scientific instruments to other institutions, which enables students to run virtual lab experiments remotely.

Libraries have traditionally been centers for out-of-classroom learning, but primarily for individual study, research, and bibliographic instruction. As students seek more venues for group learning and academic programs introduce more collaborative team-based work, libraries are now transforming into vibrant centers for informal learning. On many campuses they have even become the most important place to tap all the various services that support learning.

The Evolving Library

Some types of university libraries have been subject to rapid change more quickly than others. Medical, science, engineering, and business libraries have led the way, by converting to extensively digital resources and revealing patterns of usage libraries are likely to exhibit over the next decade. Journals and reference collections have typically been the first to be converted into digital formats—leaving many empty shelves. Although monograph (book) collections will likely remain in most libraries, acquisition of print monographs is slowing, reflecting the changing nature of the collections and user interests. Some new libraries are being founded without any books at all.[4]

Libraries with humanities, art and social science collections have been slower to convert to digital formats. Researchers in these disciplines often prefer to browse print materials and humanities content ages gracefully, unlike scientific data. However, the growing development of digital humanities initiatives at many institutions over the last five years is now exploring the potential of technological tools for analysis, textual data mining, and visualization of social science research. This may lead to more acceptance of digital formats, but it is likely that the convenience of delivery to the desktop and improvement in annotation tools will be the primary factors that win scholars over.

Undergraduate libraries traditionally have provided multiple copies of textbooks, limited collections for student research, and browsable leisure titles. As more basic texts become available online or are provided to students in electronic or downloadable form, the need to house such print material will decrease.

Teaching program needs drive community college collections, and collections development for them is not focused on supporting advanced research purposes. Although some community college libraries are experimenting with e-books, many students lack funds to purchase laptops or e-book readers yet many are also taking online courses, so resources must be designed to be universally accessible.

4 For further discussion on recent libraries that are being planned to be predominantly digital, refer to the Council on Library and Information Resources (CLIR) publication, *The Idea of Order: Transforming Research Collections for 21st Century Scholarship* (Washington, DC: Council on Library and Information Resources, 2010).

Retrospective responsibility for maintenance of print collections depends on the context and type of library. Some medical libraries, for example, act as regional libraries in the National Network of Libraries of Medicine, enabling others to divest themselves of low-usage material, knowing it will be available through the system. Some libraries are joining together in consortiums to optimize negotiating power, operational efficiencies, shared storage facilities, and reduction of collection duplications, such as the Five College Consortium in Massachusetts.

As retrieval from other libraries becomes easier (as print volumes, as electronic scans, or archived electronic files) and pressures to use space more effectively mounts, libraries are gradually reducing low-usage material if it can be sourced from another location. Concurrently, many libraries are moving to highlight and grow unique or special collections reflecting the history of their community, campus, and centers for excellence.

Many other trends will impact library planning over the next decade. The Google Books Library Project and other initiatives to develop large-scale digital libraries are making an extraordinary amount of literature available. Publishers are making publications available in electronic archives. Better reading devices like the Kindle and iPad have fueled the growing popularity of e-books. Print-on-demand services are making microscale publication feasible along with customized course textbooks. Textbooks in digital formats are easier for students to carry and use at any time. Better annotation tools encourage students and scholars to annotate in digital form. When these trends are considered along with advances in high-density storage technology, it is clear that the academic research library building type is likely to undergo significant changes in the next decade.

PROGRAM COMPONENTS

User Facilities and the Shift to More Collaborative Activities

The Learning Commons

The "information commons" model, developed in the early 1990s, was originally conceived as the place where library users could access computers and electronic resources. The concept was to provide integrated support services from both reference and information technology (IT) services, but users for the most part were assumed to be working at individual workstations. Those wishing to work in groups used adjacent enclosed group study rooms.

As the role of the library in the educational process increased, the learning commons concept emerged in the late 1990s and encouraged new forms of partnerships in support of learning. These commons introduced writing or tutoring services, media labs, more space for teaching (especially computer classrooms for hands-on teaching for information literacy), and many open settings for collaborative group work.[5]

At the same time, despite the new mobility that now empowers users to work anywhere, on or off campus, the learning commons in many campus libraries has become the central hub of informal, out-of-classroom learning. Furnished with more collaborative and group study settings, it is a place where students can study together and be seen by friends while working on projects or problem sets. The commons excels as a vital physical place that enhances the student academic experience and complements learners' increasingly virtual and distributed experience.

5 For a good summary description, see the EDUCAUSE Learning Initiative's "Seven Things You Should Know About . . . The Modern Learning Commons" http://www.educause.edu/library/resources/7-things-you-should-know-about-modern-learning-commons

LIBRARIES AND LEARNING CENTERS **CASE STUDY 2**

SALTIRE CENTRE

Glasgow Caledonian University, Glasgow, Scotland

Architect: Building Design Partnership
Completion date: 2006
Size: 10,500 sq m on five levels
Construction cost: £23 million
Capacity: 1,800 seats, 400 workstations

Key Features

- Services Mall
- Commons seating areas
- Café
- Five-story circulation atrium
- Library on multiple levels, zoned from consultative to quiet
- Stacks capacity for 350,000 volumes, currently 260,000 books
- Connectors to adjacent buildings

Saltire Centre was envisioned as an innovative facility to support learning combined with the flexibility to change over time. It was designed to provide open flexible space that would foster interaction and respond to a range of learning styles, blended together with library and other learning support services. The building is adjacent to other teaching buildings and so acts as a hub of the campus.

The strong, award-winning design uses iconic forms, vibrant color, and hanging artwork to convey the purpose of each floor. The Services Mall on the ground floor (see Figure 4.8) is the most active area, providing access to all university services at either kiosks or open staff service desks highlighted with colored neon. Together with the working café, the popular mall has 600 seats in a variety of types, small consultation rooms for meeting with advisors along one edge, and some of the print collection. Within the high 2-story space, playful objects like the inflatable igloo meeting spaces and the umbrella lighting structures create semiprivate spaces for small groups (see Figure 4.9), but are easily moved or dismantled so the space can be changed or used for other special functions. About 400 desktop computing stations were originally provided, complemented by laptop checkout. External social spaces are also provided in the plaza out front and on a large south-facing roof terrace (see Figure 4.10).

Figure 4.8 Commons and Student Services Mall. BDP, Architects; David Barbour, Photographer.

Figure 4.9 Interior landscape. BDP, Architects; David Barbour, Photographer.

Figure 4.10 Exterior view. BDP, Architects; David Barbour, Photographer.

> *The primary aim of a Learning Centre is to support people in the process of learning. This support is extended to learners in their individual endeavours and to the institution in its development of approaches to learning. What is being proposed for Glasgow Caledonian University is therefore not a new library, not a Learning Resource(s) Centre but a Learning Centre.*
>
> —Les Watson, Former Pro Vice Chancellor, Glasgow Caledonian University

A dramatic 5-story atrium provides views down into the ground-floor Services Mall and across into other areas, making activity visible and bringing natural light into the building. The upper floors, levels 2 to 4, house more quiet study venues, the rest of the print collections, print/copy spaces, and library staff offices. The facade treatment uses translucent panels with color accents to provide an even natural light within the library spaces. The facility has become a model of a robust learning center that has added value with its student-centered social learning spaces, the provision of training to assist its users with the production of new materials, and the provision of a wide variety of settings and services.

The Research Commons

With all the recent emphasis on developing learning commons, many libraries are now recognizing that researchers, scholars, and graduate students also need a central place to go for expert consulting in scholarly communications, intellectual property and copyright issues, as well as research and data curation services.

As the need for these services and better research data management grows, librarians are forming partnerships and creating physical hubs where development collaborators can come together. At the University of Massachusetts

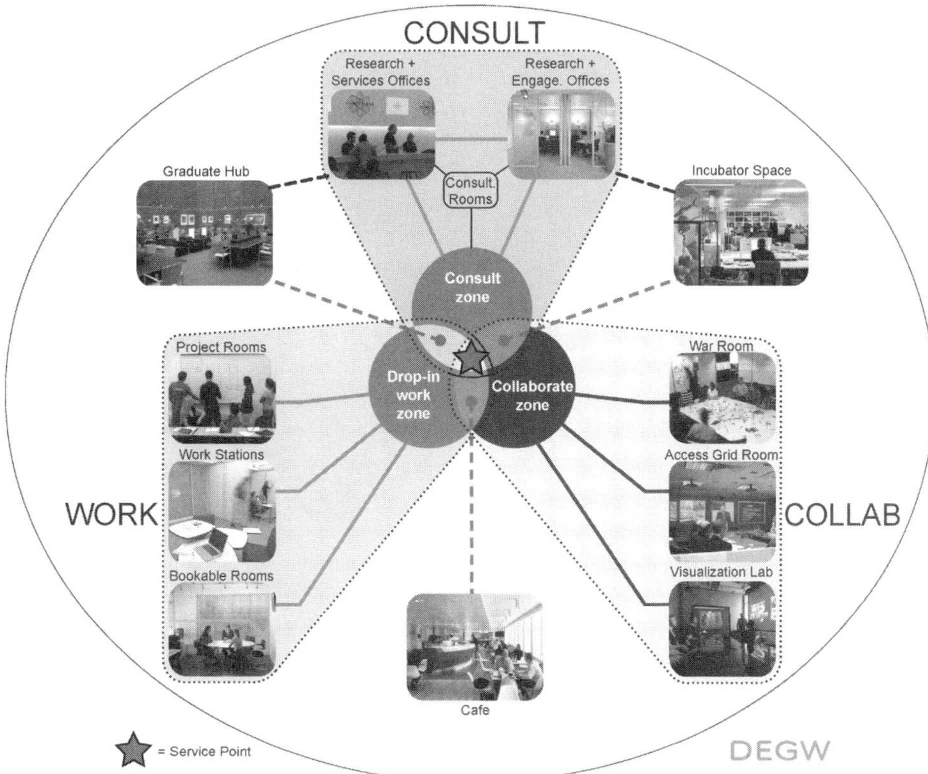

Figure 4.11 Research commons concept. University of Massachusetts Amherst/DEGW.

Amherst, a strategic master plan for the libraries developed the concept of a research commons that will not only bring researchers together with scholarly communications librarians, but also with the administrative groups that help manage research grants institution-wide. These will be co-located in a suite that offers "war room" collaborative workspace for interdisciplinary grant submittal teams, "incubator" space for grant-funded projects in collaboration with the library, and bookable workspaces for faculty and graduate students (see concept diagram in Figure 4.11).

Computing and Media Hubs

As multimedia becomes more integrated into teaching it will drive demand for more technology-enabled work settings for collaborative design and multimedia authoring. These settings will be intentionally designed to support learning and production, individually or in groups, with expert staff support nearby. Work areas may feature dual-screen monitors, scanners, video editing equipment, sound studios for audio recordings, and rooms for group viewing (see Figure 4.12).

Many institutions now question the value of providing computer labs with desktop computers which require significant maintenance costs at a time when students arrive with multiple personal devices—from laptops and smart phones to tablets and gaming systems. While cloud computing may soon render traditional computer labs obsolete for drop-in access to the network or productivity software, specialized facilities such as those supporting engineering or other disciplines will endure. With the growth of informatics in various fields and the need to analyze complex research data, innovative spaces optimized to promote the visualization of information will become increasingly sophisticated.

Social and Meeting Hubs

Many libraries have enthusiastically embraced the café as a social hub that supports informal interaction and provides a welcoming place to take a break and eat,

▸ *Figure 4.12 Vitale Digital Media Lab, University of Pennsylvania Weigle Information Commons.* Vitale Digital Medial Lab; David Toccafondi, photographer.

Figure 4.13 Georgia Institute of Technology Library East Commons Café.

enabling users to remain longer in the building, especially at night or during exam periods. Cafés play an important function as a place for students to study together or work on projects, and serve as a gathering spot for teaching assistants or faculty to connect with students. Social hubs, like symposium centers or informal presentation spaces, support the library's mission to provide neutral space to encourage interdisciplinary sharing and collaboration. Georgia Tech's Library East Commons has a centrally located café flanked by an adjacent room used for informal presentations, gatherings, and group study activities (Figure 4.13). Many libraries host events and provide reservable spaces with videoconferencing capabilities to engage off campus participants. Some libraries are being planned as multipurpose facilities combined with other organizations with an outreach mission, such as the new Hunt Library at North Carolina State University (see Case Study 1).

Other Learning Support Hubs

Learning centers can include many different types of support facilities, including: writing centers; student success advising centers; peer tutoring centers; information literacy training areas; centers for teaching and learning or faculty development; experimental learning spaces; and tech support service points. Libraries are integrating such centers and even student-managed facilities, such as the Learning Grid at the University of Warwick. Open since 2004, this facility is staffed by student advisors trained to serve as learning facilitators and media coaches.

Distributed Work Hubs

Mobility and distributed work is a growing influence on planning work environments across campuses. Libraries offer drop-in work space to support the increasingly mobile work patterns of students, faculty, and even staff who need to gather in places other than their offices or travel between campuses. Meeting rooms and shared video-conferencing centers also serve those on campus who may not have access to such space within their departmental areas.

Accommodating Collections in the Digital Age

Since about 2000, academic libraries have been acquiring print materials at a rate that has, on average, been decreasing, depending on type of library and subject matter. Acquisition of journals and reference resources in print form has been reduced significantly as more are published in electronic form. Larger research collections will continue to acquire print material, but increasing budgetary constraints are often forcing libraries to choose between formats. Community college libraries will continue to acquire print materials for those who do not have personal devices and basic texts to support the programs they offer, rather than research-related materials.

Journals

Initial conversion from print to digital resources has predominantly been in the shift to electronic periodicals and reference materials, especially in medical, scientific and engineering collections. Publishers have not only converted many current journals into electronic form but also offer back issues via an electronic archive. Librarians with confidence in these archives, or other forms of archival storage, such as services like JSTOR,[6] have started to move their bound journals off-site or even removed them from their physical collections.

6 JSTOR (short for Journal Storage) is a not-for-profit service that works with publishers and libraries to create a trusted digital archive of over 1,300 academic journals and other scholarly content: http://about.jstor.org/.

Monographs

Although acquisition of monographs (books) has generally slowed, many libraries anticipate that growth in print monographs collections will continue for the foreseeable future, especially in research libraries and in scholarly subjects like the humanities. However, depending on the rate of development of digital humanities scholarship and new digital methods of publication and research dissemination, acquisition rates may soon change in these types of collections.

Special Collections

Where resources and space are available, special collections will continue to grow as libraries value and take responsibility to conserve collections that are unique to the institution. In addition to rare books, special collections can include folios, objects, paintings, and other ephemera as well as archival collections. Archival collections can consist of a variety of materials, such as manuscripts or photographs, many in folders or archival boxes. Sometimes, if acting as steward of institutional archives, a library must continue to accumulate administrative files until digital record keeping becomes more widespread.

Browsable Open Shelving

Browsable collections are usually stored on ranges of double-faced units. Shelving capacities traditionally include the addition of a working capacity factor that provides extra open space per shelf to add volumes over time. Depending on collection type, academic research libraries are considered full once they have reached that working capacity limit, approximately 80–85 percent. In reference areas, zones with half-height shelving were common, to allow readers to pull heavy volumes and rest them on top of the three-shelf-high storage units for browsing. Many libraries are removing this type of shelving as reference materials go electronic in order to recapture space on a primary floor for other purposes.

Ranges need to be a reasonable length and ideally laid out in blocks with a rational distribution such that users can easily understand the logic of the collection. Historically, designers sized library building modules to optimize the most efficient stack configurations. As digital collections grow and print collections get transferred into high-density storage, stack layout will become less of a driver in designing new library design.

Where older buildings are renovated, dealing with nonconforming stacks is subject to code interpretation and the specific situation. Old self-supporting stack structures are particularly difficult to deal with, as they do not conform to current structural and egress codes, often are not sprinklered, and the clearance between their thin slabs is extremely tight. Often the steel stack columns were also used as conduits for electricity to light switches, an added safety concern.

Movable compact shelving operated by users allows browsing but requires far less space. However, compact shelving requires structure that can support 300 lb/sq ft live load; it is generally installed in basement areas with slab-on-grade conditions. (Regular shelving, by comparison, requires 150 lb/sq ft live load capacity.) Both manual and motorized systems have been used successfully for many years. The compact form also offers protection from ultraviolet (UV) exposure and dust, so it is beneficial over time for conservation of collections.

High-Density Storage Strategies

Many institutions pressed for space at the center of their campus turn to alternative storage strategies for their collections. Moving lesser used materials to a high-density facility, either on- or off-site, is now common. In addition space saving, these repositories offer superior environmental conditions for print materials, with colder temperature and more stable humidity, compared with those of spaces occupied by people. They may help address the problems with early 20th Century print collections that were not printed on acid-free paper and are currently deteriorating on standard shelving in most locations. Off-site storage, however, requires long-term investment in staff to manage the facility and to transport volumes, so carbon neutrality issues should be considered as options are weighed. Journal articles are usually retrieved by scanning with a document delivery service.

The advantages of high-density systems include the following:

- *Space savings*, which can free up existing stack space on campus so it can be converted to space for users
- *Convenience for users*, with delivery of electronically paged material to a service desk or even directly to faculty offices
- *Preservation*, with stable environmental conditions ideal for book storage, fireproof construction, vapor-retarding detailing, and tight envelope control
- *Reduced construction costs*, in comparison to the amount of new construction that would be required to house the same capacity of volumes in a standard structure, and reduced exterior surface area in relation to volume
- *Reduced long-term costs*, for environmental conditioning, lighting, and operation costs by consolidation into massive compact volumes
- *Efficiency of accommodation*, through automated location control systems that enable storage by book size to achieve the most dense arrangement
- *Future expansion*, with modular design that can add bays as needed over time

High-density facilities fall into two types. One type is the "Harvard depository" type developed for Harvard University in 1986,[7]

7 http://hul.harvard.edu/hd/pages/facility.html.

which uses "high-bay" shelving over 30 ft high, with bin storage and forklift retrieval by humans. The design was modular to allow the addition of future modules for expansion, and by 2009 seven modules had been added. This model has now been copied by many institutions.

The other type of high-density facility is a warehouse equipped with an automated retrieval system (ARS), which also uses bin storage but with robotic retrieval equipment (see Figure 4.14). A number of institutions have chosen to build these on campus (see Mansueto Library, Case Study 3) in response to constituents' concerns about response time for accessing requested materials and for efficiency of staffing. These can be up to 50 ft high, enabled by the development of the robotic equipment. Some libraries are showcasing the integration of an ARS into the design of their library building on campus (see Hunt Library, Case Study 1). Those that have provided a place for library users to view the robotic equipment in action have found that watching them is quite a novelty attraction.

▸ *Figure 4.14 Automated retrieval system.* DEGW.

LIBRARIES AND LEARNING CENTERS
CASE STUDY 3

JOE AND RIKA MANSUETO LIBRARY
University of Chicago, Chicago, Illinois

Architect: Murphy/Jahn Architects
Completion date: 2011
Size: 240 ft long by 120 ft wide by 55 ft deep
Construction cost: approximately $81 million
Seating capacity: 184 seats

Key Features

Grand Reading Room: 8,000 sf, 184 seats
Circulation Service Center desk
Preservation Department
Conservation Laboratory
Digitization Laboratory
Automated Storage and Retrieval System (equivalent to 330,000 linear feet)

Figure 4.15 Exterior view at sunset. Tom Rossiter © 2011 University of Chicago.

The Mansueto Library was designed to provide extensive storage for print materials in the heart of the University of Chicago campus immediately adjacent to the main Regenstein Library (see Figure 4.15). The Regenstein Library, one of the finest research libraries in the world, holds over 4.4 million volumes on both regular shelving and a full lower level of compact shelving. The strong research focus of the university is an important driver for the continuing need to grow the print collections, currently at about 150,000 volumes per year, and the faculty values highly the ability to browse the collections and wanted collection growth to be accommodated on campus. The Mansueto Library addressed these needs by creating a high-density facility that could store locally materials not needing to be browsed and free up space in existing open shelving areas for browsing. It has an automated storage and retrieval system (ASRS), which extends 50 ft underground. Its only expression aboveground is a dramatic, gently sloped elliptical glass dome over a sunlit reading room.

The Mansueto Library will provide scholars and students quick access to 3.5 million volume equivalents, typically retrieving a paged volume in 5 minutes—less time than it takes to walk between the buildings. It will be used to accommodate materials not needing to be browsed from all the libraries, such as old runs of bound journals, oversized folios, archival boxes, and other special materials that will benefit from being stored in more stable environmental conditions. It will enable shifting of collections to free up space in other libraries' browsable stack areas for new materials or for renovations to create more collaborative user spaces.

The design reduced the building carbon footprint through a compact form enabled by the ASRS and buried deep into stable ground conditions (see cross section in Figure 4.16), minimizing exposure to variable exterior conditions and allowing high-efficiency heating, ventilation, and air conditioning (HVAC) systems.[8] The initial capital investment in the ASRS will be offset by the reduced staff

8 For a summary of the energy savings analysis, see James Vaughan and B. Todd Hunter, "How the University of Chicago Is Addressing 'Sustainability Now!' with Its New Library Building," Society of College and University Planners Conference, July 2011.

Figure 4.16 Cross section. Murphy/Jahn Architects © 2007.

labor time over the life of the building, speed of delivery to a service desk, and elimination of the transportation costs typically generated by off-site facilities. This ASRS facility requires one-seventh of the space of regular stacks, making it extremely compact as well as secure.

The stable underground conditions are designed for a temperature of 60° F and a relative humidity of 30 percent. There are five rows, each with a robotic crane that retrieves bins from the 50 ft high storage racks. Each of the 24,000 bins is tracked by a bar code system, and materials are stored by size rather than by library classification. Bins are delivered to the service desk in the center of the reading room, where the paged items are extracted and held for pickup and the bins returned to the storage below.

The dome over the Grand Reading Room is composed of 691 glass panels, each 2 × 2 m with three layers of glass (see Figure 4.17). The fritted glass enclosure admits 50 percent of the visible light, rejects 73 percent of the solar heat, and filters 98 percent of the UV rays.

Figure 4.17 Side view of reader seating in the Reading Room. Jason Smith © 2011 University of Chicago.

Comparative Costs of Keeping a Book

Where they have a choice, institutions weigh the initial cost of investing in a physical book compared with its electronic form (knowing they must face the still challenging technical and economic difficulties with digital preservation), but the long-term cost for storing a print book should be considered as well. Paul Courant and Matthew Nielsen completed a study comparing the long-term cost of keeping a book in different types of storage facilities.[9] They looked at not only construction costs, but also functionality and operating costs such as maintenance, utilities, staff operations, and transportation. They analyzed four shelving models for storing a book: open shelving, high-density shelving, hybrid shelving with 10 years on open stacks (then transferred to high-density shelving), and hybrid shelving with 20 years on open stacks. ("Hybrid" models incur an additional cost of transferring the materials into storage.)

The authors conclude that space is the single largest cost associated with storing books. Open-stack facilities are much more expensive to construct on a per-book basis than high-density facilities, which require less construction, are more compact volumes with less exterior wall, and reduce environmental conditioning and cleaning services. High-density facilities do, however, cost more per book for staffing. The analysis demonstrates that keeping a book on open shelving costs about five times more than putting it in high-density storage. The authors conclude, "If an item circulates infrequently, a high-density facility may save a great deal of money, even though circulating from that facility is ten times as expensive as circulating from open stacks" (where users retrieve the materials).

Other important factors to be considered are the time required for retrieval and whether it is acceptable to a particular library's faculty and user population, and loss of ability to browse physical material with subsequent need to rely on digital browsing methods, though the potential for better electronic searching capabilities will improve and increase demand for those print materials over time.

Libraries are collaborating to form regional consortiums for storage of shared materials as an alternative strategy. Large regional consortiums of research libraries are now under discussion, and are likely to develop over the next couple of decades. Groups of universities and other organizations will develop shared print and digital repositories and share the costs of storing and managing print collections. This is likely to impact staffing at individual libraries.

9 Paul N. Courant and Matthew "Buzzy" Nielsen, "On the Cost of Keeping a Book," *The Idea of Order: Transforming Research Collections for 21st Century Scholarship* (Washington, DC: Council on Library and Information Resources, June 2010, pp. 81–105).

Staff Space to Support Changing Roles

Staff roles are changing not only within the library itself but also externally in relation to other campus organizations as boundaries between them blur. The following sections address how typical staff groups are evolving while distinctions between them erode. Developing the service strategy, defining how staff will deliver services in an integrated way, and designing the future user experience all impact library and learning center planning. See Figure 4.18 for an example diagram illustrating one of several alternative approaches to service point strategy in a library.

Information Services

Traditional reference services directed students or faculty to resources and assisted

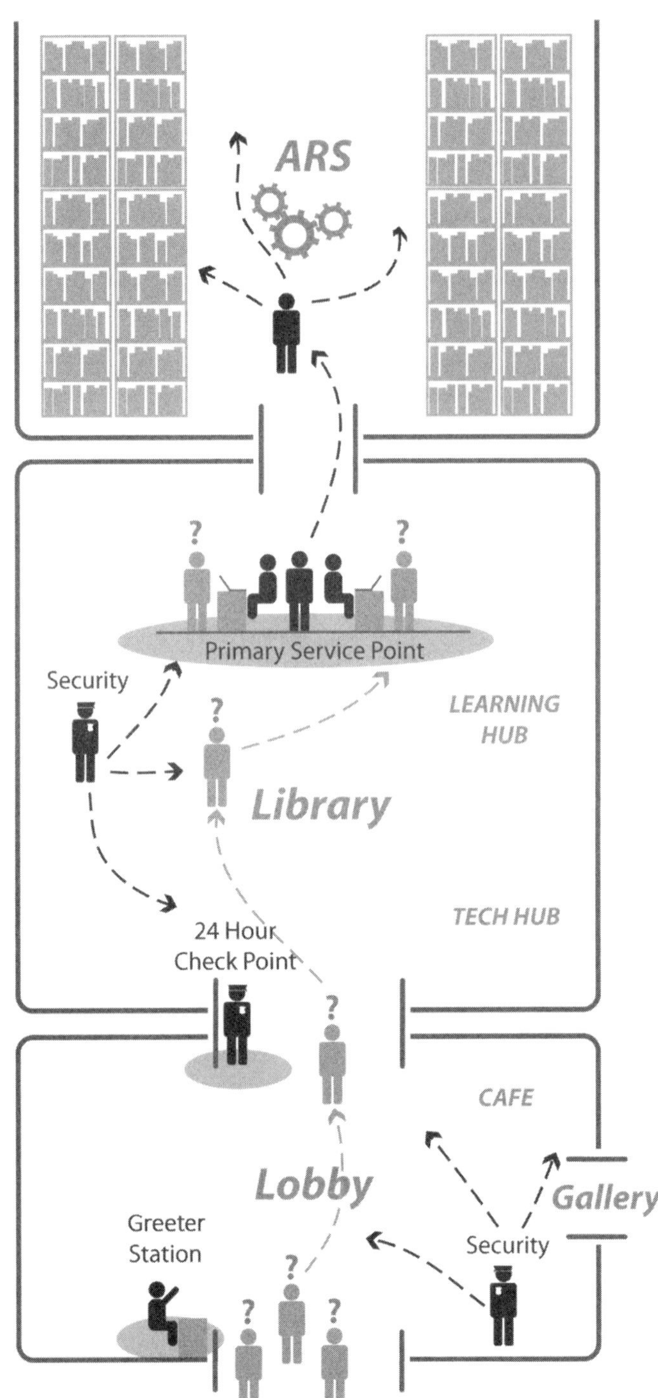

▸ *Figure 4.18 Service Point Strategy. An example from the Hunt Library workshop process, which explored alternative service point strategies.* North Carolina State University Libraries/ DEGW.

them with research queries, usually at a prominently located reference desk or by appointment. These information services are now more likely to be provided by virtual reference services or at an integrated service desk. Work space needs for information services staff consist of a mix of quiet work space for concentrated searches and collaborative areas where staff can work together and share knowledge, plus consultation rooms to meet with patrons.

Information services staff, particularly subject area experts serving as liaisons to a discipline or school within the institution, are often actively involved in collections development. This liaison role has, in some contexts like academic medical centers, been extended into the concept of the "informationist"[10] (or information specialist), as at Johns Hopkins University's Welch Medical Library or Vanderbilt University's Eskind Biomedical Library. The informationist provides knowledge management services to specific departments or groups, and functions as an embedded part of the clinical or research team. As the field of informatics becomes more developed, the boundary between informatics and information services will become less clear.

The spatial implications for this role redefinition are radical: it implies a distributed work model with roving information specialists, so space needs will be very different. The master plan for the Welch Medical Library[11] envisioned shared collaborative spaces called "touchdown" suites distributed in clinical and research departments complemented by a centrally located knowledge management hub where informationists can connect with colleagues (see Case Study 4).

10 The term "informationist" was proposed by Davidoff and Florance in 2000. See F. Davidoff and V. Florance, "The Informationist: A New Health Profession?" *Annals of Internal Medicine* 132, no. 12 (2000): 996–998.

11 See Shirley Dugdale and Kate Oliver, "Applying the SANE Study Findings: A Master Plan for the Health Sciences Libraries at Johns Hopkins University," presented at the Society for College and University Planning (SCUP) conference, July 2002.

LIBRARIES AND LEARNING CENTERS
CASE STUDY 4

WELCH MEDICAL LIBRARY
Johns Hopkins University, Baltimore, Maryland

Master plan date: 2002

Library Planners: DEGW, with Hillier Architects

The online journal frees the content from its physical container and similarly frees the library from its physical container—the building.

—Nancy Roderer, Director of Welch Medical Library

Johns Hopkins University needed to develop a master plan for the health sciences libraries that would respond to a rapid conversion from print to electronic resources. The plan needed to support evidence-based medicine, new ways of providing services, and the emergence of the virtual library. A series of facilitated workshops explored how services might change. The Welch librarians, led by Nancy Roderer, Director of Welch Library, envisioned the new role of the "informationist" as a more active and mobile participant in clinical and research teams in the future.

A space strategy was developed to support this new distributed work model, proposing a network of informationist "touchdown" suites throughout the clinical and research buildings. This was intended to be an opportunistic strategy, proposing to repurpose languishing departmental library spaces that no longer had print materials into technology-enhanced suites for one-on-one consultation, training, and knowledge sharing between the informationists and the teams they supported. These suites were to be complemented by a central knowledge center hub for staff managing the digital library operations located centrally in the medical center campus. Prototype settings for various activities were envisioned and then used to develop the space program that projected future space needs for staff, collections, and user facilities.

After conversion to electronic journals accelerated in 2000, visitation to the library building itself has declined precipitously while sources for digital archives have increased. The historic Welch Building had originally been built for the Institute of the History of Medicine in 1929 and housed the historical collections there as well, so the master plan proposed that by 2015 a reduced (and aging) print collection become integrated into the historical collections.

Other strategies were explored to revitalize vacated space in the building. One concept was to convert part of the historic Welch Building into a "center for facilitated discovery," incorporating new technology-rich collaborative spaces in which information services professionals would play a role in capturing and making retrievable the interdisciplinary discourse taking place there. This may be complemented by converting part of the existing building into a center for the graduate programs, which could provide the whole research precinct with a range of technology-enhanced collaborative settings.

Access Services

Access services include circulation, stacks management, reserves, and other user service functions, and traditionally deals with checkout, return, and reshelving of print materials as well as monitoring alarms at the exit/entry security gates. Some libraries have aggregated their reference and access/circulation services into a unit called "public services." With less print material circulating, service desks are taking on new functions, such as the checkout of laptops, e-readers, and other equipment. Many of these main service desks have cross-trained staff who assist users with basic IT questions or direct those with more difficult questions to the right expert elsewhere. They also hold requested materials for pickup. Although circulation desks are traditionally near the entry, self-checkout machines, radio-frequency identification (RFID) tags, and other service-oriented improvements can enable alternative locations.

Access services employ temporary student assistants each semester to assist with circulation tasks. As print usage declines and more material goes into off-site storage facilities, fewer book handlers will be needed, requiring less work space behind service desks. Student staff roles will likely shift to providing support to groups dealing with digital resources management, helping patrons with use of media equipment, and other new functions for which they have been trained.

Technological improvements, such RFID tag systems, will improve efficiency in management of materials on stacks as well as in circulation or storage. RFID tools can scan shelves and identify missing or out of place books as well as other useful data. Initial investment in converting a collection to RFID tags may be high, but may offer management efficiencies for certain types of collections.

Technical Services and Collections Development

The library department in charge of processing materials was traditionally called "technical services." It encompassed acquisitions, cataloging, serials processing, shelving and bindery preparation, preservation/conservation, and, in some cases, shipping and receiving. Their work space needs to be designed for a logical flow of materials through the various stages of processing, plus holding shelving for books. Design must provide convenient access to a loading dock, or service elevator connecting to it, for deliveries of daily shipments as well as packing for the bindery. A convenient service-side access path to the circulation desk and the staff who shelve materials is also important. Workstations in these areas need to be 100 NSF minimum to accommodate book trucks for work in progress, supplemented by meeting spaces and other processing areas. In large libraries, conservation areas must accommodate large tables, glue and chemical storage, sinks, and specialized equipment.

Now that libraries are ordering more journals in electronic form, print journal processing has decreased significantly over the last decade as has the need to bind these publications. Although this reduces staff time, negotiating licenses and managing access to digital materials has become increasingly burdensome. These developments force libraries to reorganize, retrain staff to new roles, and form work groups around digital assets management. (See Figure 4.19

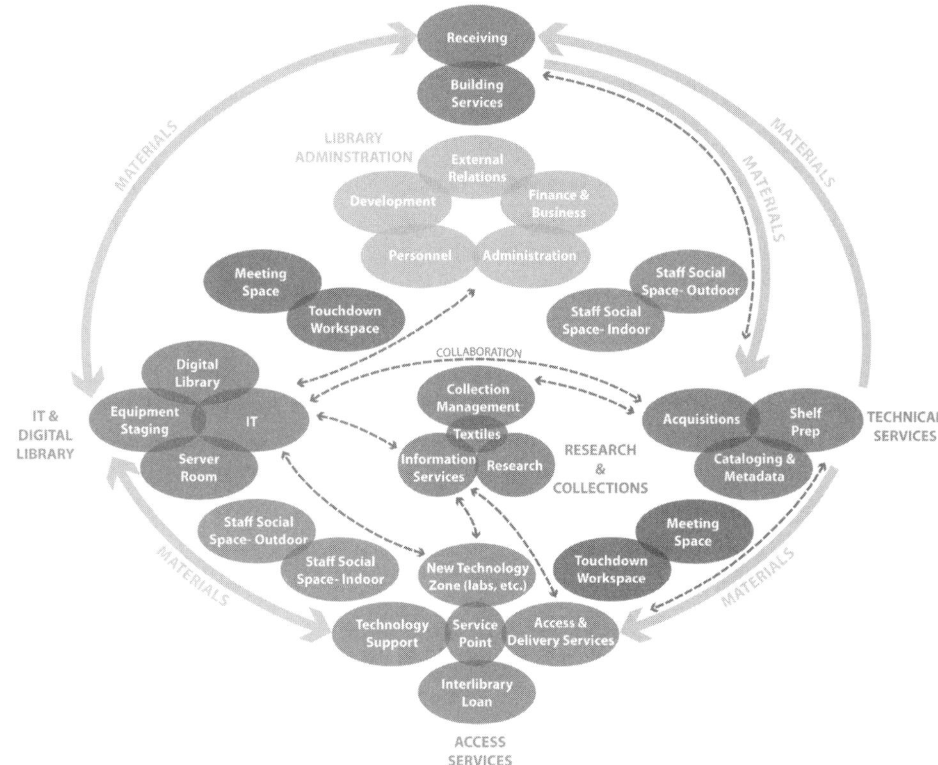

Figure 4.19 Relationships between staff groups. North Carolina State University/DEGW.

as a sample diagram illustrating relationships between staff groups.) As a "back-of-house" function, technical services groups generally do not interface with library users except through occasional virtual contact. Processing groups have less need to be physically proximate to the library stacks. Large campuses with multiple libraries have moved to consolidate processing units, in some cases by shifting operations to less central or off-site facilities or by forming institutional consortiums.

Library and IT Services

Librarians and IT organizations have worked in parallel as networked information systems developed. Organizational structures have evolved differently at each institution, but in most cases, libraries formed their own IT groups responsible for systems operations. These groups coordinate with campus IT units who manage the network infrastructure and academic computing.

Rapid technological change and the convergence of various IT-related services are redefining the boundaries between groups, which will likely lead to new organizational structures over the next decade. Closer coordination between library and campus IT services and other partners is emerging to develop new digital educational materials, academic computing capabilities, institutional research repositories, data curation strategies, digital media services, and technology sandbox labs for users. In response, campus planners must address potential future relationships and partnerships. These groups have work space requirements similar to those of software programmers—flexible, open environments that support collaboration, complemented by areas for quiet, concentrated work.

Educational Services

While librarians have always supported the educational mission of the university, they are now even more directly involved in the teaching process itself. Specialists focus on enhancing the educational program and teaching information literacy. Many now also collaborate with faculty by instructing classes on subject-specific resources or research methods. Technological developments and social media offer librarians alternate virtual ways to stay connected to classes without the need to be physically present.

BUILDING AND SYSTEMS DESIGN

Building Organization and Circulation

A key challenge of library design is functional planning, which addresses relationships between user seating, staff areas, and stacks while also taking into account circulation issues. The logic of the library's organization and layout should be simple and obvious to users, reducing dependence on signage, and transitions from public to privates zones should be evident (see Figure 4.20). Service desks should be in visible and convenient locations. Figure 4.21 illustrates how users in a workshop envisioned the library's organization.

An important wayfinding aide is a clear stack that provides logical orientation for users moving from one range to another during a search for materials. As cell phones and group study proliferate, some libraries use a system of icons to distinguish quiet from conversation-tolerant areas and zones where mobile phones can be used. Ideally, library users should be able to find repetitive spaces like toilets or printer rooms in a consistent location on each floor. On large-footprint floors a centrally located space or atrium can provide orientation, sight lines through the building, and natural light to user seating.

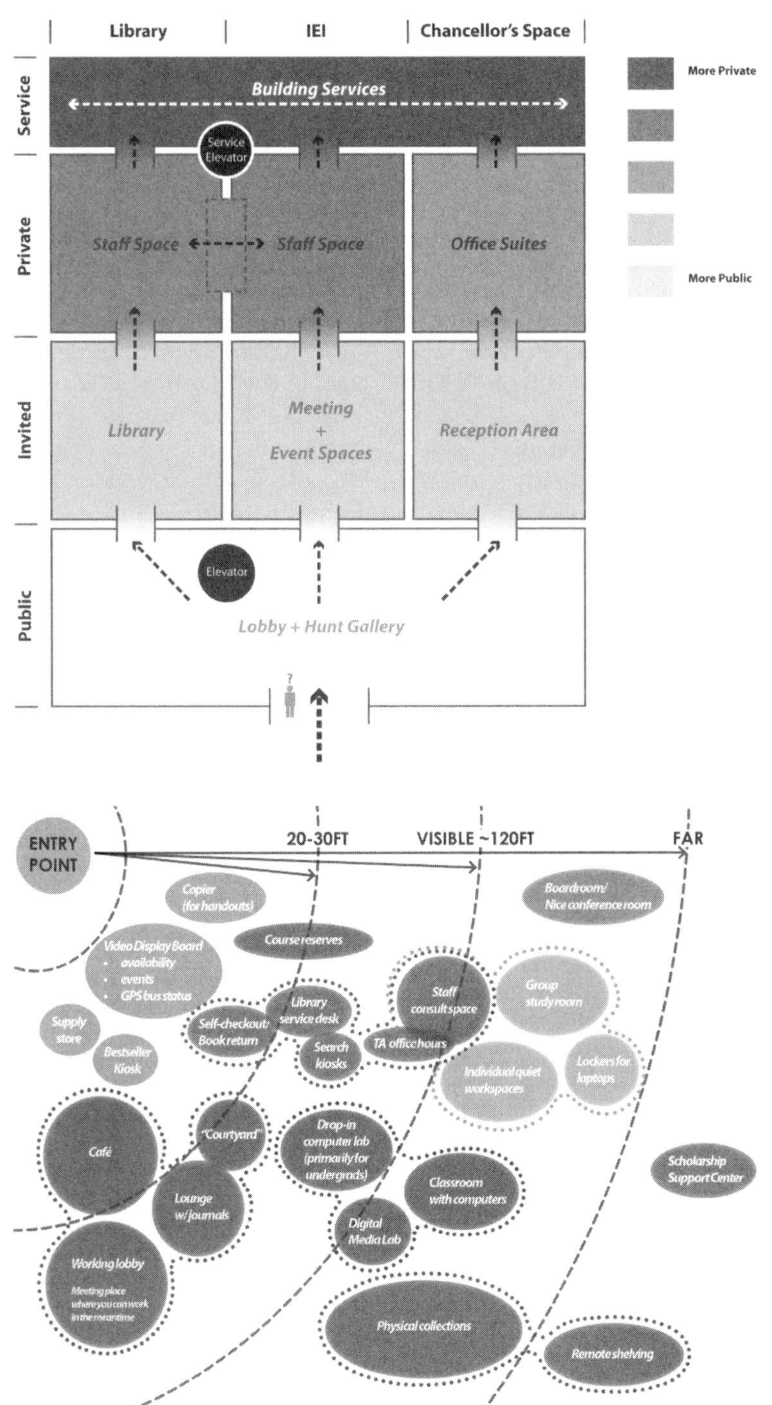

◀ *Figure 4.20 Public-to-private transitions.* North Carolina State University/ DEGW.

◀ *Figure 4.21 Building organization from the user's perspective.* North Carolina State University/ DEGW.

Movement through the buildings can become an enhanced experience for users and staff with carefully planned circulation elements. Successful library designs exploit transparency of form and materials to encourage interaction by making activity visible and service points evident. However, as libraries transform into learning centers, their teaching spaces, commons, and other gathering spots often generate significant traffic. These spaces and their traffic must be analyzed during schematic design (for example, as in Figure 4.22). Classrooms must be easy to find, accessible, and located to avoid disturbing study zones.

Materials-Handling Flows

Materials-handling flows are an important design concern even in an era of electronic resources. Special circulation requirements maintain the integrity of the library security envelope. Collection items get tagged with bar codes or, more recently, RFID tags, requiring users to check materials out before passing through the security gate. As libraries reduce print collections and stack areas, the security gate can be located deeper into the building with other functions "outside the gate" placed between it and the entry. However, staff still needs to be adjacent in case the alarm is tripped. As libraries introduce checkout of laptops and other electronic devices, service desks must monitor a wider variety of materials.

Back-of-house materials processing presents another important design challenge. The technical services group that deals with cataloging and processing of materials coming into the library needs easy access to the loading dock and to the access services staff responsible for shelving. The technical services group also prepares shipments of unbound journals for

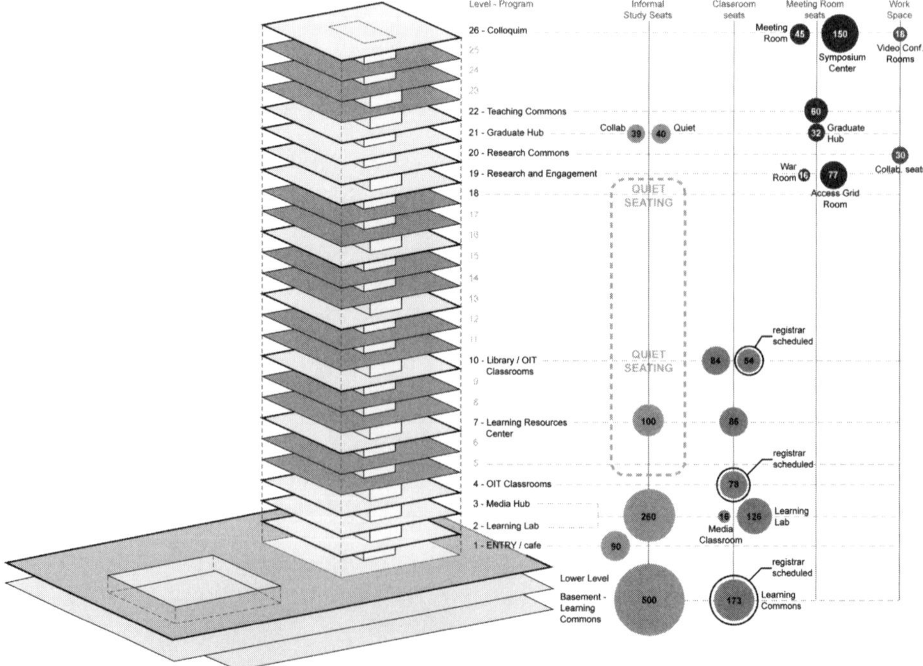

▸ *Figure 4.22 Seating distribution analysis.* University of Massachusetts Amherst/DEGW.

the bindery. (See Figure 4.23 for an illustration of these flows.) With the significant drop in print title subscriptions at many libraries, this function will likely decrease.

In place of bindery shipments, many libraries are now handling books being transported to and from off-site storage facilities on a daily basis. Others have committed to special scanning projects, which can require large staging areas with shelving to amass and return large shipments of books for scanning.

Planning for Flexibility and Adaptability

Library planners must now provide optimal flexibility—both to augment the ways spaces can be used and to enable their adaptability as systems and technologies change. Planning addresses change from the start, such as removable open stack design that allows easy space conversion for user seating. For example, by hanging aisle task light fixtures off removable stacks, spaces can be quickly and easily cleared for another use while power grids in the floor accommodate alternative furniture layouts.

Energy and Environmental Issues

In addition to good architectural practice for energy conservation, planning for sustainable library and learning center design needs to maximize the introduction of daylight in reader seating areas, especially with large floor plates. While interior atriums can bring daylight to the center of a large building, their design must ensure adequate acoustical control. Occupancy sensors can be used to control lighting in large, low-usage stack

INTAKE

1. Books arrive by truck and delivered via loading dock
2. All deliveries received and sorted in Shipping and Receiving, with books and other circulating materials separated from other deliveries
3. Books and other library materials gathered onto book trucks for subsequent processing
   - 3b Existing library materials that do not need processing placed directly into ARS from Collections Staging access point
4. Materials transported to 5th floor library staff workspace to be processed by Library Technical Services

PROCESSING AND PLACEMENT IN ARS

5. Books/materials processed by Acquisitions, Metadata & Cataloging, and Collection Management in preparation for circulation
6. Books/materials transported to 2nd Floor Central Service Point for placement in ARS
7. Processed books/materials gathered and queued for deposit
   - 7b Books/materials returned by faculty and students placed in queue
8. Materials placed into ARS

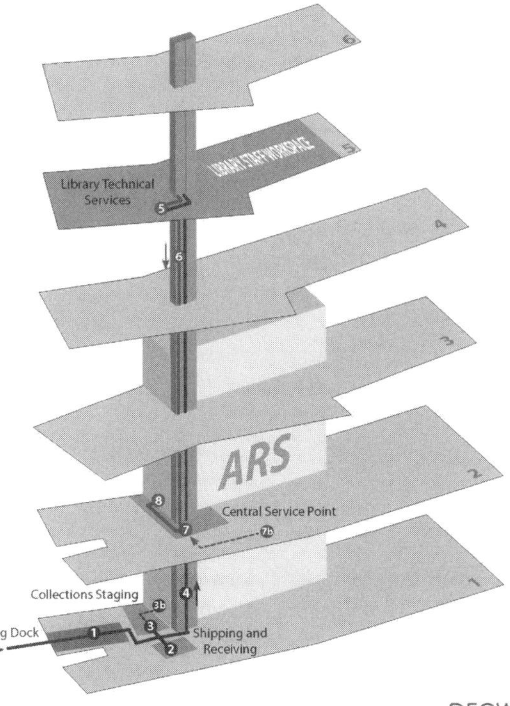

Figure 4.23 Library materials flow analysis. North Carolina State University/ DEGW.

DEGW

blocks, in group study rooms, and in other locations when not in active use.

Stable climate control for print collections is essential not just for older rare materials but also for the bulk of the early-twentieth-century books not printed on acid-free paper. Ideal conditions for print materials don't support a comfortable reader environment, so strategies to separate stack blocks from seating areas can address both sets of needs. Compact shelving zones offer better protection from light, enhanced environmental control, and a more compact footprint, reducing the required area of new construction.

Relocation of print materials to off-site storage facilities ensures optimal storage conditions. As campuses commit to carbon neutrality targets, the added cost of daily travel to and from these facilities must be taken into account. This expense is ultimately outweighed by their energy efficiency, which has been clearly documented compared with that of open stack storage.

Structural Systems

Library buildings can be designed with a wide range of structural system types, so their selection will often depend on the effect of local market forces on construction costs. Designers usually locate compact shelving in an on-grade structure at the lowest levels to reduce structural costs, but location on an upper level is feasible if functional requirements justify it.

Older university research library buildings may have a self-supporting steel stack structure where the multitier shelving actually supports the floor above. These are often surrounded on three sides by grand rooms with high ceilings that have different elevations than the stack floors. These stack blocks, designed for efficient storage with very low ceilings and tight aisle spacing and stairs, do not meet current codes. Sprinklering this type of multitier facility may require running sprinklers down each aisle due to headroom constraints. The vertical supports of self-supporting stack structures may also house conduits for electrical power with switches at the end of ranges—an added safety concern. The floors are very thin slabs or even open metal grating. It is very difficult to convert these types of structures to other purposes, so demolition to replace them will provide greater flexibility over time.

Mechanical and Fire Protection Systems Issues

Design of building systems needs to anticipate the potential for future 24-hour/7 days a week activity, even if it is not seen a strong need by the institution at the time of design. Student demand for 24/7 usage of facilities is growing, academic institutions are involved in programs with partners overseas, and libraries are becoming mixed-use facilities. As the facilities on campus most likely to stay open late, libraries and learning centers maintain staff well into the evening, providing supervision as well as service.

The mechanical systems for special collections and rare book collections must provide constant control of temperature, humidity, and filtration of contaminants. These are paged collections, with staff access only. The temperature design standard for preservation is usually 60° F (16° C). Relative humidity (RH) should be kept as stable as possible to avoid stressing materials, with 30 percent RH now thought to be ideal for paper preservation and film-based collections (with a slightly higher RH for vellum and leather materials, which can become brittle below 30 percent RH).

A preservation environment can also save deteriorating volumes printed on acidic paper from the mid-nineteenth century to the 1980s, which unfortunately predominate in many research collections. Various techniques slow their deterioration (such as deacidification treatments or electronic scanning before their paper becomes too brittle to handle), but these are expensive. Otherwise, storing volumes in a stable, cool, and light-free environment is the most practical approach until better preservation methods become more affordable.

Sprinklers need to clear stack tops by at least 18 inches, which can be a challenge when retrofitting them into an older library built without a fire protection system. In special collections areas, halon fire protection systems have been discontinued due to environmental and safety concerns. Preaction sprinkler systems are preferable, as they send an alarm signal before the water is actually released.

Electrical/Communication Systems

Migration to digital formats and increasing use of electronic resources are driving demand for server rooms, distributed closets, and related cooling systems. Uninterrupted power supply (UPS) systems are essential to protect vital library operations serving the university.

Electrical distribution systems must provide power over large open areas of library seating unobtrusively with a logic that anticipates multiple movable furnishing layouts. To accommodate the pervasive use of personal devices, buildings for informal study and collaborative activities should ideally provide access to power for every user seat. This challenges the designer to provide sufficient saturation of outlets across open floor areas as well as to all work surfaces, especially in renovation of existing buildings. Power provided only at wall outlets has limitations (even in meeting rooms this can generate tripping hazards) and ideally should be accessible at the work surface.

The growth in sophisticated academic technology systems will continue to demand more power and higher bandwidth in the communication networks required by this building type. As collaboration with remote academic colleagues increases, videoconferencing in libraries will become more important. With libraries taking on more responsibility for data curation and management of institutional repositories, demand will increase for more robust network infrastructure, either in the library facilities or at a campus data center. To support collaboration and group visualization of complex data, high definition displays or projection systems and staff trained in new types of support will become the norm.

Lighting

Lighting design must address several conditions: the stack aisles, open work areas, service zones, and zones for computing. Distribution of daylight to most user seating is desirable. Glare on computer screens can be controlled by indirect lighting (assuming sufficient ceiling height) in combination with task lighting. Readers should be able to adjust work surface lighting with controls.

Exposure to UV light damages print collections, so stack zones have traditionally been located away from facades or protected by reducing window area. As more print material gets housed on compact shelving or shifted to off-site storage, this becomes less of an issue. Protection against UV exposure should be considered in the selection of glazing systems and in areas where rare books are handled and stored.

Acoustic Control

The balance of activities in libraries has shifted as they evolve from quiet sanctuaries to active learning centers. It is important to create zones for collaborative group work versus quiet individual work. Conversation-tolerant spaces can have a pleasant buzz of activity, but white-noise systems are an option if needed. Acoustic control through circulation planning, choice of finishes, and space configuration can dampen noise levels and keep noise from traveling. For atriums in particular, architects need to consider material finishes, volume configuration, and other aspects to make sure that noise in the open levels does not travel and disturb quiet reading areas. Teaching areas and group viewing rooms fitted with audiovisual systems require good acoustical design.

Quiet study areas are still very much in demand, not only by students but also by others in the campus community wishing to escape busy office settings to do concentrated work. The traditional layout of the quiet open library with enclosed group rooms is reversing: open areas are becoming conversation-tolerant while special reading rooms serve as secluded quiet sanctuaries, reducing conflicts. Good acoustical design practice includes sound isolation and appropriate partition construction to separate spaces. Areas that are too quiet can be objectionable too, where the slightest rustle of papers or footsteps is disturbing.[12]

12 Leighton and Weber indicate that designing for 40–45 dB in quiet zones is considered prudent. See Philip D. Leighton and David C. Weber, *Planning Academic and Research Library Buildings*, 3rd ed. (New York: American Library Association, 1999), 141. A source for information about acoustic design for libraries is Charles M. Salter, "Acoustics for Libraries," written in 2002 for the Libris Design Project (http://www.librisdesign.org/) and supported by the U.S. Institute of Museum and Library Services. He explains Noise Criteria (NC) ratings and recommends an NC rating of NC 35–40 for open work areas and NC 25–30 for reading rooms and training rooms. http://librisdesign.org/docs/AcousticsLibraries.pdf.

HVAC systems can provide gentle background sound as long as disturbing vibration from equipment is avoided. Carpeting, sound-absorbent materials, and wall treatments or bookshelves all reduce noise in quiet spaces. Students seeking quiet study space sometimes advocate for reading rooms as opposed to tables scattered throughout stack areas because the space itself suggests a protocol for quiet use, which tends to be self-policing, whereas students may have a tendency to talk in groups within stack zones. Similarly, people tend to lower their voices in open workplace areas where the partitions are low enough to make them aware of people nearby.

Interior Design

The vision for the library should guide the interior design to be appropriate for a particular library building in its institutional context. Users often associate libraries with traditional materials such as wood, which convey comfort and academic ambiance. Other types of library spaces successfully express the energy of a new generation of collaborative learning activities driven by technology. Library design can be done in a wide range of materials, so a key choice is determining where to use timeless materials (e.g., stone) versus those that will allow change over time. Material choice is important for effective acoustical environmental control in library design. Flexible furnishings that are easy to move around support collaboration in commons areas and teaching spaces.

Code Issues

Libraries need to be designed based on good practice and standard code conformance, particularly with respect to fire prevention. Special issues involve seismic codes in vulnerable locations and the Americans with Disabilities Act (ADA) requirements. The ADA has primarily impacted service desk design where wheelchair users need to consult with seated staff. Also affected are current periodicals displays, which must be accessible from a wheelchair, and aisle width in stack zones. Libraries generally provide retrieval services to users who are unable to reach the upper shelves of standard stack ranges.

Special Equipment

Library equipment is either built-in (specified as part of the architectural design) or movable, the latter usually allocated out of a furniture, fixtures, and equipment (FF&E) or technology budget. Built-in equipment includes the stack shelving units, whether fixed or movable compact shelving types. Standard stack shelving units are typically 3 ft. wide, 90 inches tall and fitted out with six shelves for bound journals and seven shelves for monographs. Modular components are available to store media, archival boxes, folios, or other materials on the same shelving frameworks. Widths of aisles between ranges need to conform to ADA requirements—a minimum of 36 inches wide from base to base, which can project out by 1 inch on each side of a freestanding range. Shelf detailing and installation need to be appropriate for the seismic zoning of the building location.

Technology and audiovisual equipment budgets can be significant, particularly in a multipurpose building. These items can include: audiovisual systems, equipment and controls; projection and display tools, academic technology, collaborative technology and work settings; media lab equipment; servers; usability labs; and other types of equipment. Conservation labs not only have traditional equipment for the repair and preservation of print materials but also can have sophisticated scanning equipment to make special collections more accessible. Some research libraries have extremely high-resolution equipment for documenting large items, such as artwork.

Project planning must address computing equipment, ideally specified as late as possible to anticipate the latest generation of technology. Many librarians feel that it is no longer necessary to provide as many desktop computers as in the past, and instead are turning to new strategies such as laptop checkout or enterprise-wide cloud computing. However, for the time being libraries will still need to provide some equipment to accommodate walk-in traffic not carrying personal devices or disabled users needing assistive technologies.

Operations and Maintenance Issues

Growing student demand for 24-hour access, especially in learning commons areas, not only requires longer staff hours but also raises operational and planning issues. Maintenance procedures must address food consumption in study and work areas and schedule cleaning crews' hours around extended hours during exam periods. Zones designed for 24/7 use provide a place for students working late to study in secure locations. These are usually separated from collections areas to avoid book circulation control problems. Careful analysis of circulation flows within these mixed-use building types will uncover and address operations and security issues during design.

When users reposition lightweight furniture to suit their needs, it can migrate around, so some managers tag furnishings or color-code them to cue maintenance crews to their original location. Other managers encourage users to modify their study environment and welcome the shifting interior landscape, especially to better understand user response during the period of adjustment after a building opens.

The introduction of technology "sandbox" spaces into libraries and learning centers for tinkering with technology has operational and support implications. Where experimental classrooms are developed, they are more successful if staff are assigned to assist faculty with use of the space and its technology, to observe how the space is being used, and to gather data about the teaching activities taking place there.

LOOKING TO THE FUTURE

There are great opportunities today for partnerships among libraries, academic computing groups, centers for teaching excellence, student services, and other learning support units. Where these relationships thrive, they will influence the evolution of new, more effective learning environments and the organizations to support them. Many forces—growth in digital resources and scholarship, changes in publishing, reduced print collections, more storage options, demand for more collaborative settings, and an increasingly mobile population—are driving a complex process of change. Libraries and computing areas, once designed for individual use, are being converted into vibrant learning centers, whether as centralized facilities or distributed commons.

The academic library of the future promises not only to create settings for richer learning experiences, but also to model a better integration of formal and informal learning spaces across a campus. With integrated staffing strategies these centers can provide better services at point of need and, by colocating staff groups, help them to collaborate more productively. As libraries welcome a growing array of partners, the traditional distinctions between the library and other types of learning space will blur, redefining the future of college and university libraries.

CHAPTER 5

ACADEMIC BUILDINGS AND PROFESSIONAL SCHOOLS

Graham S. Wyatt, Partner, Robert A.M. Stern Architects

HISTORICAL PERSPECTIVE

When Charles Klauder and Herbert Wise wrote *College Architecture in America*[1] in 1929, 4 pages of text within the 300-page volume were dedicated to the design of academic buildings and only two types of rooms were discussed: a "classroom" (generally with 30 seats or less) and a "lecture room" (with more seats and a sloped or tiered floor).

The intervening decades have seen a revolution in educational theory, practice, and technology, and an accompanying explosion in the variety and complexity of academic buildings and classrooms. Some recent literature suggests that the term "classroom" unnecessarily narrows discussion and that the linguistically challenging "learning environment" more accurately reflects that much learning takes place outside the classroom. But while changes in technology and pedagogy have broadened the educational playing field, classrooms, in a multitude of forms, are still at the core of the university academic experience and promise to remain there for the foreseeable future.

ROLE OF ACADEMIC BUILDINGS ON CAMPUS

Academic buildings occupy the physical core of most campuses, and while residence halls, athletic facilities, and campus centers all support student life, academic buildings are the reason for student life. The 10- to 15-minute pass time between classes, typical on even the largest campuses, determines the central campus location required by academic buildings.

The earliest generation of American universities housed their primary activities (classrooms, library, student residences, and administration) within a single building—the Wren Building at the College of William and Mary, Nassau Hall at the College of New Jersey (now Princeton University), and "Old Main" on so many campuses across the continent. As colleges and universities grew to include several buildings, a second generation of campuses gave the library pride of place—Low Library at Columbia; Baker Library at Dartmouth and the huge libraries of the University of Illinois at Urbana-Champaign; and the University of Michigan, Ann Arbor, among others. The newest campuses—the University of Central Florida, Orlando, and the University of California, Merced, for example—place their campus centers on an equal footing with libraries, both within a dense pudding of academic buildings located at the heart of campus. Through each of these eras, the central campus location of classrooms has remained constant.

CURRENT TRENDS

While the campus core location and essential function of academic buildings have remained largely unchanged, several trends are

1 Charles Z. Klauder and Herbert C. Wise, *College Architecture in America* (New York: Charles Scribner's Sons, 1929).

driving the evolution of these buildings and the classrooms they contain:

- More than 70 percent of high school graduates now continue on to postsecondary education.[2] Universities and colleges, in short, have become a mass cultural phenomenon, and more postsecondary classrooms are needed than at any time in the history of this country.
- A broad spectrum of postsecondary instruction is now offered, ranging from highly theoretical to largely vocational, often within a single institution. Classroom and academic building design must rise to this diversity of subject matter and a corresponding diversity of teaching and learning styles.
- The growing use of interactive, team-based, and problem-based learning is affecting classroom design profoundly, favoring designs that support both student-to-instructor and student-to-student interaction within the classroom.
- The rapid evolution of information and instructional technologies continues to transform learning both in the classroom and beyond.

Changes in technology have given rise to a range of teaching and learning methods often referred to as "distance learning." Students and instructors in several locations can now share course material and communicate with each other online either during a scheduled class period ("synchronously") or as individuals and subgroups at times that suit their own schedules ("nonsynchronously"). Large courses can be subdivided into sections that meet simultaneously in remotely located classrooms within a campus or are distributed among different institutions. This ability to share educational content among locations and institutions has altered significantly the way in which universities are organized and marketed. Instructors can now provide, and students can receive, course material from and at almost any location with Internet access—a "virtual" university.

The logistics involved in effectively providing a high-quality virtual educational experience are daunting, and although virtual education methods may serve people who might otherwise lack educational access, they are generally supplementing and enhancing the face-to-face classroom experience, not replacing it. While universities must now provide distance learning capabilities and support the distance learning model, properly designed classrooms and campuses continue to provide universities with a powerful competitive advantage over the virtual learning environment.

Even the form of the face-to-face classroom has been affected profoundly by technological transformation. It is now assumed that instructors and students have their own computers and use these to communicate and share information during and between classes. Computers also support a move away from didactic teaching—lecturing—and toward problem-based learning, team learning, and various methods of individual learning. These trends often favor highly specific classroom designs, yet this move toward classroom specificity conflicts with a parallel trend: the need to maximize classroom utilization.

SPACE PROGRAMMING

A specific and well-considered architectural space program is essential to the design of a successful academic building. Basic issues regarding teaching methods must be defined and the relationship between these

2 Bureau of Labor Statistics, U.S. Department of Labor, "College Enrollment and Work Activity of 2009 High School Graduates," April 27, 2010.

and the physical form of the proposed building considered:

- What range of class sizes is to be housed?
- What subjects are to be taught?
- To what extent will instructional methods appropriate to some subjects be allowed to determine specific designs that may be at odds with the use of other methods or the teaching of other subjects?
- What nonclassroom facilities are necessary to optimally support teaching and learning?

These questions, and others, must be asked of an appropriate spectrum of stakeholders—the opinions of the registrar who schedules classroom use for many disciplines may differ greatly from those of an instructor who teaches a specific subject. Careful attention during the space programming phase must also be paid to technical issues, including lighting, furnishing, acoustics, and informational and instructional technologies, as these determine basic design decisions related to this building type.

The preparation of detailed room data sheets is important during space programming for academic buildings. Classrooms have specific dimensions and configurations related to furnishing, sight lines, and the integration of technology. These desired characteristics should be documented with text, floor plans, and room sections. Tiered classrooms present accessibility challenges that need to be addressed during space programming, and classrooms with a rated occupancy exceeding 50 people require two, suitably remote, means of egress. In short, a successful space program for an academic building is far more than a tabulation of floor areas.

Conceptual space programs for academic buildings should generally assume the following:

Room Type	Net Square Feet/Student[3]
Auditorium	12–15
Flat-floor classroom	26–28
Tiered case classroom	26–28
Tiered cluster classroom	32–36
Common room or lounge	15–20

Careful attention must be paid to common areas: academic buildings accommodate many occupants who arrive and depart during the brief periods between classes, so lobbies, corridors, and stairs must be wide and organized clearly. Elevator cabs should also be oversized but should be located so as to encourage use of stairs. Academic buildings are places of assembly, so toilet rooms need to be accordingly large. These factors cause most well-designed academic buildings to have a net-to-gross floor area ratio of approximately 58 percent (net floor area/0.58 = gross floor area).

3 For tiered classrooms and auditoriums these include floor area required for accessibility.

ACADEMIC BUILDINGS **CASE STUDY 1**

PARK CENTER FOR BUSINESS AND SUSTAINABLE ENTERPRISE

Ithaca College School of Business, Ithaca, New York

Architect: Robert A.M. Stern Architects

The Park Center for Business and Sustainable Enterprise (see Figure 5.1) showcases Ithaca College's commitment to environmental responsibility and education by achieving the U.S. Green Building Council's Leadership in Energy and Environmental Design (LEED) Platinum certification while supporting the college's collaborative, team-based approach to business education with a suite of efficient, highly effective classrooms that support lecture, teamwork, and a variety of information technologies (see Figures 5.1–5.5). The building's use of displacement ventilation provides exceptional energy efficiency with top-quality acoustics in its classrooms, offices, and common areas, while its combined use of natural light and artificial light both reduce energy use and place light where it is most needed, particularly within classrooms.

Key Academic Spaces

Trading room	1,200 NSF	40 seats
Large classroom	2,160 NSF	110 seats
Case study tiered classroom	1,440 NSF	60 seats
Cluster classroom	1,440 NSF	60 seats
Small classroom	660 NSF	30 seats
Breakout rooms	6 @ 240 NSF	
Flexible technology room	1,000 NSF	40 seats
Small classroom	1,010 NSF	46 seats
Moot boardroom	840 NSF	25 seats

Figure 5.1 *View from the south.* © Peter Aaron/Esto.

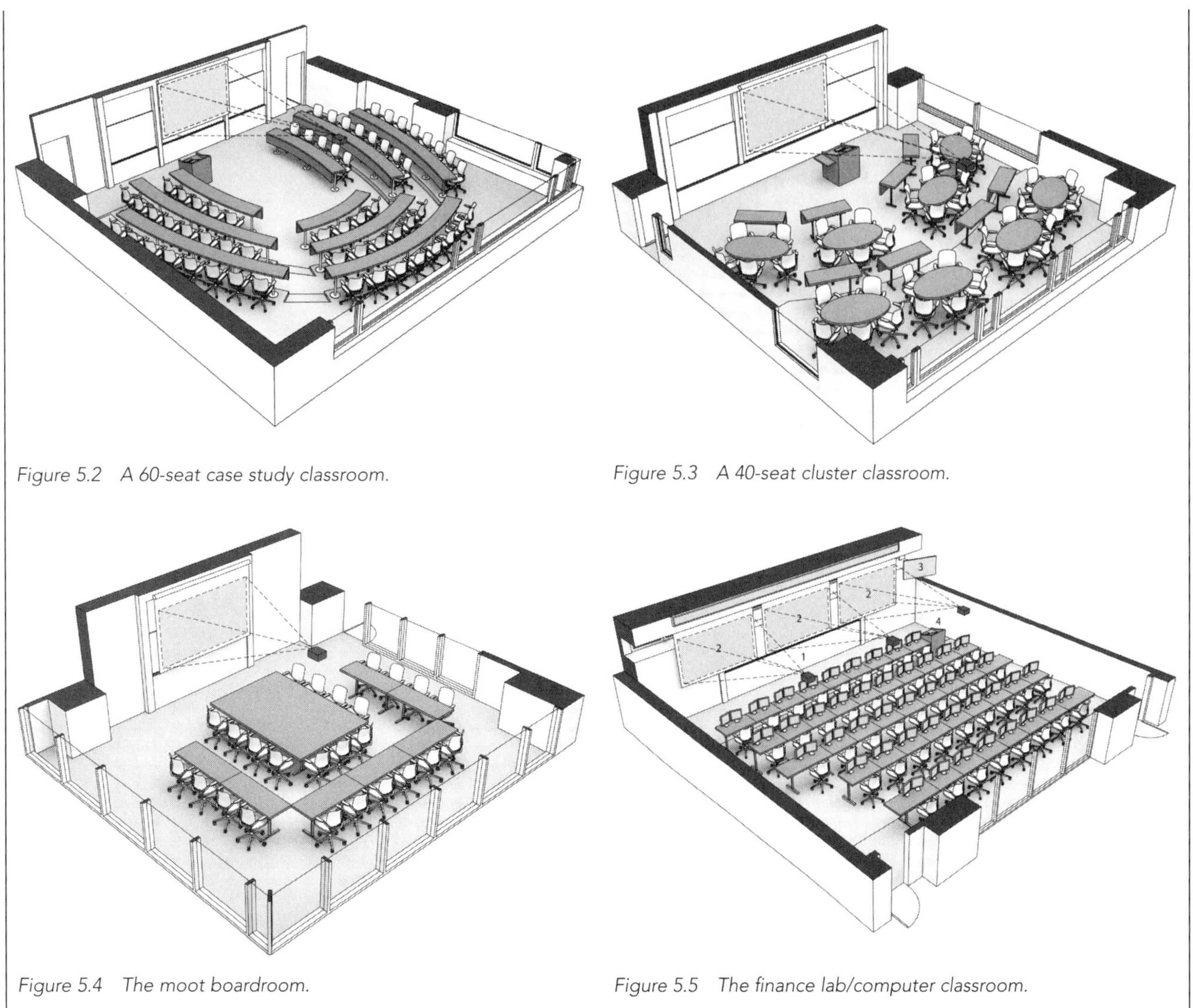

Figure 5.2 A 60-seat case study classroom.

Figure 5.3 A 40-seat cluster classroom.

Figure 5.4 The moot boardroom.

Figure 5.5 The finance lab/computer classroom.

ROOM TYPES

Eighty years after Klauder and Wise wrote *College Architecture in America*, classroom types can still be reduced to two categories: those with flat floors and those with tiered or sloped floors. Within these two broad categories, however, a spectrum of subcategories now exists.

Flat-Floor Classrooms

The "Traditional" Classroom

The most enduring advantage of the basic, rectangular, flat-floor classroom is its adaptability. It can be reconfigured rapidly and inexpensively to accommodate a variety of class sizes and formats (see Figure 5.6).

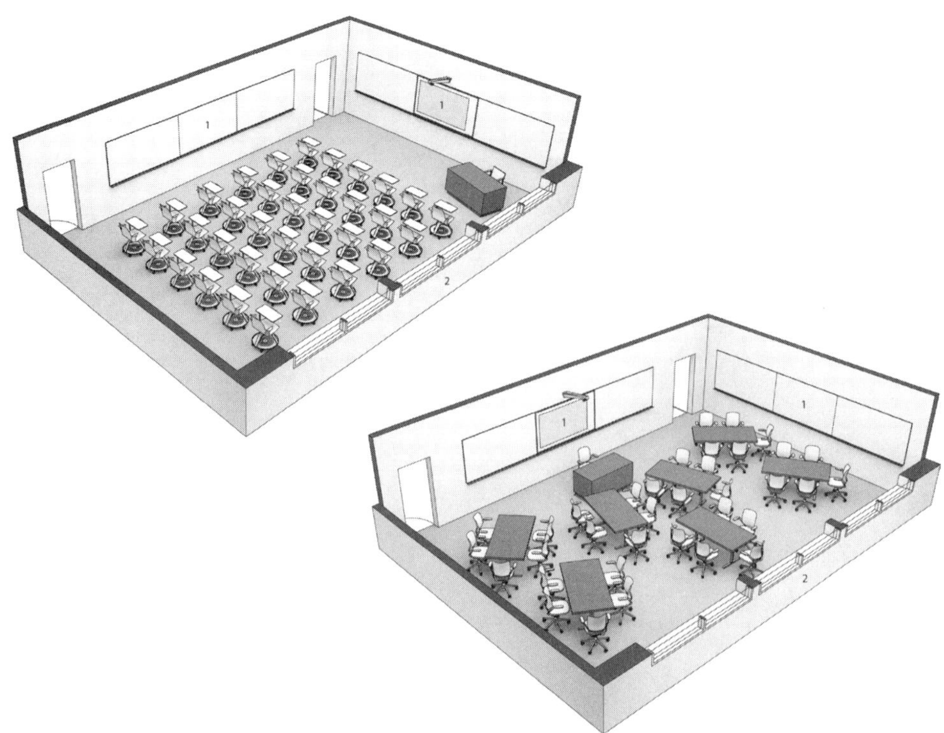

▸ *Figure 5.6 Traditional classroom in lecture and teamwork format.*
Legend
1 Presentation surface
2 Natural light
Robert A.M. Stern Architects

Lecture format:
Seats: 36
Floor Area: 982 ASF
ASF/ Seat: 27.3

Teamwork format:
Seats: 35
Floor Area: 982 ASF
ASF/ Seat: 28.1.

Certain time-tested planning principles apply: the length-to-width ratio of the room should be approximately 3:2, as deeper or shallower proportions are less accommodating to a variety of furniture configurations; ceiling heights should be at least 9 ft for even the smallest rooms and generally not less than half the room width for all but the largest classrooms; and points of entrance and exit should be located at the front and rear of the room, if possible, even in rooms small enough not to require two means of egress.

In order to accommodate teaching styles that encourage discussion among students, this basic classroom type can be reconfigured in a horseshoe seating plan, while for team-based instruction or group work, it can be refurnished with clusters of seats. Each of these configurations focuses on a "presentation wall," including a writing board and a variety of audiovisual or computer-based instructional devices.

The rapid adaptability promised by flat-floor classrooms is rarely realized, however. In reality, the tablet-arm chairs or personal desks that have been the staple of classroom furnishing for more than a century do not lend themselves to rapid reorganization, and the basic classroom, all too often, is arranged with rows of chairs and desks most suited to didactic modes of teaching. Recent advances in furniture design offer some promise, and a variety of alternative room types have arisen to more appropriately suit evolving attitudes about teaching and learning.

The Harkness Table and Classroom

In 1933, just 4 years after the publication of Klauder and Wise's *College Architecture in America*, Jens Fredrick Larson published the equally exhaustive *Architectural Planning of the American College*. Like Klauder, Larson was a successful architect who designed buildings for more than 30 college and university campuses and is most known for his work at Dartmouth, Bucknell, Colby, Lehigh, and Wake Forest.[4] Larson gave academic buildings, which he refers to as "recitation halls," minor attention: only 4 pages in his 181-page volume.[5] But during the 4 years between the publication of these two books, a frontal assault on recitation teaching occurred in Exeter, New Hampshire.

4 Thomas C. Jester, "Jens Larson, 1891–1982," *Biographical Dictionary of the Maine Olmsted Alliance for Parks and Landscape*, http://www.maineolmsted.com/ad/Larsen/html (accessed February 12, 2011).

5 Jens Fredrick Larson and Archie MacInnes Palmer, *Architectural Planning of the American College* (New York: McGraw-Hill, 1933).

The "Harkness method" and accompanying Harkness table (see Figure 5.7) were developed for the Phillips Exeter Academy, during 1930–1931, under the leadership of philanthropist Edward S. Harkness. The Harkness method, as educationally significant today as it was during the 1930s, emphasizes discussion among students, guided and facilitated, but not led, by an instructor. For Harkness, "the method" was intended to lead to a revolution in direct reaction against the all-faces-to-the-front teaching methods then prevalent. The lozenge-shaped Harkness table seats between 12 and 18 students in a nonhierarchical arrangement allowing all students to see one another and encouraging the instructor, both physically and pedagogically, to withdraw from a position of sole authority.[6]

6 Richard F. Niebling, "Edward S. Harkness, 1874–1940," Fall 1982, http://www.exeter.edu/documents/HarknessNiebling.pdf (accessed December 14, 2010).

Figure 5.7 The Harkness table in a physics lab, Phillips Exeter Academy, Exeter, New Hampshire. Courtesy of Phillips Exeter Academy. Photo by Brian F. Crowley.

Harkness tables are now used in a broad spectrum of schools, colleges, and universities for small-class instruction in both the humanities and the sciences. Harkness's "revolution in methods" failed to transform American secondary education, however, as few can afford the large tables, small class sizes, and additional teachers that the method requires, but the principles behind the revolution—student-centered, instructor-facilitated, discussion-based learning—have been central to the development of classroom design since Harkness's time.[7]

The Clarke Writing Lab

The Ronald J. Clarke Writing Lab at the St. Paul's School in Concord, New Hampshire, is a computer-based adaptation of the Harkness classroom in which students work on writing assignments that can be projected from each student's computer onto a screen for discussion or editing by other students or an instructor.

This format allows students to move quickly among work on their own computers, presentation or discussion of projected text, or more traditional seminar-style discussion around a single, large table. Student computers are located on a continuous counter mounted on three of the room's four walls. Students may be given a writing assignment during the class, which they complete on these computers before turning to the central table for Harkness method discussion. In use since 1994, the Clarke Writing Lab now supports many disciplines beyond writing instruction and is popular during the evening as an informal computer lab.

The Kiva

The Kiva is a flat-floor or tiered classroom-in-the-round, supporting an instructor-focused version of the Harkness method (see Figure 5.30). Few instructors who are unfamiliar with this classroom type are initially attracted to the Kiva classroom, but among those who have used it, many are passionately positive about its benefits. Like the Harkness classroom, the Kiva creates a compact setting for nonhierarchical discussion among students, but, unlike the Harkness classroom, it places the instructor at the center of the room, favoring those with a theatrical flair and a willingness to spend much of the class walking. In the Kiva classroom, all student seats are easily accessible for one-on-one, student/instructor discussion, but, unlike the Harkness classroom, the Kiva's design means that instructors frequently face away from at least some students, and the lack of a defined presentation wall leaves some students with poor sight lines to some of the writing boards and projection screens that line the room's walls. This last issue can be addressed, at least in part, by suspending display monitors from the ceiling at the center of the room.

The Group Dynamics Classroom

Another classroom type evolving in response to developments in technology is the group dynamics classroom, a specialized classroom in which the observation of in-class communication among students and instructors is central to the learning experience (see Fig. 5.31).

Group dynamics classrooms, used frequently for business, law, education, and psychology instruction, consist of a classroom paired with an observation room, which, for best viewing angles, is located along one of the classroom's long walls. The classroom is generally furnished with movable chairs and tables, which can be organized to support instruction in negotiation, cooperative teamwork, or a variety of other group situations. A group within the classroom undertakes an assigned task while

7 "Harkness" is a registered trademark of Phillips Exeter Academy.

students and instructors within the observation room watch and discuss the classroom activity. The observation room and the classroom must be acoustically isolated from each other, and the observation room must have full view of the classroom by means of a large, one-way window often supplemented with video cameras and monitors.

Divisible Flat-Floor Rooms: The "Multipurpose Room"

The idea of increasing classroom adaptability and utilization by building large, divisible classrooms (often referred to as "multipurpose rooms") remains popular, although this approach presents many challenges (see Figures 5.8 and 5.9). All too often, the multipurpose room, in attempting to serve many functions, serves none well.

These rooms generally consist of a large, rectangular space that can be subdivided by movable partitions. In the past, serious problems occurred with the mechanical operation and acoustic performance of these partitions. Mechanized folding partitions that are relatively easy to operate, require little maintenance, and offer acceptable acoustic performance are now available; however, the operation of these partitions is still a task that neither instructors nor students generally undertake on their own, and the acoustic performance of these partitions, although improved, is still inferior to the performance that can be achieved easily with a fixed partition.

Divisible multipurpose rooms must be provided with doors adequate to allow access to and egress from each of the subdivided parts, and lighting and mechanical systems and their controls must be designed to function for the room as a whole and for its parts. In spite of their disadvantages, multipurpose rooms remain popular because they accommodate large, if infrequent, events but need not sit unused at other times.

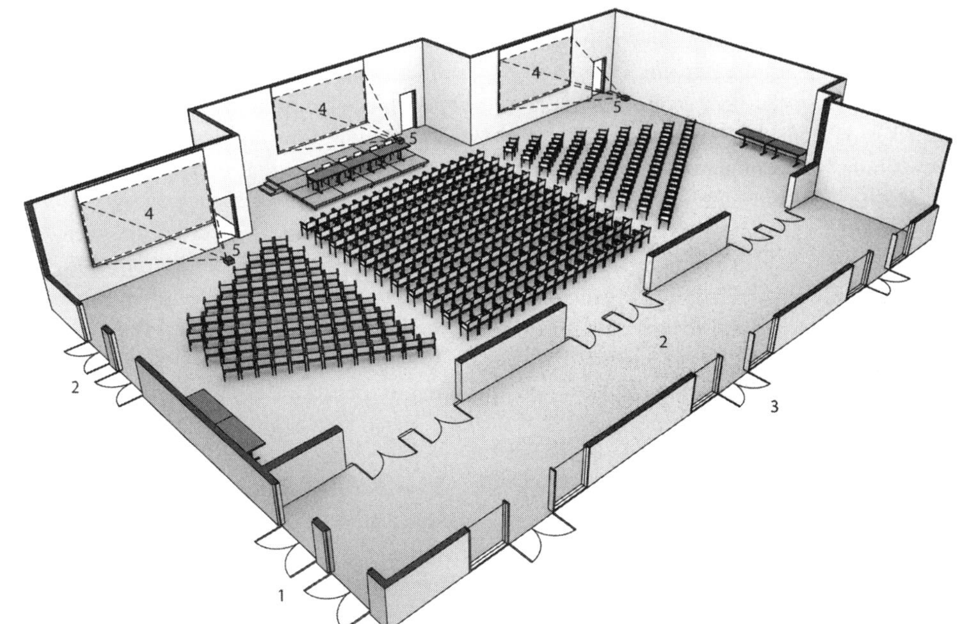

Figure 5.8 A 7,100 sq ft divisible multipurpose room suite, shown in lecture or panel format.
Legend
1 Conference center entrance
2 Prefunction areas
3 Courtyard/outdoor event space
4 Projection screen
5 Access to service, furniture storage, and kitchen
Wasserstein Hall, Harvard Law School, Harvard University, Cambridge, Massachusetts.
Robert A.M. Stern Architects.
Seats: 366
Floor Area: 7,136 ASF
ASF/ Seat: 19.6.

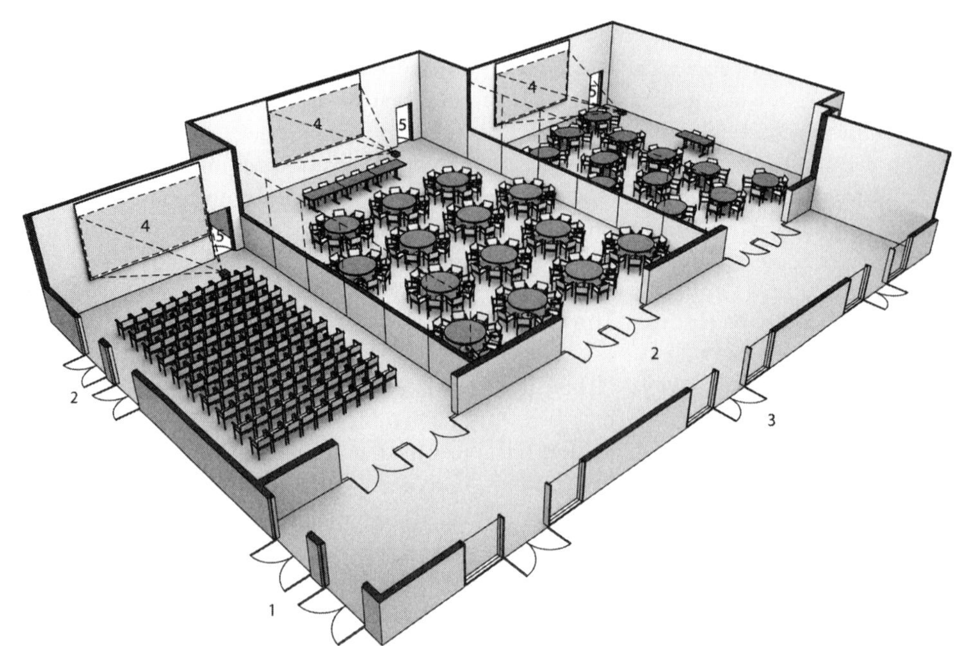

▸ *Figure 5.9 A 7,100 sq ft divisible multipurpose room suite, shown with three separate functions set-up.*
Legend
1 Conference center entrance
2 Prefunction areas
3 Courtyard/outdoor event space
4 Projection screen
5 Access to service, furniture, storage, and kitchen
Wasserstein Hall, Harvard Law School, Harvard University, Cambridge, Massachusetts. Robert A.M. Stern Architects.
Seats: 286
Floor Area: 7,136 ASF
ASF/ Seat: 24.9.

Tiered or Sloped-Floor Classrooms

Tiered or sloped-floor classrooms are appropriate when class size exceeds the point at which all members of a class can see each other clearly in a flat-floor room. Tiered or sloped-floor rooms have the disadvantage that they cannot be reconfigured easily to accommodate different furniture arrangements, but, when properly designed, they allow large classes to have clear lines of sight among students and between students and instructor. These classrooms are also acoustically superior to flat-floor classrooms (see Figure 5.10).

When the slope of the floor is low—not more than 3 in. between rows or 1 in./ft—the floor can be continuously sloped without the use of steps. With slopes exceeding this amount, steps or tiers are necessary. Slopes of less than 3 in. between rows are generally not desirable: at these shallow pitches, the benefits of sloping the floor at all start to be lost, and the transition between sloped and flat floor is so subtle that it can be overlooked and result in tripping. Although many users find a continuously sloped floor of around 3 in. slope per row to be too shallow, this classroom type does have the advantage that it does away with steps, and it allows wheelchair access to every row. The change in elevation between the front and back of these classrooms is also shallow enough that they often fit within the height of a single, typical floor.

When the slope of the floor is greater than 3 in. per row, steps or tiers are necessary. Tiered classrooms with one or two steps per tier are common (see Figure 5.11).

Tiered or sloped-floor classrooms generally have 40 seats or more. At numbers less than this, the acoustic and sight-line disadvantages of flat-floor classrooms rarely justify the expense and constrained flexibility of a

Figure 5.10 The 60-seat, tiered, Greenberg Conference Center Auditorium, Yale University, New Haven, Connecticut. Robert A.M. Stern Architects. © Michael Marsland.

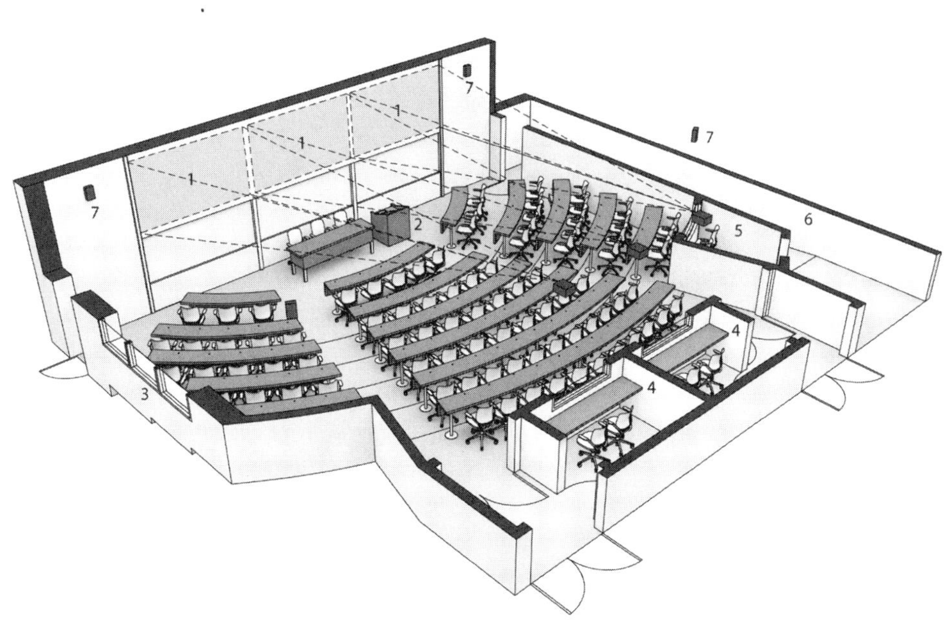

Figure 5.11 A 60-seat tiered classroom with distance learning/lecture capture and simultaneous translation capabilities.
Legend
1 Presentation surface
2 AV/IT controls
3 Natural light
4 Projection room space/ interpreters
5 AV control room
6 Ramp
7 Video cameras
Greenberg Conference Center Auditorium, Yale University, New Haven, Connecticut. Robert A.M. Stern Architects.
Seats: 60
Floor area: 2,130 ASF
ASF/ Seat: 35.5.

tiered room. Tiered classrooms in the 100-seat range can feel surprisingly intimate and allow a level of discourse within a class not possible when this number of students is seated in a flat-floor room: the much-copied Harvard Business School case study classroom, for example, seats 90. Tiered classrooms with up to 150 seats can be designed to allow unamplified student-to-student discourse (see Figure 5.12), and classrooms with up to 250 seats can be designed to allow unamplified student-to-instructor discussion.

Auditoriums

In sizes above 250 seats, a classroom is generally referred to as an "auditorium," and serious theater design considerations come into play, expensive and complex audiovisual equipment is necessary, and student-to-instructor and student-to-student conversation takes on a distance learning character even within a single room. Auditoriums in excess of 350 seats begin to justify the construction of a balcony, and in excess of 500 seats, the functioning of the auditorium is seriously compromised if a balcony is not included (see Figure 5.14).

Tiered classrooms at this size also require theater design features, including light and sound vestibules at their entrances, and lobby or prefunction areas generally sized at 7 sq ft per seat. Disruptions caused by late-arriving attendees can be minimized by providing both rear and front access doors and by providing viewing windows in classroom doors. For auditoriums, these are often supplemented by "late arrival" video monitors located in the prefunction area.

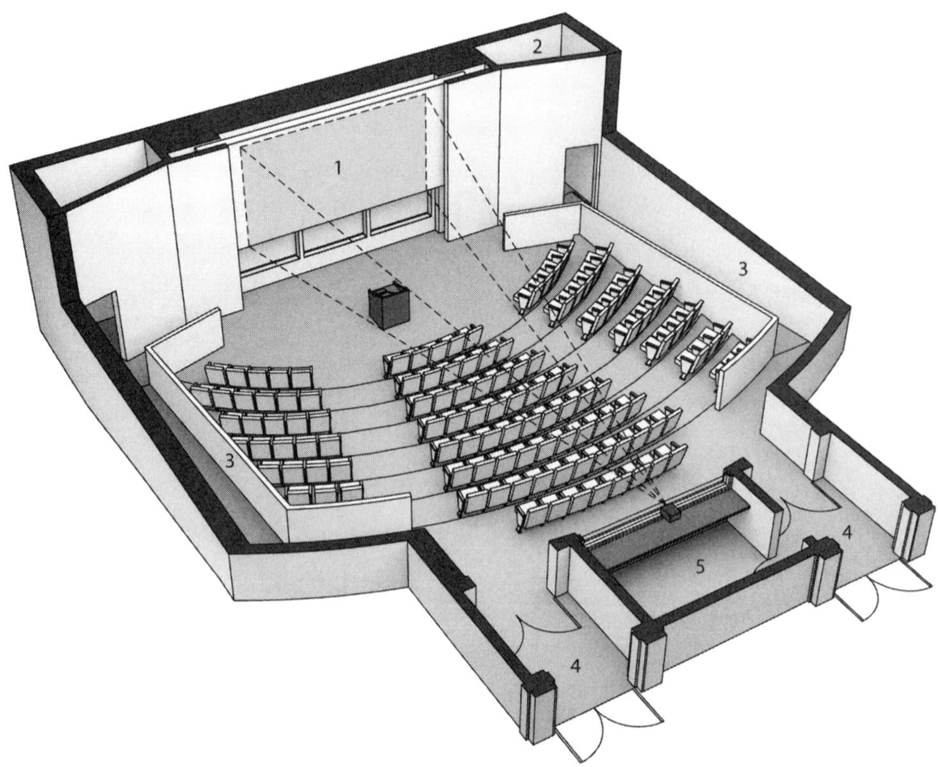

▸ *Figure 5.12 A 126-seat tiered auditorium with dual acoustic locks.*
Legend
1 Presentation surface
2 AV closet
3 Ramp
4 Rear access
5 Projection room
K. C. Irving Environmental Science Center, Acadia University, Wolfville, Nova Scotia, Canada. Robert A.M. Stern Architects.
Seats: 126
Floor area: 2,297 ASF
ASF/ Seat: 18.2.

Aisles and Continental Seating

The well-considered placement of seats and aisles within a tiered classroom is essential to its success. Most building codes require that the distance between rows be increased incrementally for each seat that is distant by more than seven seats from an aisle. Large fields of auditorium seating with aisles at the edges of the room only and larger-than-minimum row-to-row dimensions are referred to as "continental seating" (see Figure 5.13).

This configuration has the benefit that it allows aisles to be kept to the sides of a classroom, avoiding the loss of prime seats near the center of the room. It has the disadvantage that center seats are often distant from an aisle, resulting in an undesirable distribution of students around the perimeter of the room. This is not a problem in a continental-seating theater or music hall, where seats are assigned, but the use of continental seating in classrooms where seats are not assigned results in disruption by latecomers who pass in front of occupied seats in order to find an available seat. For this reason, the construction of large, continental-seating classrooms and teaching auditoriums is rare.

Careful consideration should be given to the curvature in plan of the seating rows within a tiered classroom. Straight rows are unusual in all but the smallest such rooms and are not advisable in rooms with over 150 seats, as they result in seats at the edge of the seating field with uncomfortably angled sight lines. The principal benefit of straight seating rows is the simplicity and economy that accompany a rectangular plan.

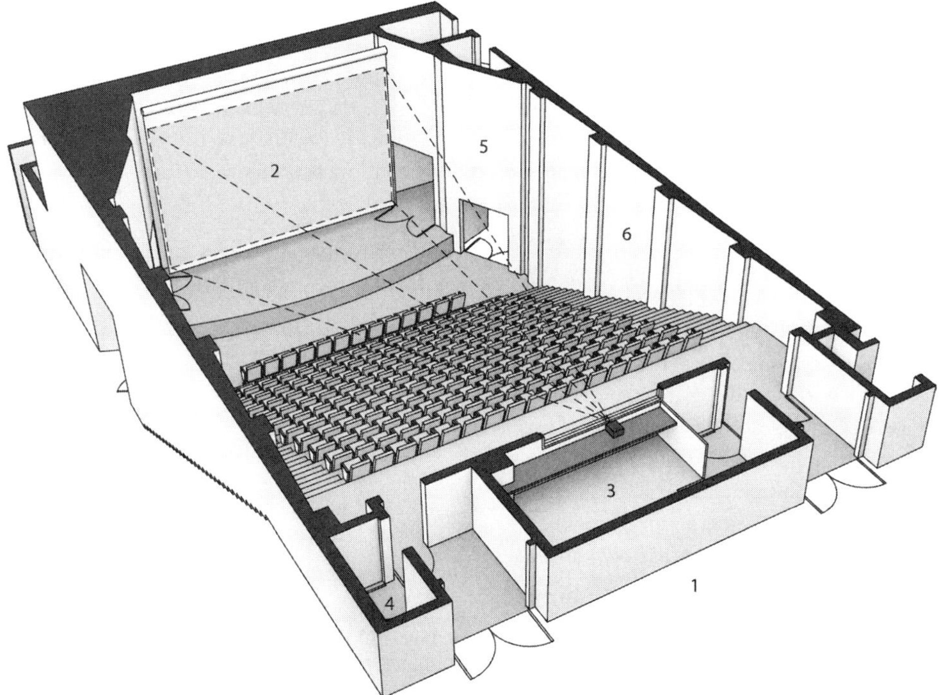

Figure 5.13 A 200-seat, steeply-tiered auditorium designed for lecture, film, and musical performance.
Legend
1 Prefunction area
2 Presentation surface
3 Projection room
4 Storage
5 Acoustic reflecting walls
6 Acoustic absorbing walls
Informatics and Communications Technology Complex, Indiana University–Purdue University Indianapolis, Indianapolis, Indiana. Robert A.M. Stern Architects.
Seats: 200
Floor area: 3,096 ASF
ASF/ Seat: 15.5

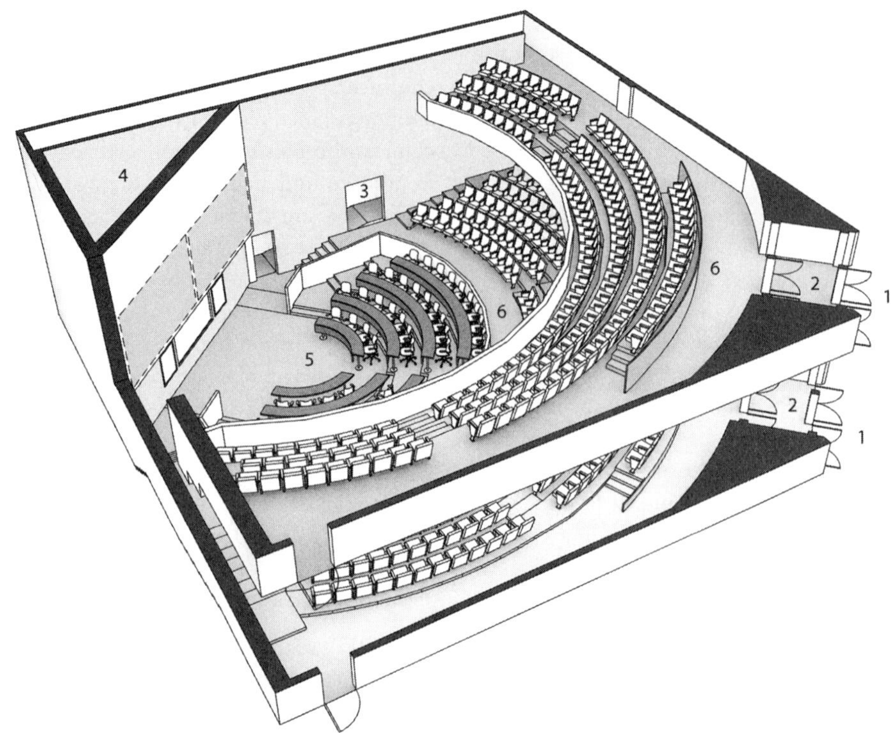

▸ *Figure 5.14 A 450-seat auditorium with balcony and fixed desk top for front section seats.*
Legend
1 Prefunction area
2 Vestibule
3 Ramp
4 Rear projector room
5 Desk seating
6 Auditorium seating
Jesse H. Jones Graduate School of Business, Rice University, Houston, Texas.
Robert A.M. Stern Architects.
Seats: 450
Floor area: 6,593 ASF
ASF/ Seat: 14.6.

When seating rows are curved, the degree of curvature affects the use of the room significantly (see Figure 5.32). For a room dedicated mainly to didactic instruction all seats should be arranged with direct sight lines to the front of the room. In the United States, this classroom type was developed and refined during the second half of the nineteenth century based on European, and primarily German, precedents, and reached its zenith in the 1880s under the dean of Harvard Law School Christopher Columbus Langdell. Langdell, an Exeter graduate of the pre-Harkness era, advocated a "Socratic" teaching method—instruction through questioning rather than lecturing—and applied this method at Harvard to legal education based on actual judicial opinions. Classes were large and combined one-on-one "cold-calling" with Langdell's version of meritocracy, which valued the final exam highly. The Langdellian method dominates American law schools to this day and casts a long shadow over undergraduate education.[8]

Case Study Classrooms

Where a room is intended for a combination of didactic presentation and discussion among students, the curvature of the rows of seats and fixed desktops creates a horseshoe-shaped plan, balancing sight lines to the front of the room with those among students. This "tighter" configuration—now generally called the "case study classroom," although it is not what Langdell used for his case method instruction—is common among schools of business, where the case method involves a

8 Bruce A. Kimball, *The Inception of Modern Professional Education: C. C. Langdell, 1826–1906* (Chapel Hill: University of North Carolina Press, 2009).

high degree of discussion among students during class. In Langdell's pedagogy, a professor questions students in search of answers leading to conclusions that the professor knows. The horseshoe-shaped case study classroom supports a pedagogy in which the give-and-take among students—the Harkness method at a large scale—leads to conclusions neither predetermined nor previously known by the instructor (see Figure 5.15).

Harvard Business School has been central to the development and refinement of this method and its corresponding classroom type. When the school moved from Cambridge, Massachusetts, to its campus in Allston, Massachusetts, in 1927, Dean Wallace Donham, working with Harvard architecture professor Charles W. Killam and architecture student Harry J. Korslund, developed a design for a 177-seat, horseshoe-shaped classroom with 6-inch tiers. Built in the basement of the school's Baker Library (McKim, Mead & White, 1927), this classroom was primitive by today's standards—acoustics and lighting were poor, students sat at wooden tablet-arm chairs, and the professor sat behind a fixed podium—but the horseshoe shape supported the school's student-centered, case study method.

The school took advantage of the construction of a new classroom building (Aldrich Hall, Perry, Shaw & Hepburn, 1953) to refine the 1927 classroom design. A committee of professors and administrators developed functional specifications and studied a variety of corporate and academic classroom precedents. A 110-seat, full-scale and furnished mock-up classroom was built in the school's parking lot, tested, and refined during a 5-week period, and a variety of new features, including a continuous fixed desktop with name card slot, were integrated into the 17 Aldrich Hall classrooms (see Figure 5.16).[9]

9 An excellent history of the Harvard Business School case study method and classroom can be found at "Inquiry and Innovation: 1908–2008, Classrooms, In Depth," http://hbs.edu/centennial/im/sections/2/c/ (accessed December 10, 2010).

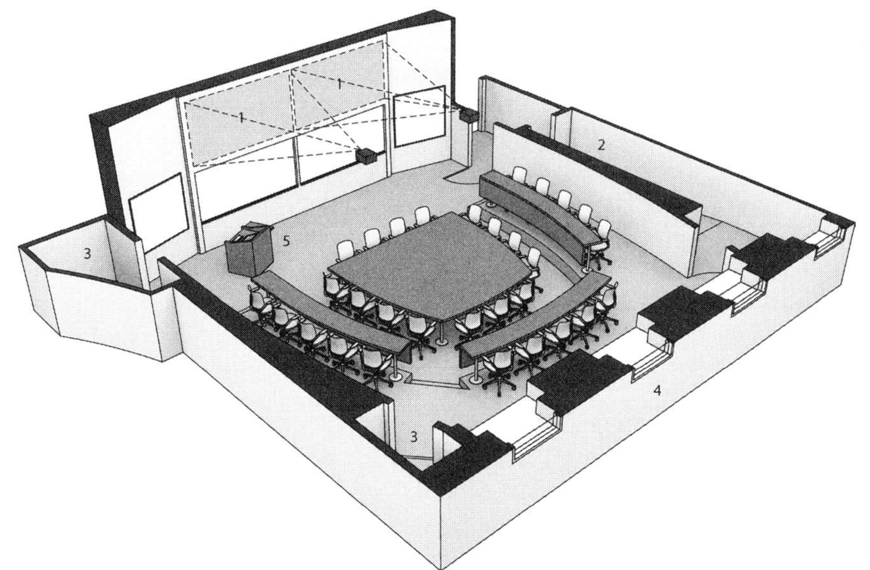

◀ *Figure 5.15 A 30-seat, single-tier case study classroom with dual, fixed projection surfaces and a 15-seat seminar table.*
Legend
1 Presentation surface
2 Closet
3 Projector
4 Podium
George Herbert Walker School of Business & Technology, Webster University, St. Louis, Missouri. Robert A.M. Stern Architects.
Seats: 30
Floor area: 849 ASF
ASF/ Seat: 28.3.

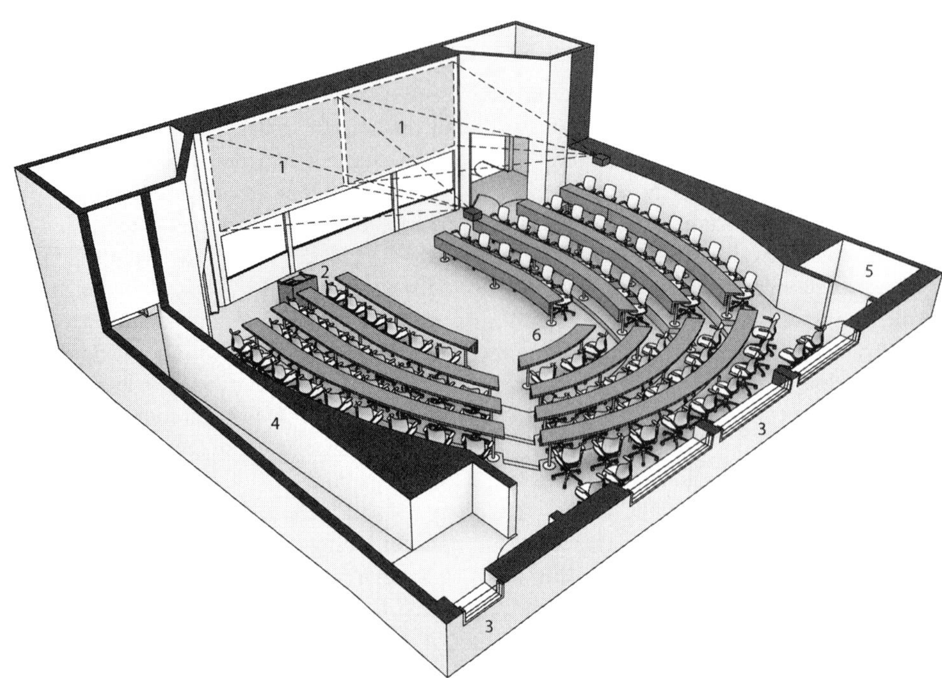

Figure 5.16 A 90-seat, 3-tier case study classroom with dual, fixed projection surfaces.
Legend
1 Presentation surface
2 AV/IT controls
3 Natural light
4 Ramp
5 Storage
6 Confidence monitor
Wasserstein Hall, Harvard Law School, Harvard University, Cambridge, Massachusetts. Robert A.M. Stern Architects.
Seats: 90
Floor area: 2,204 ASF
ASF/ Seat: 24.5.

The case study classroom is now popular among a variety of professional and graduate schools as well as for undergraduate disciplines, including language instruction. As other institutions have adopted this classroom type, and have addressed accessibility, instructional technology, and expanded teaching zone requirements often without the benefit of full-scale mock-ups, case study classrooms have become larger and less intimate than the Harvard Business School prototype. There is a natural but ill-advised tendency in classroom design to believe that bigger is better; in fact, case study classroom desktops should be narrow (ideally 18 in. or less) and row-to-row dimensions kept to a reasonable minimum (48 in. or less). Even minor increases in these dimensions can compromise the intimacy that makes the best case study classrooms so successful.

Cluster Classrooms

A relative newcomer to the tiered classroom family is the cluster classroom. First developed in 1999 by architect Carl Luckenbach, working with Dean Gilbert Whitaker and Wil Uecker of the Jesse Jones School of Management (now the Jones Graduate School of Business) at Rice University, this room captures many of the benefits of the case study classroom while allowing a class to work effectively in subgroups without leaving the classroom. The tiered cluster classroom is organized around fixed tables sized to accommodate five or six students. Three students around each table face the instructor while the remaining two or three students swivel their chairs to either face the instructor across a fixed desk or face their group table (see Figure 5.17).

The cluster classroom accommodates didactic instruction, discussion within the full

Figure 5.17 *A 45-seat cluster classroom in teamwork mode, Alan B. Miller Hall, Mason School of Business, College of William and Mary, Williamsburg, Virginia. Robert A.M. Stern Architects.* © Peter Aaron/Esto.

class, and discussion within subgroups, all within a single classroom. In so doing, it saves space otherwise needed for team rooms (discussed below) and saves valuable class time, which students might otherwise spend moving between their classroom and team rooms. The cluster classroom has the disadvantage that it requires approximately 25 percent more floor area per student than the traditional case study classroom; consequently, it both costs more to build per student and is less intimate than the case study room. This floor area per student inefficiency is largely offset, however, by the fact that the cluster classroom accommodates groups of students working together during nonclass hours; while case study classrooms generally sit vacant after class, cluster classrooms do not (see Figure 5.18).

Peninsula Clusters

A technologically enhanced adaptation of the cluster classroom—the peninsula cluster—is appropriate for classes in which student teams work on computer-based projects (see Figure 5.19).

Trapezoidal tables ("peninsulas") are organized radially around a presentation wall with their short ends facing the presentation wall and large computer monitors mounted on their long ends. Students sitting around each peninsula swivel their chairs to face the presentation wall, the table, or the monitor. Data connection points or a wireless network allow students to display content from their computers either on the peninsula monitor or on a screen at the classroom presentation wall. The peninsula cluster is popular for finance and accounting instruction and for classes that require teamwork using expensive and specialized software. Although the peninsula classroom accommodates didactic instruction poorly, as none of the students' seats face the presentation wall, it is extremely effective for computer-based group instruction and for group study during nonclass hours.

Figure 5.18 A 45-seat cluster classroom with a single tier and fixed projection surfaces.
Legend
1 Presentation surface
2 Instructor
3 Natural light
4 Projector
5 Storage
6 Rear access
Alan B. Miller Hall, Mason School of Business, College of William and Mary, Williamsburg, Virginia. Robert A.M. Stern Architects.
Seats: 45
Floor area: 1,553 ASF
ASF/ Seat: 34.5.

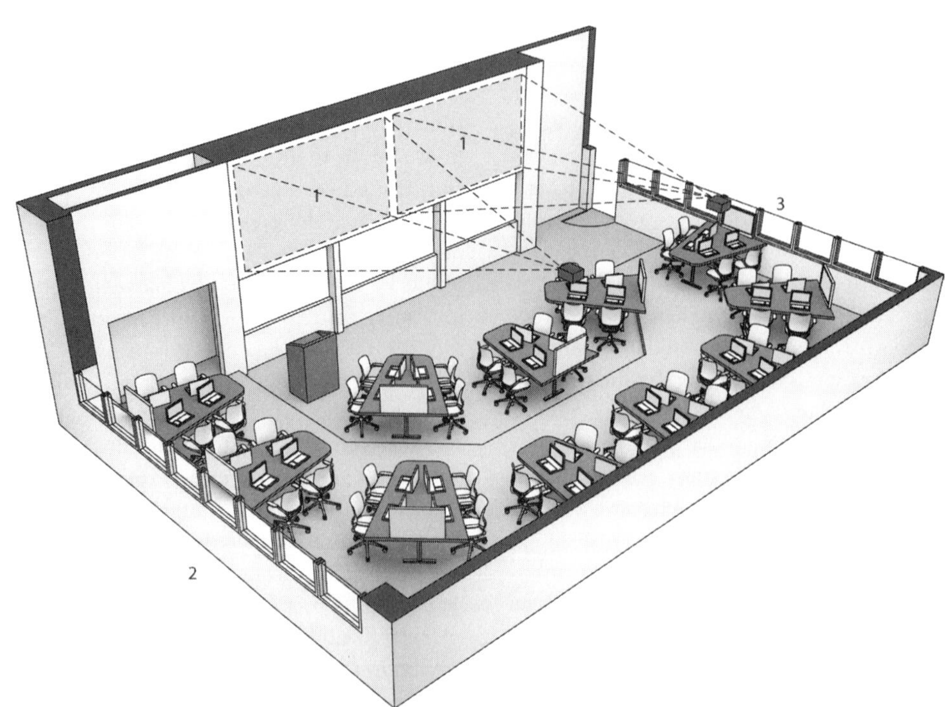

Figure 5.19 A 44-seat, single-tier accounting classroom.
Legend
1 Presentation surface
2 Natural light
3 View from corridor/lounge
Smeal College of Business, Pennsylvania State University, State College, Pennsylvania. Robert A.M. Stern Architects.
Seats: 44
Floor area: 1,288 ASF
ASF/ Seat: 29.3.

ACADEMIC BUILDINGS
CASE STUDY 2

JOAN AND SANFORD WEILL HALL
Gerald R. Ford School of Public Policy, University of Michigan, Ann Arbor

Architect: Robert A.M. Stern Architects

Located on a steeply sloping site at the southern edge of the University of Michigan's Central Campus, the 80,000 GSF home of the Gerald R. Ford School of Public Policy unites the school's physically divided research centers and faculty under a single roof. The building marks a gateway to the university with a tower at its southern end housing, among other spaces, the Great Hall and a library, two important public rooms that, together with an adjacent skylit stair tower, serve as a beacon for the university as a whole both day and night. (See Figures 5.20–22.)

Figure 5.20 The Ford School's south entrance marks the State Street entrance to the University of Michigan's Ann Arbor campus. © Peter Aaron/Esto.

A 200-seat auditorium, a 100-seat lecture hall, and other classrooms are located on the ground floor.

Key Academic Spaces

Auditorium	2,740 NSF	197 seats
Large classroom	1,990 NSF	100 seats
Medium classroom	1,290 NSF	49 seats
Small classroom	970 NSF	30 seats
Small classroom	1,000 NSF	32 seats
Great Hall	1,820 NSF	
Building area	85,622 GSF	

Figure 5.21 The double-height Great Hall connects the school's two principal floors and opens to a south-facing plaza.©Peter Aaron/Esto.

Figure 5.22 A 100-seat tiered classroom adjacent to the Ford School's Great Hall. © Peter Aaron/Esto.

Specialized Rooms

The Mathematics Emporium

While case study and cluster classrooms supplement lecture-based instruction with in-class discussion and teamwork, other classroom types, including the Math Emporium at Virginia Polytechnic Institute and State University (Virginia Tech), replace the lecture format with individually directed instruction. Opened in 1997, the Math Emporium is a converted 58,000 sq ft department store equipped with 540 computers on which students self-administer prepackaged but course-specific, computer-based instructional software covering virtually all undergraduate mathematics courses (see Figure 5.23).[10]

Open around the clock, the Math Emporium is staffed by mathematics faculty who assist students with specific questions. Students work at their own pace on a variety of courses, so the Math Emporium has neither a presentation wall nor even a defined front. Lounges, meeting rooms, and technical support spaces are located around the central sea of computers, drawing students at almost all hours for group study and team projects.[11]

The Math Emporium was conceived as a means of increasing individualized instruction and improving student performance through interactive, self-paced,

10 Michael Williams, "When Is a New Paradigm Really a New Paradigm?" http://www.math.vt.edu/people/Wwlliams/files/webct_article.html (accessed November 12, 2010).

11 Barbara L. Robinson and Anne H. Moore, "Virginia Tech: Math Emporium," in *Learning Spaces*, ed. Diana G. Oblinger, an EDUCAUSE e-book, http://www.educause.edu/LearningSpaces#copyright (accessed November 12, 2010).

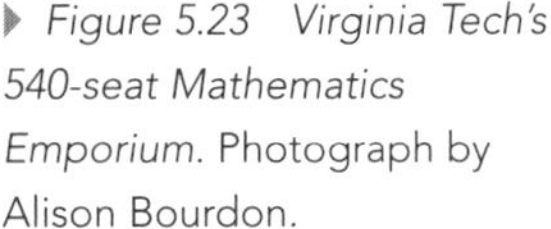

▸ *Figure 5.23 Virginia Tech's 540-seat Mathematics Emporium.* Photograph by Alison Bourdon.

and self-directed learning and not with the goal of cost cutting or instructing more students with fewer faculty. Before opening the Math Emporium, Virginia Tech found that a significant percentage of students in lecture-format mathematics courses did not learn at the pace of their class and hence either missed key concepts or spent part of their class time listening to questions and explanations that were not relevant to their own learning needs. Most students prefer the Math Emporium over lecture-format instruction because they feel that the Math Emporium allows them to pace their own learning, receive immediate performance feedback through online quizzes and tests, and have access to personal assistance with specific questions.

The Math Emporium environment requires faculty to learn new teaching techniques, working as coaches and tutors, not as lecturers. Virginia Tech now uses the emporium for some business and basic science courses but has found that its success is closely linked to its narrow focus and to the fact that almost all instructors are qualified to assist students with almost all courses offered at the emporium. It is unlikely that a "Learning Emporium," covering all subjects, is the appropriate next step in the evolution of this learning concept.

Self-directed learning modules similar to those developed for the Math Emporium are increasingly available over the Internet. A leader in this movement is Khan Academy, a not-for-profit educational organization created in 2006 by financier-turned-educator Salman Khan. Khan Academy, as of May 2012, offers 3,100 video tutorials, each approximately 10 minutes in length, covering mathematics, physics, chemistry, biology, astronomy, economics, computer science, history, and finance.

Computer Labs and Finance Labs

When computers entered academia, first as mainframes and then as personal computers, academic institutions needed facilities—computer labs—where students could be trained in computer use and could find computers and printers that they did not own themselves. With virtually all college and university students now owning a computer,[12] the function of computer labs has transformed. These labs are now focused largely on advanced or specialized computers (e.g., dual-screen monitors, Bloomberg terminals for business and finance, or advanced graphic computers for design disciplines) that allow students to be trained on specialized software that they may not own or to be instructed in disciplines that require networked computers for team projects (see Figures 5.24 and 5.25).

Even when high-speed wireless network access is available, these labs are typically built with raised, tiered access floors and with underfloor air supply. Sight lines must be studied carefully, allowing students to view their own monitors, one or more wall- or ceiling-mounted projection screens, and the faces of the instructor and other students. The technical complexity of these labs requires ongoing technical support, and the high cost of equipment generally means that these rooms are designed and managed to accommodate both classes and individual and small-group work during nonclass hours.

12 2010 EDUCAUSE study of 36,950 undergraduate students in the United States found that 98 percent owned a computer. Shannon D. Smith and Judith Borreson Caruso, with an introduction by Joshua Kim, *The ECAR Study of Undergraduate Students and Information Technology, 2010* (Research Study, Vol. 6) (Boulder, CO: EDUCAUSE Center for Applied Research, 2010), available from http://www.educause.edu/ecar.

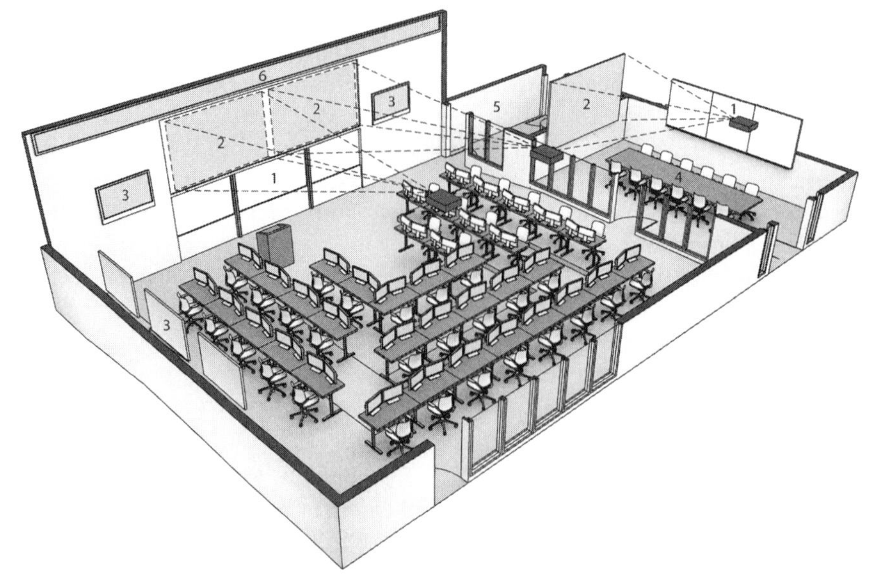

▸ *Figure 5.24 A 38-seat, 2-tier finance lab with adjacent finance seminar room.*
Legend
1 Whiteboard
2 Projection screens
3 Display monitor
4 Conference/seminar
5 AV/IT control
6 Stock "crawl"
Alan B. Miller Hall, Mason School of Business, College of William and Mary, Williamsburg, Virginia. Robert A.M. Stern Architects.
Seats: 38
Floor area: 2,311 ASF
ASF/ Seat: 60.8.

▸ *Figure 5.25 The J. David and Patricia Rogers Finance Lab is used for classes, for clubs, and as an extended-hours computer lab: Smeal College of Business, Pennsylvania State University, State College, Pennsylvania. Robert A.M. Stern Architects.*
© Peter Aaron/Esto.

As of late 2010, trading rooms, equipped with the computers and graphic displays found in the financial services industry, were in operation at more than 200 U.S. schools of business.[13] Designed to simulate the real-world trading experience, these function as specialized computer classrooms, support student clubs and organizations related to the financial services market, and serve as visible symbols of a university's or school's stature and technical prowess.

13 "Business Schools Add Mock Trading Floors," *New York Times*, December 30, 2010.

The SCALE-UP Classroom

The most significant recent advance in team-based active learning for the sciences is the SCALE-UP classroom, developed under the leadership of Dr. Robert J. Beichner at North Carolina State University between 1997 and 2001.

SCALE-UP (Student-Centered Active Learning Environment for Undergraduate Programs)[14] was conceived as an alternative to lecture-based introductory undergraduate physics and is now used by over 100 colleges and universities worldwide for large-enrollment science and mathematics courses.[15] Unlike the Math Emporium, which replaces large lectures with enriched individual learning, SCALE-UP uses the team-based techniques of the cluster and Harkness classrooms.

14 North Carolina State University, "About the SCALE-UP Project," http://www.ncsu.edu/per/scaleup.html (accessed January 2, 2011).

15 Robert J. Beichner, "The Student-Centered Activities for Large Enrollment Undergraduate Programs (SCALE-UP) Project."

The SCALE-UP classroom consists of round tables approximately 7 ft in diameter (the width of a Harkness table) and typically seating up to nine students subdivided into three groups of three. Each group is provided with a laptop computer. The classroom has no front, and instructors either work from a podium located near the center of the room or roam from table to table. Whiteboards and projection screens cover most of the room's walls (see Figure 5.26).

Like the Harkness and case study methods, SCALE-UP assumes that students complete assigned readings and come prepared to discuss them in class. Online quizzes consolidate class preparation. During class, brief lecture segments are interspersed with desktop experiments, group problem solving, and discussion, all supported by customized instructional software and simulations.[16]

16 Robert J. Beichner, "Student-Centered Activities for Large Enrollment Physics (SCALE-UP)," *Proceedings of the Sigma XI Forum on Reforming Undergraduate Education*, ftp://ftp.ncsu.edu/pub/ncsu/beichner/RB/SigmaXi.pdf (accessed January 5, 2011).

Figure 5.26 A divisible, 99-seat SCALE-UP classroom.
Legend
1 Presentation surface
2 Instructor
3 Projectors
4 Equipment storage
5 Preparation room
The Center for Natural Sciences, Ithaca College, Ithaca, New York. Robert A.M. Stern Architects.
Seats: 99
Floor area: 2,751 ASF
ASF/ Seat: 27.8.

Testing Centers

As developments in educational technology increasingly support teaching and learning in locations other than the classroom, new methods of testing have developed, accompanied by new facilities—"testing centers" (see Figure 5.27). These generally consist of large rooms furnished with rows of desk-mounted computer testing stations. Testing for a particular subject can take place over a period of hours, or even days, allowing students to take tests at times that best fit their schedules. Test takers arriving at a testing center check in at a reception desk, provide verification of identity, and are directed to a specific testing station. Personal belongings, including electronic communication devices, are generally not allowed into the testing room, so storage lockers are often provided. Test locations are assigned so as to avoid the same test being administered at adjacent testing stations. The testing room is monitored by video cameras and is designed to be free of obstructions, allowing ease of supervision. A test center manager can initiate a testing session, monitor progress during the test, and ensure that the test is completed at the appropriate time.

Testing center technology reduces or eliminates the need for an instructor to grade tests but requires that tests be suitably formatted for administration in a testing center. Frequently, several different tests are administered simultaneously for a particular class or subject, thereby reducing the likelihood of cheating. In some cases, testing center software is programmed to ask increasingly difficult questions as a test taker demonstrates proficiency with test material.

Figure 5.27 The 164-seat testing center at the College of Business Administration, University of Central Florida, Orlando. Courtesy of University of Central Florida. Photo by Graham S. Wyatt.

Space use efficiency can be achieved by designing a computer classroom to double as a testing center, capitalizing on the fact that testing centers are often used heavily at times when classrooms are used least.

Collegial Gathering Spaces

Academic buildings increasingly include collegial common spaces where students gather before or after class, obtain food, and work individually or in groups (see Figure 5.28). These spaces should be identified in an academic building's space program and should generally be of varied character: large and small, active and quiet, furnished with lounge furniture or with tables and study carrels. Appropriately designed acoustics and lighting (both artificial and natural) are important, and it is essential to provide many convenient electric outlets—data may be wireless, but to date power is not. A central lounge or "living room" is generally popular in an academic building, but other desirable common spaces include wide, furnished corridors; banquettes or furnished bay windows; and cafés or other types of food service facilities. Collegial spaces of these types should generally be programmed to provide 15 sq ft per person although building code egress requirements generally assume 7 sq ft per person, so there is a significant benefit to placing the largest of these collegial gathering spaces at ground level, where they are convenient to arriving and departing students and their heavy occupant load will not require enlarged fire stairs.

Where site constraints and climate are suitable, outdoor spaces associated with academic buildings should be designed to encourage collegial gathering and should be provided with suitable furniture, power, and computer network access.

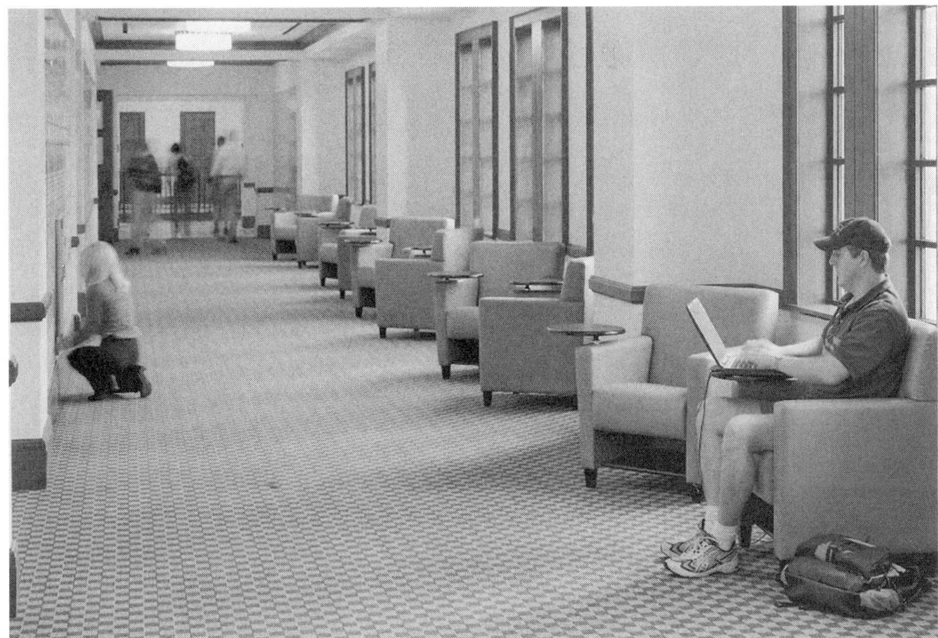

Figure 5.28 Collegial gathering in a wide, naturally lit corridor adjacent to classrooms and team rooms, Jones Graduate School of Business, Rice University, Houston, Texas. Robert A.M. Stern Architects. © Peter Aaron/Esto.

ACADEMIC BUILDINGS **CASE STUDY 3**

FARMER HALL

Richard T. Farmer School of Business, Miami University, Oxford, Ohio

Architect: Robert A.M. Stern Architects with Moody Nolan, Inc.

Introduction

The new 223,000 sq ft home of the Farmer School of Business occupies a prominent site at the heart of the Miami University campus.

Farmer Hall's main entrance, centered on a colonnaded porch (see Figure 5.29), leads to the double-height Forsythe Commons, with adjacent study and dining rooms. A broad skylit stair atrium connects the below-grade classroom floor to the office floors above.

Figure 5.29 View of the main entrance from the south. © Francis Dzikowski/Esto.

The variety of instructional spaces (see Figures. 5.30, 5.31)—case study rooms, cluster classrooms, breakout rooms, a trading room, and a Kiva—reflects the school's pedagogical style, which emphasizes small-group work, seminar instruction, and experiential learning. A prominent, separate entrance to the school's 515-seat auditorium (see Figure 5.32) is visible from Uptown Oxford's High Street.

Figure 5.30 A 36-seat, single-tier Kiva classroom.
Legend
1 Presentation surface
2 Ceiling-mounted monitors.
Robert A.M. Stern Architects.

Figure 5.31 A group dynamics observation room.
© Peter Aaron/Esto.

Figure 5.32 A 515-seat theater/ auditorium with a balcony and a 60-seat case study configuration in the first four rows: Richard T. Farmer School of Business, Miami University, Oxford, Ohio. Robert A.M. Stern Architects. © Peter Aaron/Esto.

Team Rooms

Team rooms (also referred to as "breakout rooms") continue to hold an important place in graduate and professional school education and are of growing importance among undergraduate disciplines (see Figure 5.33). Business school case study instruction and some law school classes are taught in a format that requires students to divide into groups and then reconvene during a class.

Team rooms should be sized to accommodate five or six students around a single table and should be clustered so all members of a class can move rapidly from their classroom to the necessary number of team rooms and back again. Team rooms should also be located so they can be used during nonclass hours and should typically have glass doors or sidelights to allow supervision of activity within the room. These rooms are generally equipped with a whiteboard and large, shared monitor. The efficiency of team room use is increased when these rooms can be scheduled through a networked room-scheduling system with a scheduling tablet located adjacent to each team room door. These systems allow university administrators to determine patterns of team room use and student preferences for different team room types and locations.

Team tables, banquettes, and upholstered seating groups in open lounge spaces frequently supplement enclosed team rooms, as do cluster classrooms and several other classroom types described above. All of these team room alternatives should be considered when gauging how many team rooms will be necessary in an academic building.

Figure 5.33 Team rooms with glass doors and side lights along a wide, furnished, and naturally illuminated gallery, Alan B. Miller Hall, Mason School of Business, College of William and Mary, Williamsburg, Virginia. Robert A.M. Stern Architects. © Peter Aaron/Esto.

Faculty Offices

Faculty offices represent a major program element in most academic buildings, and the wise architect will remember that, after tenure and parking, few things are more sacred to a faculty member than this office. Many academic institutions attempt to standardize office sizes and configurations. This goal is often difficult to achieve, as the expected size of a faculty office has grown during recent years. An office of 120 assignable square feet (ASF) is considered small but is still standard for many state university systems. Faculty offices of 170–180 ASF now represent the norm among top, private institutions, and offices of 180–200 ASF are becoming standard in top-ranked professional school and science research facilities. Faculty offices are sometimes clustered around administrative support areas, but a simple double-loaded configuration along a central corridor is efficient and helps to foster faculty collegiality. In this configuration, faculty offices are placed with their long dimension perpendicular to the corridor and have a clear width of approximately 10 ft. This arrangement maximizes the number of faculty offices for a given length of building facade and in offices of more than 150 ASF accommodates a desk in the portion of the office closest to the window, and a table or other furniture group in the portion of the office closest to the door.

Architectural programmers often seek to differentiate office size according to faculty seniority, with junior, adjunct, or part-time faculty assigned smaller offices than full-time or tenured faculty. This can lead to an overly specific building design, which will not easily accommodate changes in faculty demographics. It is generally preferable to provide a single size of office that will house comfortably one senior faculty member, two junior or adjunct faculty members, or three graduate or doctoral students.

The adjacency between classrooms and faculty offices is an important and often politically sensitive subject. Faculty members rarely want to have offices located near the noise and activity of classrooms, yet the offices of teaching faculty must be accessible to students. The desirable depth of a faculty office from corridor to exterior wall is also less than the desirable depth for all but the smallest classrooms. These two considerations often result in academic buildings where classrooms and offices are located in different wings or where a double-loaded arrangement of faculty offices is placed above a single-loaded arrangement of classrooms. Regardless of the configuration selected, it is desirable to provide suitably furnished areas near faculty offices where students can wait during faculty visiting hours.

Academic faculty members are the last closed-office holdouts in an era when even senior members of most business enterprises are housed in open offices. At the recently completed Bavaro Hall at the University of Virginia's Curry School of Education, four clusters of faculty offices house a total of 30 faculty members. Two of these clusters are designed for closed offices and two for open offices. The open-office configuration accommodates more faculty and provides more shared space per faculty member because the floor area required by fixed partitions and circulation is reduced in comparison to the closed-office configuration. Security is achieved in the open-office setting by providing lockable file cabinets and cupboards for each faculty member and by locking the entire suite during nonbusiness hours.

A similar arrangement is currently being built for the Schools of Business at Wake Forest University. The Wake Forest configuration differs from the Curry School of Education configuration because Wake Forest faculty members will not sit in truly open offices but will have lockable, 90 sq ft private offices with sliding glass fronts, opening to shared common space. Security is achieved in this configuration by locking the individual faculty "offices." Acoustic privacy is achieved by providing conference rooms and small enclave rooms adjacent to each cluster of offices (see Figure 5.34).

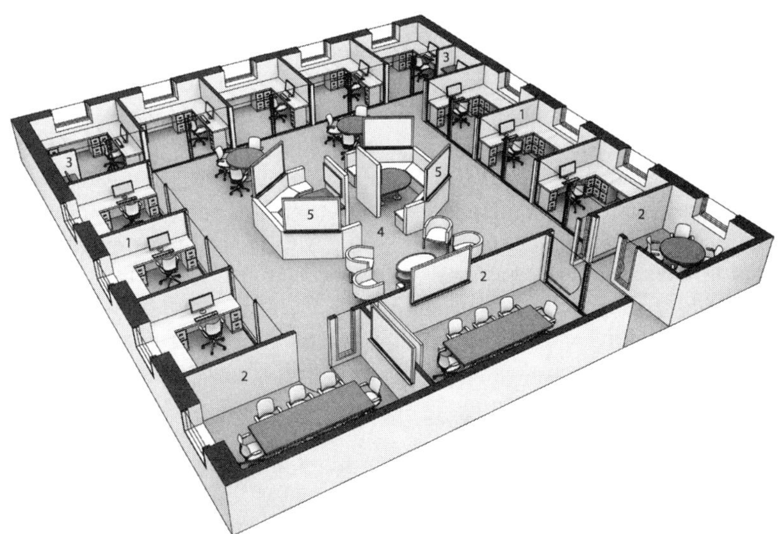

Figure 5.34 A cluster of 11 faculty offices in an "open" configuration.
Legend
1 90 sq ft offices with sliding glass entrance walls
2 Shared conference rooms (3)
3 Printer station
4 Teamwork area (1,264 sq ft)
5 Double-sided white board
Farrell Hall, Wake Forest School of Business, Wake Forest University, Winston-Salem, North Carolina. Robert A.M. Stern Architects.

TECHNICAL CONSIDERATIONS

Consultants

The design of a successful academic building requires a team including suitably qualified and experienced technical consultants. The team's mechanical engineer must be familiar with the highly variable heating and cooling loads inherent to academic buildings and with unconventional air distribution systems, such as displacement ventilation, which increase comfort, energy efficiency, and indoor air quality while reducing ventilation-based noise in classrooms. The team's lighting designer and acoustician should be experienced with classroom-specific issues related to their disciplines, and even the most experienced owners and architects should obtain the services of an audiovisual/information technology consultant.

Information and Instructional Technology

Today's students embrace technology, and academic buildings should be designed to accommodate information and instructional technologies, yet should avoid features that are so specifically suited to today's technologies that they will not easily accept tomorrow's. These technologies can be expensive and their useful life limited, so although generic or performance specification of this equipment should occur early during the design phase of an academic building project, final specification and purchasing should be delayed as long as reasonable, allowing the project to benefit from improvements in technology and reductions in cost as technology matures. The design team for an academic building should consult closely with both the university's information technology department and the instructors, as the needs and perspectives of those who will teach with these systems is often quite different from those who specify and maintain them.

While in the past, academic institutions determined technologies that students incorporated into their educational experience, these decisions today are increasingly driven by students. Students bring their own technologies, and universities increasingly adapt, incorporating these into their teaching methods and supporting them at the information technology (IT) help desk. "Educational technology" can no longer be cleanly separated from technology in general—students and instructors use the same devices to teach, learn, socialize, and organize their personal lives.

Audiovisual technology continues to converge with information technology, and these two systems—AV and IT—should be considered as one and integrated carefully with lighting systems and controls. Classroom IT, AV, and lighting controls should be simple, intuitive, and consistent among classrooms and academic disciplines—instructors should not be expected to learn different technologies for different classrooms. While rapid developments in technology make standardization challenging, maximized "interoperability" should be the goal. IT and AV devices that are compatible with a broad array of other systems and devices should be specified: students and instructors will bring an array of their own devices and expect these to interact seamlessly with the building's systems.

Classroom controls traditionally have been decentralized: light switches on walls, projector controls on projectors. The current trend is toward centralization, with content access and the control of lights, projection, window blinds, and even room ventilation on a single touch screen. These screens, with supporting devices such as document cameras, are generally located on a lectern, sometimes at a fixed location at the front of a classroom but increasingly to one side. Mobile lecterns are popular in principle but difficult in reality—most are tethered by power and data cables and so their mobility is limited. Wireless technology now allows classroom controls to be located on handheld tablets, but this technology continues to develop and basic issues remain unresolved at this time.

The increased use of information and instructional technology requires increased support and training. IT departments at academic institutions have evolved to meet this need by providing hardware and software help desk services for both students and instructors, long-term planning and implementation services related to the upgrading and maintenance of IT hardware and software, IT support during class time, and control and editing of both real-time classroom content and lectures captured for streaming or later download. In order to provide these and a variety of related services, IT departments need offices, help desks, training rooms, equipment service areas, editing rooms, control rooms, and storage. All of these should be considered carefully during the space programming phase and should be counted as net floor area. Sizable and centrally located IT network rooms will be required on each floor, and an IT/AV closet, ideally with dedicated ventilation and rear access for cabling, will generally be required for each classroom or cluster of classrooms.

Instructors increasingly receive support as they prepare coursework. While traditionally this support consisted of research and basic administrative tasks, it now often includes the preparation and training required to allow instructors to move among software packages, use Internet links, or project and manipulate content from students' computers during a class. Video studio space may be required in which instructors can prepare course content for on-line instruction. These studios are often no larger than a faculty office, but they require appropriate equipment, lighting, and proximity to a control room. An appropriately equipped classroom can double as a studio.

Classroom Response Systems

Handheld classroom response systems, or "classroom clickers," are growing in popularity as a means of engaging students and obtaining rapid assessment of educational effectiveness. Instructors use classroom clickers to monitor learning ("Did you understand that explanation?"), poll students ("Do you agree with the author's conclusion?"), or verify attendance ("Remember to click when you enter the room or you will be counted as absent"). With proper controls, classroom clickers can also be used to administer quizzes or tests. Several educational technology companies market classroom clickers, and students are generally required to purchase them for classes in which they are used. Basic models support yes/no or multiple-choice questions, while more advanced models support alphanumeric responses. Classroom response system technology can be incorporated easily into existing classrooms and can be integrated with interactive whiteboard technology.

Videoconferencing and Distance Learning

Videoconference, distance learning, and TelePresence technology, although expensive, continues to grow in popularity. Classroom-based videoconferencing allows guest speakers or students to participate in a class from remote locations.

With proper design, small-classroom videoconferencing simulates the effect of a group around a conference table.

Large-classroom videoconferencing systems are more complex and expensive, and specific attention must be paid to seating layout; sight lines; and the location of screens, cameras, and microphones. Rooms above approximately 50 seats generally require a staffed control room. For the best systems, a control room monitoring a single classroom is located at a back corner of the classroom and is provided with a viewing window to the classroom. For less expensive systems, a control room is shared by several classrooms with which it may have video camera observation only. Control room capabilities are particularly important for classes in which audience member participation is expected to be captured by cameras and microphones. For these situations, several remotely directed cameras are required per classroom, and microphones are either installed in the ceiling or on desktops. Lighting design must be coordinated carefully with video system design, and acoustic absorption within the room and noise produced by ventilation systems or transmitted from adjacent spaces must be controlled. As videoconferencing technologies evolve, they offer an increasingly immersive experience. High-definition floor-to-ceiling screens are now available, and the quality and simultaneity of both sound and image are significantly improved over what was available only a few years ago.

Confidence Monitors

Confidence monitors are now a standard classroom feature. These monitors (typically a flat-screen display) are mounted on the modesty panel in front of the first row of seats, suspended from the ceiling, or located high on the wall at the rear of the classroom—all locations that allow the instructor to see the projected image without turning away from the class.

Projectors and Screens

Video projectors have become smaller, quieter, and less expensive. They are also brighter, which means that natural light is acceptable in classrooms in a way that it was not until recently. It is now common to have two or even three projectors in a single, large classroom. Flat-screen monitors are also larger, brighter, and less expensive than they used to be and are increasingly replacing projection screens in small classrooms and in seminar and team rooms.

Writing Boards: Black and White

Instructors often have strong opinions about the choice between blackboards (chalkboards) and whiteboards (dry-erase boards), although this is rarely a decision that is made by individual instructors on a classroom-by-classroom basis. Blackboards, first used at Bowdoin College around 1823,[17] were a technological innovation in their day. They supported the transition in American education from recitation and disputation. Although they are more expensive than blackboards, whiteboards currently outsell blackboards by 3 to 1, and the long-term trend favors whiteboards. Yet the game is far from over; Harvard Business School continues to use blackboards (and yellow chalk) in all classrooms and is far from alone in this loyalty.

Specialized paints now produce a glossy surface suitable for dry-erase markers or a spectrally reflective surface suitable for image projection. Both of these products work well and are low-cost, low-maintenance replacements for whiteboards and roll-down projector screens, although they require careful preparation of the surface on which they are applied.

17 Arthur Levine, *Handbook on Undergraduate Curriculum* (San Francisco: Jossey-Bass, 1978), 171.

Interactive Whiteboards

Interactive whiteboards (also known as "Smart Boards," a registered trademark) combine a projector, computer, and writing board. Interactive whiteboard advocates claim that they combine the best of the traditional writing board with image projectors and that they facilitate student-instructor interaction. Instructors who are new to interactive whiteboards require initial training, and many instructors feel that these devices supplement, rather than replace, a whiteboard. Interactive whiteboards are now common in K–12 classrooms, and so they are increasingly expected by a rising generation of university students. They are particularly useful in small classrooms in which students are mobile and can interact with the board, and they are a convenient medium for a class website.

AV, IT, and Classroom Planning

A few general guidelines apply to the planning of classrooms that include projection screens. The minimum distance between a screen surface and the front row of seats should be at least two times the height of the image, while the maximum distance to the back row should be not more than six times the image height (see Figure 5.35).

These guidelines are used to establish the required size for projection screens and the need for multiple screens. A spectrally reflective projection screen should not be viewed at an angle shallower than 30 degrees; therefore, a plan diagram with lines drawn at 30 degrees from the edges of the screen surface defines the acceptable seating zone within a classroom. The application of these rules becomes more complicated when multiple

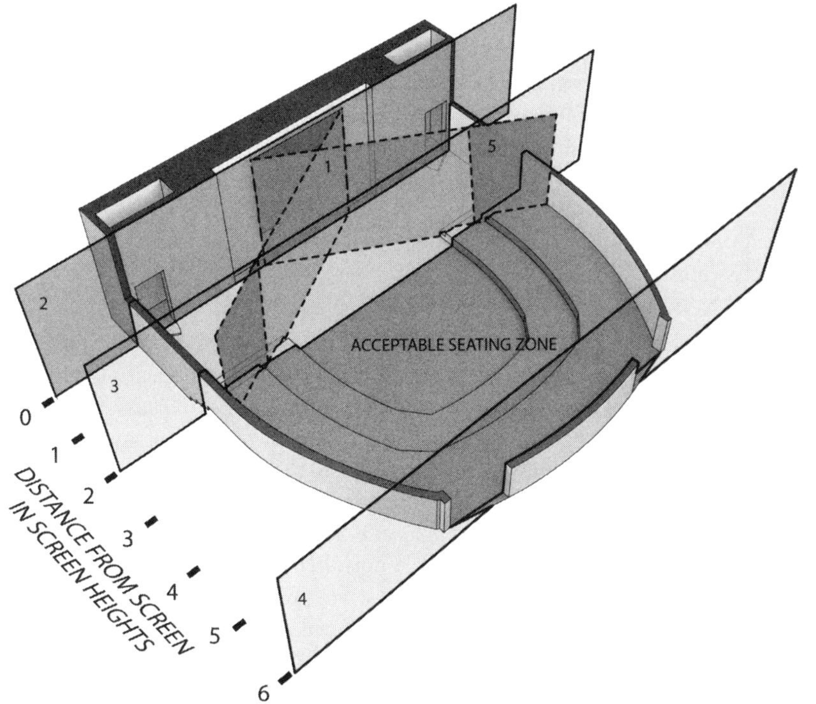

Figure 5.35 Projection screen and seat placement: optimal classroom seats are located not less than two and not more than six screen heights from the screen.
Legend
1 Projection screen
2 Plane of projection screen
3 Closest seat to projection screen
4 Farthest seat from projection screen
5 30-degree horizontal view cone from projection screen

screens are used and depends on whether students are intended to view one screen only (all screens show the same content) or all screens (each screen is intended to show different content). This 30-degree rule also varies slightly depending on the projection surface being used and is different for various flat screen monitors, for which maximum recommended viewing angles are published. For comfortable viewing, the sight line from eye level at each classroom seat to the top of a projection screen should not exceed 30 degrees above horizontal. This guideline, which is related more to viewer comfort than screen visibility, is frequently relaxed for at least some seats within a room.[18]

Classroom plans and presentation wall designs should take into consideration the relationship between writing boards and projection screens. The top portion of a writing board is rarely used if it is more than 6 ft, 8 in. above the floor—a height that establishes the bottom of the projection screen if the presentation wall is designed to allow the highly desirable ability to use writing boards and projection screens simultaneously. This rule, combined with the viewing distance rules outlined previously, determines the required ceiling height for these simultaneous-use classrooms.

Acoustics

Acoustic requirements and control strategies for academic buildings should be established during space programming and the early phases of building design. Architects should educate themselves about basic acoustical principles (e.g., reverberation time, speech intelligibility, and sound transmittance), and they should work with an acoustician to review the acoustical performance of both architectural and mechanical systems. Superior speech intelligibility—the primary measure of a classroom's acoustic success—is a function of low reverberation time, freedom from echoes, and low levels of background noise.

Speech intelligibility falls as background noise levels rise, and a noisy mechanical system is the common downfall of an otherwise well-designed classroom. The use of fan coil ventilators in classrooms is discouraged strongly. These units are inherently noisy, and no effective means of quieting them exists without destroying their heating and cooling performance. Centralized mechanical systems (e.g., variable air volume systems) with terminal units located outside the classrooms are recommended. Displacement ventilation systems are particularly appropriate for tiered classrooms where raised flooring can be used to distribute ventilation air. Ducts leading to and inside classrooms should be oversized in comparison to typical commercial applications to reduce the air velocity that creates noise. Ventilation system registers and grilles should be selected for low Noise Criteria (NC) levels. An NC level of 25 is recommended for classrooms, and this level should not exceed NC 30.

The walls that separate classrooms from adjacent rooms and from the building's exterior must be designed carefully. The Sound Transmission Class (STC) rating is the accepted measure of a wall's ability to impede the transmission of sound, and walls between classrooms with STC ratings of 45–50 are acceptable in most cases when noisy activities such as music or multimedia use are programmed. An otherwise well-designed and built wall, ceiling, or window can fail acoustically if key details are overlooked. Walls in classrooms and faculty

18 Thanks to Mark Holden of Jaffee Holden Acoustics.

offices should extend from floor to ceiling structure and be acoustically sealed at the top, bottom, and at any penetrations. Partitions, particularly in classrooms, should be either masonry or, if frame construction is used, should have staggered studs, acoustic insulation, staggered and gasketed electrical and data outlets, and double gypsum board or acoustic gypsum board. Acoustic gaskets on doors reduce noise infiltration from hallways and should be specified on most classrooms. Triple-glazed acoustic windows should be specified where outdoor noise is present.

The internal acoustic characteristics of a classroom are as important as the reduction of sound transmission from outside. Speech intelligibility is improved by reducing reverberation time, a function of both the room volume and the acoustic absorbability of its surfaces. Carpeted floors and acoustically treated ceilings are generally not enough to achieve the required reductions and need to be supplemented with the absorption provided by upholstered seats and acoustically treated rear and/or side walls. A high level of acoustic absorption is particularly important in classrooms intended for videoconferencing, distance learning, or lecture capture. In large classrooms, the front wall and ceiling above the instructor should be of a hard, acoustically reflective material and angled to direct the instructor's voice to the back of the classroom.

While an acoustically well-designed classroom of up to 150 seats can function without the need for voice amplification, distance learning and lecture capture increasingly require that classrooms, even those below this size, be outfitted with instructor and student voice amplification. For student seating areas, ambient microphones serve this function well. Individual student microphones are generally impractical, although they may be appropriate in classrooms that focus on debate or extensive student discussion.

The importance of acoustic isolation between adjacent faculty offices and between faculty offices and corridors is overlooked frequently. A design that ends partitions at the underside of a suspended acoustic ceiling, gangs several offices on a single straight ventilation duct, or deletes acoustic insulation from partitions is a recipe for postoccupancy complaints.

Lighting

Careful control of both natural and artificial lighting within classrooms is essential. In the past, high "industry standard" lighting levels often resulted in glare or excess light at surfaces, such as the ceiling, where light is not needed. These standards are changing. A well-designed classroom lighting system will deliver light where it is required: at the desktop and presentation wall. Lighting at desktops should be primarily vertical to avoid glare on computer screens. For similar reasons, classroom walls should generally not be white or near-white.

Good lighting design creates visual hierarchy in a classroom. A 5:1 ratio between the brightest part of the room and the dimmest creates an aesthetically pleasing light environment and an appropriate contrast between surfaces that require light (desks and presentation walls) and those that do not (projection screens, walls, and ceilings).

In order to achieve these differences, classroom lighting systems should create lighting zones which can operate in different modes. For the simplest classrooms, this may consist of two zones with two sets of controls, one for the seating area and one for the presentation wall. Within the presentation wall area, two zones of lighting are generally desirable, however, one for writing boards and another for projection screens.

Lighting at the presentation wall should allow different lighting modes. If a multi-level writing board is used, both upper and lower tiers of the board should be illuminated and glare free. Lighting configurations should also allow an instructor to write on a well-illuminated board while projecting presentation material on an adjacent screen with minimal illumination from sources other than the projector. It is desirable to have separate lighting controls for the presentation wall and for the student seating areas. In an auditorium, which, at times, may be used for significantly less than its full seating capacity, separate lighting zones should be provided for the front and rear seating areas. Each lighting zone will require several lighting modes (e.g., lights off, low-level lighting for viewing projected content, midlevel lighting for discussion among students or audience members, high-level lighting for before and after class and for cleaning and maintenance).

Light fixture and control technology is now adequate to meet the most sophisticated classroom lighting designs. Today's challenge is to achieve simplicity: Does your design meet the many needs of students and instructors while still remaining affordable, maintainable, and easy to operate without the assistance of a lighting specialist?

During the past decade, recommended average light levels for classrooms have decreased by as much as a half. Standards developed in the 1960s have shifted as a result of interest in energy efficiency combined with improved understanding of desirable light conditions for classrooms. High-performance standards require that natural and artificial lighting be considered as a single system. While, until recently, 50 fc was considered a necessary minimum for ambient lighting within a classroom, 50 fc is now considered a maximum. The comparable level for teaching laboratories, previously an average of 100 fc minimum, is now 50–80 fc. A classroom that focuses on student-to-student interaction has an even lower requirement for ambient light levels (around 15 fc), provided 50 fc is present at desktops and writing boards.

A significant development in classroom lighting in recent years has been the increasing availability and falling cost of LED lighting. LEDs are more "control friendly" than fluorescent or halogen lights, allowing smooth dimming across a broad range of intensities. They are also well suited to applications where a high degree of directionality is desired. They are less suitable for providing ambient lighting and so are unlikely to replace fluorescent ceiling light fixtures in the near future.[19]

Daylight in Classrooms

Once considered undesirable in classrooms designed to feature projected images, classroom daylighting is now championed by colleges and universities that cite studies showing positive correlations between daylit classrooms and improved academic performance.[20] Although classroom daylighting presents unique challenges—natural light varies in intensity and direction and can be difficult to control—properly controlled natural light in classrooms is almost always desirable and is compatible with today's bright projectors.

19 Thanks to Mark Loeffler, Associate Director of Atelier Ten Consulting Designers.

20 A variety of books and journal articles on this topic are available from the National Clearinghouse for Educational Facilities at http://www.ncef.org/rl/impact_research_studies.cfm?date=4 and http://www.ncef.org/rl/impact_learning.cfm?date=4.

Windows designed for daylighting should be above eye level. Light shelves help to reduce glare and to aid the appropriate distribution of daylight within a classroom. For classrooms with a fixed presentation wall and front-facing seating plan, daylight should come from high on a side wall.

ACADEMIC BUILDINGS CASE STUDY 4

GREENSPUN HALL

Greenspun College of Urban Affairs, University of Nevada, Las Vegas

Architect: Robert A.M. Stern Architects with HKS Architects

Introduction

The LEED Gold-certified home for the Greenspun College of Urban Affairs commands a prominent corner where the southern boundary of the UNLV campus meets Maryland Parkway, marking the campus's re-engagement of the city that has grown up around it (see Figure 5.36). Two expansive landscaped stairs at the southeast and northwest corners of the site ascend to a broad courtyard shaded by a louvered photovoltaic canopy that tames the harsh desert sun.

The 120,000 sq ft building provides classrooms, labs, departmental suites, faculty offices, and radio and television broadcasting facilities (see Figures 5.37–5.39) for the college, which is composed of the Departments of Communications Studies, Criminal Justice, and Marriage and Family Therapy as well as the Hank Greenspun School of Journalism and Media Studies, the School of Environmental and Public Affairs, and the School of Social Work. A 2-story entry commons links the ground floor to the elevated courtyard at the northwest corner of the site. Classrooms line the courtyard to the west, and the L-shaped office wing defines the courtyard's north and east edges.

Figure 5.36 View from the northwest. © Peter Aaron/Esto.

Figure 5.37 A video control room classroom. Courtesy of UNLV. Photo by R. Marsh Starks.

Figure 5.38 An audio editing laboratory. Courtesy of UNLV. Photo by R. Marsh Starks.

Figure 5.39 A broadcast studio. Courtesy of UNLV. Photo by Aaron Mayes.

Interior Finishes

Interior design issues that must be considered during the design of academic buildings:

- Academic buildings house an assembly use. They are occupied by young people who often feel little sense of ownership toward the building; therefore, finishes should be durable and easy to maintain.
- Interior finishes should also be attractive. An academic building that looks like a fortress will convey a negative impression of the institution it serves and will be treated roughly by those who use it.

- The entrance lobbies of academic buildings should generally have hard, water-resistant floor surfaces.
- Corridors, faculty offices, and classrooms should wherever practical be carpeted for acoustic reasons, even though in heavily used academic buildings carpet will need to be cleaned and replaced frequently.

Furniture

In flat-floor classrooms, modular tables and stacking or rolling chairs have generally replaced the tablet-arm chair of past generations. Stacking chairs with tablet arms are available, but the tablet surfaces are generally too small for computers. Several manufacturers now sell modular tables with wire management and a variety of top shapes that are marketed as allowing rapid reconfiguration of a classroom's seating plan. In reality, classroom furniture is rarely reconfigured. Instructors have neither the time nor inclination to rearrange furniture between classes, and support staff are neither available nor trained to perform this task. Far too often, the flexible classroom is either flexible in name only or is a furniture mess.

A broad spectrum of fixed, auditorium-style seats is available that will suit almost any budget, with hard or upholstered seats and with or without tablet arms. Almost all auditorium-style seats are available with power and data connections. If a tablet arm is specified, it should be large enough to accommodate a computer and should be finished with a nonslip surface. Auditorium seats come in a variety of widths, typically between 19 and 22 in. from center to center. Most seat manufacturers will provide a classroom or auditorium layout showing the combination of different seat widths necessary to fit within a given classroom or auditorium plan and allowing for the smooth alignment of seats along the ends of rows. These plans should maximize the number of wide seats and should be reviewed carefully to assure that seats are staggered between rows to minimize the number of seats where sight lines are compromised by the head of an audience member in front.

Case study classrooms and cluster classrooms, are generally furnished with movable chairs on casters and fixed desks with wire management and often with a slot at the front edge of the desk suitable for holding a name card. As an alternative to this furniture combination, several manufacturers (most notably Sedia Systems) produce fixed seating systems with fold-down desktops and upholstered seats. These achieve the same seating density as auditorium seats with tablet arms, but lack the desk surface area and seat comfort of the movable chair/fixed desk design.

Building Organization

The best academic buildings are designed with careful consideration given to the placement of classrooms, team rooms, and common areas. Each of the various arrangements responds to the needs of a different academic institution, and each represents a carefully studied solution chosen from among many options. Building owners and academics may have clear ideas about what they like or dislike about their existing facilities, but they are rarely able on their own to translate these ideas into improved designs. The architect of an academic building should be prepared to listen carefully to many stakeholders, to present a variety of planning arrangements, and to assist stakeholders as they define the criteria used to assess these options.

A CLOSING THOUGHT

This chapter might appear to suggest that there is a formula: choose the appropriate classroom types and supporting amenities, apply the appropriate technical standards, and you're done. This kind of thinking will lead you astray. Classrooms are at the heart of the college experience, both academically and socially. The design principles and precedents outlined in this chapter provide only the starting point. The design of an enduringly successful academic building must apply to the needs, aspirations, and culture of each academic institution. The best classrooms, and the academic buildings that house them, are comfortable settings for relaxed collegiality and for free-flowing discourse. Ask anyone who has attended college to tell you an anecdote or two about his or her experience, and invariably you will hear something about a memorable classroom. Former students will remember where they chose to sit, whom they met, and what they learned in a specific room. This association occurs because the design was right, responding to the character of the place and the needs of the people and setting the stage for enduring alumni loyalty and for a lifelong love of learning.

REFERENCES

Astin, Alexander W. 1993. *What Matters in College? Four Critical Years Revisited.* San Francisco: Jossey-Bass.

Boyer, Ernest L. 1988. *College: The Undergraduate Experience in America.* New York: Carnegie Foundation for the Advancement of Learning/Harper & Row.

Heskel, Julia, and Davis Dyer. 2008. *After the Harkness Gift: A History of Phillips Exeter Academy since 1930.* Lebanon, NH: University Press of New England.

Klauder, Charles Z., and Herbert C. Wise. 1929. *College Architecture in America.* New York: Charles Scribner's Sons.

Larson, Jens Fredrick, and Archie MacInnes Palmer. 1933. *Architectural Planning of the American College.* New York: McGraw-Hill.

Oblinger, Diana G., ed. 2006. *Learning Spaces*, an EDUCAUSE e-book. www.educause.edu/learningpsaces.

Turner, Paul Venable. 1984. *Campus: An American Tradition.* Cambridge, MA: MIT Press.

ACKNOWLEDGMENTS

I am grateful to the many friends and collaborators who have assisted me with the preparation of this chapter and who, over the years, have supported my obsession with the relationship between the design of learning spaces and effective learning. Thanks to Mark Loeffler of Atelier Ten for his insights on lighting design and to Mark Holden of Jaffe Holden for insights on acoustics and audiovisual systems. Within my own office, I thank Alex Newman-Wise who assisted with research, both Robert A.M. Stern and Peter Morris Dixon for their big-picture perspective, and Delia Conache, who is solely responsible for our firm's ever-expanding collection of classroom diagrams, which are central to this chapter and to our own work for academic institutions around the world.

CHAPTER 6

INTERDISCIPLINARY RESEARCH FACILITIES

Scott Kelsey and Andrew Labov, CO Architects

Discoveries cannot be planned; they pop up, like Puck, in unexpected corners.
—Max Perutz, who shared the 1962 Nobel Prize in Chemistry with John Kendrew for their studies of the structural of globular proteins, which established the modern field of structural biology

The past few decades have seen a significant global push to expand the core scientific knowledge base. This push, manifested through public pressures—and, by extension, funding—has created an abundance of knowledge that has led to breakthroughs such as the mapping of the human genome, the ability to work at the molecular level, and advanced understanding of the interconnectedness of all natural sciences. Advances in technology have also enabled scientists to work with precision at a scale that was previously unknown. Computing power, the proliferation of data, as well as the ability to access and share it, have facilitated advancements that previously would have taken years longer to achieve.

Our shrinking world has also moved scientific focus to solving real-world problems, which requires an abundance of basic science knowledge and the consideration and participation of a broad array of other disciplines. Therefore, new opportunities demand reaching far beyond the defined walls of medical and engineering schools and technology centers into areas such as mathematics, ethics and policy, and the humanities. Robust computing power and communication technologies can carry the integration of knowledge a long way, but allowing researchers close proximity in their work environment remains a critical component of advancing scientific missions. The need to bring varying disciplines together in order to collaborate and apply their knowledge bases toward a collective goal has created not only new ways of researching and developing solutions but also a new building typology.

The new interdisciplinary model of undergraduate science research was pioneered by Project Kaleidoscope (www.pkal.org). This organization, founded in the early 1990s, placed a heavy emphasis on undergraduate science reform through curriculum, faculty development, and facilities. New interdisciplinary approaches are indebted to the specialization of the traditional disciplines of basic science, which provides the knowledge base on which they are built. Previously unconsidered opportunities for scientific application abound as disciplines begin collaborating. However, sometimes the need to shift focus to scientific application comes simply from the maturing of the process. Needs change as organizations evolve from the basic research stage to a mix of research and product development, therapies, and manufacturing. Although the research world leads these shifts in scientific focus, the educational world must quickly follow to train tomorrow's scientists. Interdisciplinary science education, aided by advancing teaching technologies and emerging pedagogical changes, is rapidly becoming the foundation for the next generation of young scientists.

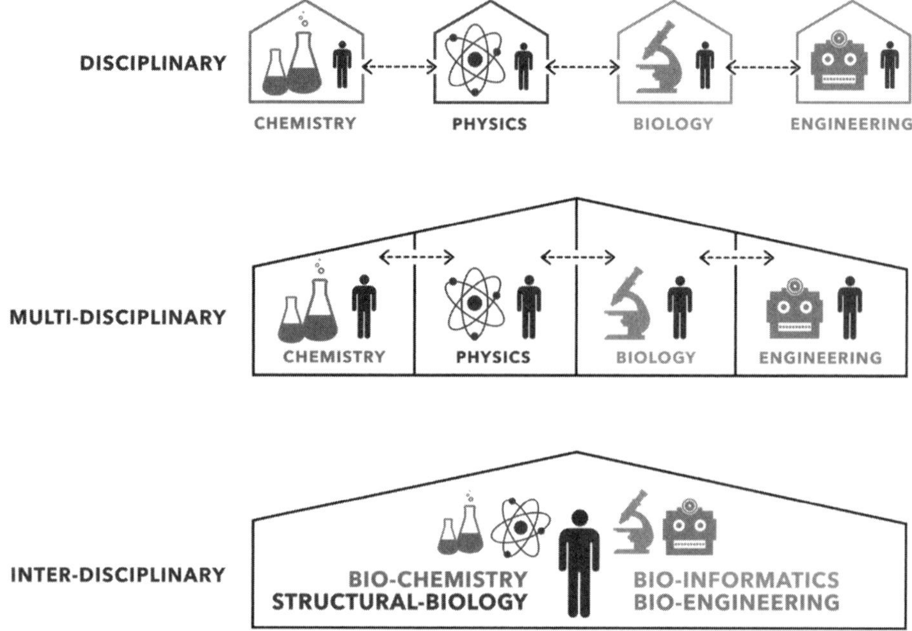

▸ *Figure 6.1 Disciplines.*

The following definitions provide a context to fully understand the idea of interdisciplinary science and the types of scientific (see Figure 6.1).

Disciplinary studies. Projects that take place within the bounds of a single, currently recognized, academic discipline. We fully appreciate the artificial nature of subject boundaries and that they are dynamic. Research activity is oriented toward one specific goal: finding an answer to a specific research question.

Multidisciplinary studies. Projects that involve several different academic disciplines researching one theme or problem, but with multiple disciplinary goals. Participants exchange knowledge, but do not aim to cross subject boundaries to create new knowledge or theory. The research process progresses as parallel disciplinary efforts without integration, but usually with the aim to compare results.

Interdisciplinary studies. Projects that involve several *unrelated* academic disciplines and force them to cross subject boundaries to create new knowledge and theory and to solve a common research goal. By "unrelated," we mean that they have contrasting research paradigms. We might consider the differences between qualitative and quantitative approaches or between analytical and interpretive approaches that join disciplines from the sciences and the humanities.

In short, interdisciplinary studies

- Cross disciplinary boundaries.
- Set common goals.

- Integrate varied disciplines.
- Develop integrated knowledge and theory.

The results of this integrated approach, therefore, are greater than the sum of the parts.

A significant factor in the success of interdisciplinary scientific learning and discovery is the ability of scientists and students to collaborate in common spaces. The new interdisciplinary venture breaks from traditional university organizational structure. The increasing creation of centers and institutes with problem- and solution-based missions is blurring academic departments' boundaries. These new interdisciplinary groups are better able to respond to the demands and opportunities of a changing world through flexible and dynamic scientific environments. Institutions are embracing this direction and fostering research-based learning by integrating research and teaching environments from all parts of their previously segregated campuses. The emerging interdisciplinary science building should therefore transfer its mission to the larger campus and promote a community that brings together constituents from all walks of the scientific and academic worlds.

THE EVOLUTION OF SCIENCE TEACHING AND RESEARCH FACILITIES

The facility infrastructure that for years has supported the organizational structure for basic science and traditional disciplines is inadequate and unable to accommodate interdisciplinary science. Traditional undergraduate sciences buildings placed a heavy emphasis on department-specific organization. This approach organized departments by building floors, with physics typically on the lower level, biology at mid-level, and chemistry on the upper level (due to higher hood usage). Faculty office and administration space also followed this silo approach. Often there was little, if any, connection between these floors, beyond stair shafts and elevators. Under this model, key scientists and their programs are separated by walls and floors, by buildings, and even by campus sectors. These barriers inhibit effective collaboration.

Another significant challenge is presented by facilities designed for a specific purpose that now must accommodate the physical, spatial, and technological requirements of a much wider range of science and collaborative work processes. The interdisciplinary science facility, therefore, was not so much *born*, but rather *evolved* over time as scientific groups and their larger institutions came to understand the benefits of having well-designed facilities to accommodate emerging fields of interdisciplinary study, including bioengineering, biophysics, nanotechnology, biofuels, and structural biology, among others.

The principles of interdisciplinary science apply equally to the arenas of teaching and research. In fact, along with developing pedagogical approaches, interdisciplinary programs have brought teaching and research environments closer together, most often incorporating research much earlier in the learning process and curriculum through problem-based techniques, group-based studies, and interactive and virtual technologies. Many of the new generation of science facilities strive to "tear down the walls"—literally and metaphorically—between instruction and research, promoting research conducted in one lab to provide content for the curriculum taught in an adjacent lab.

CASE STUDIES: AN EVALUATION OF THE INTERDISCIPLINARY RESEARCH AND TEACHING MODEL

The implications of the modern interdisciplinary science facility can best be illustrated using case studies of actual projects. Each of the four case studies throughout this chapter examines a project that was developed in response to the specific research and teaching mission of the institution. But all also share a common vision to bring existing disciplines and methods into combination. Each building represents a new milestone in shaping a vision of team-based research that cuts across the traditional boundaries between academic disciplines or schools.

Each of these case studies has been evaluated from the standpoint of four criteria:

Campus-scale planning. What role does the project play in a consolidation strategy for the science disciplines across the campus? Does the project either reinforce or create a new center or science precinct? How does the project's organizational strategy reinforce the importance of science on the campus? Does the project contain programmatic elements that reach beyond traditional science programs to create new public amenities for the campus? What design strategies emphasize openness, consolidation, and campus engagement?

Collaborative environments. How has the program been developed to acknowledge the need for team- and problem-based learning spaces? What are the characteristics of these spaces, their technologies, and their location within the building? Does the building contain programmed informal interaction space? What are the characteristics of these spaces and their location in relation to the more formal learning and research environments?

Interdisciplinary lab concepts. How has the traditional laboratory been organized to promote team-based learning and research? What are its organizational principles and metrics? How is the engineering infrastructure organized to maximize flexibility and adaptability? What organizational strategies create securable research environments where needed, while allowing for openness and flexibility?

Evolving role of laboratory support. How has laboratory support changed and adapted in response to the interdisciplinary research concepts? What are its characteristics and metrics? To what extent has laboratory support become less "dedicated" and more shared? What role does the emergence of the high-technology and dedicated core facility play?

INTERDISCIPLINARY RESEARCH FACILITIES
CASE STUDY 1

MICROBIAL SCIENCES BUILDING
University of Wisconsin, Madison

The University of Wisconsin Microbial Sciences Building comprises approximately 190,000 assignable square feet (ASF) and 330,000 gross square feet (GSF), and is part of the Biostar Initiative, a 10-year program to support biotechnology research, development, and education in the state of Wisconsin. Design began in 2002, and the project was completed in 2007 at a construction cost of $90 million, or $273 per sq ft, as measured in 2004 dollars. The new building replaced outdated and overcrowded departmental facilities and acts as a catalyst for interdepartmental collaboration and academic interaction, while maintaining the unique identity and programmatic organization of each department. It contributes to the institution's increased focus on microbiology, a discipline whose faculty and programs were previously distributed throughout several different facilities on the campus.

The programmatic objectives of this project were to capitalize on the existing strengths of research and teaching in microbiology. Two interactive and complementary departments—bacteriology, and medical microbiology and immunology—serve as the microbial research core of the campus. These two departments have unified to create an integrated and interdisciplinary training program.

Campus-Scale Planning

The Microbial Sciences Building is located at the junction of an existing group of research facilities. It not only consolidates existing departments under one roof but also strengthens connections between existing facilities through its carefully positioned circulation and core facilities, which are shared by all research buildings.

A circulation path that connects the eastern parts of the campus and the residential hall to the northwest is an important generator of form for this building. This pedestrian path is routed through the building to both enliven its public spaces and create a strong visual connection with the scientific research and teaching happening inside (see Figure 6.2). This "northwest passage" connects two atriums that serve as focal points as well as the building's living rooms and social spaces. The dual-atrium concept is both a model of social and interactive space—well used in the Wisconsin winter—and an organizing element for the five laboratory neighborhoods.

Collaborative Environments

Formal learning spaces are organized throughout the project in conjunction with both research and teaching environments. These include a large 450-seat symposium center with a sophisticated multimedia audiovisual system. Its design promotes long-duration conferences with aisles and seating that allow participants to move freely within the room without disrupting ongoing proceedings. A number of smaller-scale conference rooms seating 12–30 people are located throughout the building to promote both scheduled and drop-in meetings and discussions. Each room is equipped with audiovisual and teleconferencing capabilities. The north atrium and café serve as the social hub of this scientific community as well as providing breakout space for the symposium center's poster sessions and receptions (see Figures 6.2 and 6.3). Relaxed seating areas with mobile marker boards on every floor encourage informal shoptalk and brainstorming.

Interdisciplinary Lab Concepts

Interdisciplinary research communities should promote interaction and exchange of ideas among scientists with different perspectives. To this end, faculty members for each department are comingled on each of the five research floors. Each floor is organized as a series of five self-contained laboratory neighborhoods, and each of these neighborhoods contains an open, generic loft lab approximately 32 ft deep by 120 ft long, or five contiguous lab modules. Casework in the laboratory is a combination of both fixed and flexible. Shared laboratory support and student workstations are adjacent to

Figure 6.2 North atrium and café—view 1. © Robert Canfield Photography.

Figure 6.3 North atrium and café—view 2. © Robert Canfield Photography

the lab, and a block of faculty offices is located at the ends of each laboratory neighborhood. The offices are positioned to provide direct access to laboratories, but are separated to avoid territoriality and to allow for flexible use over time. Given the potential security risk associated with some of the research activities, each laboratory neighborhood is a lockable security zone (see Figure 6.4).

The planning module accommodates the organized and systematic delivery of laboratory services; heating, ventilation, and air conditioning (HVAC) equipment; fume hoods; exhaust ducts; and power and data. The distribution of services and infrastructure above the main corridor provides the needed flexibility to add or delete services to individual labs or lab modules. The laboratory space itself can also accommodate both faculty and programmatic adjustments and, at the same time, was optimally designed and equipped for the first occupants.

Evolving Role of Laboratory Support

Each self-contained laboratory neighborhood has both shared and customizable, dedicated laboratory support. For this project, the laboratory support to laboratory space ratio is 0.5:1. And the organizational concept promotes a distributed model of lab support, which has immediacy and adjacency to the laboratories and contributes to interdisciplinary use throughout the floor. Student offices are located off a dedicated service corridor, separate from the laboratory to promote safety.

The building also contains a 10,000 sq ft vivarium core facility with 22 animal holding rooms with biosafety levels 3 and 3Ag (agricultural) capabilities. It is security capable for use with select agents and is located on the basement level with dedicated elevator access to the research floor.

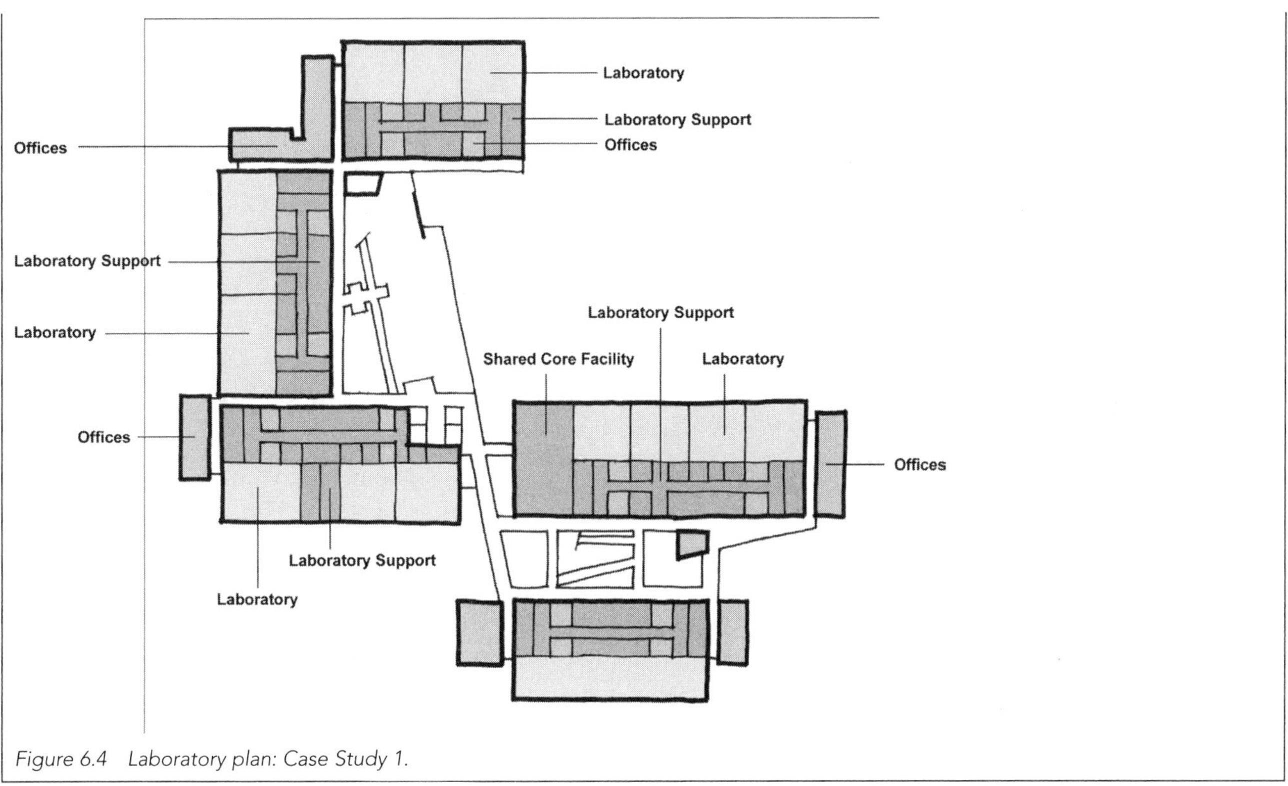

Figure 6.4 Laboratory plan: Case Study 1.

Facility requirements for both interdisciplinary teaching and research are based on the same conceptual planning principles. Four primary concepts have emerged as vital to the success of interdisciplinary science. The detailed planning requirements of teaching and research environments can then be built on the foundation of these concepts.

1. *Access by a broad range of participants to high-technology and, often very costly, core resources.* Shared core facilities supporting research and teaching spaces are an important component of the new generation of science facilities and include specialized central scientific resources. Because scientific core resources are shared to spread their cost, operations, and use across several users, they also bring varied users—students, faculty, and researchers—into close proximity. Core facilities, which serve all building users and often campus users as well, should be placed close to major circulation and gathering areas because they play a crucial role in providing new scientific centers within the building and campus.
2. *Making traditional barriers between space types and scientific activities more permeable and transparent.* Providing easier access while maintaining separations necessary for safety, security, and specific physical and environmental needs includes pairing research activities in close proximity to teaching activities, but, more commonly, simply integrates classroom,

▸ *Figure 6.5 Transparency—research, Howard Hughes Medical Institute, Virginia.*

teaching lab, and independent work group activities. On the research side, the ease of moving between labs, core facilities, and collaborative meeting and office environments becomes essential to the effective integration of individuals or groups in disciplines that have been historically separated. A simple reduction of distance between scientists is the first step in overcoming many traditional barriers. The new generation of interdisciplinary labs must incorporate more transparency not only by using more glass and open work spaces but also by promoting access, exposure, and display of the science that is taking place (see Figure 6.5).

3. *Creating more spaces for collaboration and centers for the exchange of knowledge.* Places of exchange such as student group rooms, commons, and coffee lounges are genuinely important to today's students and should be strategically placed to maximize a highly collaborative environment. The relationship of the building's components (i.e., office to laboratory to shared support to classrooms to public spaces) can encourage serendipitous encounters among faculty, students, and staff (see Figure 6.6).

Soft spaces that include generous and well-designed staircases, pleasant corridors, and recesses to accommodate the accidental conversation all play a role in the collaborative environment.

Hard, high-tech spaces, such as videoconferencing, distance learning, and multimedia-capable auditoriums and meeting spaces, are a necessary complement. They must incorporate the latest information and communication technologies and be able to adapt as technology advances over time.

Organizing individual work spaces, both private and open, in arrangements and proximities that promote interaction

◀ *Figure 6.6 Collaboration. Engineering Sciences Building, UC Santa Cruz.* © Robert Canfield Photography.

is also vital. No longer can the science student or researcher "hole up" in the back room for his or her life's work. The entire building should be considered as a "place to do science." However, because the movement toward greater openness does not obviate the need for quiet space, small private workrooms and meeting spaces must be interwoven with public spaces.

4. *Adaptability and flexibility in spaces and supporting building systems.* Research laboratories must economically accommodate both the demands of new technologies and the growth, contraction, or reconfiguration of research groups. Reconfigurable classrooms and teaching labs are essential in adapting to future trends in science curricula and pedagogies. Similarly, engineered systems (e.g., structural, mechanical, electrical, plumbing, and low-voltage technologies) are crucial to a successful project. In planning for these systems, it is important to note that although a 100 percent flexible facility may sound ideal, that flexibility comes at a cost. Strategies must be developed to identify institutional goals and priorities, which, in turn, inform planning for flexibility that is cost effective. Institutions should strive to create sustainable strategies that provide an efficient, functional facility for the future without compromising safety. Integrating robust infrastructure systems into the essential nature of the scientific environment can ensure future flexibility.

INTERDISCIPLINARY RESEARCH FACILITIES **CASE STUDY 2**

WILLIAM H. FOEGE BIOENGINEERING AND GENOME SCIENCES BUILDING *University of Washington, Seattle*

The Foege Bioengineering and Genome Sciences Building comprises 148,000 ASF and 220,000 GSF to consolidate and enhance the university's scientific initiatives of genome sciences and bioengineering. Design began in 2002 and was completed in 2007, at a construction cost of $98.6 million, or $380 per sq ft, as measured in 2005 dollars. This building replaces outdated and scattered research and teaching environments for both departments and the medical school. The project was a rare opportunity to co-locate two renowned programs under one roof to support interdisciplinary research and shared resources.

Programmatic objectives were unique to each department. Bioengineering consolidated a program spread among nine buildings on the University of Washington campus and created the opportunity for state-of-the-art interdisciplinary teaching and research that fuses the activities of the College of Engineering and School of Medicine. For genome sciences, the key driver was the creation of leading-edge research space designed to accommodate team-based interdisciplinary research in a field of study still in its infancy with a rapidly growing faculty.

Campus-Scale Planning

The Foege Building occupies an important gateway site at the south of the main campus and to the east of the University of Washington School of Medicine. This parcel of land was the last remaining significant open space adjacent to the medical school, and the building was positioned to its east side to support the development of a contiguous green space and vista connecting Portage Bay to the north main campus. This vista maintains sight lines and physical connections to the unique waterfront feature of this portion of the campus and creates a central organizing space for its science research and teaching buildings (see Figure 6.7). The building's entrance system and internal circulation allows student, staff, researcher, or visitor to circulate inside the east edge of the building, especially in inclement weather, creating an internal street that follows the slope down from the north and terminates at Portage Bay to the south. Here the circulation path leads to a café and symposium center that are amenities for the larger campus. Breaking the building mass at the center creates a cross-axis connecting this building to the main east–west pedestrian circulation system for the hospital and School of Medicine. The physical path system actively engages and reinforces the campus through the use of enriched paving, wayfinding, and transparency to building interiors.

Collaborative Environments

In conjunction with research and teaching laboratories, the building contains a range of meeting spaces, including a 200-seat symposium center with adjacent breakout space for poster sessions and gatherings. This center contains sophisticated data and audiovisual systems providing distributed technology and videoconferencing. Smaller conference rooms for 10–20 people are located throughout

Figure 6.7 Exterior. Foege Building, University of Washington, Seattle. Lara Swimmer, Photographer.

the building. Informal, drop-in spaces are also strategically located to take advantage of crossing circulation areas, natural light, and distant views. These spaces are outfitted with writing surfaces, power/data access, and soft seating. The café, an important programmatic element of the project, is positioned near the terminus of the north–south internal circulation spine connecting directly to the symposium center. It provides stand-up tables, café-style seating, and group tables as well as an outdoor terrace with seating that affords panoramic views to the waterfront. The café provides complementary meeting environments, where teams of researchers can join together to share ideas over food and coffee, and has become an important destination for all students at the School of Medicine.

Interdisciplinary Lab Concepts

The facility contains two unique yet complementary strategies of laboratory planning. Each represents a specific response to the research and teaching activity, its use of laboratory support, intensity of engineering services, and position of faculty offices.

In bioengineering, the typical laboratory floor contains an L-shaped laboratory space with adjacent support and student workstations. Faculty offices and computational and administrative space are located across a central corridor. Laboratories are 30 ft deep with four to six modules of contiguous laboratory space. Fifty percent of the lab floor has wet service accessibility. Interrupting the laboratory at strategic modules are bars of laboratory support. Laboratories contain primarily fixed casework systems, and teaching laboratories are co-located throughout the building with research space (see Figure 6.8).

The typical laboratory floor for genome sciences contains an open, loftlike organization. These lab lofts have been devised to support team-based interdisciplinary research. Given the relative newness of the genome sciences research initiative, the labs are highly adaptable to a range of activities, from wet bench to dry computational. These labs are 32 ft deep with six to eight modules of contiguous laboratory space. Twenty-five percent of the lab floor has wet service accessibility; the east wall of the laboratory zone is a wet wall containing sinks, hoods, equipment, and access points to the support zone. A "ghost" corridor runs adjacent to this wet wall. On each floor, two zones of swing space can be devised to contain laboratories, lab support, or office space. Laboratories contain all movable, flexible casework, and overhead service carriers maximize flexibility and plug-and-play capability (see Figure 6.9).

Evolving Role of Laboratory Support

Laboratory support plays a unique role in each wing. Bioengineering demands less dedicated laboratory support, as much of the instrumentation occurs directly within the lab. Its ratio of lab support to lab therefore is 0.35:1. By comparison, genome sciences requires extensive lab support and a ratio of lab support to lab of 0.75:1, which can increase to 1.0:1 when the "swing spaces" are fully utilized. In addition, given the emerging nature of interdisciplinary

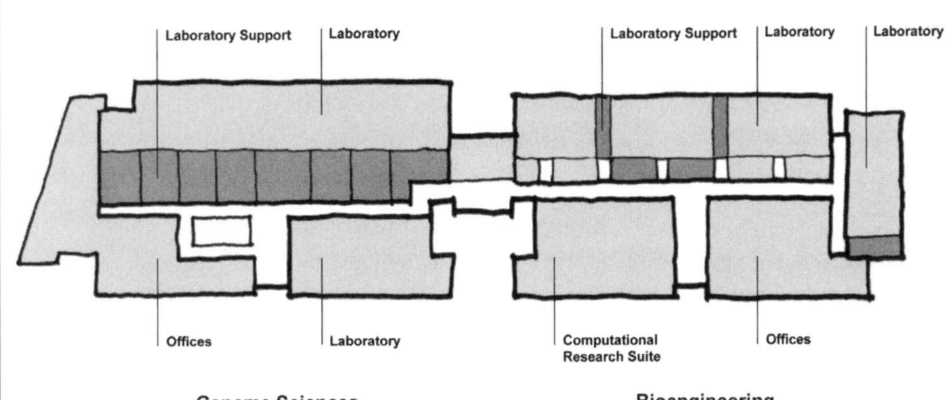

Figure 6.8 Laboratory plan.

▸ *Figure 6.9 Flexible Laboratory Systems.* Lara Swimmer, Photographer.

genome research, dedicated areas in the laboratory support zone contain even higher levels of engineering infrastructure—power, data, and cooling—creating "hot zones," a planning strategy that promotes long-term flexibility for the research mission.

A unique characteristic of this project is its abundance of core facilities. These cores are located in the basement level and are shared resources for this building and the School of Medicine. These include a 20,000 sq ft vivarium and a data center.

TEACHING/LEARNING FACILITIES

A better learning environment equates to positive outcomes that prepare students for jobs demanding analytical ability, creativity, and familiarity with new technologies. Experiential, hands-on teaching methods educate the next generation of workers to be flexible, adaptable, and able to respond to changing economic and technological circumstances. This corresponds with trends that indicate students want to be active participants in their learning experience, rather than passive recipients of course material. This calls for interactive and technology-laden instruction that offers innovative hands-on learning in the science disciplines.

The power of interdisciplinary learning lies in students' abilities to solve problems by taking information and processes from multiple disciplines and integrating them into a unique solution. This is why interdisciplinary teaching and research is one of the fastest-growing trends in science, technology, engineering, arts, and mathematics (STEAM) pedagogy. These approaches teach students how to "think outside the box" and

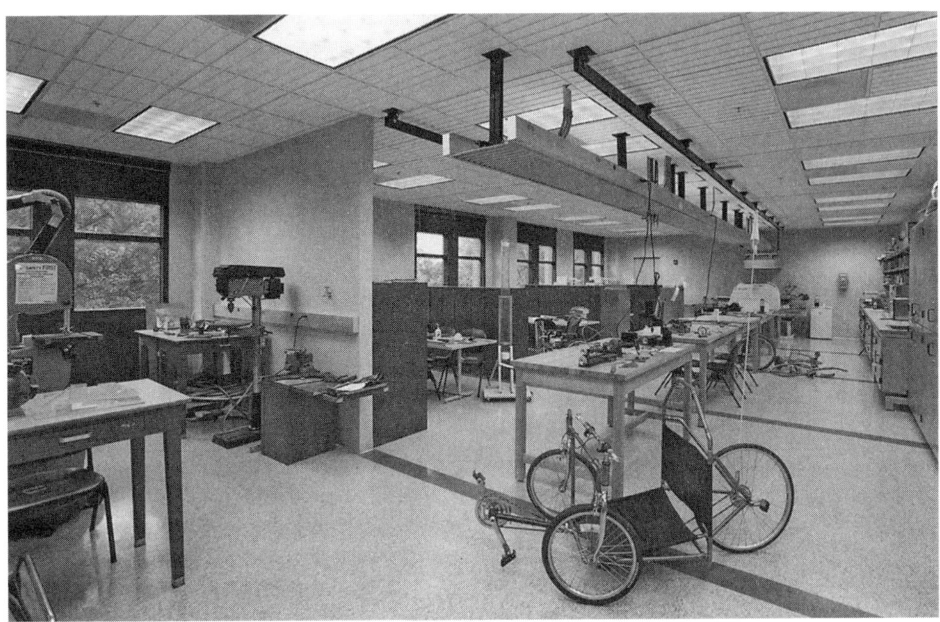

◀ *Figure 6.10 Breaking barriers between space types. Engineering Student Projects Laboratory, University of Kentucky.*

how to solve real-world problems. The challenge for architects is to create learning environments that foster thinking that transcends traditional disciplinary boundaries (see Figure 6.10).

The primary goal of the building design is to *increase* opportunities for interaction among faculty and students and to create non-traditional spaces that promote the frequency of "effective intellectual collisions" among all building users.

Traditionally, the laboratory is the place where science "happens." However, it is important to remember that much discovery in science happens when scientists, both faculty and students, are thinking about their projects or working out solutions with colleagues outside of the laboratory. The new buildings should redefine the notion of the "laboratory." Although the laboratory bench is the place to conduct experiments and acquire data, much scientific learning should take place away from the bench. For higher-level science curricula, this starts by moving individual student workstations outside the laboratory and consolidating them into easily accessible adjacent spaces in areas that have high student traffic. This arrangement has a practical advantage: it reduces the amount of "wet lab" space that needs to be maintained, heated, and ventilated, resulting in an overall reduction in operating costs. Conceptually, it creates a comfortable and inviting space that enables students to sit down outside of the formal and restrictive lab bench and discuss scientific concepts and ideas (see Figure 6.11).

The traditional teaching lab and lecture halls are no longer the only effective spaces for entry- and lower-level students. An ever-increasing body of research shows that traditional lecture-style learning environments are not effective for all students. Teaching methods have developed varied learning methodologies and technologies, such as group, problem-based, distance,

▶ *Figure 6.11 Wisconsin Institutes for Discovery, University of Wisconsin, Madison.* Ballinger Architects.

and virtual reality. For all students, the emergence of spaces like student group rooms and learning studios have demanded technology-intensive programs that incorporate wireless networks, distance learning, videoconferencing, classrooms wired at each seat, multimedia technology, and web streaming (see Figures 6.12 and 6.13, Color Plate 11).

A survey conducted by the EDUCAUSE Center for Applied Research (ECAR) of approximately 30,000 students at 100 universities produced results that illustrate that new science buildings require design solutions that support these new learning paradigms. The survey revealed that students want immediate access to real data and expect information technology to be integrated into all aspects of the learning process. They want sufficient table space for a variety of information technology tools, and they prefer integrated laboratory facilities. Having access to faculty members and experts is equally important to them. The need for social space, including access to small-group work spaces, shared screens, and work group facilitation, also ranked high on the list of expectations.

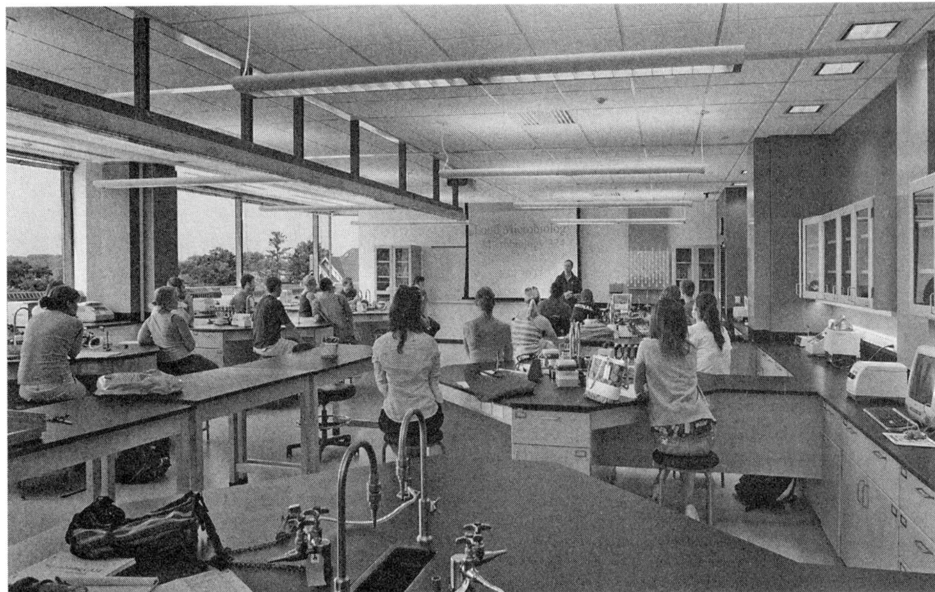

◀ *Figure 6.12 Teaching/learning facilities, University of Wisconsin, Madison.* © Robert Canfield Photography.

◀ *Figure 6.13 Technology Enabled, Problem Based Learning Studio, School of Medicine, University of Virginia, Charlottesville.*

INTERDISCIPLINARY RESEARCH FACILITIES
CASE STUDY 3

LIFE SCIENCES CENTER
Loyola Marymount University, Los Angeles, California

The Life Sciences Center at Loyola Marymount University (LMU) is a 110,000 GSF state-of-the-art science facility with three levels of subterranean parking. It is designed to house teaching laboratories, research laboratories, laboratory support spaces, faculty offices, classrooms, shared public spaces, and a large auditorium. As the first new building for the Seaver College of Science and Engineering in many decades, this high-profile project will not only establish new standards for undergraduate science education but will also contribute to the establishment of new building and site standards for the entire LMU campus.

Five main project objectives were established to guide the design team throughout all phases of the project:

1. Create a new, state-of-the-art science center on campus.
2. Promote interdisciplinary collaboration between the fields of science, their faculty and students, and researchers.
3. Promote sustainability throughout the design, construction, and life of the building.
4. Foster indoor and outdoor connectivity.
5. Use the building as a teaching tool for sustainable practices and other learning experiences through "science on display" design.

Campus-Scale Planning

The LMU master plan proposes that the campus become an assembly of courtyards connected via a series of pedestrian-oriented walks and allées. To respond to this concept, the new building and adjacent Seaver Hall defines a central courtyard. The notion of the courtyard—and, by implication, the indoor-outdoor relationship of the Southern California lifestyle—is extended up the building by way of a planted roof, which connects all three floors of the building. A passageway, overlaid on the site, maintains a pedestrian route between existing science buildings and creates an entry point from the adjacent campus roadway. The building program is thus split around the entryway into two primary structures: an academic wing and a public pavilion.

The "front door" to the building is off the courtyard and is further defined by a 3-story, L-shaped building comprising the academic program spaces. Articulated as a glazed atrium housing the primary circulation stair and study spaces, the entry and first floor glazed areas are conceived as an 80 ft door that opens at the ground floor to promote indoor-outdoor connectivity and provide natural ventilation for the interior double-loaded corridor. The building is topped by a large trellis system, which serves to disguise mechanical equipment and support solar panels.

The northern pavilion houses the 292-seat auditorium under a green roof. A 2-story exterior lobby provides access to the auditorium and a second-floor terrace, which provides two more access points to the rear of the auditorium. As a university-wide amenity, the building connects directly to a palm walk proposed in the master plan (see Figure 6.14).

The three-level subterranean garage underneath the building contains approximately 370 parking spaces for faculty, students, and staff and is accessed off the main circulation drive at the northeast corner of the site.

Figure 6.14 Exterior.

Collaborative Environments

One important driver in the development of this science facility is the need for a rich array of collaborative environments. As previously stated, research has shown activities outside the laboratory—casual exchange, poster sessions, and display—and places that accommodate them, such as cafés and soft seating, are critically important to cultivating a sense of discovery and learning. Therefore, the building's circulation systems promote connectivity, openness, and spatial experience, and work in conjunction with formal teaching laboratories and student-faculty research spaces. The building's main entry is conceived as a place where students will gather before or after class. To promote connections to the landscape and take advantage of the mild climate, four vertically articulated doors allow the front door and entry to open directly onto the court and promote pedestrian movement between the building and the garden, creating a unique spatial experience. The primary vertical circulation stair rises to the upper floors of the building from this main entry and gathering point and can be easily seen through the large expanse of glass curtain wall that rises 3 stories adjacent to the stairway.

The primary circulation system is a generous double-loaded corridor that is wide enough to accommodate the influx of students during cyclical class changes. Designed as a kind of internal street, it connects laboratories, classrooms, and faculty offices as well as study areas, support spaces, and a large connective stair. This corridor is suffused with natural light and views to the campus.

"Science on display" is an important concept that teaches and illustrates scientific principles through the use of artwork and architectural features placed throughout the building. On the first floor, large windows allow for direct sight lines into the laboratories (see Figure 6.15). This direct connection between the public realm and the semiprivate laboratory space will enhance knowledge of laboratory activities for students and visitors. Another benefit of the open sight lines is that faculty and staff will have an "eyes-on" view of all laboratories throughout the day.

One unique characteristic of this project is its green roof ramp. This elongated, sloped plane extends from grade at the central courtyard up to level 3, with a connection at level 2. It is a combination of intensive and extensive planting systems and will define areas for pedestrian circulation. Plantings include sedums, succulents and low meadow grasses or drought tolerant lawn grasses, and will contain science demonstration gardens that support the center's teaching mission. Its lower portion includes an informal amphitheatre with pavement and seat walls integrated into the planted roof. The roof edge extends into the landscape at grade, thereby anchoring the landscape with the adjacent courtyard.

Figure 6.15 Science on display.

Interdisciplinary Lab Concepts

The new science center is organized to intentionally blur traditional departmental boundaries. It was determined early in the planning process that all introductory curriculum classrooms would be located on the first floor of the building to facilitate the large number of students who pass through these classrooms on a daily basis. Both the general biology and the chemistry classrooms are located at the northern end of the building to promote cross-disciplinary interest and interaction and to consolidate laboratory support for the sharing of stockroom services.

Faculty offices are located on levels 2 and 3, adjacent to casual seating and study areas, and are positioned to be open and welcoming to the internal corridor system. They are anchored on both the north and the south ends of the floor plate. To further interdisciplinary interaction, administrative support is centralized on the ground floor.

Both teaching and research laboratories are interchangeably located on the outer perimeter of the floor plate. The principle of collocating research and teaching labs promotes greater interaction of student and faculty. An added benefit is greater flexibility and utilization over time.

Evolving Role of Laboratory Support

Laboratory support is distributed on all three levels and is organized to be directly accessible to adjacent teaching and research laboratories. A small, shared vivarium suite is located at the basement level directly accessed by a service elevator. Other support spaces include stockrooms, freezer farms, and instrumentation suites.

It is also important to allow students and faculty from different academic disciplines to mix. Locating traditional disciplines on separate floors is not conducive to the interdisciplinary mission. Larger floor plates, communicating public stairs, transparency, and technology help balance the need for integrating multiple departments and emerging problem-based centers of focus within the curriculum. In addition to potential in-lab problem-based activities that achieve this, the new building programs include several study and "social spaces," designed to be comfortable, welcoming, and accessible to everyone. A "town center" provides a major gathering space, while others are spread throughout the building at locations where students and faculty are likely to gravitate. Therefore, these spaces conceptually expand the "laboratory space" beyond the laboratory bench to the student study areas and the social spaces that exist throughout the building (see Figure 6.16).

The concept of "science on display" leads to features such as exhibition spaces and views into classrooms and labs, and even incorporates scientific-based features into the architecture, engineering, and surrounding landscape. In addition, high-tech auditoriums, virtual-reality rooms, and conference rooms are capable of fully immersing students and visitors of all disciplines into the work at hand.

RESEARCH FACILITIES

As research needs and their related facilities become more complex and specialized, and research changes become more frequent, institutions tend to set aside their long-range plans for ad hoc initiatives. However, planning new research facilities for the long-term and wide-ranging needs of interdisciplinary science will quickly pay off because future renovations will be easily accommodated. As a result, long-range planning methodologies to manage life-cycle cost control, facility flexibility, and evolving research requirements are well worth the time and consideration of both scientific and facility leaders. The new generation of research facilities can contribute to solving growth-related issues such as disparity and inefficiency. Interdisciplinary research buildings are often seen as scientific town centers with social interaction spaces such as restaurants and conferencing centers with breakout rooms, as well as technical interaction components such as scientific cores shared by institutional users. These are features that attract building occupants as well as the larger institutional population. As research programs expand faster than the supporting infrastructure, scientific and facility leaders must come up with new solutions to accommodate them in existing research facilities. Attempts to resolve these issues include increasing lab automation, sharing

◀ *Figure 6.16 Town center/ Main Street, Health Sciences Education Building, University of Arizona, Phoenix. ©* Timmerman Photography.

equipment and labs, and experimenting with alternative work arrangements. The design of the new interdisciplinary research building responds to the same issues more effectively by employing the previously described concepts of centralized core resources, collaborative work environments, and flexibility contained in an energy-efficient package.

Integrating research from varied disciplines that typically have not previously worked together can be a difficult logistical task for scientific leaders. Close proximity of participants is clearly necessary to foster the most effective collaboration. However, simply co-locating or grouping these disparate programs is not enough. Spaces must *encourage* interaction. Placing people, labs, and amenities around pleasant, light-filled spaces is essential to fostering this interaction. Truly collaborative spaces begin with open, shared, and flexible laboratories and extend to individual work spaces for lab workers. These workstations, traditionally inside the lab, are now more effective as adjacent, open, office-like environments, allowing food and drink, with more comfortable spaces provided for write-up and computational activities as well as conversations between co-workers.

Private offices, group workrooms, and high-tech conferencing facilities are located in close proximity along common travel paths. The next level of collaborative spaces include amenities that attract the larger scientific population, such as comfortable group seating areas, cafés and restaurants, lobbies, open stairs and atriums, and larger multimedia auditoriums. Researchers inside labs should have the opportunity to be inspired by chance intellectual exchanges with those working in other environments through these soft, pleasant social spaces (see Figure 6.17).

Another trend is a move toward larger floor plates, which accommodate a larger population per floor and allow a high level of transparency between space types through the use of glass walls. Internal transparency is critical to larger floor plates, and their higher cost is offset by less exterior facade area. The gain is a highly collaborative environment that still meets safety and security needs. And, transparency allows landlocked interior spaces to borrow natural light from those at the perimeter.

Shared research cores are simply a means of leveraging capital and operational costs as well as the space needed across a greater number of users. Cores include specialized spaces, equipment, and/or processes that are too demanding for a single research program to support. They may be as small as a single piece of equipment or as complex as an entire vivarium. With the emergence of many new areas of research and the rapid advancement of high-technology solutions to traditional problems, the opportunity for the effective use of cores is so great that some institutions have created entire facilities that house only research cores. Strategic, institutional perspective on the development of these cores can directly benefit a large number of individual research programs, and their location will bring varied users to a common setting and promote scientific collaboration.

▸ *Figure 6.17 Social spaces, University of Texas, Austin. All laboratories and offices open onto atrium and outdoor terrace, allowing year-round gathering.* © Tom Bonner.

Research programs experiencing rapid growth, such as bioengineering, nanotechnology, and biofuels, demand highly specialized equipment with above-average requirements for power, water, environmental control, vibration, portability, and technical support. This growth and evolution also equates to rapid changes in scientific equipment and frequent lab modifications, making facility flexibility of utmost importance. Flexibility is necessary because change is inevitable. More facilities are using mixed-reality environments where research is conducted in both the physical world and the virtual world, each of which requires specialized lab space. The recent trend toward generic lab space is being overshadowed by the growing need to support engineering applications, imaging, biocontainment, computational science, nanotechnology, rapid prototyping, small-scale industrial processes, and other specialized functions. The impact of automation and miniaturization means individual pieces of high-cost, high-throughput equipment are replacing large generic spaces for performing many routine tasks by people at a bench. Although the generic lab remains a necessary component, it must be carefully programmed to accommodate the varied mainstream needs of research programs, while balancing the need for specialty research spaces. Flexible, adaptable structural spaces and engineered systems must be appropriate for both generic and specialty spaces. These systems must have a robust capacity and be easy to access for upgrades and maintenance.

One effective strategy for future flexibility is to design a percentage of research labs as generic space with a limited range of flexibility to accommodate most needs. The remaining percentage can then be designed as highly flexible and more capable of performing a wider range of specialized functions. The balance of these percentages must be carefully considered. Striking the right balance can also optimize the cost of the interdisciplinary facility, whereas a 100 percent flexible building may be prohibitively expensive for many institutions.

Another approach to achieving flexibility in interdisciplinary research buildings is "just-in-time" programming and design. This can avoid disparity between early programming needs and the actual construction project, which is typically completed years after the planning and design process. "Just-in-time" simply means performing detailed programming and design of spaces at the last possible date to ensure that additional changes or renovations will not already be needed on move-in day. To achieve just-in-time programming, architects design a generic, flexible facility and finalize detailed programming just before procurement of the fit-out elements toward the end of construction. The additional costs incurred by this method are justified in a life-cycle cost analysis by savings on move-in day renovations and a better fit. This approach is effective to a degree, but often it cannot accommodate as many specialty research needs.

In all approaches, the goal is constant: consider the future needs of the building and create a facility that will be functional for many years, even as its program changes.

INTERDISCIPLINARY RESEARCH FACILITIES CASE STUDY 4

NORMAN HACKERMAN EXPERIMENTAL SCIENCE BUILDING

University of Texas, Austin

The new Experimental Science Building (ESB) replaced the existing, obsolete ESB, which was located on the same site and completely demolished. The new ESB comprises 284,000 GSF and 156,000 ASF, providing for an integrated and interdisciplinary approach to education, research, and development for the College of Natural Sciences, including Neuroscience, the Center for Learning and Memory, and Organic Chemistry Teaching and Research. The facility will fulfill the college's new initiatives in curricular mission as well as academic goals for growth. The college will also provide advanced infrastructure to serve current and future programs with sophisticated and technologically advanced core facilities that will serve the larger campus research community.

Campus-Scale Planning

The location of the ESB immediately adjacent to the campus's original 40 acres complies with the primary objective of the campus master plan by increasing the density of the existing core campus. It reinforces the existing quality of the campus by maintaining existing pedestrian pathways around and through the site. The site occupies a strategically and physically important urban location on the overall campus and within the College of Natural Sciences precinct: it represents the last major opportunity to build a new science facility of any significance in this location.

The design responds to and reflects this context in terms of form, scale, massing, materials, and proportion, as well as how it meets the sloping ground plane, touches the sky, and relates to its architectural neighbors. It also contributes to and interacts with its campus context to enhance the public realm and quality of the external environment, especially the new pedestrian mall, while the existing urban scale and ambience of 24th Street provide an elegant and appropriate foreground setting for the new building (see Figure 6.18).

Organized into a 500 ft long narrow bar, the building's shape is dictated by site development constraints such as setbacks and limitations imposed by the position of adjacent buildings and streets. The building is 6 stories, with a mechanical penthouse and a basement level. This vertical organization allows public access at the first floor, while creating the ability to control access to upper research floors and the basement-level core facilities.

Collaborative Environments

Two atriums are located at strategic positions to provide informal meeting and interaction spaces and to access views and bring natural light into the center of this very large building. The central atrium is located proximate to research laboratories and office spaces with an adjacent open stairwell to promote communication between floor levels. A second atrium at the east end of the building opens onto a landscaped terrace overlooking the pedestrian mall (see Figure 6.19). Each of the atriums is appointed with casual seating and whiteboards, and supported by glass-enclosed conference rooms and a break room for casual interaction and engagement to provide respite from the intensity of the research environment.

Figure 6.18 Exterior. © Tom Bonner.

Figure 6.19 Casual interaction space. © Tom Bonner.

In conjunction with research and teaching laboratories, the ESB contains a range of small, medium, and large conferencing spaces, including a 130-seat seminar room with flat floor and movable seating. Additional small meeting rooms are specifically designed and located adjacent to faculty offices to facilitate drop-ins and unscheduled meetings.

Interdisciplinary Lab Concepts

The ESB is an example of a highly flexible, interdisciplinary research building that can accommodate a broad range of research, from computation and neurosciences to wet chemistry, within the same planning depth, readily allowing reconfiguration of space and changes in use over time (see Figure 6.20).

The building contains 250 fume hoods, primarily in the chemistry research and teaching laboratories, providing the building's infrastructure with significant capacity that can be easily accessed from walk-in mechanical shafts with internal catwalks that enable maintenance and replacement without significant disruption to ongoing research.

Neuroscience laboratories are interdisciplinary, team-based research environments that are configured into various combinations of wet bench, write-up, computation, team meeting, and electrophysiology setups, all within a single laboratory.

Evolving Role of Laboratory Support

Laboratory support characteristics between neurosciences and chemistry are very different, but both disciplines require a 1:1 ratio of laboratory support to laboratory space. Chemistry laboratories are supported by dry and wet instrument rooms opening onto a common equipment

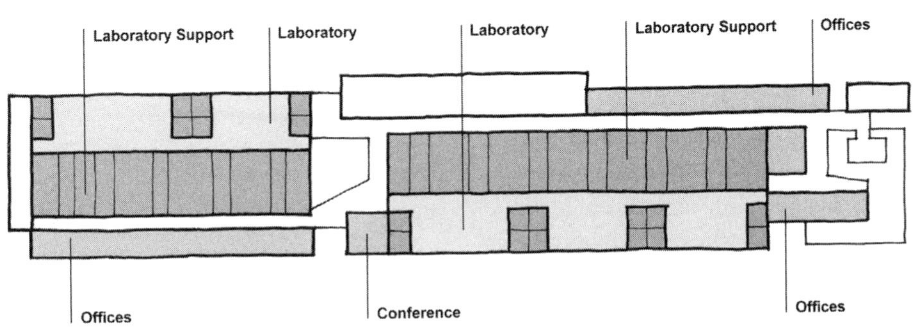

Figure 6.20 Floor plan.

galley that also provides access to dedicated workrooms for graduate students, with direct visual access to and from the open lab. Neurosciences is supported by highly flexible, open areas separated by blackout curtains, allowing controlled light experiments in areas of various sizes.

Core laboratories supporting neurosciences and chemistry include a large vivarium, a nuclear magnetic resonance (NMR) facility, a magnetic resonance imaging (MRI) facility, and an electron microscopy core facility. They are located in the basement, which has a floor height of 25 ft, allowing maintenance access to all areas from an overhead catwalk within a full-height interstitial floor, without interrupting ongoing activities or affecting operational protocols for cleanliness.

PLANNING BUILDING INFRASTRUCTURE FOR INTERDISCIPLINARY SCIENCE

Many of the fundamental technical and engineering issues that one should consider for the programming and design of a laboratory building are detailed in the first edition of *Building Types Basics for College and University Facilities* by David J. Neuman. This section will expand on those considerations as they specifically influence the programming and design of leading-edge interdisciplinary research or teaching laboratory buildings, and discuss innovations that have emerged since the publication of that book, especially in the area of energy efficiency and sustainability.

Interdisciplinary research places unique demands on the design of a building's infrastructure. These demands should be addressed as early as possible in the design process, beginning at the programming phase, so that all stakeholders fully understand and agree on the implications of their decisions to future research. Ideally, an interdisciplinary science building contains infrastructure to allow disparate types of research activities to be co-located anywhere so as to generate synergies of thought and ideas. These should be easily reconfigurable over time to house different methods of research and teaching, many of which are unknown and cannot even be anticipated.

Many approaches and solutions provide various levels of flexibility and adaptability, which ultimately must be balanced against cost. Some examples are illustrated in the case studies, and others are described below. It is important to recognize that these solutions are the result of a methodology and approach that begins during programming and that the success of the final result depends on this rigorous effort. It is also worth noting that MEP systems offer the greatest opportunity for supporting those synergies, but also the greatest challenges to balance the constraints of first costs, operational costs, and future renovation costs, and so must be carefully considered from the outset.

The various approaches begin with the following questions:

- Can the general direction of research be anticipated?
- Are the themes of research already identified?
- Are the users of the building currently identified?
- Is the priority maximizing flexibility or maximizing space?

Laboratories

Perhaps the most difficult aspect of programming the infrastructure of an interdisciplinary science building is anticipating the future types of research that may eventually take place in the building. This is challenging enough when the general type of research and research teams are already known, but more so when potential users have not been recruited, or specific directions of research defined. This is especially the case with interdisciplinary research, whose purpose is to bring together groups who do not usually work together to generate new ideas and, sometimes, new and emerging fields of funded research. However, a number of strategies can be applied from the outset.

Zoning Services by Lab Type

Generally more suited to the team-based open labs required for biomedical, biochemical, neuroscience, and computational work, this zoning method accommodates various types of labs within the same footprint, so they can be relocated over time, if adequate supporting utilities are provided.

- *Themes of research.* The programming process starts by creating a chart that matches various themes of research that may be anticipated for a building and the disciplines that are generally needed to support those themes (see Figure 6.21).
- *Laboratory types.* The next step is to associate the research disciplines identified previously with the various laboratory types needed to support those activities, recognizing that more than one type is usually needed for any discipline (see Figure 6.22). While most laboratories share common characteristics set out by modular planning and flexibility strategies, they are differentiated not only by the actual activity but also by the infrastructure (power, piped gases, specialty water, telecom) and the special equipment (fume hoods, biosafety cabinets, etc.) particular to that research. Ranging from most to least expensive, they are often categorized as "wet" (chemistry), "damp" (biomedical), and "dry" (computational).
- *Scenario modeling.* Using this information, it is then possible to model

THEMES OF RESEARCH

	UA COM				UA COP	ASU	
SUPPORTING DISCIPLINES	Cancer Biology	Cardiovascular Disease	Neurological Disorders	Diabetes	Medical Chemistry	Cancer Biology	Cardiovascular Disease
Genomics	●	●	●	●	●	●	●
Proteomics	●	●	●	●	●	●	●
Biomedical Informatics	●	●	●	●	●	●	●
Pharmacogenomics					●		
Pharmacogenetics					●		
Molecular Biology	●				●	●	
Systems Biology	●	●		●		●	●
Synthetic Biology	●	●				●	●
Biomedical Engineering	●	●		●		●	●
Virology	●	●				●	●
Immunology	●			●		●	
Microbiology					●		
Biochemistry					●		
Neuroscience			●				
Electrophysiology			●				

◀ *Figure 6.21 Themes of research.*

▸ *Figure 6.22* Laboratory types.

LABORATORY TYPES

MEDICAL RESEARCH DISCIPLINE	WET			DAMP		DRY	
	Chemistry Hood Sensitive	Biochemistry Pharmacology	Biomedical Wet Bench	Flexible Wet/Dry Zoning	Instrumentation	Computation	Engineering
Molecular & Cellular Biology		●	●		●	●	
Genomics				●	●		
Proteomics				●		●	
Biomedical Informatics				●		●	
Pharmacogenics				●		●	
Pharmacokinetics				●		●	
Medicial Chemistry		●				●	
Systems Biology			●	●		●	
Neuro-Biology			●	●	●	●	
Synthetic Chemistry	●			●	●	●	
Toxicology		●					
Computational Biology		●	●		●	●	
Computational Chemistry			●		●	●	
Virology		●	●			●	
Immunology		●	●				
Metabolic Biology			●				
Biomolecular Engineering		●		●			●
Nano-scaled Research	●						●

"what-if" scenarios, build out the program with various combinations of laboratory types, and model the potential construction cost proportionally.

Zoning of Services for Flexible Activities

This approach provides a highly flexible, highly adaptable service platform that can change over time, and it allows for a wide variety of activities, even within a single lab, with disparate and sometimes incompatible activities in adjacent labs. This approach is generally more suited to the physical science, computation, and engineering disciplines, with their many hybridizations (e.g., bioengineering, biofuels, and nanobiology).

Scientific Capacity

Aggregating a variety of types proportionally within a single building establishes the building's scientific capacity, which can be defined as the range of research activities that can be supported over time by the building's utility infrastructure and physical characteristics. An effective strategy for future flexibility is to design approximately 70 percent of the building for the anticipated laboratory types. The remaining 30 percent can then be designed as highly flexible space, which is capable of performing a wider range of specialized functions.

Collaborative Relationships

Breaking down traditional barriers between scientific activities, laboratories, and collaborative working and instructional environments has implications for MEP systems and energy use. The desire to combine varied uses into a single space should be weighed against the higher cost of constructing and operating non-laboratory space as accredited laboratory space, along with potential safety and security concerns associated with locating research staff from nonrelated fields within areas where they may lack adequate training in safety protocols.

There is no right or wrong solution or one approach that is necessarily better than another. It is more important to define goals, culture, and budget, and build an infrastructure that supports them. The following three examples illustrate a range of MEP infrastructure solutions that support interdisciplinary research in very different ways.

1. *Universal flexibility: James H. Clark Center, Stanford University.* In contrast to the closed rooms and corridors of a traditional laboratory facility, the Clark Center is open and flexible: external balconies replace internal corridors, and laboratory layouts can be reconfigured at will (see Figures 6.23 and 6.24). All benches and desks are mounted on wheels and can be moved to allow ad hoc team formation to respond easily to fast-evolving research needs. This versatility is further enabled by workstations that plug into an overhead utility grid system of exposed services and flexible connections. This approach, which enables people with diverse skills and needs to work together nearly anywhere, also has a cost premium, because it provides a nearly uniform distribution of services to all locations, whether used for offices or laboratories. While the open interior environment is stimulating, it can also be considered

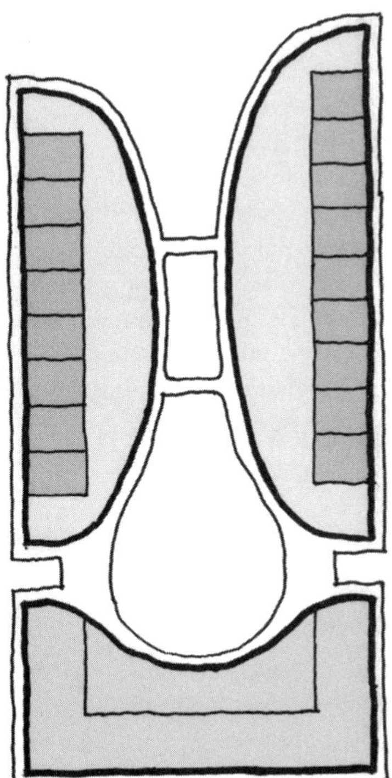

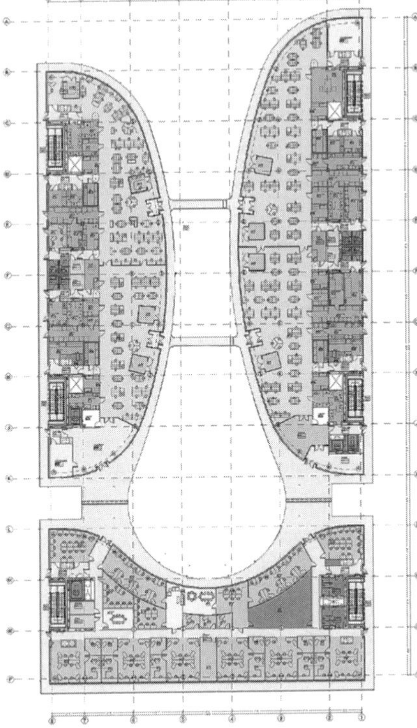

Figure 6.23 "Universal Flexibility": Floor Plan—Clark Center, Stanford University, Stanford, California.

▸ *Figure 6.24 "Universal Flexibility": Typical Laboratory—Clark Center, Stanford University, Stanford, California.*

somewhat disruptive due to the lack of acoustical privacy between research groups and noise from research equipment residing within the general work space. The spaces can be highly collaborative but not necessarily interdisciplinary. This is dependent on the management structure.

2. *Specialized and customized: Powell-Focht Bioengineering Hall, University of California, San Diego.* Due to the changeable and varied nature of bioengineering research, laboratories are distributed in flexible, generic planning modules that allow a great deal of customization to accommodate the specialized and unique needs of each individual researcher. The laboratory floors are organized in uninterrupted runs of 10 laboratory modules that also incorporate integral support (instrumentation) spaces. A heavy emphasis is placed on the provisions and capacities for engineering systems that serve the laboratories. The design of piped services, fume hood density, electrical capacity, and vibration resistance ensures that each laboratory can accommodate the broadest variety of research activities, ranging from computation to wet bench work, nuclear imaging, and benchtop nanofabrication. This is an interdisciplinary but not necessarily highly collaborative facility (see Figures 6.25 and 6.26).
3. *Innovative adjacencies: Wisconsin Institutes for Discovery, University of Wisconsin, Madison.* While this project provides a somewhat conventional range of office, laboratory, and laboratory support spaces, its innovation comes from the arrangement of these spaces within a very deep floor plate. Rather than a typical

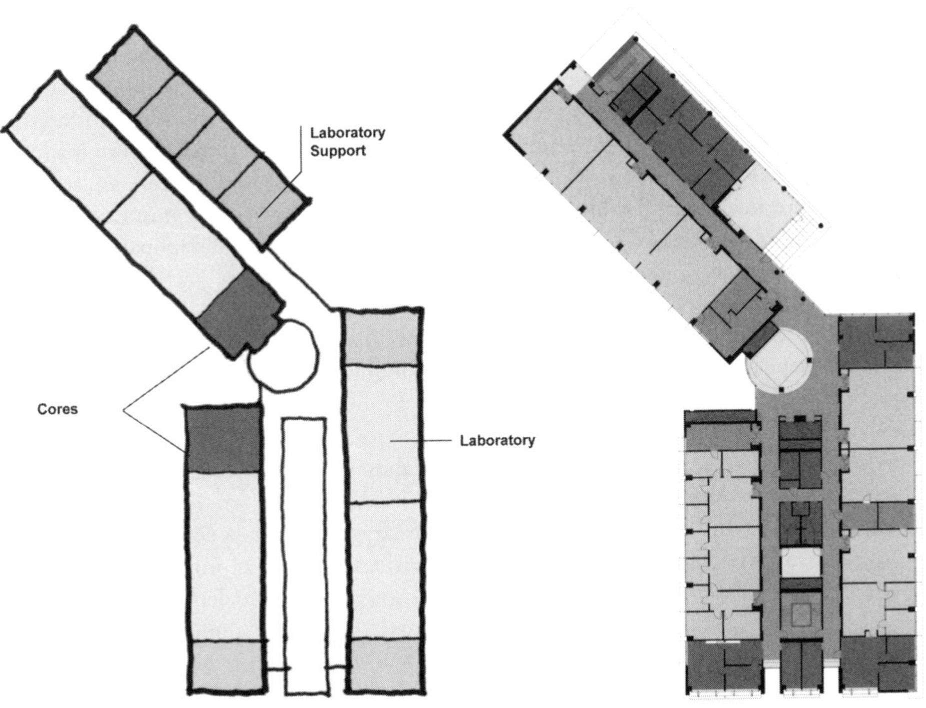

◀ *Figure 6.25 "Specialized and Customized": Floor Plan—Powell-Focht Bioengineering Hall, University of California, San Diego.*

◀ *Figure 6.26 "Specialized and Customized": Typical Laboratory—Powell-Focht Bioengineering Hall, University of California, San Diego.* © Robert Canfield Photography.

linear block of laboratories forming a corridor, the laboratories are broken up into three independent "pods," two wet and one dry, each with its own associated lab support space. Offices and research assistant workstations occupy the "in-between" space in a highly flexible open-office floor plan that serves double duty as circulation and meeting space, thus increasing opportunities for chance encounters between research teams. Each pod is independently served with its own rooftop mechanical system and shafts, allowing the open office and meeting area to have a separate, conventional HVAC system, which reduces operational costs and energy use. This is a highly collaborative, potentially interdisciplinary facility (see Figures 6.27 and 6.28).

Laboratory Planning Principles: Flexible and Adaptable Infrastructure

While the programming strategies described above can help delineate the potential uses and supporting infrastructure needed on day one, any modern laboratory building must be flexible and adaptable to changes in those uses over time. While the life cycle of the building structure should extend to 50 years, its mechanical and electrical systems should be expected to last 20–25 years, and its telecommunications systems approximately 10 years. Systems with the shortest life spans should be the most accessible, both for routine maintenance and for future replacement. Proven strategies for ensuring flexible infrastructure for interdisciplinary research include the following:

- *Modular planning.* The foundation of laboratory design rests on the concept of modular planning, which defines a "module" as the basic building block of laboratory space, consisting of two workbenches or write-up areas facing each other across a common access aisle, taking up approximately 11 ft (see Figure 6.29). The depth of the laboratory is generally a multiple of this dimension, allowing their recombination into a variety of room sizes, with a typical single laboratory module defined as 11 × 33 ft and accommodating anywhere from two to six researchers, while smaller laboratory support spaces usually range in size from a third to half of a module.
- *Scalability.* Laboratory modules can be combined into "laboratory units" that

▸ *Figure 6.27 "Innovative Adjacencies": Floor Plan—Wisconsin Institutes for Discovery, University of Wisconsin, Madison.*

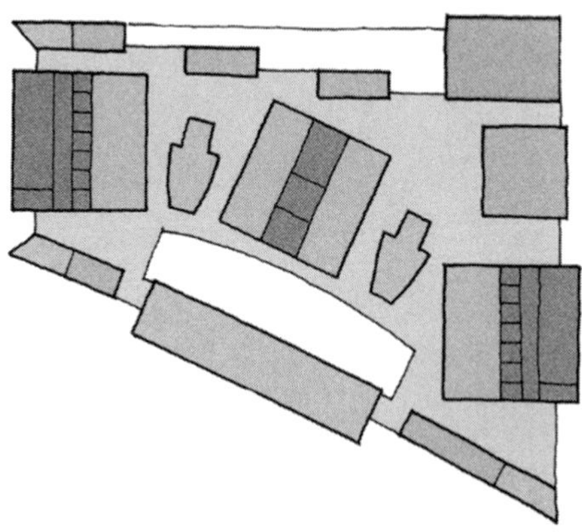

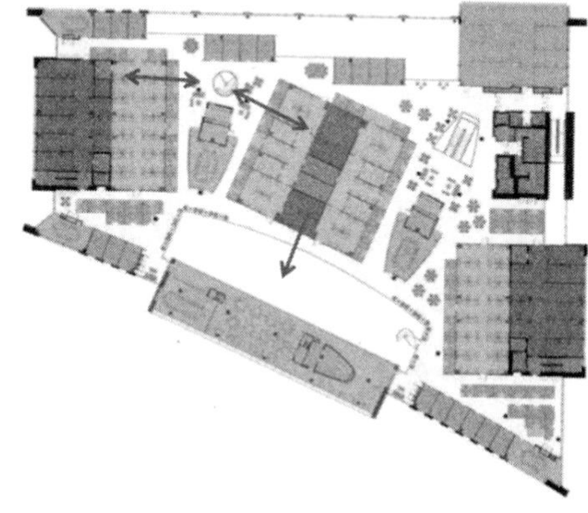

◀ *Figure 6.28 "Innovative Adjacencies": Typical laboratory—Wisconsin Institutes for Discovery, University of Wisconsin, Madison. Ballinger Architects.*

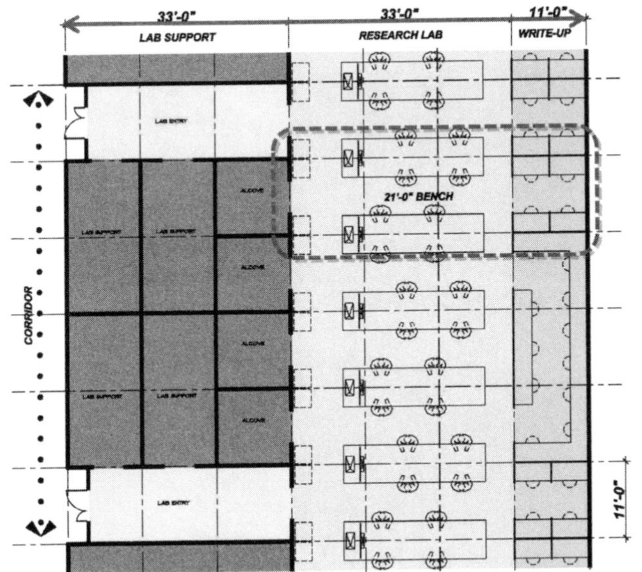

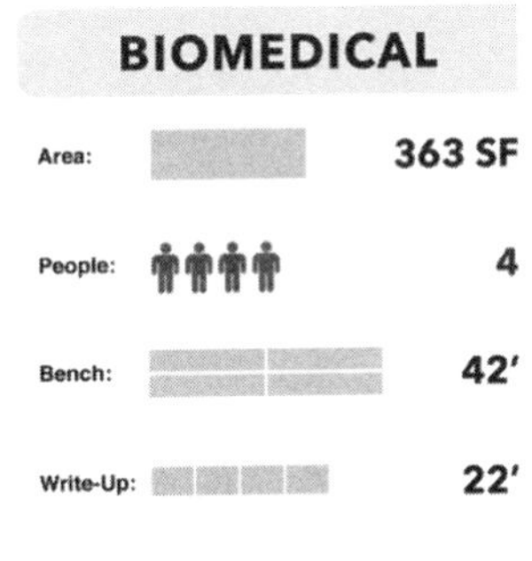

Image Courtesy of: Research Facilities Design

◀ *Figure 6.29 Modular planning – Biomedical laboratory.*

serve the needs of a variety of activities. Research laboratory units generally range from one or two module start-up labs, to three or four module labs for established teams, while a five-module instructional lab unit can accommodate 28–30 students. Similarly, the piped, power, and data systems serving laboratories and support spaces can be economically and efficiently distributed by providing a single point of service to each laboratory unit, with shutoff valves or electrical disconnects. This allows the utilities in one lab unit to be shut off for maintenance or renovation without disrupting activities in neighboring spaces.

- *Dedicated utility pathways.* It is essential that all utilities be accessible over the life of the building. Dedicating pathways from the shaft or utility closet to the laboratory, combined with careful coordination during design and construction using building information modeling (BIM), enables utilities to be combined into a common overhead service carrier that provides space for future growth and maintains zones for maintenance access (see Figure 6.30).
- *Accessible shafts.* Mechanical and piping shafts should be oversized by 20–30 percent to accommodate future growth and independent systems that may be needed over time to support special equipment or uses. Shafts should be carefully located so that they are accessible, and they should be provided with a full-sized door and internal catwalk to allow access by maintenance personnel and for renovation activities.

▸ *Figure 6.30 Dedicated utility pathways, College of Engineering, University of California, Santa Barbara.* © Robert Canfield Photography.

Flexibility within the Laboratory

A range of approaches within the laboratory provides increasing levels of flexibility, generally with an increase in associated cost:

- *Fixed systems.* For many laboratories, especially in higher education, a variety of space types often provides adequate flexibility to allow for fixed modular casework, which has the lowest initial cost, but highest cost of replacement (see Figure 6.31).
- *Flexible with a wrench.* The next level of flexibility uses modular metal casework systems and furnishings that have internal piping and power chases served from a single fixed point, and are demountable by maintenance staff using hand tools (see Figure 6.32).
- *Plug and play.* The most flexible, and most expensive, approach also uses modular metal casework systems, which are on wheels and can be moved by researchers. Utilities are provided from overhead chases suspended below the ceiling that are connected to the casework using flexible hoses with quick-disconnect fittings (see Figure 6.33).

Support Space

Support spaces commonly consist of small individual rooms containing noise- and heat-generating equipment that also have increasingly specialized MEP system requirements. These spaces include tissue culture rooms, cold rooms, dark rooms, server rooms, freezer farms, autoclaves, chemical storage, and imaging equipment. Their cellular nature does not facilitate interdisciplinary collaboration and sometimes requires restricted access to student research assistants when they cannot be visually supervised. One planning approach that addresses these

Figure 6.31 Fixed Systems: Experimental Sciences Building, Texas Tech University, Lubbock.

▸ *Figure 6.32 Flexible with a Wrench: College of Engineering, University of California, Santa Barbara.*

▸ *Figure 6.33 Plug and Play: College of Engineering, University of California, Santa Barbara.* © Robert Canfield Photography.

limitations is the "equipment galley," which locates freezers, centrifuges, instrumentation, and other benchtop equipment that can be shared by multiple research teams into a common linear aisle, often with windows to the adjacent laboratory, promoting safety and collaboration (see Figure 6.34).

Programming Support Space

Each laboratory type described previously requires some amount of support space. Benchmarking numerous facilities has revealed trends and ratios that can be helpful at the early programming phase to estimate the amount of support space that will be necessary (see Figure 6.35). These ratios show an ever-increasing amount of support space for biomedical laboratories, equal to and sometimes greater than the laboratories they support. In physical science, computation, and engineering (PSCE) research, the trend is nearly opposite, with specialized equipment becoming more affordable and located within the laboratory, which takes on the characteristics of a single, open support space with robust flexible infrastructure.

Support Space Infrastructure

Support space must not only serve diverse uses on opening day but also be flexible enough to enable changes in those uses over time. Strategies for ensuring flexibility within the support zone include:

- Increased vibration resistance of the building structure
- Localized cooling equipment such as heat pumps or chilled beams to supplement the main building HVAC system, which then does not need to be upsized to accommodate higher equipment loads in the support zone
- Separate electrical panels with medium and normal voltage dedicated to the support spaces

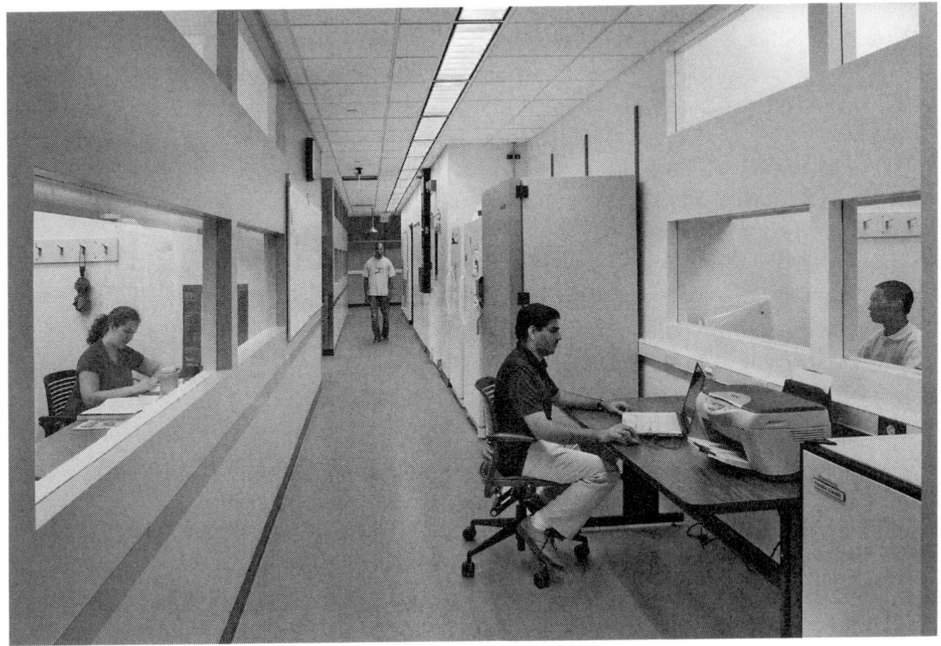

◀ *Figure 6.34 Equipment galley, Microbial Sciences Building, University of Wisconsin, Madison.* © Robert Canfield Photography.

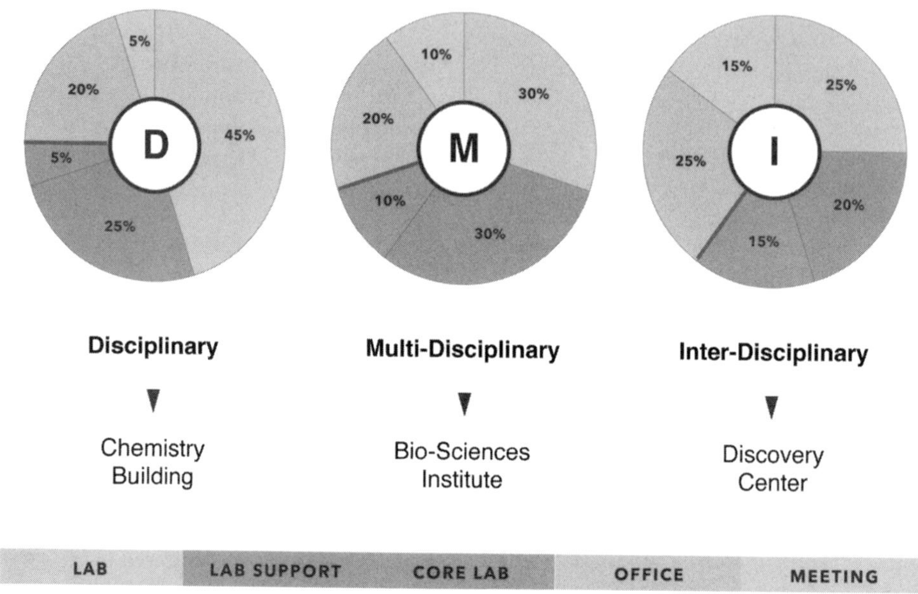

▸ *Figure 6.35 Benchmarking.*

- Overhead utility systems, including power, data, and process piping (water, gas, air, etc.)
- Modular wall systems that allow support rooms to be easily subdivided or enlarged
- Limited amounts of fixed benches and sinks, or designated special zones for fixed systems
- "Swing space," which is space within the general laboratory for additional services that can be readily changed to support space (see Case Study 2)

Core Laboratories

Core laboratories are categorized as laboratories containing highly specialized equipment that have unique and specific infrastructure requirements or other physical characteristics that make them more expensive to build than other laboratories. Because of this, they are often a shared amenity within either the building or the campus. With careful placement and planning, they offer excellent opportunities to facilitate interdisciplinary research because they can bring research groups out of their own laboratories and into a "research commons." Core laboratories fall into the following two broad categories.

Centralized Cores

Following the more traditional definition of core laboratories, centralized cores have special physical characteristics and infrastructure requirements that are difficult to provide on typical laboratory floors, including:

- *Imaging.* Nuclear magnetic resonance units, human and animal imaging, microscopy, chromatography, and other vibration-sensitive imaging and sensing equipment is most economically built on grade or in a basement on thickened concrete slabs, physically isolated from the rest of the building. Imaging cores often require special construction for radiation or electromagnetic frequency shielding, high-voltage power, localized cooling, and dedicated exhaust systems. They may also contain oversized, heavy instruments that require a high-bay space and/or special access for installation and replacement.

- *Data center.* Computation, file server, and storage racks are co-located for benefits of scale in a secured and environmentally controlled space. Redundant backup MEP systems (including multiple and specially dedicated chillers, transformers, uninterruptible power supply [UPS] systems, dry-chemical fire suppression, and leak detection systems) ensure survivability of research data.

Distributed Cores

These are highly specialized, purpose-built spaces that with careful planning can be built on typical laboratory floors, with the obvious advantage of providing dedicated collaboration space throughout the building.

- *Biocontainment.* Laboratories with biosafety levels (BSLs) of 1–3 require increasing levels of environmental and security isolation from other spaces as well as dedicated supply air and exhaust systems, often with their own duct shafts and special air filtration.
- *Imaging.* When considered early in the design stage, it is possible to provide many types of microscopy and other imaging equipment on typical laboratory floors by increasing the capacity of the building structure to resist vibration using stiffer floors or more columns.
- *High-throughput cell screening.* Equipment supporting genomics and proteomics research can rely on single, large pieces of expensive screening equipment or repetitive racks of small sequencing robots. They are often the easiest to locate on a typical laboratory floor, often within the laboratory support zone.

Programming Core Laboratories and Infrastructure

Because of their high cost and specialized infrastructure requirements, it is important to program core laboratories carefully to ensure that they are relevant to potential users and will be used at a rate that supports their investment. A number of programming tools can facilitate this process. Figure 6.36 shows a chart that matches various types of research laboratories programmed for a building with the types of core laboratories that are generally needed to support those activities. Another tool is to conduct a survey or inventory of existing core facilities located in surrounding buildings on the campus and within other collaborating research institutions. This can quickly bring to light gaps and overlaps in research capacity within the larger institution that can be filled by the new core laboratories, making the facility more attractive to a broader pool of researchers.

Estimating the infrastructure demand for new core laboratories can be challenging, given the diverse requirements of different core laboratories. Rapid developments in specialized technology, especially in imaging equipment, sometimes means that the equipment originally specified during design is replaced with a newer model before the building is even complete. For some owners, not all core laboratories required in a new

▸ *Figure 6.36 Programming core laboratory types.*

	CORE LABORATORY TYPES									
		IMAGING CORE								
Medical Research Discipline	Animal Facility	Microscopy	Spectroscopy	Chroma-tography	Neurological Imaging	High Throughput Cell Screeing	Data Center	Bio-Containment	HPLC	Clean Room
Molecular & Cellular Biology	x	x	x			x	x			
Genomics	x			x		x	x			
Proteomics	x			x		x	x			
Biomedical Informatics				x			x			
Pharmacogenomics	x			x		x	x			
Pharmacokinetics				x			x			
Medicinal Chemistry		x					x		x	
Systems Biology	x		x	x		x	x			
Neuro-Biology	x		x	x	x	x	x			
Synthetic Chemistry	x			x			x		x	
Toxicology	x	x				x	x	x		
Computational Biology		x	x				x			
Computational Chemistry			x				x			
Virology	x	x	x			x	x	x		
Immunology	x	x	x			x	x	x		
Metabolic Biology	x		x			x	x			
Biomolecular Engineering	x	x		x			x			x
Nano-scaled Research	x						x			x

facility are completely determined in advance (or are not affordable) and are not provided on opening day. Instead, shelled space is provided to allow future growth and development and provide additional flexibility.

Sustainable Design and Energy Efficiency

Since the publication of the first edition of *Building Type Basics for College and University Facilities*, many sustainable and energy conservation strategies have moved from the "leading edge" to become "state of the industry" and are now readily adopted in contemporary laboratory buildings, particularly in the current context of reducing operational costs. One leading organization promoting energy conservation is Labs21 from the Lawrence Berkeley National Laboratory. Its website (www.labs21century.gov) provides guides for best practices in design that outline numerous criteria that should be considered by the owner and design team at various stages of a project, as well as metrics for measuring their effectiveness.

The suitability of any strategy to a particular project will be affected by many factors, including local climate, cost of energy, and the like, and will require careful study by the design team. However, Labs21 outlines principles and approaches proven to be effective over a wide range of project types and locations and should be considered at the earliest stages of a project:

- *Right sizing.* MEP equipment is often oversized in the attempt to provide flexibility, which can increase energy consumption and diminish life-cycle economics. "Right sizing" applies the principle of diversity, which is the assumption that it is unlikely that all of a laboratory's equipment will be in operation at the same time. The percentages can be established through benchmarking against other projects from information provided by Labs21 or the design professional, and by taking actual meter readings of similar existing buildings on campus.

▲ *Color Plate 1 Arts Grounds plan, University of Virginia, Charlottesville. OLIN, Al Forrestor, Illustrator*

▶ *Color Plate 2 Aerial rendering of Masdar City, Nigel Young/Foster + Partners*

◀ Color Plate 3 View of Masdar Library, Nigel Young/Foster + Partners

▼ Color Plate 4 View of Masdar City, Nigel Young/Foster + Partners

▲ *Color Plate 5 Interior after rehabilitation—Garrett Hall, University of Virginia, Charlottesville. Architectural Resources Group*

▶ *Color Plate 6 Front facade after rehabilitation—Garrett Hall, University of Virginia, Charlottesville. Architectural Resources Group*

▲ *Color Plate 7 Interior Reading Room—Joe and Rika Mansueto Library, University of Chicago, Jason Smith © 2011 University of Chicago*

▲ *Color Plate 8 Exterior At Sunset —Joe and Rika Mansueto Library, University of Chicago, Tom Rossiter © 2011 University of Chicago, Murphy/Jahn Architects*

▲ *Color Plate 9 Audio Editing Laboratory—College of Urban Affairs, University of Nevada, Las Vegas, Robert A.M. Stern Architects*

▲ *Color Plate 10 Exterior view—College of Urban Affairs, University of Nevada, Las Vegas, Robert A.M. Stern Architects*

▲ *Color Plate 11 Technology Enabled, Problem Based Learning Studio, School of Medicine, University of Virginia, Charlottesville, CO Architects, © Robert Canfield Photography*

▲ Color Plate 12 Exterior view, School of Medicine, University of Virginia, Charlottesville, CO Architects, © Robert Canfield Photography

▲ *Color Plate 13 View from courtyard, Willow Street Residence Hall, Tulane University, New Orleans, Louisiana, Mack Scogin Merrill Elam Architects*

▲ *Color Plate 14 View of courtyard, Willow Street Residence Hall, Tulane University, New Orleans, Louisiana, Mack Scogin Merrill Elam Architects*

▲ *Color Plate 15 Lap and leisure pool, Student Recreation and Fitness Center, University of Maine, Orono. Cannon Design, Hedrich Blessing Photography/Jon Miller*

▲ *Color Plate 16 Exterior, Student Recreation and Fitness Center, University of Maine, Orono.*
Cannon Design

▲ *Color Plate 17 University of South Florida, Tampa, Marshall Center Gould Evans Associates. Al Hurly, Photographer*

▸ *Color Plate 18 University of South Florida, Tampa, Gould Evans Associates Marshall Center—Exterior*

▲ *Color Plate 19 '62 Center for Theatre and Dance, Williams College, Williamstown, Massachusetts. William Rawn Associates, Architects, Inc., 2005. © Robert Benson Photography*

▲ *Color Plate 20 Gallery space in the Nerman Museum of Contemporary Art in Overland Park, Kansas*

- *Low-pressure-drop design.* The energy needed to push air through ductwork or pump water through piping is largely determined by the resistance to flow. Slightly oversizing ductwork and pipes can reduce resistance, and thereby energy consumption, while also anticipating future needs. This should be balanced against possible increased floor-to-floor heights to ensure adequate space for ductwork. During construction, the need to "make things fit" sometimes leads to reducing duct and pipe sizes below their optimal dimensions, which can actually result in higher operating costs. Allowing time in the design and construction schedule for careful coordination, especially if the architect and contractor use BIM software, can avoid this in most cases.
- *Temperature ranges.* Some experiments and specialized equipment must operate within a very narrow temperature range, which requires a high level of temperature and humidity control and places high demands on the HVAC system. Dedicating higher levels of temperature control only to specific zones, such as laboratory support, or favoring individual rooms over open laboratories, can reduce energy demand. Working with building users to allow a wider range of temperatures in open laboratories and nonlaboratory areas can also lead to substantial energy use reductions, but requires mutual agreement among users on a definition of thermal comfort.
- *Low-flow fume hoods.* New advances in fume hood design have reduced the amount of airflow required for each fume hood while maintaining worker safety. For example, at the Norman Hackerman Experimental Science Building at the University of Texas at Austin, the project's 260 low-flow fume hoods reduce airflow by 70,000 cfm and reduce associated cooling required by 530 tons (see also Case Study 4).
- *Recirculating air to labs: Segregation and cascading.* One design strategy for promoting interdisciplinary collaboration is the integration of laboratory space with office, write-up, and meeting space. This can, however, increase the potential for energy waste. An architectural solution that maintains functional adjacencies, while atmospherically segregating lab and non-lab spaces into separate zones served from separate HVAC systems, is often more efficient. This efficiency can even be improved if a portion of the unconditioned outside air usually supplied to the labs is replaced by a small percentage of the already conditioned return air drawn from the adjacent offices, a technique called "cascading."
- *Chilled beams.* One of the greatest consumers of energy use in laboratories is the fan power required by air-handling units (AHUs) to push conditioned air throughout the buildings in sufficient quantity to provide the safe number of air changes for life safety and to provide adequate cooling. Chilled beams can provide an alternative solution. These are ceiling-mounted air-conditioning units containing chilled-water coils that provide localized cooling using only a minimal quantity of air already in the room necessary for general life safety, generally six to eight air changes per hour. Chilled beams are effective in laboratories with small numbers of fume hoods and large heat loads from equipment, but not recommended for laboratories with more fume hoods

requiring high air change rates, such as chemistry laboratories.

- *Heat exchange and recovery systems.* In this system, air or water that has already been used to heat or cool a space is passed through devices that indirectly recover the latent heat or cooling and recirculate it to the main HVAC equipment, thereby reducing the amount of new heating and cooling required. This technology is very effective in buildings with large numbers of fume hoods, where the flow rates of conditioned air are highest.

CHAPTER 7

HOUSING

John Ruble, FAIA, and Jeanne Chen, AIA, Moore Ruble Yudell

From Harvard University's initial gathering of student and faculty houses and classrooms to the elevated concept of Thomas Jefferson's Academical Village, housing has historically been an integral part of almost all American campuses. Exceptions include more urban institutions, with their relative scarcity of land and reliance on external housing and transportation, following the Continental European model of the university as a component of the city. Since the 1950s, the commuter campus model has become more common for new institutions in exurban settings, yet many such campuses struggle with a desire to keep students engaged after class, and housing becomes a logical next step in their evolution.

America's post–World War II G.I. Bill began a great expansion of higher education, both in numbers and in demographics, leading to the 1963 Higher Education Facilities Act, which supported a campus building boom for housing as well as academics facilities. As the American ideal of public education has now come to include 2–4 years of college, the expansion has continued. Campus housing now accommodates a spectrum of residents and housing types, from "classic" single undergraduates to couples housing for both graduates and undergraduates to junior and senior faculty condominiums. As the varied backgrounds and lifestyles of campus residents continue to diversify, fulfilling the basic need for *community* is still the most important challenge for residential architecture.

RESIDENTIAL LIFE: EVOLVING TRENDS AND UNDERLYING CONSTANTS

> Not all the schools use housing for recruitment, but the "buzz" about student life on campus can be powerful—and when housing really works, whether it's old or new, it can become the place everyone wants to be.
>
> —*Tom Hier, Biddeson Hier Ltd., Educational Planning Consultants*

Housing for campuses is a constantly evolving subject for planning, programming, and design. As colleges and universities advance their understanding of *residential life* as an integral part of the educational experience, the quality and diversity of on-campus housing is both a critical aim and a moving target. In competing for the best students and faculty, many institutions today have launched major campaigns to improve the quality of campus housing as well as the closely related programs for dining, recreation, and student union facilities. For all but a handful of top-tier schools, it is no longer adequate simply to locate students on campus. In fact, in the twenty-first century, students and their families have increasingly demanded personal choice within vibrant communities.

In meeting today's high standards, campus housing must address a wide range of concerns—from the evolving nature of student life in the age of instant communication to the timeless issues of community and privacy. Contemporary cultural and ethical values, such as social diversity, gender neutrality, and concern for the environment, are key influences on student attitudes and surely will influence how students live in common.

Yet while understanding current trends is an inevitable part of creating new campus housing, trends need not dictate every response. The places we inhabit will outlast the times we live in. Now that modernity—in the form of laptop computers and smart phones—has become a highly movable feast of ephemera, the architecture of the residential environment might better address more timeless concerns. Indeed, for campus housing, longevity itself may be the greatest measure of success. The most sought-after housing on the Lawn at the University of Virginia offers accommodations that are virtually unchanged in almost 200 years (see Figure 7.2). Heritage buildings, from Duke

Figure 7.2 The Lawn at the University of Virginia, Charlottesville: modest accommodations with a grand tradition.

University to the California Institute of Technology (Caltech), offer a sense of belonging that can still compensate for a missing checklist of the latest features. And equally important for housing, as for virtually any other program type, creative responses to the specific qualities of locale and region provide critical opportunities to enhance the identity of the campus as a place.

AN INTRODUCTORY GUIDE

In order to be brief yet comprehensive, this chapter is organized as an introductory guide to address campus housing in two complementary modes. The first is an outline of the most basic, program-specific *concerns, concepts, and criteria,* including a discussion of the design process. Included in the outline are references that link to additional sources of information as well as comments provided by campus professionals responsible for student or residential life at different institutions around the United States. Second, a series of case studies illustrates a spectrum of current design for a range of settings, programs, and types.

A Word on Faculty Housing

While many student housing complexes incorporate faculty units, faculty and/or staff housing for most institutions is provided through private development to offer a more affordable alternative to local market-rate housing. Within the University of California system, faculty housing by not-for-profit foundations also has proven successful. Limited numbers of historic residences that exist on or near older campuses can provide a higher standard of accommodation for administrative and academic leaders, and each is a special case. Because typical faculty and staff housing is likely to be off campus, and has more in common with not-for-profit residential development, the balance of this chapter on campus housing is devoted to student housing.

PROGRAM-SPECIFIC CONCERNS

If any single objective is dominant in student housing today, it is *choice.* As students progress from their freshman year to upper classes and graduate schools, their needs evolve. Whether these variant populations are separated or mixed becomes an interesting expression of institutional philosophy. Most institutions require the first one or two years as on-campus residence, in some cases within a specific complex, such as Duke University's East Campus.

Unique design concerns include the following:

- ***Residential interior planning.*** Individual spaces that efficiently accommodate simple furnishings and allow some degree of personalization
- ***Types and styles of accommodation.*** Single- and double-occupant rooms organized into residence halls, suites, or apartment units and gathered into "houses," quads, or discrete colleges
- ***Social networks and groupings.*** The scale and order in which private spaces are assembled horizontally and vertically into houses, neighborhoods, or communities
- ***Security, controlled access, and privacy.*** How the housing district provides secure circulation and controlled entry into buildings, an issue that may be heightened depending on site and context

Durability and function of interior materials and fixtures. Striking a balance between maintenance costs and desired residential character

Group activities and interaction. Inclusion of shared lounge, dining, and activity areas, complementing private space with social spaces

Parking. Universal access and bicycle parking

Residential counselling. Inclusion of special units for faculty or resident advisors when provided

Budget. Usually expressed as project cost per bed or (more accurately) per square foot

Site planning. Considering relationships to primary student-serving facilities (e.g., recreation, student centers, retail, and dining) as well as academic centers

Resources

A number of relevant organizations maintain websites and periodically publish studies and surveys on student residential life.

Association of College and University Housing Officers—International, *Journal of College and University Student Housing*

acuho-i.org

Society for College and University Planning

scup.org

Council for the Advancement of Standards in Higher Education

cas.edu

College Planning and Management, *Living on Campus Annual College Housing Report*

webcpm.com

The Princeton Review, "Dorms Like Palaces," "Dorms Like Dungeons"

http://www.princetonreview.com/college/college-rankings.aspx

Student Housing Business

studenthousingbusiness.com/news.html

Architectural Record, Building Type Studies/Colleges and Universities

archrecord.construction.com/projects/bts/archives/universities

National Clearinghouse for Educational Facilities

ncef.org/rl/housing.cfm

RESIDENTIAL COMMUNITY: KEY CONCEPTS

A few key concepts are useful in providing a framework for the myriad small and large decisions that go into housing design. They also point to deeper, more lasting considerations in the shifting trends and styles of residential programs. How each of these concepts is to be addressed is at the core of any design process.

Concept 1: Scales of Community

More than any other campus component, housing provides a setting for *community*. What students need socially evolves quickly during the undergraduate years, and a useful response is to provide choices of community on a sliding scale. A worthy rule might be that the better the housing as a place, the more scales and kinds of community it can

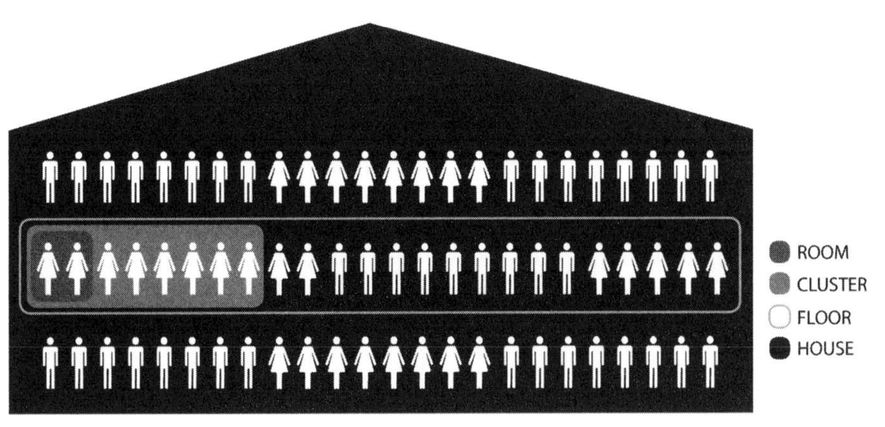

◀ *Figure 7.3 Scales of community.*

sustain (see Figure 7.3). This means that students will be brought together in different numbers in a variety of activities and settings, for example, sharing a room or suite; sharing bathrooms, lounges, and living areas on a wing of a residence hall; and/or sharing a kitchen. Residential life can also extend to participation in related programs based on language learning, cultural and academic interests, public service, or environmentally responsible lifestyles.

Design for evolving formal and informal activities calls for spaces and layouts that provide both flexibility and redundancy. Circulation nodes (entries, stairs, elevators) and shared facilities can both define and link intermediate scales of community, offering in-between places of interaction and negotiation within the whole. How these features are distributed in relation to individual dwelling units is a large part of the design challenge for student residences.

Concept 2: Housing Types

Duke's future housing model is all about the House—students will share a budget, elect officers, and take part in faculty-led programs—we're changing the assignment system to give more non-fraternity students a *home community*.

—Larry Moneta, V.P. Student Affairs, Duke University

Campus housing, like all housing, may be thought of in terms of formats or types. Each type characterizes a set of basic components (e.g., rooms or suites) and their organization, density, and patterns in terms of built areas and open space. The types also imply opportunities for different scales of community, from the nucleus of a shared room or suite, to the residence hall or house, to the overall complex or college.

The Residential College

At the most comprehensive end of the scale is the clustering of residential, social, and academic facilities into a complete college. Facilities for teaching, research, dining, and living are gathered into a well-defined complex, typically with its own enclosed or semi-enclosed outdoor space. The classic image of the residential college is the Cambridge or Oxford cloister, that is, patterns of discrete, enclosed courts surrounded by 2- and 3-story ranges of rooms that share a chapel, library, or dining hall. At the

University of California, Santa Cruz, the college type is just as strong a pattern but takes the form of small villages separated by dense redwood groves and hilly landscape (see Figure 7.4).

While the true residential college combines academic and residential programs, the form of the college is often appropriated as a place of residence alone, usually with scheduled communal dining as part of the plan. Caltech's Avery Center is an example, with enclosed courts, patios, and a multiuse dining hall, offering students a sense of separate identity within the larger institution (see Figure 7.5). The intermediate scale of community makes the residential college an attractive format for housing entering classes of freshmen.

The Residence Hall

The most generic form of student housing is the residence hall or dormitory. At its core is the basic pattern of "rooms on a path," that is, single- or double-occupancy rooms that may share bathrooms at a ratio of approximately one bathroom per two to four beds

Figure 7.4 Village in a forest, Colleges 9 and 10, University of California, Santa Cruz. Architect: EHDD.

◀ *Figure 7.5 Cloistered courts frame community, Avery Center, California Institute of Technology, Pasadena.* Architect: Moore Ruble Yudell.

or, alternatively, grouped into communal bathrooms shared by a hall or floor. The residence hall allows flexible assignment, including mixed-gender arrangements. A variant is single-occupancy rooms in pairs, allowing two students to use one room for lounging/studying and one for sleeping (see Figure 7.6).

Most commonly seen as housing for entering and lower undergraduate classes, the residence hall may be organized with a sophisticated "social plaid" of hierarchic groupings: 1–2 students per room, up to 30 students per wing or floor, two wings or floors per shared kitchen and/or study room, as many as 100 students per ground-floor lounge, and, depending on the scale and density of the context, many more per building entry.

Suites

Typically for upper-class undergraduate students, the shared occupancy of two- to four-room suites allows a next level in terms of student/household community. While kitchens usually are not included, the suite offers some flexibility of shared furnishings, bathrooms, and living arrangements.

Apartment Housing

Most commonly for upper-class undergraduate and graduate students, the apartment type includes private baths and small kitchens for each unit, typically in a compact 600–1,000 sq ft layout. Individual (one or two bedrooms) and family-oriented (two or three bedrooms) apartment units may be provided for faculty advisors who reside in student complexes. For upper-class

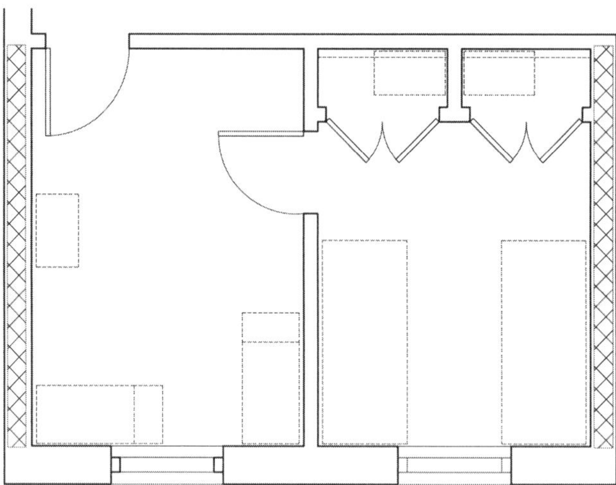

▸ *Figure 7.6 Typical double two-room plan.*

undergraduates, apartment housing provides a step toward life off campus, but maintains a closer tie to the campus community.

The House

A house is any meaningful grouping of students, usually 30 or more, which may occupy its own small building or be defined within a larger complex by some form of threshold: a clear point of entry into a hallway, floor, or wing. Shared facilities might include a lounge/study room, a kitchen, and a porch or terrace. Social or academic functions, such as an honors student program, can give the house its particular purpose and identity. Floors or wings of residence halls are often appropriated as "houses" for all kinds of student groups, including fraternities, dining clubs, and affinity groups based on lifestyle.

Concept 3: The Hierarchy of Shared Facilities

Residential life isn't just about learning, it's also about *health*—this newer generation of students is "stressed out"! They need places to de-stress, good common areas with outdoor connections—places for community and places to get away.

—Willie Brown, Executive Director Housing and Residential Services, University of California, Santa Barbara

Common areas in student housing provide a vital setting for community and, if well designed, can address many student needs, including the need to be "alone together." Shared spaces should include at least an open lounge at the ground-floor level for residents and visitors, but they may be far more elaborate, with programs for dining and recreation. (See Figure 7.7 for a recent survey of ancillary facilities.)

The essential planning principle for shared facilities is hierarchy; that is, spaces for special activities are located according to their function along the path from the building entry to the individual rooms or suites. The most unique facilities are placed

AVERAGE SPACE/STUDENT: 333 SF/BED (RANGE 250 SF/BED TO 400 SF/BED)
MEDIAN SIZE: 278 BEDS
AMENITIES: LAUNDRY 98% AC 84% KITCHEN 73% VENDING 80%
TV ROOMS 78% STUDY 78% CLASSROOMS 47% FITNESS CENTERS 16%
DINING HALLS 18% COMPUTER CENTER 28%
2010 College Housing Report, College Planning & Management

Figure 7.7 Student housing program elements.

at or near the entry to the building or at the center of the complex (see Figure 7.8). The more common or repeated facilities are located closer to rooms.

Concept 4: The 24/7 Student Environment

In the design of the campus residential environment, night and day are equally

Figure 7.8 Lounges gather at entry points. Architect: Lewis Tsurumaki Lewis.

important. Landscape lighting is just the beginning of the creation of a safe and attractive nighttime district. Shared social, academic, and recreational activities with glassy facades toward common exterior spaces can serve as "lanterns" guiding the way to building entrances. Nighttime acoustics pose more of a problem (e.g., closed courtyards and operable windows in warm weather) for which nonparallel building walls and landscape screening may scarcely help. Choreographing student movement and carefully locating lounges and other spaces used at night near the points of entry can mitigate conflicts.

Concept 5: Fundamental Needs

Student needs are basic. They will respond to the simple generosity of natural light, views outside, enough room to move furnishings around from time to time, and hallways wide enough to sit down on the floor and talk to their neighbors (see Figure 7.9). Interiors need not be precious or fragile, but neither should the environment express bulletproof durability. Commonplace materials that age reasonably well, such as durable hardwoods and sustainable alternatives like bamboo flooring, can also accumulate an attractive patina of having

▸ *Figure 7.9 Simple generosity, Bornhuetter Hall, College of Wooster, Wooster, Ohio.* Architect: Lewis Tsurumaki Lewis.

been lived in. Some aspects of generosity do have cost implications. A critical one is ceiling height. Older buildings (pre-1960) inevitably offer more attractively proportioned spaces because they predate air conditioning and the current assumption that 8 ft ceilings are adequate for any size room. Some strategies can help, such as allowing some lounge areas to span vertically two floors with a connecting stair and using careful energy modeling to balance taller rooms and lower refrigeration tonnage works in some climates.

DELIVERY OPTIONS: THE PROGRAMMING/DESIGN/PROCUREMENT PROCESS

The design and delivery process for campus housing may be highly participatory—involving students, faculty, and campus professionals and leaders—*or* it can be driven by management with predetermined aspirations, criteria, and budgets. While the design should be guided by all of these concerns, the budget may be an overriding issue for many institutions. Depending on the type of institution, program goals, and constraints, the overall programming/design/procurement process may take one of several forms as outlined below.

Design/Build Approach

Campus housing may be produced by a design/build process or through a private developer with a special focus on student residential programs. In the latter case, it is even more critical for the campus institution to thoroughly research comparable facilities; tour the work of the candidate firms; and establish clear, detailed criteria. Any reliable design/build process should include the following minimum set of steps and requirements:

- Needs assessment and feasibility study by in-house campus professionals and/or independent consultants
- Benchmarking: a study of relevant comparable facilities recently completed
- Program development/budgeting with stakeholder participation and professional assistance
- Detailed programming: room-by-room requirements and specifications to establish quality standards and/or performance criteria
- Qualifications-based design/build or developer team selection, or design competition, with competitive bidding
- Independent peer review of the work of the design/build or developer team
- Long-term maintenance or warranty phase continuity from the developer team

Design/Bid/Build Approach

If greater control of the final result is a priority, some version of design/bid/build is still a reliable process, allowing a balance of quality, program criteria, and cost. An idealized process might include the following:

- Needs assessment and feasibility study by in-house campus professionals and/or independent consultants
- Design team (architects and consultants) selection based on qualifications
- Benchmarking: a study of relevant comparable facilities recently completed
- Program development/budgeting with broad stakeholder participation (students, faculty/staff, campus professionals, and administrative leadership) led by the design team and/or program consultant
- Detailed programming: room-by-room requirements and specifications to establish quality standards and/or performance criteria

- Continuous stakeholder involvement in the design phase work
- Qualifications-based bidders in a competitive-bid contractor selection process
- Construction phase services by the design team
- Independent commissioning as well as warranty phase continuity by contractor and design team

Integrated Project Delivery

A promising newer approach to design and delivery is integrated project delivery (IPD)—the contractually defined collaboration of client, design professionals, and construction team. This relatively new process is strongly underwritten by the American Institute of Architects and some construction organizations as an effective way to join the three parties to any construction project in a cooperative effort. For a campus residential project, the overall process under an IPD approach might include the following:

- Initial campus needs assessment with independent program consultant.
- Identification of a core team of campus stakeholders committed to working collaboratively on the project.
- Qualifications-based selection of design professionals with emphasis on collaborative approaches and, specifically, relevant staff experience in teamwork.
- Qualifications-based selection of lead construction team with appropriate selected staff.
- Team engaged in contract-based collaborative approach with similar steps/phases as the design/build approach . . . *except*:
- Budget is managed as guaranteed maximum construction cost, with a shared reward system for cost savings and shared liability for maintenance of budget and related performance.
- The collaborative design work, documentation, and construction are enhanced by using building information modeling (BIM).
- Bids on systems and components are taken from subcontractors who participate in design/specifications as appropriate.
- Project-specific professional liability insurance is relevant for this approach.
- Preestablished funding for an extended warranty/maintenance contract with construction team/subcontractors may be part of the overall project budget.

SITE PLANNING

Housing is typically a part of the original core of heritage campuses and close to the heart of newer campuses. But as institutions and facilities grow, campus housing tends to be pushed to the periphery. The quality of site planning can have enormous impact on the flow of student life from residence to academic, social, and recreational centers.

Site planning is also central to the response to place. Conceptually, every campus housing complex is part of a larger whole; therefore, how the layout of buildings and site reinforces the defining qualities of campus character or, conversely, how it can introduce new forms are crucial questions. Often new housing intervenes in and around existing older fabric, and these issues are heightened.

Specific concerns for residential site planning include the following:

- *Context*, in terms of how the project's massing and layout respond to the scale and character of existing campus development as well as adjacent neighborhoods in urban settings.
- *Project scale and density* in relation to overall campus development plans and policies.

- *Climate* and its interpretation of seasonal variation, accommodating or mediating weather extremes and maintaining access to sunlight between buildings.
- *Pedestrian, bicycle, and vehicular access* relate to linking building entrances to the network of walkways and roads.
- *Bicycle parking* on most campuses is a great challenge, accommodating large numbers of bikes as close as possible to building entrances and providing secure, covered, and lockable bike storage.
- *Fire/emergency access* includes emergency vehicle access to all sides of buildings as well as required clear dimensions for roads and gateways and access into closed courtyards.
- *Open space* uses building layouts to shape iconic, functional exterior spaces, responding to existing patterns of building and landscape as well as existing topography.
- *Landscape design* includes responses to an existing or iconic campus landscape character; programmable exterior spaces and/or outdoor rooms as required; planting to provide shelter and mediate building mass; campuswide systems of paving, lighting, and furnishings; seasonal character and climate; and water use/conservation and site hydrology; as well as balancing the priorities of landscape character and maintenance.
- *Security* establishes clear visibility along paths into and out of the buildings and site; organizes residents' windows to overlook public areas; provides secure enclosure with controlled access where required; activates ground-floor building edges with views into and out of public rooms; and determines the locations of emergency call boxes.
- *Service* allows discrete loading/trash/recycling points served by accessible roads; "moving day" access with temporary vehicular use of main pedestrian paths; and specialized service access for shared dining and/or event facilities.
- *Placement of dining and other shared social activities* to "capture the energy" at points of arrival from the surrounding campus or to energize the center of a large complex.

HOUSING FORMATS: RESIDENTIAL INTERIORS' PLANNING

Students should be brought together in natural ways that appeal to basic human nature—comfort, natural light, generous spaces, and wide corridors.

—*Tom Hier, Biddeson Hier Ltd., Educational Planning Consultants*

Student Room Types

For residence halls, the basic unit of planning is the single- or double-occupancy room with approximately 100 sq ft per bed. For each student, the minimum furnishings are a single bed, a small desk and chair, and a closet or wardrobe with both hanging and drawer storage. Some institutions prefer wardrobes to built-in closets, allowing for more flexibility for the inhabitants, sometimes in combination with bunk beds or a system that allows a bed to be stacked over a desk. For upper-class and graduate students, larger single-occupancy rooms with private baths may be most appropriate.

"Rooms on a Path"

Residence halls for first- and second-year students typically provide rooms along a double-loaded corridor with up to 20–24 beds per length of hallway. Such a grouping typically shares both a central bathroom and lounge. Bathrooms may also be distributed separately as a series of single-fixture rooms shared by the hall. Either way, one set of fixtures (shower, toilet, and lavatory) per four or five students is typical.

Two-Room Suites

Two single-occupancy rooms may be adjoined and share a bathroom. The adjoining rooms allow students the option of using one room for sleeping and the other as a study or lounge.

Larger Suites

For third- and fourth-year students, two- and four-room suites address their desire for greater privacy and choice of roommates. Each suite may have a small living area, a single bathroom, and two double-occupancy rooms or up to four single-occupancy rooms and two bathrooms. Larger combinations may be created by adjoining the living areas of two suites to form a "house," possibly with a shared kitchen.

Apartments

The defining quality of apartment-style housing is the provision of a larger living/dining area and a kitchen. A plan with one single- and one double-occupancy room allows flexible conversion from three students—or two graduate students—to a resident faculty unit.

Mixed Occupancy

Some mixing of residence types within a building or floor is often useful, particularly for older undergraduates and graduate students. This allows affinity groups to form more flexibly; for example, a group of five or six friends may be accommodated in a four-person apartment plus one or two adjacent single rooms, with a range of privacy to suit different needs.

Corridors and Stairways

Hallways are possibly the most social spaces in any residence scheme and should be laid out with some variation in width to allow places for spontaneous conversation. At intervals, or at the ends, natural light is extremely valuable, even as borrowed light from lounge/study rooms and stairways. Some articulation at entries to bathrooms and even student rooms allows for an important sense of threshold. In some climates, exterior single-loaded galleries and open stairs are appropriate, facilitating natural ventilation for rooms and suites. In addition to exit stairs, open stairs linking lounges can enhance social life. At least one stair and/or elevator should provide additional width for moving furniture and for emergency/disabled access.

Lounges and Study Rooms

The basic kit of the residence hall includes multiuse lounges for study and social contact (see Figure 7.10). Each cluster of bedrooms will benefit from at least 10–15 sq ft of lounge area per bed—particularly where rooms are mainly double occupancy. Larger lounges provide more active space; smaller ones offer quiet retreats for late-night work. Such spaces can also function as the hinge between floors or corridor suites. Smaller workrooms can be distributed as hideaways or clustered to bring students together.

Laundries and Kitchens

Laundry and kitchen facilities also promote community, linking separate suites and groups by bringing students upstairs or down and inviting interaction. As with other factors, entering freshmen may benefit from larger facilities shared by more neighbors, and returning undergraduates may prefer the greater privacy and convenience of smaller, more distributed facilities. Nevertheless, in apartment-style housing,

◀ *Figure 7.10 Comfort, natural light, and quiet space, Infill Student Housing, University of California, Berkeley.* Architect: EHDD.

with a kitchen in every unit, a common laundry may provide a critical complement as a place of interaction. Shared kitchens are typically equipped like residential kitchens, with additional care for durable finishes. Laundries serving larger numbers of students are treated and equipped like commercial laundromats (and may be operated by commercial firms), but benefit from additional space for seating, television viewing, and conversation.

Ancillary Support Spaces

Janitorial facilities, as well as electrical and data closets, should be provided on each floor. Vending machines need special accommodation with acoustic separation, floor drains, and waterproof floors. Recycling facilities may be centralized in each building, but should be convenient and offer an opportunity for informational "biofeedback," giving students periodic updates on how their community is performing in terms of energy use, waste, and water conservation.

CAMPUS DINING: ACCOMMODATING CHOICE AND STYLE

Housing needs a strong connection to dining. When you think about what a student's day is like—choice is important. So is flexibility, having options. *The most precious commodity for students today is Time.*

—Marty Redman, Executive Director, College Houses and Academic Services, University of Pennsylvania

Dining is itself a dynamic topic for campus planners and student life professionals. Central campus dining facilities are integral to student unions or campus "community centers," and complement the spectrum of dining that may be provided within residential complexes. Virtually all campuses provide both.

Residential dining also appears in several formats, related to the type of housing it serves. As there is continuous innovation and development of campus dining styles, planning consultants who specialize in food service are essential to the design of any new or remodeled facility.

The Refectory Hall

For residential colleges, the classic dining hall with long tables and scheduled menus can still be relevant, providing younger students with a regimen for mealtimes and reinforcing a sense of participation in the identity of the college. Romanticized in the image of Hogwarts School of Witchcraft and Wizardry (in reality, Oxford University), the dining hall provides a quality of ritual that coming generations of students may yearn for (see Figure 7.11). However, the dining hall may also be attached to any number of food service formats, from table service to trays (or trayless) and counter service to food courts.

▸ *Figure 7.11 Modern refectory hall, Vanderbilt University, Nashville, Tennessee.* Architect: Bruner Cott.

The Dining Commons

Similar to the refectory hall in scale, but different in layout, the more contemporary dining commons provides either a formal or a free-flowing mix of larger and smaller spaces—including separable rooms. Varied ceiling heights and lots of edges and corners make for a richer choice of places to dine, and the open visual flow throughout the commons allows students to easily find each other (see Figure 7.12).

The Market Hall

The multicentered format of the marché-style servery (or food court) has widely replaced the cafeteria line in contemporary campus food service, with the attraction of open prep stations and a wider variety of food choices. As the servery itself takes over a large portion of food preparation, foods are fresher—often made to order—and the centralized kitchen facilities are reduced. While typical for large facilities, multistation food service has been applied to dining areas as small as 100 seats.

The Café, Franchise, and Grab-and-Go

Smaller, more casual dining outlets play an important role in activating residential settings and offering convenience and choice to busy students. Whether living in dorms or apartments, students still commonly need quick and convenient meal options as well as basic supplies. Increasingly, the common franchise café not only serves breakfast but also provides a venue for study groups. How many such outlets can a given population sustain? Retail consultants can provide planning guidelines as well as information on current trends.

RECREATIONAL AMENITIES: THE 24/7 STUDENT LIFE

Campus residences seeking to outpace the competition increasingly offer recreational

◀ *Figure 7.12 Dining commons, Ernie Davis Hall, Syracuse University, Syracuse, New York.* Architect: Mack Scogin Merrill Elam.

facilities close to, or in, the housing complex. At one extreme is the Campus Recreation Center at the University of Cincinnati, which includes student housing in a campus and regional recreational center (see Figure 7.13).

However it is packaged, student recreation is a larger campus planning issue, and placing housing and recreation in relative proximity is an important first step. Within the housing complex, smaller facilities may be more effective, such as game rooms and multiuse rooms suitable for aerobics or other less equipment-intensive exercise. Encouraging outdoor recreation may be accomplished by providing well-planned open space.

Recreation can also include cultural events and gatherings, both large and small. Music performances need not be confined to the stadium or arts center. Again, the scale and outfitting of venues for any kind of performance is a complex topic in its own right, covered in Chapter 10, and qualified consultants in theater design, acoustics, and audiovisual systems should be included in the planning and programming process.

HOUSING FABRIC: SETTING PERFORMANCE CRITERIA

The basic program requirements for housing establish a full range of concerns for the building fabric—its quality of construction, performance, safety, and economy. Building codes for multiunit residential uses set minimum standards for a majority of construction factors, but many institutions may exceed code minimums with their own standards for systems and materials as well as having their own in-house fire/life safety officials. The following sections provide a preliminary outline of criteria in terms of codes, building systems, and performance and sustainability, and should be followed up by detailed research into the regulations and requirements of given locations and campuses.

▸ *Figure 7.13 Recreation on a regional scale activates new housing and "Main Street," University of Cincinnati, Cincinnati, Ohio.* Architect: Morphosis.

Code-Based Criteria

In addition to fire prevention and life safety, many aspects of building quality and performance are also covered by building codes. Most states have adopted the International Building Code (IBC), which describes building construction requirements for classified types of use or occupancy, according to the floor area and height, and consolidates the regulations of several previous regional codes. A notable exception is California, where annually updated provisions for seismic safety, energy use, and sustainability exceed the requirements of many other states and may set new standards in years to come.

Code-based criteria of particular relevance for campus housing include the following:

Building construction type. Based on the overall structural/construction system, the IBC places limits on building height and/or area. Limits may be extended by adding a fire sprinkler system to the building. Figure 7.14 shows construction types commonly used for student residence halls, an R occupancy for most codes, with area/height limitations that may apply.

Building spacing and setbacks. Site planning is also affected by construction type limitations. Typically, building exterior walls with windows must be set at least 40 ft apart, and some constraints apply to windows adjacent to exit stairs and balconies. But such code minimums may easily be exceeded by considerations for daylight and the proportion of open space between taller buildings.

Building height. Construction systems for buildings above 4 stories are more restricted and generally more expensive. High-rise requirements may be triggered above 6 stories, affecting exiting requirements and elevator sizes significantly.

Room-to-corridor relations. Openings into rooms along the hallway are very much controlled by fire safety regulations, which typically call for mechanical door closers and positive air pressure from the hall toward the rooms. All of these items can make some energy-saving strategies like natural ventilation difficult.

CONSTRUCTION TYPE/HEIGHT, RELATIVE COSTS

TYPE	NO. OF STORIES
Wood Frame	1–4
Steel Frame and Wood Composite	4–6
Brick or Concrete Masonry Units (CMU) with Concrete Slabs	2+
Concrete Frame with Concrete Slabs	4+
Steel Frame, Metal Deck	4+

Figure 7.14 Construction types are related to building scale and height.

Building Systems

With an overlay of both code-based and performance-based criteria, the selection of building systems has the greatest impact on achieving a successful project and meeting budget. When projects have serious budget problems, it is often due to a "disconnect" between the cost per square foot and the basic design approach in terms of scale, construction type, and the overall structural and mechanical systems that are chosen. Early design and feasibility studies should consider significant alternatives as site planning leads to massing, which, in turn, sets the building type, which then leads to a host of other choices.

Structural System

The choice of structural system is typically based on the massing of the facility and the least expensive construction type allowed by code for the height and typical floor area of the project. Type V/1-hour wood frame construction is still the most economical for housing under 4 stories, but critical issues of acoustic separation and long-term durability and maintenance must be considered. Type III/1-hour (noncombustible masonry walls with protected combustible floor construction) allows more floors and area and is cheaper than all-noncombustible construction. But within the overall construction approach, quality can vary greatly according to performance-based criteria. Other hybrid systems that have proven effective include the following:

- Steel frame/wood composite structures
- Concrete masonry units with post-tensioned concrete slabs
- Concrete masonry units with precast/prestressed concrete planks
- Concrete or steel frame with post-tensioned concrete slabs

In some regions, such as the western United States, seismic design is a dominant concern. Every aspect of construction, from foundation system to suspended lighting, must meet detailed requirements, and the cost of basic structural systems consumes a much greater proportion of the budget.

Mechanical Systems

The choice of systems for heating, ventilation, and/or air conditioning depends entirely on regional practice based on climate, but each institution may have its own preferred approach. Low-initial-cost approaches typically include unit fans in each bedroom served by warm and/or chilled water piping. Overall building ventilation and/or conditioning systems may be more economical to operate or may be required due to ambient humidity conditions. Fire regulations may call for mechanically pressurized exit corridors and stairs. Contemporary goals for energy efficiency may lead to newer approaches or simpler solutions like baseboard radiant heating, ceiling fans, and operable windows in milder climates.

Plumbing Systems

Plumbing system choices, like many other decisions, generally fall between the competing priorities of initial cost and long-term serviceability. Metal piping systems cost more and perform longer with less maintenance. Plastic systems, when allowable by code, should be specified as Schedule 40 or Schedule 80 polyvinyl chloride (PVC) pipe. Fixtures must be chosen for serviceability and low water use. Many institutions are adapting waterless urinals, for example. Layout and type of fixtures should be based on proven dimensions for ease of maintenance, and detailing for installation—especially wall mounting—should be carefully vetted with campus facilities professionals.

Electrical Systems

Power usage in student housing has greatly expanded with the continuing development of personal computing and entertainment systems. Students may also use small cooking apparatus, refrigerators, and other appliances, and campus policies may or may not be effective in reducing loads. Power cabling, like plumbing materials, is a cost-for-value consideration. While some codes still allow exposed wrapped cable (Romex), long-term service strongly favors the use of rigid or flexible conduit with changeable wiring.

Lighting options continue to evolve, with newer requirements for energy efficiency having a real impact on practice. Fluorescent and light-emitting diode (LED) fixture types have greatly improved service and replacement, and are available for virtually all interior and exterior conditions. Within the residential environment, two issues are critical. The layout of fixed lighting, wall or ceiling, must be carefully coordinated with anticipated furnishings. The use of occupancy sensors or hotel-type, card-operated on-off switches should be considered for significant energy savings.

Telecommunications and Information Technology

While cable trays are not yet common in student housing, significant provisions for information and telecom infrastructure are. Starting with a ground-floor data room and stacked data closets, telecom and data are distributed to each floor via oversized rigid or flexible conduit. Provision of wireless data requires adequate transmission, the rates of which may vary depending on building construction and scale. As each institution will have its own evolving approach and standards, early consultation with campus information technology (IT) systems personnel is key to a successful outcome.

Fire and Life Safety

While the essential concerns of fire protection are code-based, detailed requirements affect choices of building systems. For plumbing and ductwork, penetrations into fire-rated construction must be adequately—and expensively—detailed, and access panels for maintenance in ceilings and walls must use approved products. Piping may need fire protection, and door and window systems may need to meet specific fire ratings. Sprinkler systems are commonly used, whether required by code or not, and alarm and smoke detection systems will follow the standards of each campus or institution.

Performance-Based Criteria

Building Envelope

Within the selection of exterior systems and materials are complex decisions relating to aesthetics and building performance. Contextually relevant materials, such as stone at Duke University or blended red brick at the University of Virginia, may be virtually mandated by campus stakeholders, and may or may not be valid in terms of responding to regional climate conditions. Current goals or requirements for sustainability consistently call for a more robust exterior envelope. Contemporary best practice emphasizes an airtight enclosure, impervious to moisture or vapor, with high thermal resistance and, depending on climate, high thermal mass. Windows should be chosen for quality and energy efficiency, which typically means double glazing and factory-finished metal framing or exterior cladding.

Roofing systems offer many choices, but quality and cost are most often directly correlated. For flat roofs, built-up asphalt is viable, but reinforced single-ply or heat-welded membranes and various multilayered systems for planted roofs offer Leadership in Energy and Environmental Design (LEED) green building points as well as increased performance. For more visible sloping roofs, the look of which may be mandated by campus heritage, a wide array of composition and natural tile materials, as well as raised-seam metal systems, provide many options. The critical point is to clarify expectations for performance and cost. As always, specifics of climate and the maintenance budget of the institution must be considered.

Interior Systems

Interiors come into heavy use in student dorms, and expectations for performance, maintenance, and replacement must be carefully reviewed at the outset of programming and budgeting (see Figure 7.15). Nevertheless, gypsum wallboard systems with wood or metal studs and joists remain the ubiquitous choice for interior partitions and ceilings. The detailing of corners; baseboards; wainscoting, if provided; and interior door frames will have important consequences for both performance and aesthetics. Interior wall finishes range from paint and synthetic wall coverings in rooms and hallways to epoxy paint and tile for bathrooms and showers.

Flooring is the most critical wear surface. Carpet and carpet tiles are widely standard, but traditional linoleum is highly sustainable and can provide a more hypoallergenic environment, which may be an increasing concern in coming years. Bathroom floors call for ceramic tile over waterproof membranes. In temperate or cold climates, providing

Figure 7.15 Natural wood complements a durable interior, Bornhuetter Hall, College of Wooster, Wooster, Ohio. Architect: Lewis Tsurumaki Lewis.

adequate walk-off mats and/or grates at entrances, together with concrete, stone, or ceramic flooring where traffic is highest, helps protect interior flooring.

Casework and Furnishings

Closets and shelving may be built-in or provided as furniture. Either way, durable hardwood or "fin-ply" solid-stock plywood should be considered for long-term wear. Use the early design process to study modular furniture systems that allow reconfiguration within room dimensions. Larger institutions typically have established standards and preferred systems.

Acoustics

At the top of the performance-related criteria is acoustic separation between walls and floors. Wood-framed flooring can be augmented with a shallow cement topping slab. Walls between rooms or suites must be framed to meet sound transmission minimums per code, and ideally use staggered studs, batt insulation, double layers of drywall, acoustic sealant, or all of the above. Layouts of rooms for sleeping must consider adjacencies, which means avoiding stairways, elevator shafts, vending machine rooms, and other human or mechanical noise generators. Solid-core doors with soundproof stripping and reinforced framing at the door opening are basic.

Indoor Air Quality

Contemporary standards for indoor finishes and products have risen in the sustainability era. Even if LEED certification is not required, similar standards for healthy building materials should be followed. Low-VOC (volatile organic compound) finishes, mildew prevention, and the use of natural materials wherever suitable will continue to be basic to good practice for residential buildings.

Operational Costs

Maintenance for various systems and materials can be thought of in 3-, 5-, and 10-year cycles. Clear criteria should be established during programming and budgeting, in close consultation with campus facility and maintenance professionals. Regardless of the initial planning, many campuses defer maintenance, and buildings designed for a 50-year lifetime may be in use, remodeled or not, much longer. Design building systems and finishes with replacement in mind, using a hierarchy of more and less permanent components. Keep floor layouts and primary structure reasonably independent, with simple, logical arrangements of highly serviced spaces like bathrooms and laundries. Put sufficient resources into all the moving parts (e.g., doors, windows, elevators, mechanical systems, and furniture).

Sustainability: The Behavior Factor

Student residential life can provide important early education in sustainable living. New projects that include information monitoring—such as an online power/energy use "dashboard"—can provide student communities with the feedback they need for behavior modification. At Dartmouth's McLaughlin Cluster Housing, students, on their own initiative, created a web page with interpretive graphics—a polar bear's fate on a fragile ice cap demonstrates how well each house has reduced its carbon use on a daily basis—which has led to house-by-house competition for building performance (see Figure 7.16).

Renovation and Reuse

Renovation programs provide necessary upgrades to older housing stock. As such, there may be more of a focus on basic building fabric and systems, and less on new concepts and styles of accommodation. A typical project may need to be

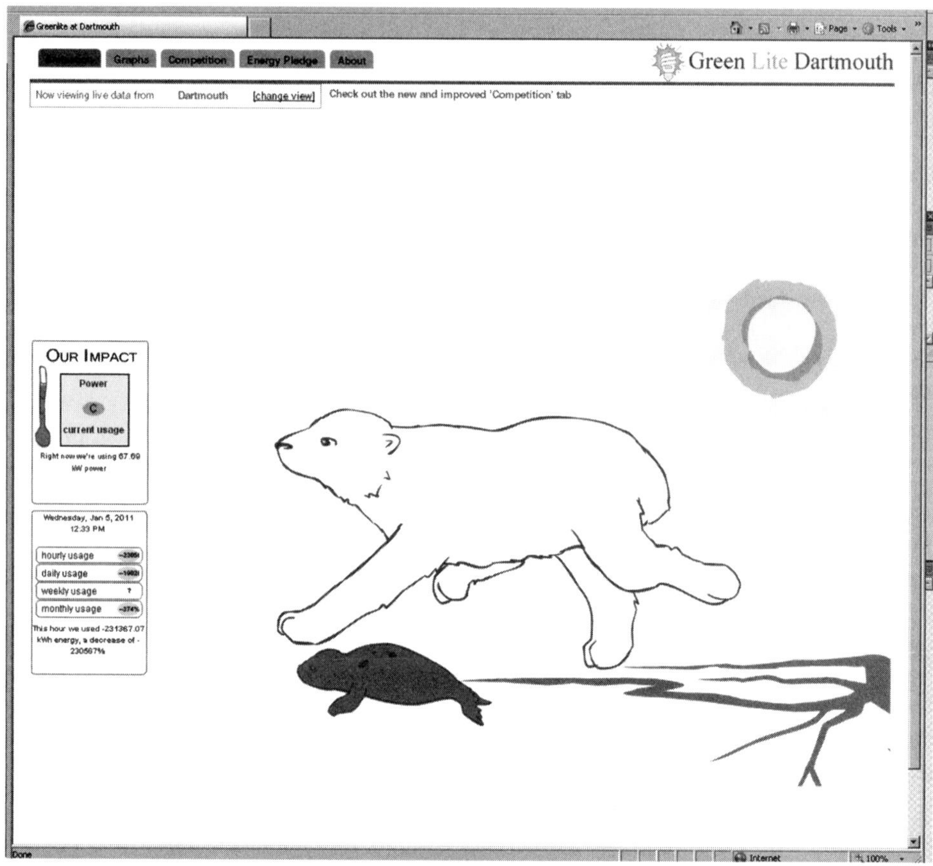

▸ *Figure 7.16 Website "dashboard" encourages a more sustainable student lifestyle. McLaughlin Cluster Housing, Dartmouth College, Hanover, New Hampshire.*

completed in the field during summer recess and should be designed with expedient construction in mind. In some states, major structural upgrades to meet new seismic design codes may make renovation impractical, and careful analysis of costs and benefits is critical. In any renovation project, the need to minimize loss of housing units is part of the problem. Construction phasing and the logistics of constrained sites must be planned around. Early programming should explore whether remodeling is best combined with new construction, to maintain available occupancy levels and to keep housing revenues up during the overall process.

CAMPUS HOUSING
CASE STUDY 1

SMART HOME
Duke University, Durham, North Carolina
smarthomeduke.edu
Architect: Frank Harmon, FAIA

> *Why Build a Smart Home at Duke? . . . One of the most important aspects of this project is that it is a living laboratory—students actually reside in the Home Depot Smart Home, and live with the benefits and consequences of their technology design and deployment decisions. . . . Smart homes can improve the quality of life for people of all ages and incomes.*
>
> —Larry Moneta, V.P. Student Affairs, Duke University

Led by engineering students Mark Younger and Tom Rose, the Smart Home is a 6,000 sq ft, live-in research laboratory that provides students at Duke with opportunities for real-life, hands-on engineering outside the classroom; broad cross-disciplinary interaction; and industry/university partnerships in a living and learning community.

- Year completed: Fall 2007
- Building area: 6,000 sq ft, live-in research lab for students and faculty
- Number of beds: 10 student residents
- Room types: five reconfigurable double bedrooms at 250 sq ft each
- Cost (in 2007 dollars): $1.2 million
- LEED Platinum Sustainable Student Community
- Operated by Duke's Pratt School of Engineering

Smart Home Goals

- Commit to and explore an energy-efficient lifestyle.
- Compare, use, and develop smart and sustainable technology.
- Provide insight to homeowners for "do-it-yourself" technology integration and control.

Key Spaces

Ground Floor: Mix of Public and Private Space

- *Commons area*: interconnects first and second levels with 2-story social lounge space while enabling passive thermal cooling
- *Clean lab:* computer room with control and monitor panels, including smart panels
- *Media room:* multimedia experience space
- *Dirty lab:* place to build and test products
- Double bedroom and shared bathroom

Second Floor: Private Space

- Four double bedrooms
- Approximately 250 sq ft per double
- Two bedrooms sharing a bathroom
- Bedrooms separated by movable panels to allow reconfiguration into suite arrangements

Basement: Mechanical Space

- HVAC systems
- Energy recovery ventilator
- Air purification system
- Six 350-gallon rain harvesting tanks and solar water collection tanks

(See Figures 7.17–7.19.)

Figure 7.17 Smart home, Duke University © Duke University Photography—used with permission.

▸ *Figure 7.18 Commons area connecting first and second floors.* © Duke University Photography—used with permission.

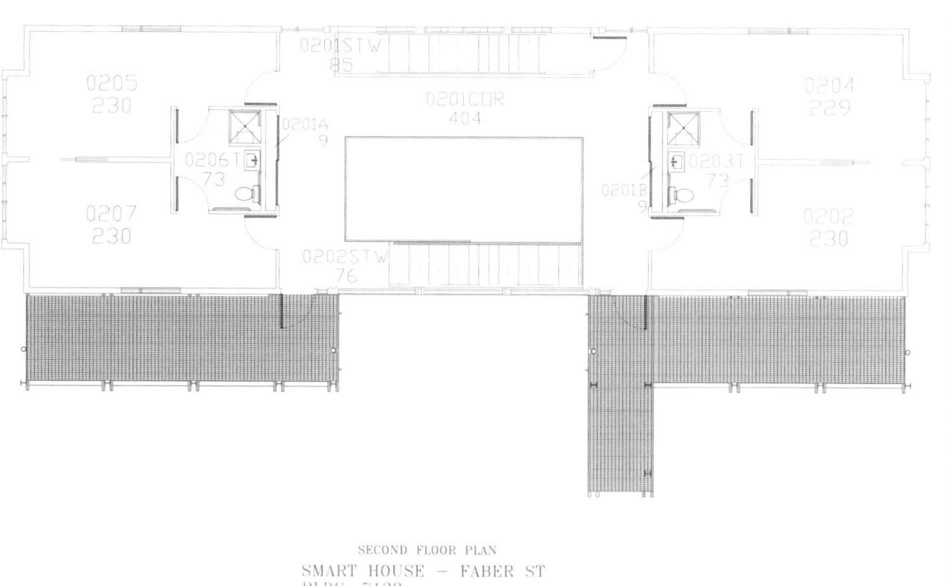

▸ *Figure 7.19 Smart home floor plan.*

CAMPUS HOUSING
CASE STUDY 2

BORNHUETTER HALL
College of Wooster, Wooster, Ohio
Architect: Lewis Tsurumaki, Lewis Architects

Contrary to the prevailing trend at residential colleges toward apartment style living, extensive discussions with students, residential life staff and college administration led to the unanticipated conclusion that a double-loaded corridor type actually encourages the greatest degree of socialization and the most positive student experience.

—Lewis Tsurumaki, Lewis Architects

Bornhuetter Hall enriches the academic experience by providing a balance between private spaces for study and public gathering areas for communal discussion. The hallways are designed to encourage social interaction and widen at the ends to embrace public lounges and intimate sitting areas. The outdoor courtyard is the heart of the building with wood-clad study nooks that cantilever like box seats into this theatrical space.

- Year completed: 2004
- Site area: 1.5 acres
- Building area: 47,500 sq ft
- Number of beds: 185 beds/4 stories in two housing wings
- Room types: doubles and singles
- Average square footage/bed: 256 sq ft/bed total building area; 115 sq ft/bed in rooms
- Bathroom type: communal
- Cost/bed (in 2004 dollars): approximately $37,000

Transforming the Conventions of the Double-Loaded Corridor

- Ideal number of rooms along a single corridor: 25–30 rooms/hall
- Creates two separate housing wings—to allow ideal hall unit
- Corridor should be wide enough to accommodate informal interaction and interconnect shared social spaces at either end
- Corridor should be integrated with major building circulation paths
- Provides balance of social spaces to include larger shared lounges, kitchenette, and intimate study areas

Key Spaces

- Outdoor space as an exterior room
- Housing wings shape outdoor room
- Contains social and private spaces
- Enhances movement to the student housing entry and provides connections through to an adjacent public park

Ground Floor (Partially below Grade)

- Double bedrooms and singles
- Lounges with kitchenettes
- Cantilever study nooks
- Multipurpose space
- Computer lab
- Hall director's apartment
- Shared laundry
- Shared storage
- Mechanical/service/receiving

Typical Housing Floor

- Double bedrooms and singles
- Multifixture bathrooms centrally located in each wing
- Hall lounges at inside corner with shared visual connection
- Study nooks
- Entries to housing wings at first floor

(See Figures 7.20–7.22.)

Figure 7.20 Bornhuetter Hall courtyard © Michael Moran.

Figure 7.22 Bornhuetter Hall entrance.

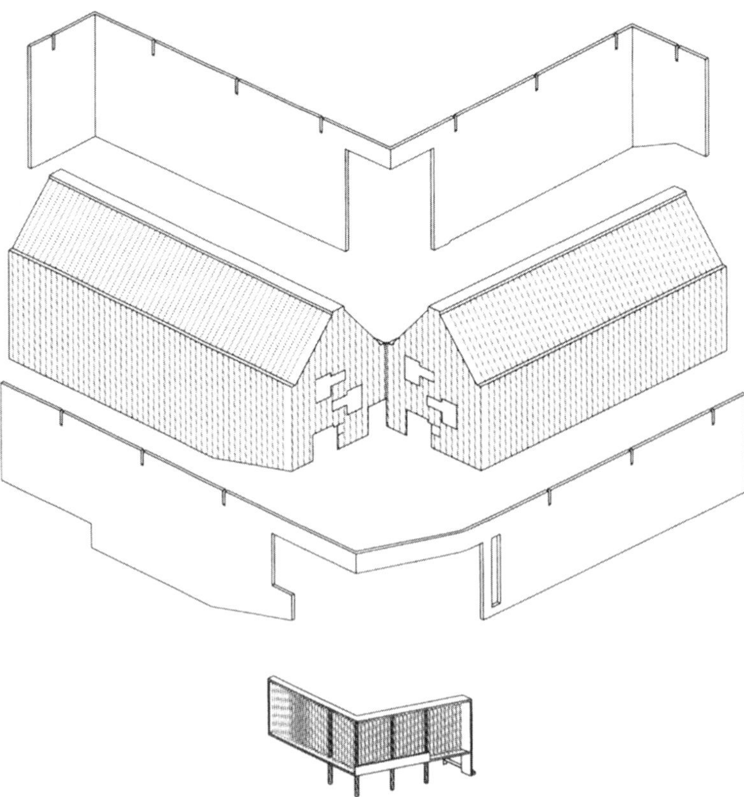

Figure 7.21 Bornhuetter Hall diagram.

CAMPUS HOUSING
CASE STUDY 3

MCLAUGHLIN CLUSTER HOUSING
Dartmouth College, Hanover, New Hampshire

Architect: Moore Ruble Yudell Architect & Planners
Executive architect: Bruner/Cott & Associates

> *This team was able to marry Dartmouth's past and future in an organic way. They've created environmentally sound, wonderful spaces that speak to the nature of our visually simple campus. . . . The planning incorporated strategies to mitigate the impact of very large buildings within the context of an intimate pedestrian oriented campus.*
>
> *— Nancy Jeton, Chair of the Board of Trustees Committee on Master Plan and Facilities*

The McLaughlin Cluster Housing provides 343 new beds within a new residential community that allows choices for living and study and mixes lower and upper classmates. The housing is composed of simple brick forms with gabled copper roof containing the student rooms, which are linked by transparent connectors containing living and kitchen spaces. The buildings form a central courtyard used for outdoor play and study, while multiple entries animate the street and internal courtyard and allow for connections across campus.

- Year completed: Fall 2006
- Site area: 3.2 acres
- Building area: 134,000 sq ft
- Number of beds: 343 beds/3–4 stories
- Six residential halls/three halls linked in two housing wings
- Average square footage/bed: 390 sq ft/bed total building area; 135 sq ft/bed in rooms
- Room types: multiple room types—doubles, singles, suites
- Bathroom type: individual gender neutral
- LEED Gold
- Cost/bed (in 2006 dollars): approximately $113,700

Creating a Social Plaid to Support Student Community

- Distribute social living, lounge, kitchen, and dining areas horizontally on each floor along a common path to encourage informal encounters.
- Promote interaction vertically between floors by limiting housing to primarily four levels, with social stairs interconnecting shared study and lounge spaces.
- Centrally locate the student commons within the housing cluster to provide a social heart for the complex.
- Provide student choice with a variety of room types.
- Facilitate movement and provide opportunities for identity with multiple building entrances to each hall.
- Program outdoor gathering spaces.

Living Sustainably

- Integrated design considers human aspects of comfort, maintainability, durability, and New England's harsh winters. High-performance building systems include radiant heating and cooling, heat recovery from hot water, and use of renewable energy.
- The McLaughlin Cluster project was used as a case study in the college's environmental studies curriculum during the design process.
- Greenlite, an online web page developed by students and faculty, allows students to instantly monitor energy usage in the McLaughlin Cluster, increasing awareness and creating competition between halls to reduce energy use.

Key Spaces on Typical Floor

- Variety of room types encourages mix of upper and lower classmates
- Two-room doubles at 265 sq ft
- Singles at 130 sq ft
- Suites with 4–5 bedrooms and with living area and bathroom
- Three halls of 15–20 beds interconnected by shared living rooms within each wing
- Individual gender-neutral bathrooms and showers: 1 fixture per every 4–6 beds
- Living rooms with kitchen/dining—one kitchen per floor encourages interaction

- Small studies and informal lounges
- Trash/recycling

Shared Amenities

- Student commons and commons kitchen for entire cluster
- Faculty apartment
- Graduate student apartment
- Cluster housing offices
- Campuswide conference room
- Shared laundry in basement of each wing
- Shared storage in basement of each wing

(See Figures 7.23 –7.26.)

Figure 7.23 Dartmouth College housing. © Timothy Hursley.

Figure 7.24 Site plan.

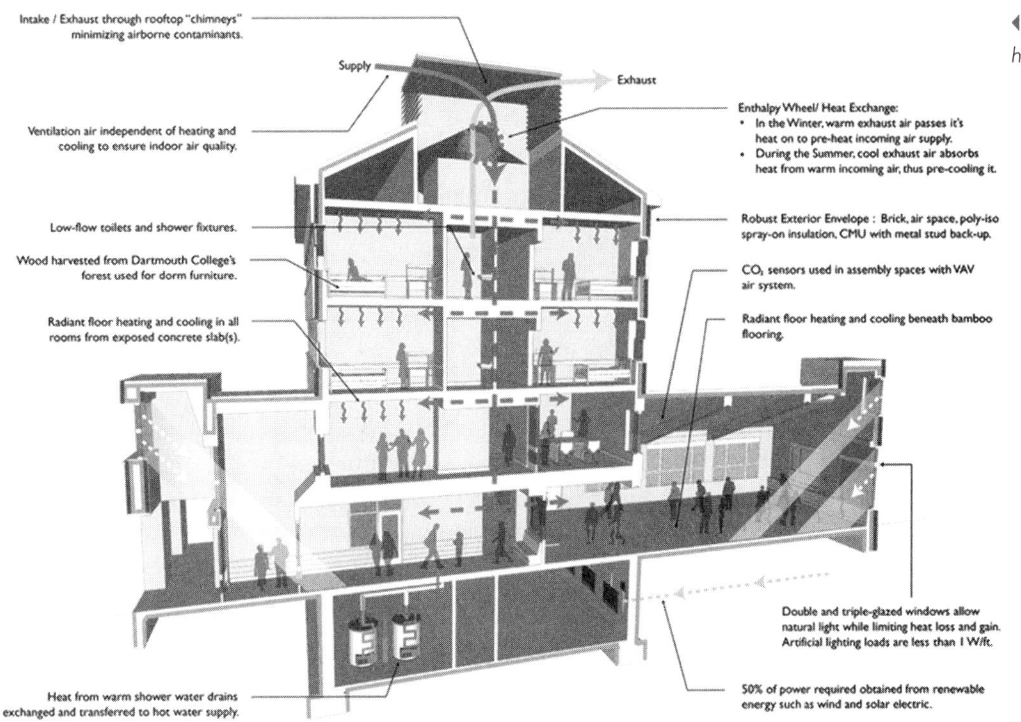

◀ *Figure 7.25 Dartmouth housing diagram.*

◀ *Figure 7.26 Dartmouth housing area.*

CAMPUS HOUSING
CASE STUDY 4

WILLOW STREET RESIDENCE HALL
Tulane University, New Orleans, Louisiana

Architect: Mack Scogin Merrill Elam Architects

> *The Student Housing at Willow Street project is one of highly divergent and seemingly incompatible requirements. . . . The "ranges," a term borrowed from the second tier of buildings off the lawn at the University of Virginia, serve as a garden wall, screening the student housing from the Audubon neighbors. Bringing comfort to the homeowners, the "ranges" provide unique living environments for honor students.*
>
> —Mack Scogin Merrill Elam Architects

The design of the Willow Street Residence Hall is informed by the distinctive features of traditional New Orleans buildings, including, most importantly, the exterior courtyard. Of similar size and proportion to local French Quarter spaces, these courtyards provide necessary shade and planting. They also create social spaces for student interaction, an extremely important consideration for the university, and establish clear zones of security within this colorful and often tough port city.

- Year completed: 1999
- Site area: 90,000 sq ft
- Building area: 108,000 sq ft
- Number of beds: 330 beds divided among four buildings/3–4 stories
- Courtyard houses: single-room and double-room suites
- Ranges private flats, 2-story lofts as duplex units
- Average square footage/bed: 327 sq ft/bed total building area; 160–200 sq ft/bed in rooms
- Bathroom type: shared within two-room suite
- Cost/bed (in 1999 dollars): approximately $36,400

Developing Solutions Informed by New Orleans Traditions

- Campus goal to create housing that attracts students to live on campus and return a collegiate atmosphere to this north campus area
- Respect Audubon neighbors to the west, where student housing coexists with the back fences of adjacent homes
- Architecture influenced by New Orleans buildings, including tall, generous windows; interior wood shutters; metal work details; stairs and balconies; and exterior courtyards

Breaking Down Scale/Restating the Problem Ranges as Garden Wall

- Establishes buffer zone between neighbors and denser student housing courts
- Screens student housing so students cannot be seen or heard
- Ranges create unique living environment for honor students

Exterior Courtyard Typology

- Secure outdoor zones for students within potentially tough city context
- Similar size and proportion to local French Quarter spaces

Key Spaces on Typical Floor

- Three courtyard buildings
- Two-room suites with:
  - Two double rooms sharing a bath
  - Two single rooms sharing a bath
  - One single and one double room sharing a bath
- Social lounge
- Kitchen
- Study rooms
- Balconies
- Laundry

Ranges: Leadership Village (By Application Only)

- 20 students in single-room suites
- 40 students in 2-story, double-occupancy loft suites
- Spiral stairs and balconies

Shared Amenities
- Classrooms
- Community space
- Conference room
- Computer concierge/cybercafé on ground floor
- Café and specialty shops
- Laundry room
- Trash/recycling center
- Vending machines
- Two ground-level apartments
- Terraces and courtyards

(See Figures 7.28–7.30.)

Figure 7.27 Tulane University housing rendering.

Figure 7.28 Tulane University housing detail.

▸ *Figure 7.29 Tulane University housing unit.*

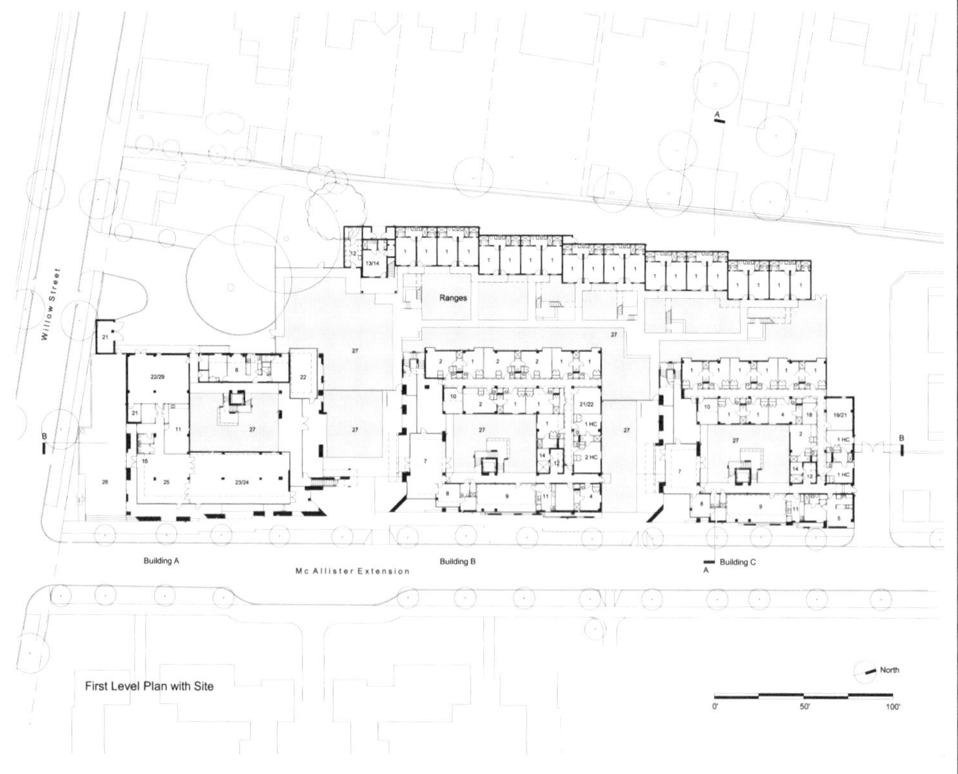

▸ *Figure 7.30 Tulane University plan.*

CAMPUS HOUSING
CASE STUDY 5

MANZANITA VILLAGE

University of California, Santa Barbara

Architect: Moore Ruble Yudell Architect & Planners
Executive architect: DesignARC

> *"Great effort was made to balance individuality and community. The buildings are conceived as a three dimensional social plaid encouraging more dynamic social interaction."*

Manzanita Village is an 800-bed undergraduate residential complex primarily for returning second- and third-year students. Rooms are organized into smaller-scale houses to create an intimate environment that lends itself to special student communities and affinity groups. The planning is shaped to enhance and express community at multiple scales. In response to a site where the campus meets the ocean, we inflected the typologies of the courtyard and the urban square to establish strong social places and connect to the power of the landscape.

- Year completed: 2002
- Site area: 14.5 acres
- Building area: 233,400 sq ft
- Number of beds: 800 beds in 17 residential houses, creating three quads
- Room types: doubles and singles
- Average square footage/bed: 290 sq ft/bed total building area
- Bathroom type: communal
- Cost/bed (in 2002 dollars): approximately $62,300
- Built to surpass California Title 24

Balancing the Individual and the Community

- Active pedestrian paths intersecting at a central plaza where housing, dining, and academic uses all have a strong presence
- Exterior paths and courtyards shaped to contain community and oriented toward the landscape
- Three-dimensional social plaid of vertical social magnets composed of entries, lounges, studies, kitchens, and laundries collected into a hub of activity
- Six houses per quad linked in three pairs of 40–60 students
- Approximately 270 students per each of three quads

Key Spaces on Typical Floor

- Mix of single and double rooms
- Typical double 180 sq ft
- Typical single 130 sq ft
- Small communal bathrooms: ratio of one per four beds at 100 sq ft
- Lounges/study
- Laundry/vending (one per house)
- Kitchen (one per house)

Shared Amenities

- Carrillo Dining Commons
- Interior and exterior dining seating areas
- Housing complex administration offices
- Live-in resident director
- Technology center with computer and study hall
- Multipurpose rooms
- Storage
- Swimming pool and deck area
- Volleyball courts
- Surf showers
- Barbeque areas

(See Figures 7.31–7.34.)

Figure 7.31 Manzanita Village housing © Art Gray.

▶ *Figure 7.32 Manzanita housing aerial.* © Werner Huthmacher, Berlin.

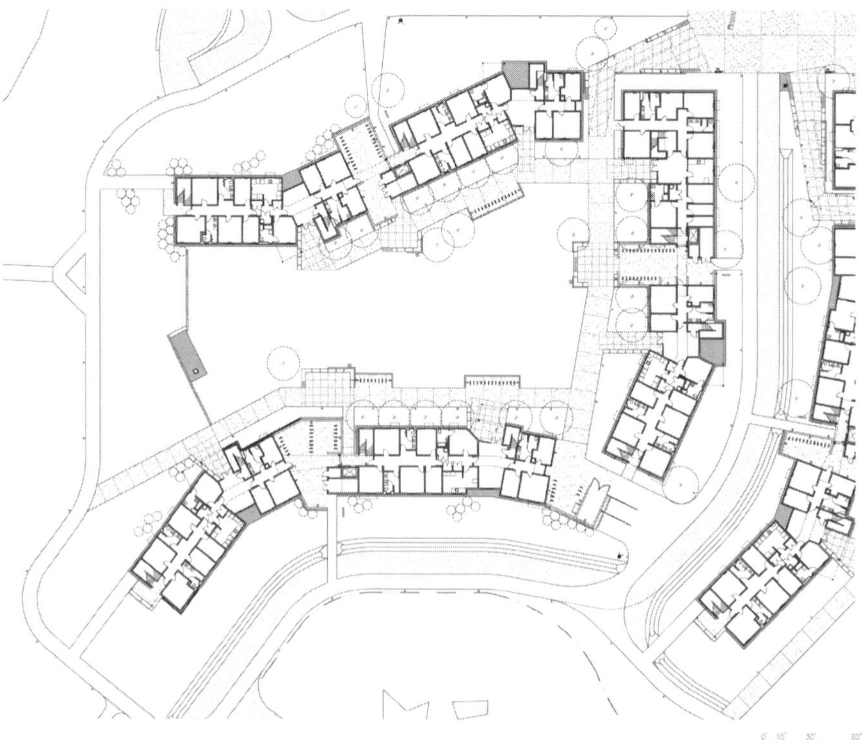

▶ *Figure 7.33 Site plan.*

◀ *Figure 7.34* *Manzanita Village outdoor dining.*

◀ *Figure 7.35* *Manzanita Village housing.*

CAMPUS HOUSING **CASE STUDY 6**

CHARLES DAVID KEELING APARTMENTS

University of California, San Diego

Architect: KieranTimberlake

> *The design truly capitalizes on San Diego's ideal climate. Together with the recent renovation of the adjacent Fleet residence halls, Revelle College is now more unified with old and new structures that create shared spaces and define the west edge of the campus.*
>
> —KieranTimberlake

The Charles David Keeling Apartments, located within Revelle College on the southwestern edge of the University of California San Diego campus overlooking the coastal cliffs of La Jolla, are designed to promote social interaction and outdoor living. Three cast-in-place concrete structures—one 10-story, one 8-story, and one 5-story—provide new housing for 510 students and two resident deans in 85 six-person apartments. Apartments are arranged along a single-loaded exterior corridor so that each space receives abundant daylight, natural ventilation, and views.

- Year completed: Summer 2011
- Site area: 3.3 acres
- Building area: 159,600 sq ft
- Number of beds: 510 beds/5, 8, and 10 stories
- Room types: six-person apartments
- Average square footage/bed: 313 sq ft/bed total building area
- Bathroom type: private bathroom in apartments with compartmentalized fixtures
- Cost/bed (in 2011 dollars): approximately $90,200 (final number witheld)

Project Goals

- Apartment-style units for undergraduate housing that support the university's long-range development plan goal of accommodating 50 percent of all students on campus and Revelle's residential college culture
- Enhances Revelle's place at the historic campus core, which is defined by its distinctive 1960s Southern California architecture
- An ambitiously sustainable building that grows out of San Diego's ideal climate and specific environmental constraints
- Outperform Title 24 by 35 percent and achieve LEED Platinum rating
- Control solar heat gain with deep overhangs on south and vertical shading on west
- Manage stormwater with green roof and biofiltration swales
- Water conservation through graywater treatment and water-efficient fixtures and plantings

Figure 7.36 Charles David Keeling housing. © Kieran Timberlake.

Shared Amenities

- Two resident dean apartments
- Floor lounges
- Meeting rooms
- Outdoor courtyard
- Usable green roof terraces/walkways

(See Figures 7.35–7.38.)

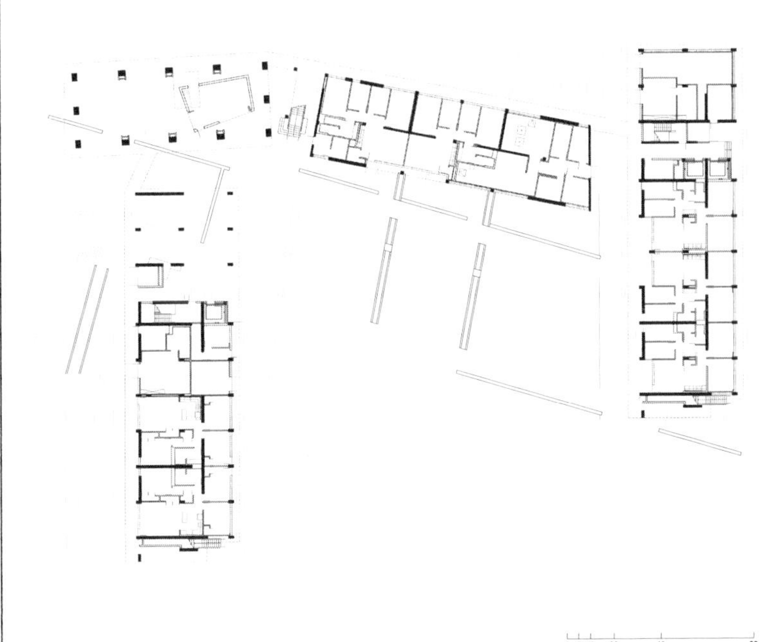

Figure 7.37 Charles David Keeling apartments plan. © Kieran Timberlake.

Figure 7.38 Controlling solar heat gain with deep overhangs. © David Harrison.

CHAPTER 8

ATHLETIC AND RECREATION FACILITIES

David Body, FAIA, RIBA, Cannon Design

> *Give about two hours a day to exercise; for health must not be sacrificed to learning. A strong body makes the mind strong.*
>
> —Thomas Jefferson

Sports facilities, ranging from large arenas for basketball and ice hockey to natatoriums and recreation centers (see Figure 8.1), share some design and planning issues and concerns. However, each type of facility has attributes unique to its use or program.

This chapter examines the range of campus facilities serving the full spectrum of programs, from intercollegiate athletics to intramural competition to recreation and fitness opportunities. Each institution's programs and goals are specific to its mission and to the current and future needs of its students, faculty, staff, and community.

SHIFTING TRENDS IN SPORTS AND FITNESS

Collegiate physical exercise and competition programs have a long tradition. Introduced to campuses in the nineteenth century and firmly entrenched by the

Figure 8.1 Entrance to Activities and Recreation Center (ARC), University of California, Davis. Cannon Design. Photography by: © Tom Bonner.

1920s, such programs were founded on the belief that building both mind and body is crucial to developing the whole person. This notion was perhaps best expressed in 1923 by Jesse Feiring Williams of Columbia University Teachers' College, who said that exercise and competition are a learning medium providing "education through the physical" rather than "education of the physical."

Physical education in the nineteenth century was organized around health, hygiene, exercise, and instruction, with an emphasis on individual activities such as gymnastics, calisthenics, and exercise programs. In the early years of the twentieth century, with baseball, basketball, volleyball, and football growing in popularity, team sports rather than calisthenics received greater emphasis. Although degree programs in physical education are offered at many institutions today, their inclusion in the everyday student core curriculum has declined sharply. Very few colleges and universities mandate even token participation in physical education courses.

Still, physical exercise and fitness are today an unquestionable part of college life. Driven by a growing interest in both entertainment and health, students in large numbers are attracted to spectator sports and are eager to participate in recreational and fitness opportunities. As a result, the programs that have strong support on campus today are intercollegiate sports for student athletes and recreation for the general student body.

A competitive college admissions environment has shaped athletic and recreation facility design. The athletic traditions and recreational opportunities offered by a college or university are often a critical point in the decision-making process of the prospective student.

Recreation facility design is largely driven by recruitment and retention and, nowadays, by the preferences of the millennial student. Thus, climbing and bouldering, outdoor activities, personal training, mind/body classes, massage therapy, indoor soccer, and more sophisticated food service options are growing trends within the recreation center. Increasingly, the recreation center is called a "wellness center," a "fitness center," a "health and fitness center," or even a "student life center," perhaps as a reaction to the "country club" connotation as well as recognition of the increased interest in fitness by students, faculty, and staff.

Other, more global, campus-planning trends are a major influence as well. One example is incorporating varying degrees of health and wellness programs within the recreation building. These range from the simple information center to the fully equipped student health services center included as a discrete but integrated component.

Another important trend has been the emergence of "fusion buildings," which combine different and often previously competitive components of student life with a traditional recreation facility, including traditional student union functions, foodservice, student health services, intercollegiate athletics, and campus events. The University Center at Nova Southeastern University in Ft. Lauderdale, Florida, which includes recreation, athletics, a 4,400-seat arena, a student union, foodservice, music and dance departments, and performance spaces, is a prime example.

ATHLETICS AND RECREATION FACILITIES
CASE STUDY 1

UNIVERSITY CENTER
Nova Southeastern University, Ft. Lauderdale, Florida

Architect: Cannon Design

> *We are beginning to build a "sense of belonging" and an affinity for NSU which we have long lacked.*
>
> *Today, students meet their best friends along the spine of the UC at orientation and professors waiting for racquetball courts chat with students who are in the free weight area. The UC is a transformational building "outside of the classroom" because of the interaction it fosters between students, faculty and staff.*
>
> —Dr. Brad A. Williams, Dean of Student Affairs, Nova Southeastern University

University Center is a "fusion" facility that combines student center functions, including campus dining facilities and student activity space, a 4,400-seat intercollegiate sports arena (see Figure 8.2) and convocation center, a recreation center (see Figure 8.3), and a performing arts center.

A 3-story, skylit galleria offers physical and visual access to all program components (see Figure 8.4). The building's location at the center of campus, between academic buildings and student residences, draws

Figure 8.2 Sports arena. University Center, Nova Southeastern University, Ft. Lauderdale, Florida. Cannon Design. Photography by Hedrich Blessing Photography/Jon Miller.

Figure 8.3 Fitness center. University Center, Nova Southeastern University, Ft. Lauderdale, Florida. Cannon Design. Photography by Hedrich Blessing Photography/Jon Miller.

Figure 8.4 Skylit galleria. University Center, Nova Southeastern University, Ft. Lauderdale, Florida. Cannon Design. Photography by Hedrich Blessing Photography/Jon Miller.

students through the galleria on their daily journeys, bringing them into contact with the varied activity inside and with one another.

Sustainability

A number of the building's sustainable strategies and components reduce operational costs, including an energy recovery system, carbon dioxide occupancy sensors, low-flow plumbing fixtures, daylighting, and high-performance glazing. The chilled-water system increases ice storage capacity so that ice can be made during off-peak hours at lower utility costs.

- 344,600 sq ft
- 309,600 sq ft new
- 35,000 sq ft renovation
- Completed in 2009
- LEED Silver equivalent

ATHLETICS, RECREATION, INTRAMURALS, AND CLUB SPORTS

Intercollegiate sports are governed by the National Collegiate Athletic Association (NCAA) and the National Association of Intercollegiate Athletics (NAIA), which are discussed in detail in the following section. Club sports thrive at a competitive level just below intercollegiate intensity.

Because intercollegiate sports entail extensive standards and regulations and are frequently important revenue generators, the design of big-ticket facilities, such as arenas or natatoriums, is typically influenced by NCAA rules or recommendations.

Intramurals are organized sports played at a recreational level strictly among an institution's general student body. Although less expensive to run than intercollegiate or club sports, they require organizational support and facilities and, along with recreational and fitness programs, are likely to serve a much higher percentage of the campus population.

Athletics

National Collegiate Athletic Association (NCAA)

The NCAA classifies institutions with similar programs in three divisions. It is not uncommon for a school to play one sport, such as ice hockey, lacrosse, or soccer, in one division and most of its other sports in a lower division.

Division I

Member institutions must sponsor at least seven sports for men and seven for women, or six for men and eight for women, including two team sports for each gender. Each playing season must be represented by both genders (see Table 8.1). Contest and participant minimums are established for each sport along with scheduling criteria. Division I schools invariably devote substantial resources to athletics, including financial aid to athletes, inasmuch as there is no restriction against giving financial aid within established limits on the basis of athletic ability.

Division II

Member institutions must sponsor at least five sports for men and five for women, or four for men and six for women, including two team sports for each gender. Again, each playing season must be represented by both genders. As in Division I, Division II specifies contest and participant minimums for each sport. Financial aid may not exceed established minimums.

Division III

Division III member institutions have regulations similar to those of Division II, with the significant difference that Division III schools may only award financial aid on the basis of need, not on the basis of athletic ability.

National Association of Intercollegiate Athletics (NAIA)

The NAIA has 300 member institutions and administers 11 men's sports and 10 women's sports. The level of competition is similar to that in NCAA Division III, but some scholarship aid is permitted. Facility needs are similar to those for the NCAA programs.

Recreation, Intramurals, and Club Sports

The administrative structure of these programs is determined generally by the size of the institution and the intercollegiate level of competition. On larger campuses with a significant athletic program, they are most frequently administered by the department of student recreation, which is a division of the department of student affairs or, less frequently, a division of Associated Students (AS).

Table 8.1 NCAA Sports by Season

Fall	Winter	Spring
Men's cross country	Men's basketball	Baseball
Women's cross country	Women's basketball	Men's golf
Field hockey	Women's bowling	Women's golf
Football	Fencing	Men's lacrosse
Men's soccer	Men's gymnastics	Women's lacrosse
Women's soccer	Women's gymnastics	Women's rowing
Women's volleyball	Men's ice hockey	Softball
Men's water polo	Women's ice hockey	Men's tennis
	Rifle	Women's tennis
	Skiing	Men's outdoor track
	Men's swimming and diving	Women's outdoor track
	Women's swimming and diving	Men's volleyball
	Men's indoor track	Women's water polo
	Women's indoor track	
	Men's wrestling	
	Men's fencing	
	Women's fencing	
	Men's rifle	
	Women's rifle	
	Men's skiing	
	Women's skiing	

On smaller campuses that compete in NCAA Division II or Division III or in the NAIA, recreation is most often a component of the department of athletics.

Most recreation departments are members of the National Intramural Recreational Sports Association (NIRSA), a national organization with over 650 institutional members. NIRSA provides guidance to its members on a wide range of topics, including facility standards, programming (see Table 8.2), staffing, and operations, and its publications are available to the public.

The student recreation center as it is understood today emerged as a distinct building type in the early 1980s, and on many campuses it has replaced the student union as a focus of campus social life for a large percentage of students. The building may also be managed by a student committee, which, because they fund it by assessing themselves an additional fee, control the programs offered and also whether and

Table 8.2 Indoor Recreational Sports		
Aerobics	Indoor triathlon	Stomp
Air pistol	Innertube water polo	Swimming
Air rifle	Jogging	Table tennis
Badminton	Korfball	Trekking
Basketball	Kumdo	Underwater hockey
Belly dancing	Martial arts	Uni-hock
Boxing	Melonball	Volleyball
Broomball	Pickleball	Walking
Capoeira	Pillow polo	Wallyball
Flickerball	Quickball	Water basketball
Floor hockey	Racquetball	Water polo
Goal ball	Roller hockey	Water volleyball
Hoover ball	Short court	Weight lifting
Indoor soccer	Spinning	Wrestling
Indoor track	Squash	Yoga/tai chi

when parts of the building can be used by athletes or physical education. Many campuses report that participation in recreational activities exceeds 70 percent. Studies are under way to correlate improved academic achievement with this type of participation.

FACILITIES

In general, the larger the institution and the higher the level of NCAA competition, the more likely it is that the athletic facilities will be dedicated exclusively to the competitive athlete, with very little sharing. The most frequent exceptions are the natatorium, fieldhouse, and practice field space due to the cost of aquatic facilities and lack of available land on many campuses.

At smaller institutions that participate in NCAA Divisions II and III or the NAIA, there may be more sharing, although the recreational use is limited to times when athletic competition or practice is not scheduled. This conflict, along with increased interest in exercise and wellness among students, has been the primary stimulus for the proliferation of the dedicated student recreation center over the past 25 years.

The discussion of facilities in this section is divided into two categories: those that serve primarily intercollegiate athletics programs and those that serve mainly recreation programs.

Facilities—Athletics

Athletics department officials grow concerned when they sense a disparity between their school's facilities and the facilities of other institutions in their conference or league. This concern is usually most evident when recruiting top athletes, who often weigh several offers and are influenced by the quality of a school's living quarters, training rooms, practice areas, and competition facilities.

Even the best programs may see the need to add and upgrade facilities, and sport-specific buildings can make all the difference. Specific training facilities for football, basketball, hockey, and other sports, together with weight training, sports medicine, and team lockers, are critical to recruiting.

The Collegiate Arena

Indoor sports arenas dominate the landscape of campus life because they house most spectator sports activity from October through March, the greater part of the academic year. Although schools with large Division I programs may have separate arenas for basketball and ice hockey, multipurpose facilities that accommodate both programs, as well as nonsport activities such as concerts, are more typical at midsize and smaller institutions. Although an arena can easily accommodate sporting competitions such as volleyball, gymnastics, and wrestling, frequently nonsport activities such as concerts and trade shows contribute much toward retiring debt or covering annual operating expenses. Further, the seating capacity and floor space of this building type make it not only suitable for activities but also equally practical for convocations, commencements, and other speaker presentations that may draw a large audience without producing revenue.

Arena Design Specifics

An arena's size and shape are guided by the sports it will house. If basketball is the sole activity, the floor dimensions are dictated by the dimensions of the competition court and the desire generally to provide two practice basketball courts, usually perpendicular to the main court (see Figure 8.5). Because sideline seating is preferred for basketball, a typical seating arrangement locates the majority of spectators along the sides of the court.

Ice hockey arena design is dictated only by rink size. The NCAA calls for an ice surface of 100 × 200 ft, but National Hockey League and American Hockey League standards are 85 × 200 ft, which requires less building area and is therefore less expensive. Collegiate hockey rinks range between 85 and 100 ft in width. Most ice hockey arenas are bowl-shaped, with equal seating all around. Open concourses are popular in hockey arenas of 7,000 seats or fewer. Larger hockey and basketball arenas exceeding 7,000 spectators usually require a second or even a third bowl of seating above the concourse, and many have both an interior and an exterior concourse.

Multipurpose Design

If an arena is to be a multi-purpose facility, the design is most frequently organized around the dimensions of the ice rink. To convert from ice hockey to basketball, the dasher boards typically remain in place, and only the glass/acrylic shielding is removed and stored (see Figures 8.6 and 8.7). Ceiling heights of 55 ft or more are generally the rule if there will be a center-hung scoreboard. The minimum clearance for a suspended scoreboard or ceiling is 25 ft, but if the building is to be used for NCAA volleyball, the clear height requirement is 41 ft.

Retractable seating around the center rink/court area results in more flat floor area, which increases seating flexibility for large events such as commencement ceremonies. Seating layout should be designed with care to optimize sight lines, and particular attention should be paid to sight lines from seats designated for spectators in wheelchairs so that their view is not obstructed when people stand in front of them.

Figure 8.5 Multipurpose arena with retractable seats, Centers for Sport and Performing Arts, Adelphi University, Garden City, New York. Cannon Design. Photography by: © David Sundberg/Esto.

Figure 8.6 6,300-seat arena in hockey configuration, Agganis Arena, Boston University. Cannon Design. Photography by: Dave Desroches.

▸ *Figure 8.7 7,300-seat arena in basketball configuration, Agganis Arena, Boston University. Cannon Design.* Photography by: Dave Desroches.

Regardless of the variety of uses contemplated, it is important to plan the operating budget for the labor and time it takes to transform a multipurpose arena from one activity to another.

Access and Parking

Large assembly spaces, such as arenas, that attract audiences from off campus are best located at the edge of campus to minimize traffic impacts on normal campus activities or to take advantage of large fields, parking lots, or nearby public transportation. A good rule of thumb is to provide one parking space for every three to four seats, although fewer spaces may be sufficient if a significant number of seats are restricted to on-campus students.

Other Considerations

Other issues that must be addressed in arena design and planning include general pedestrian circulation in relation to entrance locations; drop-off points for ticket sales; accessibility for people with disabilities; separate access accommodations for buses and teams; and separate access accommodations for deliveries, trash pickup, and television trucks. To enhance circulation and minimize line conflicts, distribute concessions throughout the arena and away from toilets (see Figures 8.8 and 8.9).

The Fieldhouse

The typical fieldhouse is 200 × 300 ft, which accommodates a six-lane, 200 m competition indoor track. Often, it contains four tennis courts or basketball courts in the infield and a system of motorized curtains to subdivide the space for multiple simultaneous activities. Batting cages and netting for practicing throwing events can also be lowered from the ceiling.

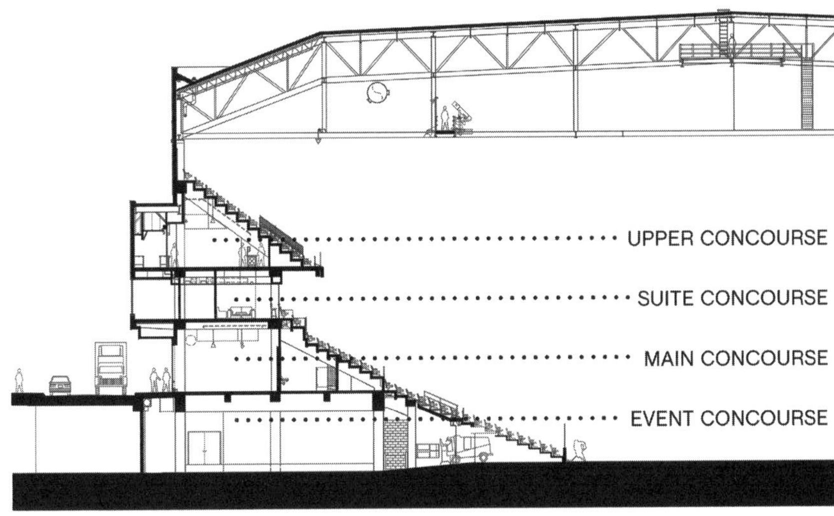

Multiple Concourse Arena Section

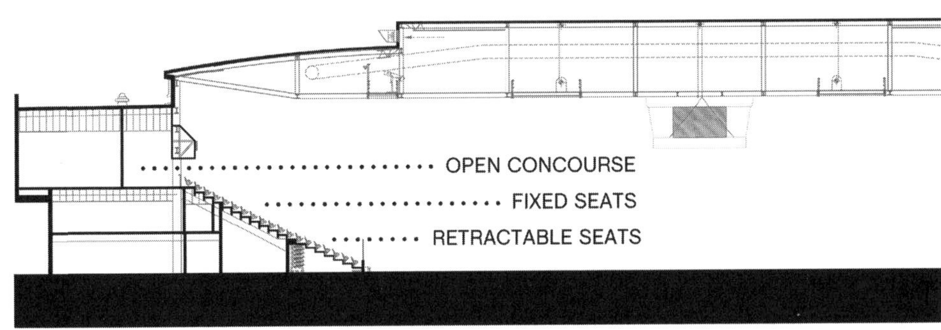

Open Concourse Arena Section

Figure 8.8 Arena concourse sections. Courtesy of Sink Combs Dethlefs, Sports Architects.

The fieldhouse is frequently shared by athletics, recreation, and club sports. Besides track and field, tennis, and basketball, it may also be used for indoor soccer, jogging, physical education, and indoor practice of outdoor sports during inclement weather (see Figure 8.10). On some smaller campuses, the fieldhouse also serves as the competitive venue for basketball and volleyball, with spectators seated on retractable or portable bleachers surrounding an inlaid or portable wood floor.

In smaller colleges and universities, the fieldhouse may be the largest single space and one of the most flexible on campus. It can accommodate as many as 6,000 people for convocations, graduations, and other large campus gatherings. Multiple functions,

▸ *Figure 8.9 Arena concourse and concessions, Agganis Arena, Boston University. Cannon Design.* Photography by Hedrich Blessing Photography/Jon Miller.

▸ *Figure 8.10 1,500-seat fieldhouse with 200 m banked track, Boston University. Cannon Design.* Photography by: Michael Hamilton for Boston University Photography.

along with the number of potential spectators, can make it difficult to meet code requirements for exiting and restroom accommodations.

Walls should be durable and capable of withstanding the impact of a soccer, lacrosse, or hockey ball. Concrete masonry units up to 12 ft in height are the most common. If corrugated or insulated metal panels are used, netting may be required to protect against denting.

Floor surfaces are usually synthetic, either poured urethane or sheet rubber. The floor's resiliency and texture are determined by its uses. If track is the primary activity, a spike-resistant material is important; if tennis, the playing surface will require the approval of the tennis coach.

Recreational basketball can be played on a synthetic surface, but players may not get the same amount of protection from injury that a resilient wood floor system provides.

Often, resilient wood floors are installed in fieldhouses to meet the needs of basketball and volleyball programs in particular. Whether to use a portable wood floor on top of the synthetic surface or to build it into the floor system is not an easy choice. Wood is not a good surface for tennis and will suffer damage from track spikes or similar athletic shoes.

Artificial lighting is usually direct metal halide lighting unless tennis and volleyball are the primary sports, in which case indirect lighting is preferable, as it prevents glare when players look up. Inserting a translucent skylight at the roof ridge can bring in natural light unobtrusively, brightening what may otherwise seem a vast and rather unfriendly box.

Storage space equivalent to 10 percent of the floor area is not too much to provide due to the multiple uses involving numerous pieces of equipment and furnishings. A large overhead, coiling door makes it easier to move large pieces of equipment in and out. If vehicles will drive on the floor, the floor material and sub-base must be able to support their weight.

The structure is usually a pre-engineered system that may be modified to add architectural features that will respond to the campus context. Carefully considered skylights and insulated translucent panels can eliminate the need for artificial lighting during daylight hours.

The Natatorium

The natatorium is the most expensive athletic and recreational facility to construct and to operate, and there should be much deliberation before committing to its configuration (see Figure 8.11). In addition to the physical choices, there is usually a scheduling conflict between athletics, recreation, and, to a lesser extent, physical education and community use.

Many larger institutions have chosen to construct both a competition pool and a separate leisure pool to avoid the compromises inherent in a shared facility (see Figure 8.12). The two major conflicts, apart from schedule, have to do with water depth—7 ft or more for the competition pool and shallower water for the recreational/lap/teaching pool—and with water temperature, which is 78–82° F for the competitive athlete and 84–86° F for the recreational swimmer.

If the pool must be shared, as is the case at some smaller institutions, conflicts and compromises should be thoroughly explored during the programming and design phase.

Competition Pool

Seven organizations govern aquatic sports, and their requirements are not always consistent. They are USA Swimming, the

▸ *Figure 8.11 Competition pool, 25 yd stretch, with movable bulkhead and 600 seats, Fitness and Recreation Center, Boston University. Cannon Design.* Photography by Hedrich Blessing Photography/Jon Miller.

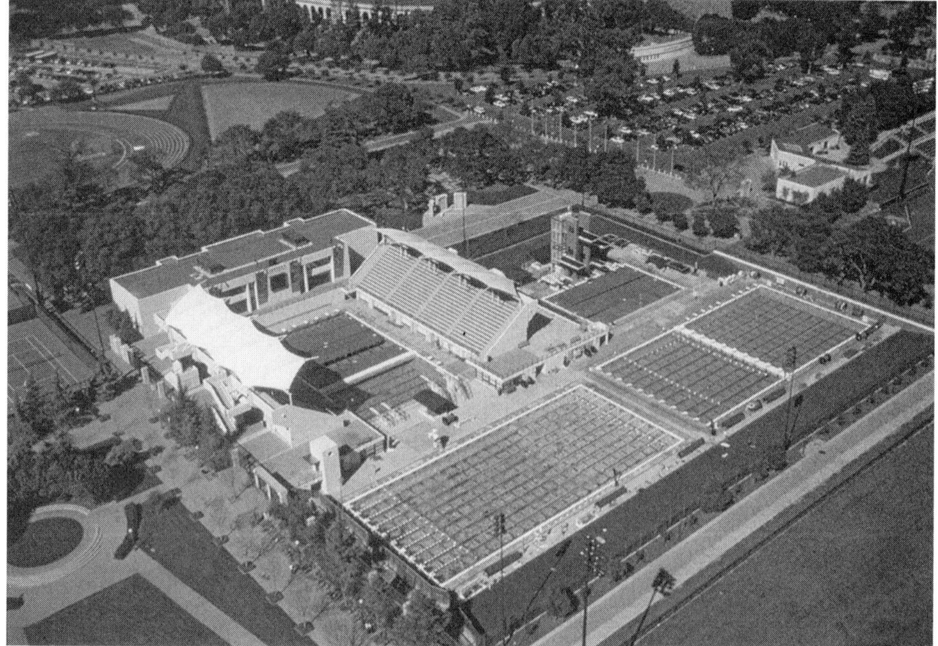

▸ *Figure 8.12 Four-pool aquatics center, Avery Aquatic and Maas Diving Center, Stanford University, Stanford, California. ELS Architecture and Urban Design.* Photography by: Proehl Studios.

National Federation of State High School Associations (NFHS), the NCAA, FINA (International Swimming Federation), USA Water Polo, USA Diving, and USA Synchronized Swimming.

An NCAA pool must be a minimum of six lanes; 75 ft, 1 in. long (1 in. for the timing system touch pad); and 45 ft wide. Each lane is 7 ft, with 1 ft, 6 in. spaces along each side equipped with wave-suppressing lane lines. The depth may vary, but a depth of about 7 ft is considered to create a "fast pool."

Pool length and depth increase if the program includes diving, scuba, or synchronized swimming and if swimming and diving practices are to run concurrently. A pool that is longer than 75 ft yet less than 50 m is termed a "stretch" pool; stretch pools vary in length but generally do not exceed 140 ft, and they have a deeper diving well at one end, depending on the configuration of diving boards and platforms. The swimming and diving sections are separated by a movable bulkhead, usually set at the 75 ft mark, which locks in place in the gutter.

Because NCAA swimming events are conducted at 25 yd (75 ft) under the current rules, pools of this size are popular. However, the training demands and the longer distances required for Olympic trials and events call for a 50 m pool. When designed to the Olympic standard of 50 m, pools are generally subdivided once or twice with bulkheads. A 50 m pool is generally 75 ft, 1 in. across (instead of 45 ft) to allow swimmers in NCAA competition to swim from one side wall to the other. The lanes increase in dimension to 9 ft. The 50 m pool allows for 22 or more lanes for practice or lap swimming, and it also accommodates water polo and, with appropriate depth, diving, synchronized swimming, and scuba.

Many top-level programs have a "dotted I" configuration, which consists of a 50 m × 25 yd pool for swimming competition and a separate 75× 60 ft diving tank.

Spectator seating should be raised above deck level to provide good sightlines and, where possible, be accessed from the rear to eliminate spectator traffic on the pool deck.

Recreation or Leisure Pools

Recreation or leisure pools have become increasingly popular on both large and small campuses (see Figure 8.13, Color Plate 15). Programming includes water volleyball, water basketball, water aerobics, teaching, and inner tube polo; the addition of a big screen is popular for watching football and other events. The pool usually has predominantly shallow water and contains several lap lanes together with leisure components such as lazy rivers, vortexes, bubble benches, and water slides (see Figure 8.14). Climbing walls also can be integrated into the pool design. The decks may also have a therapy spa and sauna. A "wet classroom," with ready access to the deck, is a desirable feature, allowing people to receive instruction on lifesaving and water safety in wet swimsuits (see Figure 8.15).

Design Details

Although bright lighting is desirable in a natatorium, minimizing glare on the surface of the water is essential so that lifeguards can see distressed swimmers below the water's surface. Placing lifeguard stations with their backs to light sources can mitigate this problem to some degree. The installation of overhead translucent skylights is another approach because the angle of reflection is not back into the lifeguards' eyes. Artificial light should be either indirect or vertical.

A second issue is corrosion. Because of the high humidity and the chemicals in the

▸ *Figure 8.13 Lap and leisure pool, Student Recreation and Fitness Center, University of Maine, Orono. Cannon Design.* Photography by: © Anton Grassi/Esto.

▸ *Figure 8.14 Outdoor pool complex with leisure and lap pools, Recreation Aquatics Center, Texas Tech University, Lubbock. Brinkley Sargent Architecture.* Photography by: © Harvey Madison.

◀ *Figure 8.15 Pool and wet classroom, Campus Recreation Center, University of Maryland, Baltimore. Sasaki Associates, Inc.* Photography by: © christopherbarnes.com

natatorium atmosphere, pool environments are highly corrosive to steel. The pool envelope must be tight, with very little to no air infiltration, and careful attention must be paid to the vapor barrier.

Regulations—competitive, environmental, and life safety—are constantly in flux. Care should be taken to design the facility to the current prevailing codes and regulations. For example, states have differing requirements for a minimum depth of pools.

Practice Facilities

Driven by the need to recruit the best athletes, dedicated practice facilities are being constructed for many sports, particularly those that compete in the campus arena (see Figure 8.16). Basketball practice facilities typically contain two competition-size courts with the same floor surface and baskets that are used in the arena. The building may house generously sized locker rooms, team meeting rooms, a players' lounge, satellite weight-training and sports medicine centers, coaches' suites, and even a dedicated hall of fame.

Other sports that may have dedicated facilities with somewhat similar amenities include volleyball, rowing, wrestling, and gymnastics. It is preferable that these programs are contiguous to, or adjacent to, the arena or performance space.

Indoor football practice fields (see Figure 8.17) are becoming a requirement at schools with a strong football program. Sized to accommodate a full-sized artificial-turf field, this kind of facility provides a secure and comfortable all-weather

▸ *Figure 8.16 Basketball Intercollegiate Practice Facility, Virginia Polytechnic Institute and State University, Blacksburg. Cannon Design.* Paul Burk/Paul Burk Photography.

▸ *Figure 8.17 Football indoor practice facility, University of Michigan, Ann Arbor. TMP Architecture, Inc.* Photo: Paul Bednarski Photographics.

environment. The building can range from an innovative and aesthetically pleasing engineering statement to a pre-engineered structure or an inflatable or cable-supported fabric structure.

Office Space Needs

Athletic departments need administrative offices. Here, it is important to consider centralizing coaches and staff in one large administrative suite or situating them in various campus locations close to their training or playing venue. Office sizes may vary according to the stature of the individual; the athletic director or head football or basketball coach may enjoy much larger accommodations than personnel involved in a nonrevenue-producing sport.

Weight Training and Sports Medicine

According to recent statistics, football, wrestling, soccer, and volleyball incur the greatest number of injuries; and football, wrestling, and women's gymnastics incur the most severe injuries. Sports medicine or training rooms are a part of the daily routine of prevention and therapy for the student athlete as well as a critical recruiting tool and, in recent years, have grown in size and complexity to respond to a greater need for treatment and rehabilitation and to incorporate preventative modalities. It includes areas for therapy and pregame or practice taping, and often contains a contiguous aquatic therapy component (see Figure 8.18).

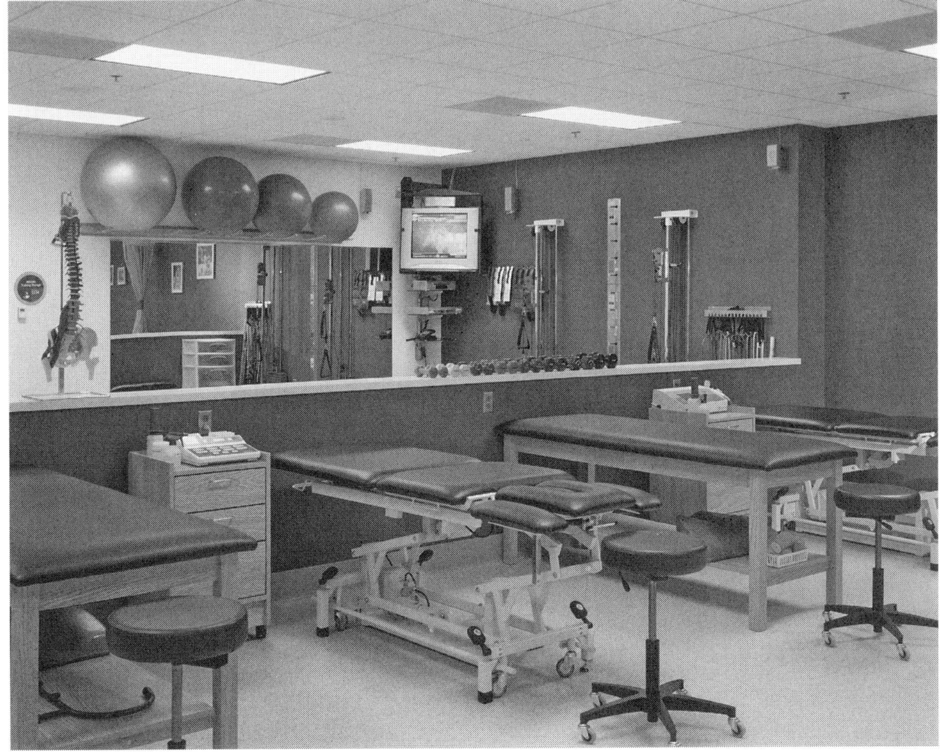

Figure 8.18 Athletic training room, Agganis Arena, Boston University. Cannon Design. Photography by: Hedrich Blessing Photography/Jon Miller.

Weight-training rooms are designed to meet the philosophy of the current strength-training coach and the general needs of the athletic program (see Figure 8.19). The weight room and associated offices can be up to 20,000 sq ft to accommodate a Division I program that includes football. In some cases, separate weight-training rooms are provided for individual sports. The space should be well lit, and it often features motivational images.

Team Locker Rooms

In the past, athletic locker rooms were provided on a seasonal basis at many schools, but because today's athletes are involved in a year-round training regimen—even at the Division III level—teams are assigned designated lockers for the entire year (see Figure 8.20).

The locker room is a home-away-from-home and a symbol of team pride. It can range from a large, lavish room with an adjacent players' lounge for football, basketball, baseball, or hockey, to more modest accommodations for non-revenue, or Olympic, sports.

Other Athletic Facilities

In response to academic eligibility requirements, academic centers for the student athlete have proliferated in recent years. Team meeting rooms to accommodate 15–120 people are required, as are locker and office suites for coaches, whose recruitment is also heavily influenced by an institution's facilities.

A hall of fame is standard for programs of all sizes and can be representative of all sports or related to a specific sport (see Figure 8.21).

▶ *Figure 8.19 Athletic weight room, Acosta Athletic Facility, University of California, Los Angeles. Cannon Design.* Photography by: © Tom Bonner.

◀ *Figure 8.20 Hockey team room, Agganis Center, Boston University.* Cannon Design. Photography by: Hedrich Blessing Photography/Jon Miller.

◀ *Figure 8.21 Basketball Hall of Fame, Basketball Intercollegiate Practice Facility, Virginia Polytechnic Institute and State University, Blacksburg. Cannon Design.* Paul Burk/Paul Burk Photography.

ATHLETICS AND RECREATION FACILITIES CASE STUDY 2

STUDENT RECREATION AND WELLNESS CENTER

California State University, Long Beach

Architect: Cannon Design

> *The Student Recreation and Wellness Center (SRWC) has transformed student life on the CSULB campus. Traditionally a commuter institution, CSULB has seen an increase in the number of students staying on campus, especially in the evenings and weekends, specifically because of this new facility. Even more exciting is the impact this "student life" facility has had on our academic program. The interface between SRWC and our campus academic programs has created educational synergies on campus which did not exist before.*
>
> —Dave Edwards, Ed.D., ASI Associate Executive Director/Director University Student Union, CSULB

CSULB's Student Recreation and Wellness Center anchors student life in a new facility that emphasizes continuity of indoors and outdoors and the belief that health and fitness are essential to academic success. A landscaped entry plaza (see Figure 8.22) with adjoining snack and juice bar provides an outdoor gathering space linked conveniently to the campus's circulation axis. Inside, an interior "street" maximizes views into the building's major functions, which include a 20,000 sq ft cardio/fitness center, a three-court gymnasium, a two-court multipurpose activity court (MAC), multipurpose rooms, two racquetball courts, a wellness center, staff offices, and a jogging track. High-activity spaces enjoy ample

Figure 8.22 Landscaped entry plaza. Student Recreation and Wellness Center, California State University, Long Beach. Cannon Design. Photography by: © Brad Feinknopf 2010.

views of playing fields entry plaza through broad expanses of windows that transform the building into an illuminated beacon at night. A walled courtyard encloses sand volleyball courts and a recreation pool.

Sustainability

The building achieved Leadership in Energy and Environmental Design (LEED) Gold certification. Glazing and sunshading options were carefully chosen to optimize the building's energy efficiency, with insulated low-emissivity (low-E) glazing, glass fins, fritted glass, translucent glass, and other features contributing to the building's energy use reduction of 21 percent below baseline. Air quality is kept high through ventilation system monitoring, low-emitting materials, and a green housekeeping program that utilizes nonhazardous cleaning products and practices.

- 130,000 sq ft
- Site size: 142,000 sq ft
- Completed in 2009
- LEED Gold

Facilities—Recreation, Intramurals, and Club Sports

As stated previously, the recreation center has become one of the primary "see-and-be-seen" spaces on campus, and circulation patterns should be designed to offer a clear view of most activities and to take advantage of the three-dimensional interplay of space that is possible due to the varying volumes of the spaces. Transparency, both internal and external, is key to the success of a recreation building, and the use of glazed walls in fitness centers, squash/racquetball courts, MACs, gymnasiums, and group exercise rooms (see Figure 8.23) can enhance the upbeat feeling. Maximizing "building efficiency" is often not the most important goal, because the building's social aspects take place as much in the "spaces between" as in the activity spaces themselves (see Figure 8.24).

Most recreation centers are designed with a single point of entry that limits access to properly credentialed students, faculty, and staff. Turnstiles activated by student registration cards and/or biometric scanning devices are typically used. A front-desk graphic monitor control can further help with occupant safety, security, and energy performance.

The recreation center has become a fixture on campus, whether located adjacent to residence halls, in the heart of the campus, or on the periphery. It is often an iconic architectural statement that is the starting or ending point for prospective student tours.

Fitness/Weight Room

The most popular space in a recreation center is the fitness/weight room. Typically, this space is organized around three basic

Figure 8.23 Multipurpose room. Student Recreation and Wellness Center, California State University, Long Beach. Cannon Design. Photography by: © Brad Feinknopf 2010.

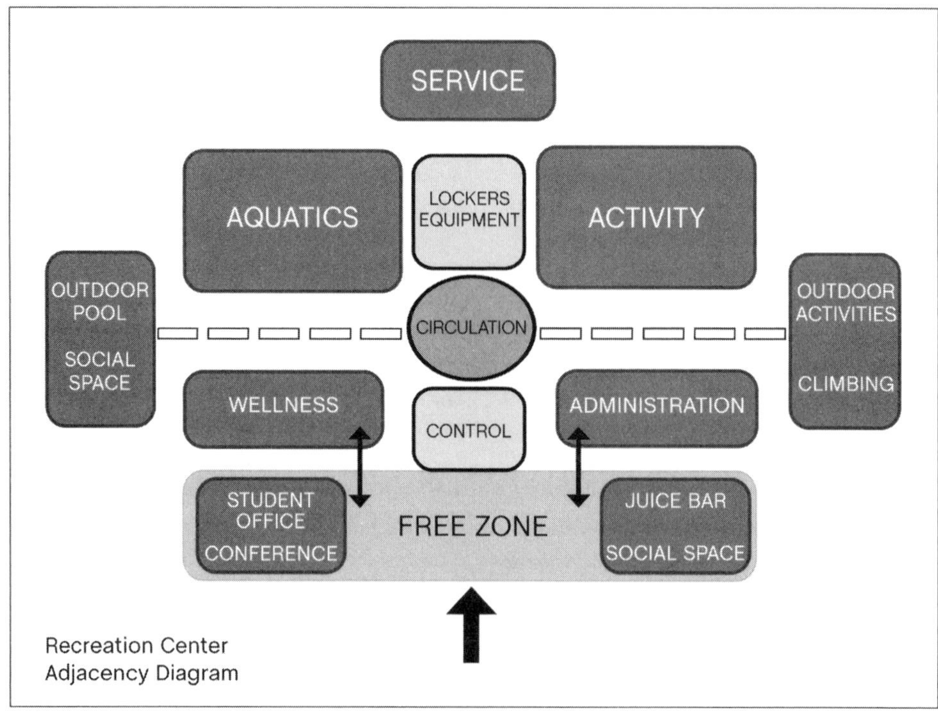

Figure 8.24 Recreation center adjacency diagram. Student Recreation and Wellness Center, California State University, Long Beach. Cannon Design. Courtesy of Cannon Design.

functions: (1) free weights, including dumbbells; (2) aerobic equipment such as treadmills, stair climbers, and stationary cycles; and (3) effort-resistive equipment involving hydraulics, pulleys, chains, or levers. Frequently, aerobic machines are equipped with individual television screens, and they can be used to generate a modest amount of electricity for the building. A control desk makes it easy to monitor users' comings and goings and to hand out items such as towels and weight belts. A stretching area should be set aside near the entrance but out of the major circulation path. Many centers now provide self-monitoring computer stations to track fitness progress such as changes in weight, blood pressure, and heart rate. To accommodate increased interest in personal training, a room is often located adjacent to the fitness weight room for testing, evaluation, and instruction. Part of the room, however, should be screened from view to accommodate those who do not wish to become part of "the show."

Lighting in these spaces is often indirect and softer, for the comfort of participants who frequently look up at the ceiling as they exercise. A 12 ft minimum ceiling is recommended, but many contemporary centers are two levels with the aerobic machines overlooking the main floor. The floor surface should be easy to clean and resilient enough to withstand the impact of free weights without major deformation. The placement of mirrors should be coordinated with the fitness equipment planner, and hydration stations must be installed in strategic locations and provided with a splash-resistant floor. Power requirements for equipment are constantly changing and should be addressed early in the design phase.

Fitness/weight rooms should be located on the lowest building level, or over unoccupied or transient spaces, to avoid the sound and vibration effects of free weights dropped from above. Views into these spaces help market the facility and enhance the see-and-be-seen attraction.

Recreation Gymnasiums

Typically, the recreation gym is sized to accommodate 50 ft wide × 84 ft long (high school standard) basketball courts, although 76 ft long courts are sometimes chosen. If the width is less than 50 ft, it precludes the three-point shot, which has a 20 ft, 9 in. arc. Occasionally, 50 ft × 94 ft NCAA regulation courts are utilized to accommodate collegiate basketball camps. A minimum safety clearance around the courts is 8 ft at the sides and 10 ft at the ends, although dimensions may increase as required by an elevated jogging track clearance or casual seating for intramurals. Clear height is typically 25 ft minimum, with 28–30 ft preferred. Baskets may be fixed or retractable.

A typical two- or three-court gymnasium can also be striped for volleyball and badminton and use portable or retractable net posts (see Figures 8.25 and 8.26). Motorized divider curtains allow different activities to occur simultaneously. Portable goals can also support indoor soccer or floor hockey.

Resilient wood flooring is standard for gymnasiums, with synthetic poured urethane or plastic tile as an alternative.

Multi-purpose Activity Courts (MACs)

Multi-purpose activity courts are enclosed or semi-enclosed spaces designed for activities that involve a projectile, such as soccer and floor hockey (see Figure 8.27). Generally, they are also equipped for basketball and volleyball.

Enclosed on all sides, MACs can accommodate a variety of sport activities that the gymnasium's vast volume cannot. MACs come in all sizes and are ideally configured according to specific requirements, such as the preferred dimensions for roller hockey (the National In-Line Hockey Association requires 80 × 180 ft) or indoor soccer (the U.S. Indoor Soccer Association recommends 75 × 180 ft for youth and amateur play). More often, they are a nonstandard size that is related to the size of a one-court (70 × 114 ft) or two-court (130 × 114 ft) recreational gymnasium that allows for programming flexibility.

A MAC will usually have rounded corners, recessed goals, and player benches. The walls are often a combination of concrete block and ice hockey-type dasher boards. The walls must be designed to resist the impact of soccer balls and other projectiles.

Floor surface options depend on primary and secondary uses. If indoor soccer, basketball, and volleyball share priority, a resilient wood floor is preferred. If indoor soccer is the primary use, a synthetic surface may be appropriate. For roller hockey and floor hockey, a plastic tile or acrylic material should be considered because they are resistant to skates and the impact of sticks.

Jogging Track

Reintroduced in the design of recreation centers in the mid-1980s, the jogging track was a basic element in older turn-of-the-century buildings.

A track works best if it runs around at least three playing courts, approximately 11 laps to a mile. Banked corners are seen occasionally, but their value for walking and jogging is debated. A flat floor with a 15 ft minimum radius is most common. Four 3 ft wide lanes are optimal, but three lanes are more common. Projections from

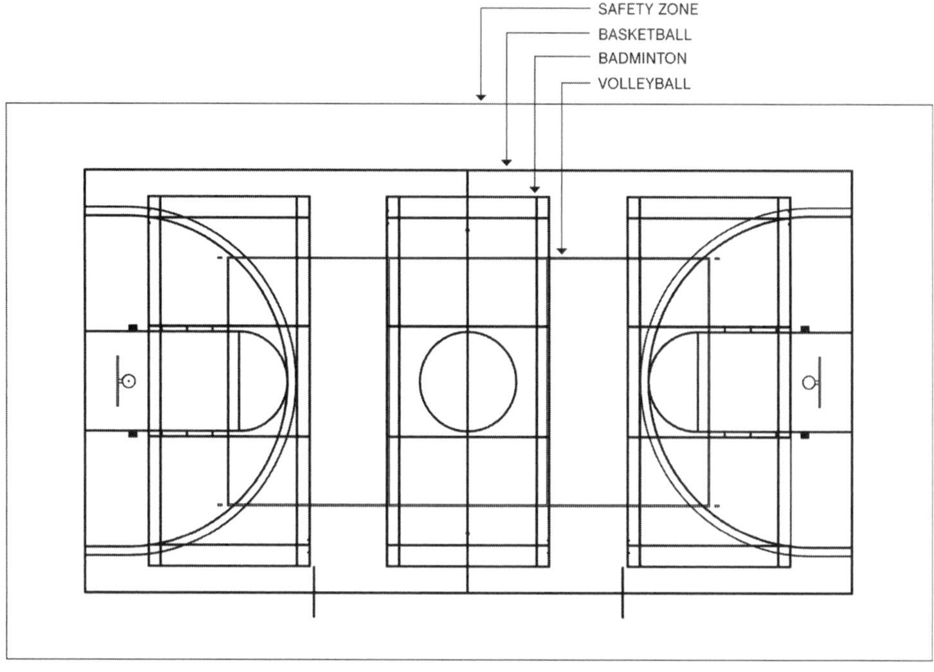

▶ *Figure 8.25 Universal court layout. Student Recreation and Wellness Center, California State University, Long Beach. Cannon Design.* Courtesy of Cannon Design.

▶ *Figure 8.26 Recreation gymnasium, Student Recreation and Wellness Center, California State University, Long Beach. Cannon Design.* Photography by: © Brad Feinknopf 2010.

◀ *Figure 8.27 Multipurpose activity court, Recreation Center, University of Alabama, Birmingham. Cannon Design/ William Blackstock Architects.* Photography by: © Rion Rizzo/Creative Sources Photography, Inc.

the wall should be padded if hazardous to joggers. Contemporary recreation centers usually allow the jogging track to escape the confines of the gymnasium and to encircle other areas of the building, such as the entrance lobby, fitness center, MAC, and natatorium (see Figure 8.28). In some cases, the track even escapes the confines of the building, capturing views over the campus (see Figure 8.29).

Track surfaces are typically sheet goods of rubber or poured urethane that provide resiliency and shock absorption. A 9–10 mm product is acceptable; a thicker material is better but more expensive. A product of 13 mm thickness, the International Amateur Athletic Federation (IAAF) standard, is preferred.

Group Exercise Rooms

Group exercise or multipurpose rooms that lend themselves to a range of activities, such as aerobics, martial arts, dance, and fencing, require minimal setup time and can easily cycle from one time slot to another within a weekly schedule (see Figure 8.30). Where possible, "spinning," or bicycle exercise classes, should occupy a separate room, often with tiered decks, so that equipment need not be moved and a more theatrical environment can be created.

Floors in these spaces are most commonly wood, designed for resiliency and shock absorption. Ceiling heights should be 12 ft minimum, sometimes higher to accommodate certain martial arts involving weapon skills. Natural light and views to the exterior

▶ *Figure 8.28 Elevated jogging track and control desk, Recreation Center, University of Alabama, Birmingham. Cannon Design/ William Blackstock Architects.* Photography by: © Rion Rizzo/Creative Sources Photography, Inc.

◀ *Figure 8.29 Jogging track exiting the Recreation Center, University of Alabama, Birmingham. Cannon Design/ William Blackstock Architects.* Photography by: © Rion Rizzo/Creative Sources Photography, Inc.

◀ *Figure 8.30 Multipurpose room and casual seating, Student Recreation and Wellness Center, California State University, Long Beach. Cannon Design.* Photography by: © Brad Feinknopf 2010.

are desirable, although views into the space may have to be controlled out of respect for the participants' modesty and concentration. Artificial light should permit different levels of illumination to suit the activity. Multipurpose rooms also demand adequate, easily accessible storage for equipment and supplies.

Racquetball, Handball, and Squash

Although racquetball has declined in recent years, it is still a popular activity. The court is 20 ft wide × 40 ft long × 20 ft high, and the game is played off all six surfaces, including the ceiling. Handball, strong in some areas of the country, uses the same court but with different floor and wall markings.

Since the adoption in the United States of the international-size court, squash has enjoyed significant growth. The court is 21 ft wide × 32 ft long and requires a clear height of 18 ft, 6 in. The North American court, which is slowly being phased out, is 18 ft, 6 in. wide × 32 ft long. Unlike racquetball, the ceiling is not in play in squash.

Tempered-glass court systems, available for both racquetball and squash, can furnish a court with one, two, three, or four glass walls. A glass back wall is the most frequently used. Although movable glass back walls can be installed to permit the speedy conversion of a racquetball court to a squash court, because racquetball courts are 20 ft wide, this converted court is 1 ft narrower than the international-size squash court. Some facilities have chosen to make convertible recreational racquetball courts 21 feet wide (see Figure 8.31).

Doubles squash courts are popular in some areas of the country. A North American doubles court is 25 × 45 × 26 ft clear height, and an international doubles court is 25 ft × 32 ft × 18 ft, 6 in. clear height.

Climbing, Bouldering, and Outdoor Activities

Participation in outdoor activities such as climbing, bouldering, kayaking, camping, and cycling is increasing. As a result, many recreation centers include an outdoor activities center that houses a trip-planning room; rental center counter; and significant storage space for tents, kayaks, and bicycles.

An indoor climbing and bouldering space is often adjacent to the outdoor activity center (see Figure 8.32). There is a wide variation in the size and complexity of the walls, and this issue should be reviewed with the staff at an early stage of planning, since the implications are wide reaching, including building mass, height, security, lighting, and environment. A synthetic turf indoor facility for soccer, softball, and so on may be located adjacent to the outdoor facilities area (see Figure 8.33).

Recreation Locker Rooms

When designing a recreation locker room, there are three main questions to consider: (1) How many lockers should be included? (2) How big should they be? (3) Should they be available for yearly or semester rental or for day use? These are three of the most difficult programming decisions to be made, each with different requirements due to culture and climate. For economy of space, the answer is day lockers related to the anticipated occupancy of the building; however, rental income for semester or yearly use may offset the cost of the initial additional building area for dedicated lockers over the building's life cycle.

The most common locker size is 12 in. wide and 15 in. deep, although options vary widely. A combination of full- and half-height lockers is typical. Smaller key lockers for backpacks, cell phones, and

Figure 8.31 Convertible racquetball/squash court, Student Recreation and Wellness Center, California State University, Long Beach. Cannon Design. A movable back wall allows both games to be played on one court. Photography by: Kevin Choi/ Courtesy of Cannon Design.

Figure 8.32 Indoor field activities, Adventure Recreation Center, Ohio State University, Columbus. Moody Nolan, Inc. Photography by: © Brad Feinknopf 2010.

▸ *Figure 8.33 Climbing wall, Adventure Recreation Center, Ohio State University, Columbus. Moody Nolan, Inc.* Photography by: © Brad Feinknopf 2010.

valuables may reduce the required number of full-size lockers. The most common locker material is painted steel, although wood, plastic, and phenolic materials are gaining in popularity.

Open gang showers are rarely seen anymore. Divided showers with plumbing on the sidewall are most common for both men and women. Increasingly, women's locker rooms also incorporate a small changing space in front of the actual shower. Gender-neutral, ADA-compliant rooms must also be provided.

Other Components

Other components frequently included in a recreation center are an administrative suite, wellness center, social space, juice bar, game room, demonstration kitchen, equipment storage and checkout, and building storage and maintenance (see Figure 8.34).

Stadiums and Outdoor Facilities

While this publication is principally dedicated to buildings, we would be remiss if we did not discuss the huge impact that stadiums and fields have on campus planning. Together, athletic and recreation buildings, stadiums, fields, and required components for spectators, amenities, such as restrooms and concession areas, parking, and other tributary components can constitute more than one-third of the total campus area (see Table 8.3).

When planning, it is important to note that competition fields have clearly defined playing dimensions and safety zones as well as strongly preferred orientations. For example,

Figure 8.34 Lounge and juice bar, Student Recreation and Wellness Center, University of Wisconsin, Oshkosh. Cannon Design/ Potter Lawson, Inc. Photography by: James Steinkamp/Steinkamp Photography.

Table 8.3 Athletic and Recreational Outdoor Facilities

Intercollegiate	Recreational
Football stadium	Slow-pitch softball complex
Football practice field(s)	Intramural/recreational fields
Baseball stadium	Club sports fields
Softball stadium	Recreational pool/social complex
Soccer stadium	Challenge course
Soccer practice field	Roller hockey
Lacrosse stadium	Skate park
Lacrosse practice field	Tennis
Field hockey stadium	
Track stadium	
Hammer/javelin field	
Tennis complex	
Aquatic complex	
Golf course	

a north–south orientation is preferred for football, soccer, and field hockey fields.

As the demand for additional competition, practice, and recreational outdoor space has grown—and land has become scarce—schools are increasingly placing both natural and synthetic-turf fields atop parking structures and, in some particularly landlocked institutions, on top of recreation or athletic facilities.

Outdoor stadiums and fields that may be found on campus are listed elsewhere in this chapter. Spectator capacity, athletes' facilities, and parking will vary based on the institution and the level of competition.

PROCESS

The basic phases for designing and delivering a sports building are the same as for most campus buildings: establish need, programming, schematic design, design development, contract documents, bidding or negotiation, and construction. The success or failure of a project is often determined by decisions made at the earliest stages. It is vital to have budget and expectations aligned.

The owner, often in collaboration with a sports facility firm, must establish a statement of goals that should include, as a minimum, aspirations for the project, budget and schedule constraints, and sustainability goals.

The preliminary budget is often established on the basis of cost per square foot applied to a preliminary list of spaces plus efficiency factor. An experienced sports firm can assist with a database of similar projects corrected for bid date and geographic location.

In comparing costs at peer institutions, it is important to understand the difference between construction cost, which is for "bricks and mortar," and project cost, which also includes "soft costs," land acquisition, permits and fees, professional services, FF+E, owner management costs, and so on. These "soft costs" can range from 15 to 40 percent of the project cost.

In the programming phase, the "wish list" is refined based on more detailed data, which is documented in the form of individual room data sheets that become the foundation for the design and documentation of the building and allow for a more detailed cost estimate. Headings include area, code capacity, critical dimensions, systems (HVAC, lighting, power, data communications, fire protection), and FF+E.

Concurrently with the building program, a detailed site analysis should be prepared. This may include ensuring conformance with the campus plan, parking requirements, pedestrian and service vehicle access routes, and availability of such utilities as electricity, steam, chilled water, and gas.

The ensuing phases will build on the detailed program and site analysis; however, it cannot be overemphasized that the key to a successful project is to establish a collaborative, transparent, and interactive process with consistent participation by key decision makers for the owner and the design team.

Renovation

Many campus athletics and recreation buildings are in need of renovation and/or expansion. Functional and aesthetic expectations have changed, and even buildings from the 1990s are frequently outdated and inadequate to meet current demands.

A study should be undertaken to examine functional, technical, and aesthetic deficiencies and to recommend which combination of demolition, renovation, and new construction is most cost effective. In addition to programmatic improvements, a total reimaging of an existing building is often required to meet the expectations of current students, faculty, staff, and spectators.

Codes and ADA Requirements

Building Codes

Building codes are constantly updated in an attempt to protect the public. The architect and the contractor should obtain the current applicable codes at the outset of a building project to ensure all requirements are met as the design proceeds. Among other things, building codes specify maximum allowable size, height, and occupant load for major program spaces. The occupant load calculation is especially critical, as it affects both exiting requirements and plumbing fixture requirements. Building codes can be unclear about the occupant load requirements for spaces such as racquetball and squash courts, gymnasiums without seating, and indoor jogging tracks, so it is recommended that the building official be consulted early in the process and negotiated occupancy loads mutually agreed on as necessary.

Providing code-required exits based on occupancy loads or seating capacity can have a significant effect on design. In an assembly building in particular, a timed egress analysis can provide substantial savings.

An aquatic facility has its own set of codes, usually separate from the building code and often found in the health code, that address issues such as maximum pool size, minimum deck size, minimum water depths, filtration, and toilet and shower. They need to be reviewed before the design proceeds.

Title IX

Signed into law by President Richard Nixon as part of the Educational Amendments to the Civil Rights Act in 1972, Title IX exerts a powerful influence on the planning and design of athletic facilities. This federal regulation reads: "No person in the United States shall, on the basis of sex, be excluded from participation in, be denied the benefits of, or be subject to discrimination under any education program or activity receiving federal financial assistance."

For designers, Title IX has come to mean that facilities of equal or similar size and quality should be provided for men and women, and sports facility planning must take this into account. This has been most visible in the extensive renovation and alteration of existing buildings undertaken to reach gender equity.

Americans with Disabilities Act

Intended to make buildings more accessible to the public, the Americans with Disabilities Act (ADA) has been expanded and more clearly defined to incorporate new requirements that affect the design of sports facilities on college campuses. The new criteria contain fewer incongruities and seemingly arbitrary measures than did the law in its original form. The updated 2010 Standards for Accessible Design include a chapter devoted to recreation facilities. It addresses disability guidelines for outdoor facilities such as golf courses (including miniature golf) and ski trails that were not previously addressed. For an explanation or clarifications of the new requirements, check the U.S. Access Board website (www.access-board.gov).

ADA Modifications

Building elements particularly affected by the new standards include exercise equipment, locker rooms, lockers, saunas and steam rooms, team and player seating areas, and swimming pools and spas. In writing their recommendations, the experts recognized that sports have participation rules and requirements that should not be modified when such a change would fundamentally alter the nature of the sport. For instance, raised structures used for lifeguard stations at pool's edge, for refereeing in volleyball and tennis, are exempted from some ADA requirements. Similarly, the old rules called for an across-the-board access that was incompatible with competition spaces, such as boxing rings, sand volleyball courts, and ice hockey rinks. The logistics of these sports received subsequent exemption at venues such as boxing rings or ice hockey rinks.

Fitness Facilities

In recreation centers and fitness/weight rooms, under the new regulations, at least one of each type of exercise equipment and machine must be provided with clear floor space around it and be reachable via an ADA-compliant access route.

Locker Rooms

At least 5 percent of locker rooms designed for public or common use—but no less than one of the rooms of each type in a cluster—will need to be ADA accessible. In these rooms, at least 5 percent of lockers, but no less than one locker of each type, must be accessible. Benches must have seats that are 20–24 in. deep, a minimum of 42 in. long, and 17–19 in. high. Aisles must have a thruway of at least 36 in., and a minimum clear floor space of 48 × 30 in. is required for a parallel approach to the bench.

Swimming Pools

Whether used for recreation or competition, swimming pools need a lift or sloped entry if the perimeter wall is less than 300 ft in length, or two means of access if the wall dimension is greater. As a result of growing appreciation of the need for accessibility by a wider range of users, many pools have already been built with zero-depth entry ramps and steps into the water. Further regulations for pools are under review and designers should consult the latest updates.

Team/Player Seating

There remains some confusion about how to best provide wheelchair spaces in team or player seating areas. Flat-floor sports such as basketball and volleyball present a minimum of difficulty, but field sports such as soccer, lacrosse, and baseball pose a greater challenge. For example, still under discussion is a possible requirement for lifts or ramps into baseball dugouts.

Wayfinding

Statutes require a number of basic signs in every building, such as "No Smoking" or "Exit." A well-designed layout directs people to most of the major activity spaces but often needs visual reinforcement to clarify specifics such as location of the ticket office, seat location, and directions to restrooms or concessions.

A wayfinding system starts outside the building, often as far away as the parking lot, directing people to a parking space, to pathways, and then to a building entrance. It frequently deals with code requirements: accessibility entrances, emergency egress, areas of refuge, and firefighting apparatus such as extinguishers and hoses.

In a recreation center, environmental graphics can energize interior spaces and also provide a subtle degree of privacy to sensitive spaces, such as group exercise rooms.

Acoustics

Arena

Acoustic considerations vary across spaces. Arenas encompassing multifunctional spaces, such as those used for concerts, athletic events, convocations, or the spoken word, can be a particular challenge. For sporting events, a certain amount of additional noise may be seen as a home-team advantage and sound can be evenly distributed. If concerts feature electric instruments, sound sources can be controlled through digital audio sound systems and placement of speakers. For lectures, the sound should come from the general direction of the person making the presentation.

The surfaces within the arena play a large role in controlling reverberation and echo. When the space is full, a certain amount of sound is absorbed by spectators and their clothing. If empty seats are fabric over foam padding, the result is similar. Sound reflection increases with hard plastic seats or benches on concrete risers. However, the single largest surface area that assists in absorbing sound is the ceiling or underside of the roof structure. If the structure is exposed, a perforated acoustical roof deck with glass fiber insulation in the cells is a basic means of controlling the unwanted reverberation and echo.

Mechanical systems can cause disruptive noise through airborne sound and structural vibration. Isolation of mechanical equipment from the structure may eliminate some or all of this low-frequency noise. Airborne sound can also be mitigated through sound attenuation in ducts or at the mechanical room.

Field House

As a large open space—often 60,000 sq ft or more—the fieldhouse presents many of the same challenges as the arena, since such spaces are used for many of the same purposes. One means of creating an absorptive surface is acoustical blocks consisting of concrete masonry units with slots and a glass fiber insert that absorbs sound; again, the ceiling or roof structure is the best location to provide absorption. In many fieldhouses, mechanical equipment is located within the space; unless properly designed, its noise can cause interference with a coach's verbal instructions or other non-sporting events.

Recreation Center

Structure-borne sound is an issue in every type of building. In recreation centers, the sounds of aerobics music, bouncing basketballs, rocketing squash or racquet balls, and squeaking sneakers may disturb adjacent activities. Avoid locating occupied or sound-sensitive spaces such as offices or mind/body studios under the gymnasium. The frequencies of a bouncing basketball or squeaking sneakers are particularly difficult to control. In a natatorium, corrosion-resistant hard surfaces and their resultant sound reflection also need mitigation by suspended acoustical materials or the like.

An acoustics consultant should review the program and work with the owner and architect to achieve the right balance for the range of proposed activities.

Sustainability

Sustainable Sites

Carefully considering pedestrian, transit, and bicycle accessibility can reduce vehicular traffic to reach facilities sited on the campus perimeter. The ground under a playing field can be used as a heat sink/source in a geothermal exchange system. Field lighting should ideally be designed to minimize light pollution.

Water Efficiency

If allowed by the local jurisdiction, collect and store rainwater or graywater for irrigation. Locker rooms use large quantities of potable water, and this can be mitigated by the use of low-flow plumbing fixtures (although these showers are not popular with athletes!) and by collecting rainwater for use in toilet flushing and hand washing.

Energy and Atmosphere

Athletic and recreational buildings enclose large volumes and have large expanses of roof, exterior wall, and glazing. Heat gain or loss can be mitigated with a high-performance building envelope that addresses solar orientation and shading, insulating materials, and glazing size and type. Many spaces within athletic and recreation buildings have specific temperature, humidity, and air flow requirements, and energy strategies should not compromise these functional requirements.

Other sustainable strategies include air-to-air heat recovery for locker rooms and other high-ventilation spaces, displacement ventilation that can deliver air directly to occupants at a higher temperature than conventional systems, and building commissioning to ensure that all systems operate correctly.

Materials and Resources

Sustainable materials include low-emitting flooring, carpets, paints, and sealants and responsibly forested wood products. Select materials that do not have to be transported long distances, are indigenous to the region, or are from renewable sources (e.g., bamboo).

Indoor Environmental Quality

Arenas have high ventilation requirements during peak occupancy. Return air bypass can dehumidify air without using reheat during periods of high humidity.

Daylight analysis should be performed to ensure that the use of artificial light can be minimized, consistent with functional issues such as glare.

Structural

Long-span roofs that are common to athletic facilities offer the opportunity to create a grand statement, limited only by the project budget and the imagination of the project team. A dramatic, fully integrated, and cost-effective roof was realized at the Richmond Olympic Oval through the use of simple sawn lumber pieces that were arranged into shallow V-shaped pre-stressed arches placed between composite steel/glulam arches spanning the width of the facility (see Figure 8.35).

When rhythmic athletic activity spaces are placed on a structured upper floor, special attention must be paid to the floor system's dynamic characteristics. Repetitive, synchronous footfalls impart dynamic energy impulses into the floor and structural framing. Care must be taken that the input frequency and associated lower harmonic frequencies do not create resonance.

On tight sites where space is at a premium, it can be cost effective to turn the facility's roof into a playing field. An artificial athletic surface is much lighter in weight and easier to design as a watertight system than is a natural grass surface. This places less demand on the structure to hold the load and is less expensive to support and maintain, but the stormwater management advantages of a "green roof" should not be overlooked.

Mechanical, Electrical, and Lighting Systems

Mechanical

Mechanical systems provide heating, cooling, and ventilation of spaces and control of humidity and odors. Since athletic and recreation centers are typically composed of many different functional spaces (arenas, fieldhouses, gymnasiums, natatoriums, fitness centers, recreation spaces, lockers, and offices), different HVAC systems are typically utilized to condition these different spaces. Climate and the load characteristics of the specific spaces should be established

◀ *Figure 8.35 Long-span structure using sustainable beetle wood, Richmond Olympic Oval, Richmond, British Columbia, Canada. Cannon Design.* Photography by: © Photography West-Stephanie Tracey.

early in the design stage, when room criteria sheets are developed.

For better energy efficiency, these systems typically incorporate energy recovery from locker areas and natatoriums, demand-controlled ventilation via CO_2 sensing to account for variable occupancy, air-handling systems zoned to match areas with similar occupancy schedules, and humidity control approaches that do not require reheat. Consider air flow modeling for natural ventilation. Computerized energy management systems have vastly improved whole-facility energy management.

Electrical and Fire Alarm

Electrical power requirements depend on the intended uses of a given space. Arenas used for concerts, for example, will need an added power load for arena ring boards, scoreboards with video displays, and performers' sound systems and specialty lighting. Broadcast truck power, satellite uplink, and electronic news gathering (ENG) truck power should be considered.

In recreation centers, specific placement of power outlets can be an issue, particularly in fitness centers where outlets on a grid can provide flexibility in placing equipment. Data network outlets should also be considered to allow programmed functionality and reporting of advanced cardio/aerobic equipment. It is possible to use fitness equipment to generate power and feed it back into the facility power system. Audio systems are often provided in fitness spaces as well as monitors with programmable headsets to access television programming.

Pool equipment and systems require special anticorrosion consideration to protect from chlorination systems and general moisture levels.

Fire alarm systems must be carefully planned in multifunctional, high-bay, and high-seating-capacity areas. Special lighting and sound systems shutdowns, smoke evacuation, fire warden stations, and special notification and detection means may be required.

Lighting and Lighting Control

The Illuminating Engineering Society (IES) guidelines establish recommended lighting levels; however, each sport has specific requirements that may or may not agree with IES standards. Performance spaces where events can be televised require not only a greater level of intensity and multidirection for depth perception but also light of a special color. As a result, metal halide, for both its color and its intensity, is most often specified in these situations. A building's lighting flexibility can be a test, too. For instance, dimming may require special fixtures or controls or the introduction of an incandescent source that can be switched off and on quickly.

Tennis centers most often use indirect lighting so that direct glare does not interfere with a player's vision. Climbing-wall lighting requires multidirectional light sources to allow depth perception and limit shadowing.

Lighting sources within a recreation center most often use metal halide or fluorescent in large spaces and fluorescent, sometimes indirect, lighting in multipurpose group exercise spaces, locker rooms, support spaces, and offices. The desire to dim lighting and create different effects for meditative group exercises has prompted multi-illumination systems that work in combination to create moods and enliven an environment with a dramatic effect on the quality of a space.

In large spaces, the need to relamp fixtures calls for careful planning, especially in natatoriums. Lights over a pool require special code safety considerations and are not easily relamped without costly catwalks.

A low-voltage networkable lighting control system with a built-in time clock and local overrides should be provided to control all lighting in the building. An occupancy sensor equipped with bi-level switches should be installed in offices, conference rooms, lounges, storage rooms, and other areas where occupancy is intermittent. Separate automatic dimming controls composed of a photocell and luminaries equipped with dimming ballasts may be provided in all daylit areas to harvest daylight savings.

Financing

The financing of collegiate athletic and recreation buildings is becoming ever more complex and creative, since very few are being built with state funds.

Collegiate arenas are usually funded by a combination of private donations, ticket income, and financial instruments supported by advertising, concessions, private suite rentals, seat licensing, and income from nonathletic events and rentals. More recently, public–private partnerships (P3) have emerged as a popular funding mechanism.

Most competition venues and support facilities, such as academic centers, intercollegiate lockers, weight rooms, sports medicine facilities, and halls of fame, are almost exclusively funded by donations.

To a large extent, recreation centers also rely on philanthropy and, most frequently, another form of financing wherein students vote by referendum to assess themselves a fee per quarter or semester to support a bond issue for 20–30 years.

Operations and Maintenance

Arenas host thousands of spectators, aquatic centers have their own specific environmental challenges, and recreation centers are typically open from 6 A.M. to midnight and can have over 8,000 visits a day on a large campus.

The importance of selecting materials, systems, and equipment that are resistant to heavy use or abuse and easily maintained and operated cannot be overstated; however, construction costs are finite, but operational costs are ongoing for the life of the building and should be addressed throughout the design process.

The collegiate arena usually has fewer spectator events than a civic or professional arena and is often managed by university staff, with student workers who must be fully trained to safely operate complex systems and equipment; however, it is becoming increasingly popular for universities to retain an outside arena management firm, particularly if the financial model requires income from touring shows.

The recreation center is usually managed by the department of campus recreation, which employs facility managers who deal with routine maintenance and repairs and coordinate with other campus entities for major repairs and upgrades. While daily cleaning is often done at night, some campuses have established schedules that permit a continuous process during hours of operation, thus allowing the building to save energy by being shut down for 6–8 hours.

Key Cost Factors

Cost factors for athletic and recreation buildings begin with site selection. At this stage, a number of factors drive up costs (topography, rock or ledge, groundwater, poor soil). The structural system is less susceptible to hidden costs except when the design emphasizes structure as a design feature. Mechanical systems and lighting costs can be equally straightforward once the client selects the desired criteria.

Sustainable design goals may add to cost, but life-cycle cost analysis helps put the investment in perspective. Because durability is a crucial factor in sports facilities, the cost of alternative abuse-resistant materials must be weighed over their life spans. Similarly, mechanical and electrical systems that can perform precise operations must be weighed against the institution's ability to operate and maintain them.

In each project, we must ask the client what value is received in return for investment. It is equally important to remember that value is not always measured in dollars. The value of the architecture and its impact on a campus should be weighed in enhancing and protecting the legacy and vitality of any given institution.

CHAPTER 9

SOCIAL AND SUPPORT FACILITIES

Brenda A. Levin, FAIA, Levin & Associates

The union is the community center of the college, serving students, faculty, staff, alumni, and guests. By whatever form or name, a college union is an organization offering a variety of programs, activities, services, and facilities that, when taken together, represent a well-considered plan for the community life of the college.

—Association of College Unions International (ACUI), "Role of the College Union," 2009[1]

In an era of rising educational costs and increased competition for students, the building type commonly known as the "campus center" has assumed a pivotal role on college and university campuses—in both a real and a symbolic sense.

Viewed as a key factor in student recruitment and retention, the campus center has the potential to define the social experience on campus, serving as a destination for students and drawing them—in this age of social media—out of their dorms or apartments and into a place of community and social engagement. Here, experiences are shared in a relaxed, collegial setting—whether for food, lounging, studying, recreation, clubs, student-driven activities, or a myriad of other functions that the building might house.

Large or small, new or renovated, the campus center is all about creating a vital crossroads for student life, celebrating an institutional culture, and building an enduring sense of community.

1 ACUI, "Role of the College Union," http://www.acui.org/content.aspx?menu_id=30&id=296.

HISTORY

As a campus building type in the United States, the campus center, or student union as it was historically known, is just over 100 years old. Although some buildings of this type predate World War II, most of these early examples were limited in the extent of programs housed.

The first American student union building, the 1896 Houston Hall at the University of Pennsylvania, was loosely modeled after the student unions at Cambridge and Oxford, originally established as debating societies. Houston Hall, however, had a distinctly different and some might say American focus. Described at the time "as a unique experiment in college education, the frank and practical recognition of the importance of the leisure hour,"[2] it contained a lounge and reception area as well as a bowling alley, swimming pool, music room, gymnasium, theater, and billiards room. This facility prototype was widely imitated in the United States at the turn of the last century, during a time that student bodies were beginning to diversify in terms of class, culture, and religion.

By the 1950s, colleges and universities found it necessary to improve and expand student services. As both the size of the institutions and the diversity of students expanded, earlier models of student support became inadequate. With increased student activism making campus administrators

2 "The Houston Club," University of Pennsylvania, 1986, http://www.archives.upenn.edu/primdocs/upf/upf8_5/upf8_5i_houstonclub1896.pdf.

aware of the need to address the social and political aspects of student life, the 1960s and early 1970s saw a wave of new campus center construction to meet a broader range of student needs. These new centers often included support space for student organizations and student life administration, food service, mostly in the form of cafeterias, as well as limited amounts of meeting space.

However, it was not until nearly a century after the first student union opened that a rethinking of the model began to emerge, fittingly enough, at Houston Hall (see Figure 9.1). Venturi, Rauch, Scott Brown and Associates introduced a new direction—inspired by the urban, commercial strip. Their lively 1981 remodel of Houston Hall's nondescript basement space featured a neon ceiling, colorful signage, and open stores and boutiques.

Perhaps the most notable shift in campus planning was the widespread acceptance of the campus center as a major focal point for the academic and intellectual mission of the college or university—the learning-living culture of the institution. In this regard, the term "campus center" has increasingly replaced the previously favored "student union" as the terminology of choice to describe this building type, reflecting its key institutional role.

Figure 9.1 Exterior, Houston Hall, University of Pennsylvania, Philadelphia. Venturi, Scott Brown and Associates. Venturi, Scott Brown Collection, The Architectural Archives, University of Pennsylvania.

◀ *Figure 9.2 Combined library and campus center functions, Athenaeum, Goucher College, Baltimore, Maryland.*

In the first decades of the twenty-first century, the campus center, as a building type, continues to evolve. The "hybrid," "fusion," or mixed-use facility has become increasingly common[3]—whether it involves combining library and campus center functions—as at Goucher College's Athenaeum (Figure 9.2; RMJM Architects, 2009)[4] —or incorporating classrooms and other academic program elements, as in Barnard College's Diana Center (Weiss/Manfredi, 2010). Many current projects are incorporating significant recreational and lifestyle uses such as fitness centers. This evolution of the campus center speaks to fundamental changes in student life, culture, and expectations that are reflected in the most recent wave of campus center renovations, additions, and new construction.

TRENDS

Any discussion of campus centers must recognize the underlying trends shaping the planning and design of buildings on college and university campuses.

- *Market forces.* The increasingly consumer-oriented marketplace of higher education today is creating pressure for institutions to sharpen their brands, creating a competitive advantage to recruit and retain the best and the brightest. Investment in amenities, such as a campus center with an iconic, or signature, architectural presence, offers a means to market the college experience to prospective students and their families.

3 Craig Hamilton, "Fusion Building: New Trend with Old Roots," *Planning for Higher Education* 37, no. 2 (2009).
4 "Is It a Library? A Student Center? The Athenaeum Opens at Goucher College," *Chronicle of Higher Education*, September 14, 2009, http://chronicle.com/article/Is-It-a-Library-A-Student/48360/.

- *Cultural changes.* Styles and modes of work, study, and play are evolving among students. Students expect a seamless social-recreational-study continuum in their collegiate experience. Studying, once a typically solitary activity, can now be mobile and collaborative. Multitasking is often viewed as the norm, and shifting attitudes regarding space are blurring the distinction between public and private.

SOCIAL AND SUPPORT FACILITIES
CASE STUDY 1

CENTER FOR COMMUNITY
University of Colorado, Boulder

Architect: Centerbrook Architects, with Davis Partnership Architects
Food service: Bakergroup

The Center for Community was designed to be a welcoming, intimate home away from home for students, faculty, and staff on a sprawling campus of more than 30,000 people. The vision was to create a destination serving diverse food, and to combine a dozen previously scattered student service departments—housing, financial aid, career counseling, etc.—into one highly sustainable building.

The Center for Community is a place to eat, meet, and be seen on campus. It includes nine microrestaurants geared to a diverse, sophisticated clientele, serving as many as 6,000 meals a day. A 375-car parking garage, offices, and meeting spaces complete the program. The design fosters connections among building users and between people and the environment. The design continues the campus aesthetic while establishing a new iconic presence.

Year completed: Fall 2010
Site area: 4.35 acres
Building area: 324,402 sq ft
Enrollment: 30,000
Institution type: public
Project cost: $84.4 million
Cost per square foot: $260
LEED Gold certified

Planning Process

Planning encompassed iterative, inclusive design workshops with various academic constituencies.

Siting Issues

The building is strategically located on a busy thoroughfare between residential and academic neighborhoods, where one-third of students pass daily.

Building Configuration: Indoor and Outdoor Spaces

- The H-configuration establishes outdoor gathering spaces: a protected north entry court; an east courtyard for large open-air events (see Figure 9.3) and a west patio facing the mountains.
- Microrestaurant fare runs the gamut from sushi, Latin, Asian, Italian, and Persian to organic local dishes, plus a to-die-for dessert destination and the only kosher venue in the city (see Figure 9.4)
- The central atrium in the entrance courtyard is capped by a dramatic bell tower; student services offices on the floors above open toward this light-giving feature (see Figure 9.5).

Design Features

- The center's exterior of rough-hewn, variegated sandstone from local quarries and terra-cotta roof tiles continues the fabric of the university's distinctive regional architecture that dates to the 1930s, while at the same time it establishes a commanding new presence on campus.

Figure 9.3 East courtyard and entrance. © Jeff Goldberg/Esto.

Figure 9.4 Grotto Restaurant. © Jeff Goldberg/Esto.

Figure 9.5 Atrium at the east entrance. © Jeff Goldberg/Esto.

- Inside, warm wood trim and paneling combine with swaths of vivid colors to enliven and distinguish spaces. Colorado materials, colors, and organic patterns serve to bring the outside indoors.

Sustainability Features

- Ample natural lighting and passive solar heating
- Low-flow plumbing fixtures used throughout, providing a 30 percent reduction in water use
- Low-VOC (volatile organic compound) adhesives, sealants, composite woods, paints, and carpets
- Carpets recycled; certified Cradle-to-Cradle products
- 18 percent regional materials
- 83 percent Forest Stewardship Council (FSC) certified woods
- 20 percent recycled material content
- 92 percent construction waste diverted from landfills

- *Technology.* The "anytime-anywhere" expectations of students today place high value on personal connectivity and flexibility. The relentless pace of technology development for communication, information access, and recreation poses special challenges for campus centers and their need to support both academic and social interests of the campus. Demands for bandwidth and wireless capabilities must be factored into planning any new facility, with accommodations for adaptability for future technologies.
- *Sustainability.* As a campuswide value and practice, sustainability is now an expectation for incoming students. The campus center must be a place that matches the environmental commitment of today's educated and conscientious students.
- *Demographics.* Diversity characterizes the student body at most institutions, whether ethnic or racial, young or old, residential or commuter, part-time or full-time, international or local. Student life facilities must be able to accommodate this range of users, both traditional and so-called nontraditional students, with their specialized needs.

IDENTIFYING THE SITE

The Campus Crossing

Site identification is the first step in the planning process. Typically, an institution's strategic or master plan will guide this decision, whose goal is to maximize opportunities for student encounters along their daily paths of travel (see Figures 9.6 and 9.7). And while the vast majority of campus center projects today involve renovation and expansion of existing facilities, or even building anew on the same site as the

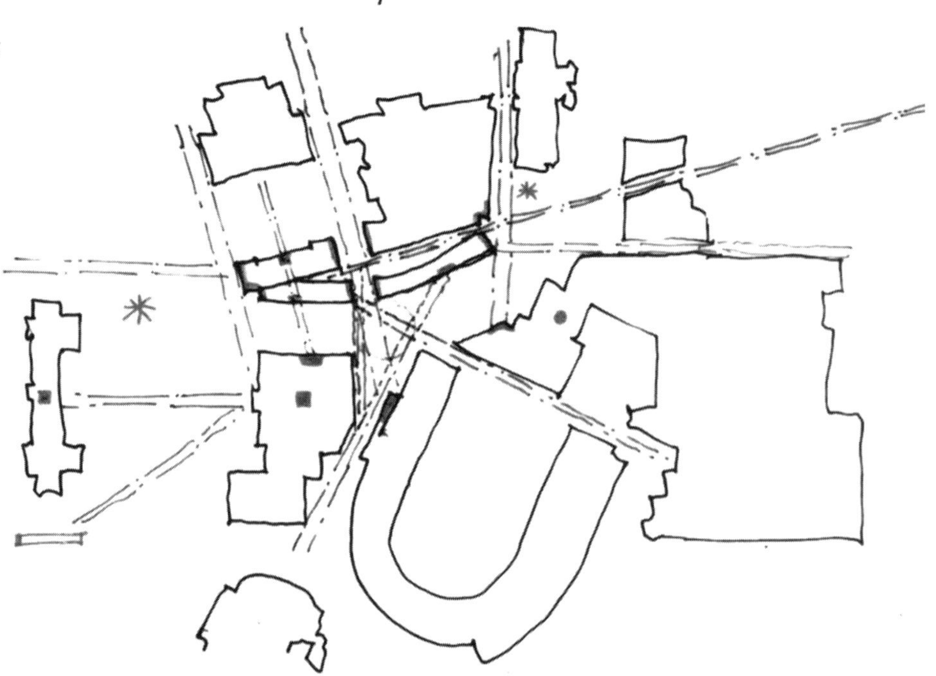

Figure 9.6 Study of axes and entries, Joseph A. Steger Student Life Center, University of Cincinnati, Cincinnati, Ohio. Moore Ruble Yudell, with Glaserworks.

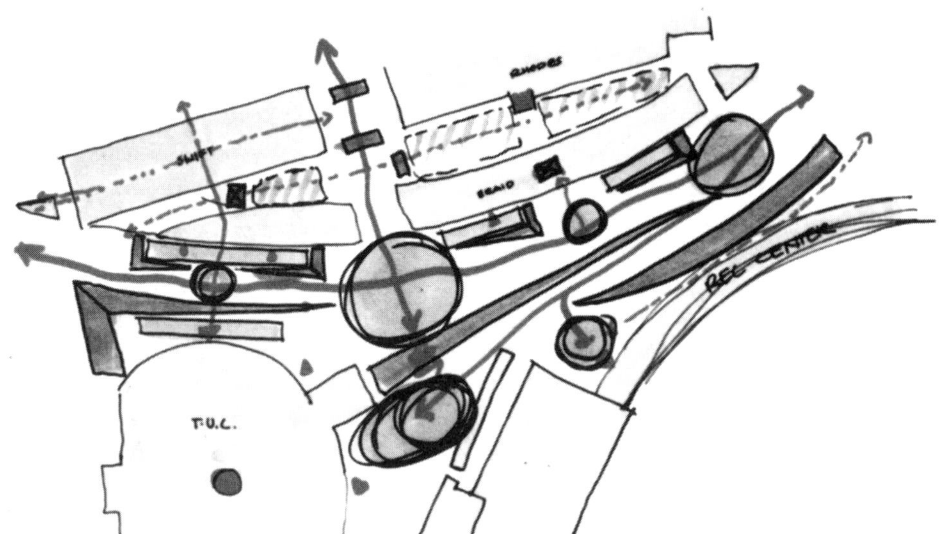

◀ *Figure 9.7 Study of axes and places, Joseph A. Steger Student Life Center, University of Cincinnati, Cincinnati, Ohio.* Moore Ruble Yudell, with Glaserworks.

previous facility, as at Ohio State University's Ohio Union (Moody Nolan, 2010) or Williams College's Paresky Center (Polshek Partnership, 2007), there is value to reviewing site criteria and evaluating feasibility to ensure that the decision to renovate, expand, or replace meets the institution's strategic goals.

Further, evaluation may suggest an alternative to the single central facility, particularly at large, geographically dispersed campuses or where space limitations at an existing student center dictate expansion elsewhere. A student center hub with an additional satellite facility (or facilities) may serve the campus community more effectively.

Key criteria for siting involve the simultaneous necessity for a central campus location, along significant paths of travel, coupled with the intensive service requirements that accompany food and retail operations. At many campuses, particularly those with substantial pedestrian cores, there are few, if any, sites that can accommodate both objectives. Service for large truck deliveries is most easily accomplished at the campus edge, whereas the best locations to maximize public access are often at the campus core.

At the Campus Center at the Illinois Institute of Technology (OMA/Rem Koolhaas, 2003), the location of the project was determined by a study of pedestrian flows on the urban campus so that the building itself functions as a crossroads (see Figure 9.8). Vehicular access and building services were facilitated through proper zoning of building program elements.

For new construction, the factors that go into determining ideal locations vary from campus to campus, depending on points of origination and the daily paths of travel along specific routes. For a largely residential campus, the best path may be along the route or routes between residential areas and the academic campus that students traverse daily. At a campus that serves commuter students, the primary path of travel may be between parking areas and the academic campus or between the campus and a public

▸ *Figure 9.8 Campus Center, Illinois Institute of Technology, Chicago. OMA.* (OMA) Ruault Philippe, Photographer.

transportation hub. The Campus Center of Indiana University–Purdue University Indianapolis (SmithGroup, 2009) occupies a site between the campus and parking facilities and offers a physical and programmatic connection between campus and community for this largely commuter campus.

Regardless of whether the site involves an existing footprint or new construction, the safety and security of the student population must be taken into account when developing siting and orientation for the facility.

Preservation and Modernization

In terms of the volume of campus center construction, the vast majority of current projects involve an existing structure rather than an entirely new building. History, cost, and location contribute to this circumstance. First, a majority of colleges and universities already have a campus center. Although these structures are occasionally either given over to new uses or demolished and rebuilt, it is far more typical—and generally less expensive—to solve the problems of building deterioration and lack of space through renovation and addition at existing sites than to develop new buildings. Existing structures may also figure prominently in the memories of alumni and thus add value to institutional character.

Second, location is one of the most important factors in the success of a campus center. While some locations become inappropriate over time as the campus evolves, most existing campus centers retain their strategic location in relation to the daily paths of students.

In some circumstances, a building that was not designed as a campus center may be adapted for this new use, as with Virginia Commonwealth University's Hunton Student Center (EYA, 2007), a renovated nineteenth-century historic church, one of three student centers on this geographically dispersed campus. Appropriate location, the degree of program fit and adjacencies, vehicular and service access, and the ease of interior alterations and insertion of new building systems and infrastructure are the most important factors in this decision for adaptive reuse as well as the feasibility to expand if needed.

Building additions are often the means to make existing campus centers work with different and expanded programs. Functions that cannot be accommodated in an existing structure owing to structural, spatial, and location constraints can often be specifically designed for an addition (see Figure 9.9). For example, a long-span multipurpose hall or flexible meeting room complex may be impossible to locate in an existing building without major structural reconfiguration but may be readily accommodated in an addition.

Additions can also provide a key to unlocking construction phasing sequences. The addition can be built first, with functions then relocated to the addition while the old building is renovated. Whether the addition is a major renovation or a renovation and addition, consideration for scheduling and operational impacts need to be factored into the construction phasing.

From a design perspective, it is incumbent on the design team to create a compelling connection between the renovated facility and the expansion. The Price Center East at the University of California, San Diego (Yazdani Studio/Cannon Design, 2008), celebrated this connection with a dazzling

Figure 9.9 New dining area created in historic courtyard, Johnson Student Center, Occidental College, Los Angeles. (Levin & Associates) Don Milici, Photographer.

yellow tunnel, bringing a playful sense of drama to the experience of moving through the building (see Figure 9.10). Furthermore, the dialogue between old and new, particularly in cases where the original building is of historic or architectural interest, is another important issue to be addressed by the design team.

DEVELOPING THE PROGRAM

Predesign and the Design Process

At the core of nearly every program for campus centers is the concept of "hearthstone," a concept promulgated by the Association of College Unions International (ACUI) in its statement of purpose.[5] Loosely interpreted, the campus center is to the campus what the "great room" is to the house, a place of warmth, gathering, conversation, and sustenance.

However, each institution is unique, and a well-orchestrated programming process is essential to creating a student life facility that is tailored to a specific campus culture and needs. What suits a 30,000-student urban research university with equal numbers of undergraduate residents, commuters, and graduate students may not suit a 5,000-student liberal arts college located in a rural community. Those that know this best are the people intimately involved with student life, student programs, and community-related programs on campus.

5 ACUI, "Role of the College Union."

▸ *Figure 9.10 Compelling connection between the renovated facility with the expansion, Price Center East, University of California, San Diego.* Image Courtesy of Yazdani Studio of Cannon Design, photography by Timothy Hursley.

SOCIAL AND SUPPORT FACILITIES
CASE STUDY 2

Figure 9.11 Before: Florence Rand Land Art Building.

Figure 9.12 Servery

ELIZABETH HUBERT MALOTT COMMONS
Scripps College, Claremont, California

Architect: Levin & Associates Architects

The new Elizabeth Hubert Malott Commons is a compelling example of successfully solidifying a sense of place and identity for Scripps College, a respected and distinguished member of the noted Claremont Colleges and one of the oldest and finest liberal arts women's colleges in the United States.

- Year completed: February 2000
- Building area: 32,000 sq ft
- Institution type: private
- Full-time enrollment: 953
- Funding source: private funds
- Project cost: $11.9 million

Planning Process

In the early 1990s, the college established a strategic plan to centralize the food services in one place, a vital new source for communal interaction.

The existing Florence Rand Lang Art Building was selected to be renovated and expanded. Designed in 1938 as the final piece of Gordon Kaufmann's campus plan, it was, unfortunately, not of the character or quality of his earlier work (see Figure 9.11).

The college community wanted a building inspired by the historic residence halls, to anchor the north-south axis of the campus. Levin drew from the rich vocabulary of architectural details, patterns, textures, and landscape to design a commons unique to Scripps (see Figure 9.12).

Guided by the Scripps tradition of creating buildings with spaces of simplicity and beauty, Levin created a complex of one- and two-story buildings and courtyards. The extensive renovation was supplemented with five individual additions. The "renewed" center houses the servery, dining rooms of differing scales, formality, and ambience; faculty lounge, offices for student organizations and government, music studios, and the career-resource center (see Figure 9.12). It has become a gathering place that fosters the intellectual and social interaction and the sense of community that the college desired.

Figure 9.13 After: Elizabeth Hubert Malott Commons.

Site Issues

The Scripps College campus is an architectural and landscape treasure, organized on major cardinal axes that terminate with a focus on a major piece of architecture. In selecting the Florence Rand Art building, which is at the south end of a large expanse of open space, as the site for the student commons, the college created the opportunity to reinforce this original campus planning principle.

Building Configuration, Indoor and Outdoor Spaces

Scripps Colleges' landscape and outdoor spaces are integral to the character and form of the campus. Open space, courtyards of varying sizes, patios, and water elements are found throughout the campus. The design of the Malott commons incorporates both existing courtyards as well as the creation of a new main entry court and fountain.

Infrastructure Considerations

While essentially reusing an existing building as a starting point, five individual additions created a composition of buildings that seismically acted to reinforce the original. All new infrastructure, including a central plant, utilities, and communication systems, were components of the project.

Program Elements/Facilities Included

To retain the Scripps traditional experience of dining in individual residence halls, several dining rooms of differing

Figure 9.14 North dining room.

sizes and formality were created. Concern over the loss of the intimacy of that experience was mitigated by the design of the following unique spaces:

Self-serve marketplace with wide variety of menu options, serving over 1000 meals a day

4 distinct dining rooms

2 meeting rooms

2 outdoor patio courtyards

Student-run coffee bar

Performance space

Student mail center

Student-run store

Key to the success of the predesign phase is a mechanism for engaging key constituencies and building consensus for the campus center plan. Interactive design workshops, visioning charrettes (see Figure 9.15), focus groups, and surveys that involve major stakeholder groups—students, faculty, administrators, facilities and security personnel, and often alumni—offer opportunities for participation that create a sense of ownership.

The process can begin by crafting a mission statement and/or a statement of shared values and goals. What is the role of the center for the campus as a whole? What are the institutional goals? What services and functions are to be provided? What is the desired architectural character of the building, inside and out—contextual, iconic, or something in between? What is the building to be called? Even the naming decision may have a long-term impact on how the facility is viewed and used. Research is typically a critical and useful accompaniment to this process, including group visits to other facilities and a thorough analysis of trends. The Association of College Unions International (ACUI), through its publications, can be enlisted as an additional resource.

While food service and lounges are the common denominator of most campus centers, the sum total of spaces and functions

Figure 9.15 Example of a visioning charrette where participants imagined a U.S. News and World Report story about the future campus commons at Scripps College, Claremont, California. Levin & Associates.

they contain are diverse, perhaps more so than those of any other campus building type. Several factors inform decisions about the configuration of functions: whether comparable facilities already exist elsewhere, planning goals articulated in the campus master plan, and campus politics. The presence or lack of specific program elements in sufficient quantity elsewhere on a campus may be the single most important program determinant.

Consolidation of previously dispersed services that pertain to student life is often the driving force in programming campus centers. At the same time, campus center programs are often shaped by the unmet needs of a campus, identified through campuswide assessment of what facilities are desired minus what exists, leaving a base program to be refined and added to by advocacy groups.

The campus master plan also plays a role in determining which facilities should be included in the campus center. For example, in some master plans the decentralization of many student life facilities may be a deliberate objective. However, if a primary goal of the master plan is to centralize all administration, then student life administration would be best located with other administrative offices, rather than with student life facilities.

The structure and interests of advocacy groups are also central to the programming process. Groups that are well organized and have a strong presence on campus are more likely to be heard than those that are less well organized, such as commuter students, who may have specific needs that may be unnoticed and ill-served. It is therefore essential that all constituencies be enlisted early in the planning process, whether or not they are organized.

Critical, too, during the programming phase, is the overall design for project management and constituent involvement that will carry the project to completion. A particular challenge concerns continuity and the need to keep the project moving forward as representatives of stakeholder groups change.

Once the broad outlines of the program are delineated, the preliminary space program for the new or renovated campus center can be articulated. This program document details the various activities and functions to be contained both within and outside the building, along with the characteristics of these spaces; physical space requirements; adjacencies; and specific requirements for technology, infrastructure, security, vehicle service access, pedestrian and bicycle accommodations, storage, and other support functions.

PROJECT MANAGEMENT

A coherent and orderly participatory process always results in the best campus building of any type. The key is involvement by the client and the users throughout the program, design, and documentation phases. It is often difficult to retain continuity of a group, but every effort should be made to anticipate transitions, such as the 4-year cycle of undergraduate students, and create some overlap to avoid having to revisit decisions that have been made. Committees with the greatest continuity often produce the best results.

Depending on the phase, the planning group may be defined as a "steering committee" (all phases), a "program committee" (program phase), or a "design committee" (schematic design through construction document phase; see Figure 9.16). Committees should be structured to enable participation and regular attendance rather than intermittent involvement.

A coherent project process will enable the design team to design a project in a thoughtful and organized way, allowing the

◀ *Figure 9.16 Design committee workshop.* Levin & Associates.

committee to comment and give input on both conceptual ideas and technical needs specific to the individual institution.

By organizing the process to coincide with the development of project documents, the committee will be involved in the evolution of the design, and the architect and design team will have the necessary feedback to maintain the schedule. It is important for the committee to have access to operations staff, who will provide the required information specific to their discipline.

For example, if food service is a major component of the project, the provider needs to be at the table at the appropriate times throughout the process. Information technology, audiovisual, retail services, security—all must be defined early in the process. The development of technical criteria documented in writing for each space is a useful way of confirming that the needs of the users will be met.

No matter what committee/project management structure is created by the institution, information flow is critical. Regularly scheduled meeting times with the committee are recommended. Minutes of the meetings, recording decisions by the committee, should be disseminated promptly to all members, enabling participants to be more effective.

KEY DESIGN CONSIDERATIONS

Given the trends and forces underlying campus center facility planning and design today, how do they translate into the actual design of the facility? What are the key considerations in shaping the plan? What values must the design of the campus center embody, and how can these be translated in architectural and engineering terms? How can the facility remain relevant to the institution and its students, and be positioned to accommodate future change (see Figure 9.17)?

While central atriums, expansive window walls, and the open intercommunicating stairway have emerged as *de rigueur* design features of many recent projects,[6] all thoughtful approaches to the design of a campus center, whether new or renovated and expanded, need to consider a range of underlying issues that impact design (see Figure 9.18).

Flexibility and Specificity

Campus buildings today are increasingly being asked to house multiple functions.[7] This may mean that the campus center could potentially hold a library or classroom space; a small performance area to be used to host a speaker, student production, or movies; meeting rooms that can be portioned into different sizes; or dining facilities incorporating zones that can function independently for a variety of uses and times of day or night. These types of multifunctional spaces can provide opportunities to activate areas that may sit empty at particular times throughout the day and help satisfy the 24/7 demands that campus facilities must often accommodate.

6 Michael J. Lewis, "Forget Classrooms: How Big Is the Atrium in the New Student Center?" *Chronicle of Higher Education*, July 11, 2003.
7 Amy Milshtein, "The Big Picture," *College Planning and Management*, January 2010, http://www.peterli.com/cpm/resources/articles/archive.php?article_id=2088.

Typically, the campus center contains a hierarchy of spaces that range from common spaces—the paths and places of informal gathering—to well-defined programmed spaces that accommodate specific functions. The challenge is to balance flexibility in all these areas with utility, with the understanding that flexibility is a value that can extend the life and relevance of the center facility itself by adapting to changing student lifestyles and service demands. The trend toward specialization, coupled with the need for flexible reconfiguration, poses an enormous challenge for the design team.

Many programs, such as food service, meeting spaces, and some lounge and office functions, have space-specific requirements, ranging from specialized equipment to acoustics to specific occupancies and sizes. At the same time, the cycle of change in other aspects of student life is rapid, thus requiring that the internal plan of the campus center, or specific room and space functions, be subject to change. A flexible infrastructure for the delivery of food services and reconfigurable meeting and office spaces that meet requirements for acoustical isolation are critical.

Connectivity and Circulation

Most campus buildings exist to accommodate specific uses. A successful campus center, however, is unique in its dependence on unprogrammed circulation space to foster student interaction and a sense of community. Arguably, the most important room in the campus center is not a room at all, but rather the space that connects the rooms—the network of lobbies, hallways, and stairs—both indoors and outdoors. The Amble, a curvilinear 3-story-tall central path through the Student Center at Morgan State University (Sasaki, 2006), orients users within the building and allows visual and

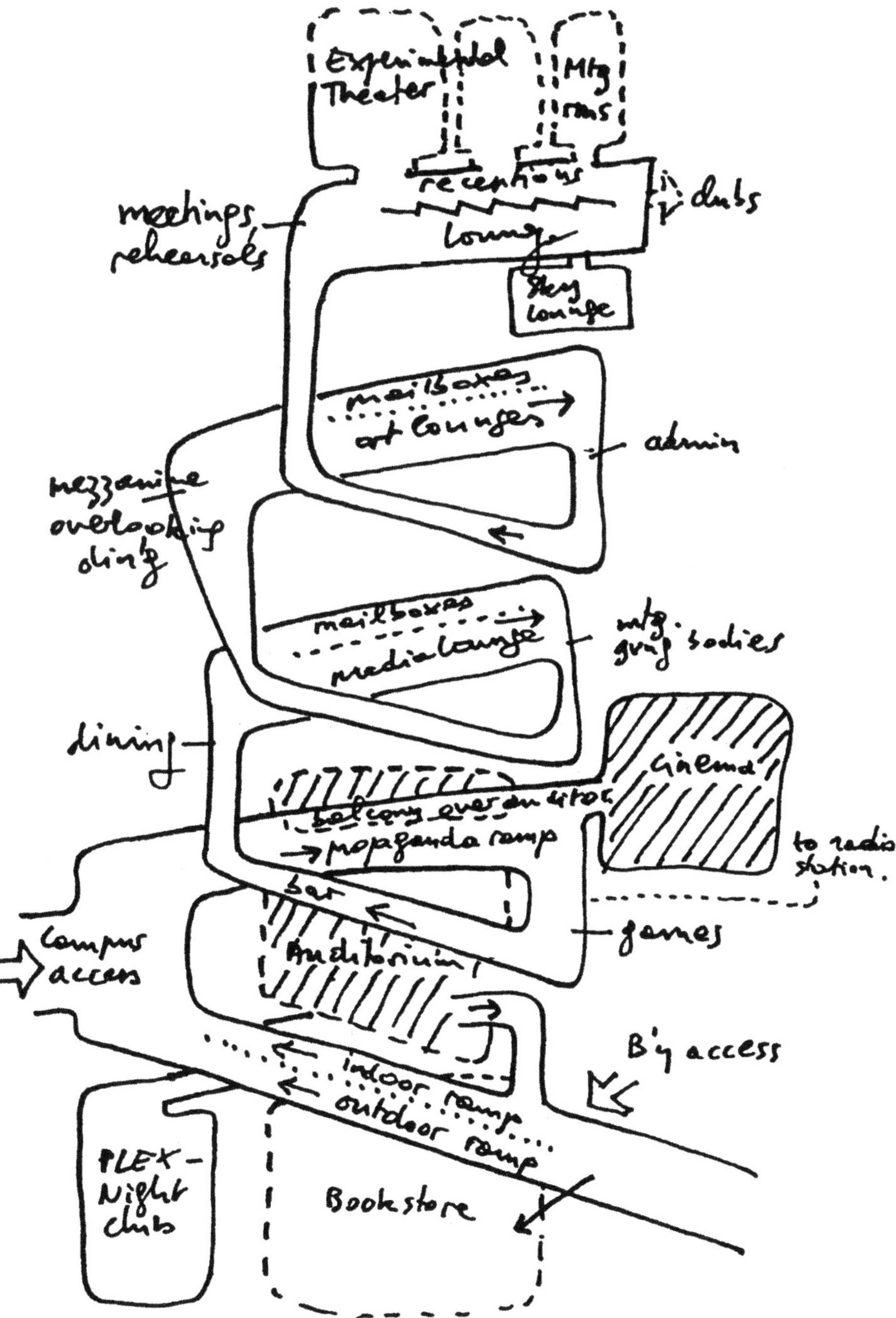

◀ *Figure 9.17 Program and circulation diagram, Lerner Hall, Columbia University, New York, New York.* Bernard Tschumi Architects.

Figure 9.18 Central atrium with open interconnecting stairways provides both circulation and the opportunity to see and be seen. Columbia University, New York, New York. (Bernard Tschumi Architects) Lydia Gould, Photographer.

physical access to all public areas as well as the outdoors (see Figure 9.19).

Although there are many specific, destination-based reasons that a student chooses to enter a campus center building, the prospect of chance encounters, the "see-and-be-seen" factor, may be the greatest attraction. A great deal of study occurs in campus centers rather than in libraries, precisely because students seek a comfortable place with a reasonable level of distraction, including occasional socializing and snacking. Properly configured circulation spaces provide this distraction. Many rooms are best interpreted not as traditional enclosures but as extensions of lobbies and halls. Examples include

◀ *Figure 9.19 The Amble, a curvilinear, 3-story, central path through the Student Center, Morgan State University, Baltimore, Maryland.* (Sasaki Associates, Inc.) Robert Benson Photography.

lounges and food service and retail spaces, which may in some cases not be rooms at all but simply extended circulation.

The objectives for building circulation are threefold: clarity, organization to extend exposure to a wide range of activities, and open viewing between circulation and activity areas to advance casual encounters. Clarity can be attained in a number of ways. Repetition of circulation paths in the same relative position and orientation from one level to the next is one method. Increasingly favored is the use of a multilevel central space—the atrium—with all spaces opening off this central area.

A second objective of circulation is drawing the user past as many activities as possible, in much the same way that shopping malls, with anchor tenants, are organized. The placement of important destinations that draw many users to them, such as food service facilities, is often the most effective way to increase activity. Instead of placing the most highly trafficked destinations at the front, it is often desirable to make them remote to extend exposure.

Third, if a student can experience activities as he or she moves through the building, then circulation is clearer and more memorable.

Adjacencies and Activities

The many programs accommodated in the campus center, combined with specific objectives for adjacency and transparency between programs, can result in contradictory design challenges. For example, the main attraction in many campus centers is the availability of food at all hours. To the extent possible, food services should be located to draw students through the building, exposing the campus community to a wide range of program activities. Many of these activities, however, have requirements that contradict the basic tenets of campus center food service delivery. Campus center dining is by design a high-traffic, noisy affair with many simultaneous conversations held amid constant comings and goings. Many other campus center programs, including meeting and conference space, some offices, and reading or study lounges, require relative quiet and fewer distractions.

SOCIAL AND SUPPORT FACILITIES
CASE STUDY 3

STUDENT UNION
University of Connecticut, Storrs

Architect: Cannon Design, in association with WTW Architects

Planning for an expanded student union at the University of Connecticut must respect the original union building's places, spaces, and memories, while embracing the principle that the campus is about people, not just about buildings and spaces. We looked to capture the past in order to create a vibrant future.

Through new connections and vistas, an opaque 1950s building capitalized on its central campus location to become more transparent and lively. The design transformed an introverted existing building into an extroverted, dynamic student union that rebrands campus life at the University of Connecticut.

Year completed: 2006

Building area: 207,750 sq ft (151,950 sq ft new; 55,800 sq ft renovated)

Institution type: public

Full-time enrollment: Fall 2010 enrollment, 30,034

Funding source: state funded

Project cost: $60 million

Maximizing an Ideal Site

Cannon Design and its team worked with multiple campus groups, including the student union staff, student organizations, campus cultural centers, and the faculty senate, to develop the program and architectural design for the student union, more than doubling the size of the existing building. From the beginning, it was evident that the existing building could not support the proposed program and that the campus required a larger facility. The existing building's central location, however, was ideally suited to accommodate an expanded student-centered facility.

Situated at one corner of a major campus quadrangle, the student union reinforces the quad's spatial identity and strengthens a new campus pedestrian street to the south. Because, in this location, the student union was such an effective unifier of the overall campus fabric, when the time came to update the facility, rather than demolishing the whole building and constructing an entirely new one, the university chose to retain and renovate one of the student union's two 1950s-era buildings, demolish the other, and build a new addition.

Figure 9.20 The student union defines one side of a major academic quadrangle in the heart of campus, reinforcing the quad's special identity. © Paul Burk Photography.

Establishing the Campus Hub to Encourage Interaction

By locating the addition primarily on the quad side of an existing building, designers define the quad with a contemporary, transparent appearance while preserving portions of the original facade flanking the outer streetscape (Figure 9.20). A 4-story pedestrian spine follows the building's north–south axis, uniting various functions with an interior streetscape. Major building entries occur at student activity centers: the theater, lounges, dining area, and ballroom (Figure 9.21).

Figure 9.21 Food court and café/restaurant: seating for 300 with multiple food selections. © Paul Burk Photography.

Intensifying the Student Union's Community-Building Influence

A major design element is the 4-story, skylit atrium linking the existing building and the new with the addition of a pedestrian spine, called "Union Street," along the building's north–south axis. Staggered balconies offer glimpses of visitors on all four floors and foster a sense of community among the building's many users (Figure 9.22). The new plan adds two points of entry to the building, further enhancing the feeling of transparency and giving people the freedom of easy passage, using it as a shortcut or indoor pathway—a particular advantage during Connecticut winters.

Features

- Food court and café/restaurant: seating for 330 with multiple food selections
- Grocery store/deli
- 5,240 sq ft of flexible ballroom space (300–450 persons)
- 500-seat multiuse theater
- 2 multiuse function rooms
- 6 large, 8 medium, and 2 small conference rooms
- Expanded student government and student life organization offices
- 6 independent multicultural centers
- Pocket student lounge spaces
- 15,000-box post office
- Game room
- Outdoor equipment room
- Art gallery

Figure 9.22 Staggered balconies offer glimpses of visitors on all four floors. © Paul Burk Photography.

Acoustics is another key factor in the analysis of adjacencies within a building. Establishing hierarchies of noise levels can be helpful when organizing programs and functions. For example, a gathering lounge may be well located adjacent to dining areas, but study lounges should be more remote. Acoustic separation can also be addressed by acoustic partitions, ranging from glass to sound-insulated wall assemblies, depending on the degree of separation required. Again, there is a contradiction between the desire for transparency and revelation of activity and the need for separation. If glass provides enough separation, both acoustically and visually, it is preferred over opaque walls, as it reveals use to the passersby.

Campus centers incorporate a range of specialized functions, often varying with the facility. So-called hybrid facilities, a term used currently to describe less typical combinations of functions and programs, in fact reflect the fluidity of programming that has characterized the campus center building type over its history. Nonetheless, it is possible to identify typical program elements that are found in many, if not most, campus centers. Each of these functions brings with it specific infrastructure needs, with the accompanying impact on flexibility.

Food Service

Food is what draws students to the campus center and is thus regarded as the most important component of the campus center services. Dining and food service delivery methods and styles are subject to continuous redevelopment. In less than a decade, between 1980 and 1990, the cafeteria line virtually disappeared in favor of the scramble-style servery, the food court, and, most recently, marché-style dining, with its wide array of offerings geared to satisfying the tastes of an increasing diverse and sophisticated student body. Additional dining options have also proliferated, such as grab-and-go, branded food concepts, cafés and diners, and prepare-your-own facilities for commuting students. Visible food preparation, fresh made-to-order options, and bakeries that produce the smell of fresh baked bread and sweets are increasingly popular (see Figure 9.23). Many campus centers offer a variety of settings in which to purchase and eat, ranging from the large dining hall with open tables to smaller dining alcoves, coffeehouses and publike lounges, stand-up

Figure 9.23 The marketplace concept provides visible food preparation, variety, and fresh made-to-order options preferred by students. (Levin & Associates) Alex Vertikoff, Photographer.

bars, and booths, often "microthemed" to offer a variety of experiences for their student users.

Lounges: Social and Study Spaces

Although a central gathering lounge is still included in most campus centers, it is often supplemented by specialized lounges offering different levels of activity and comfortable seating. Television lounges, quiet lounges, and study lounges are the most common. The study lounge is increasingly in demand today as a supplement to library space and as an alternative to the isolation (or, alternatively, the overcrowding) of the dorm room. It accommodates the collaborative forms of learning and study so prevalent today and places studying activities near food service for evening snacks and off-hours eating. Lounges may also be tailored to the needs of commuter and other nontraditional students, complete with self-serve food preparation areas and lockers to store possessions.

Student Organizations

Perhaps the most mutable area today, however, is student organization offices and support space. Student organizations wax and wane from year to year, along with their demand for types and quantities of office space. A highly flexible system that allows growth and contraction, yet provides secure storage, is necessary.

An area dedicated to student activities may contain a common lounge, reception area, and furnishings that are shared by all, while lockers or cubicles that can be secured offer storage for the individual organizations. At Columbia University's Lerner Hall (Bernard Tschumi, 1999), loft-style floors with open column-to-column structural bays enable flexible partitioning or cubicles for a variety of student-driven uses (see Figure 9.24).

Meeting and Conference Space

Meeting and conference space, always in demand, varies from day to day as to size, type, and quantity of space needed. The inflexible meeting space of the older campus center has given way to a hierarchy of meeting facilities, ranging from very large multipurpose ballrooms to flexibly sized conference rooms, fixed-seat lecture and projection rooms, and small seminar-type conference rooms. The campus center has, in part, become a conference center to support campus life, with the added benefit of outside rental opportunities when not in use by the campus community.

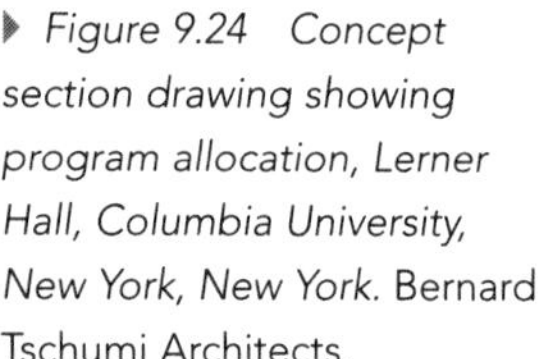

▸ *Figure 9.24 Concept section drawing showing program allocation, Lerner Hall, Columbia University, New York, New York.* Bernard Tschumi Architects.

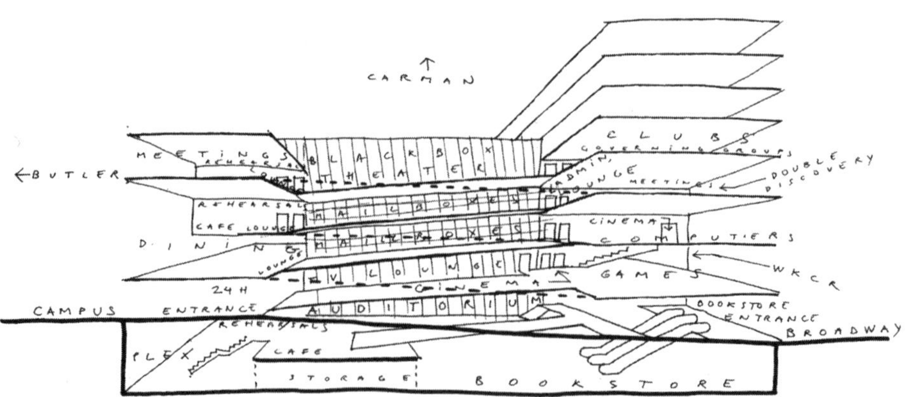

Examples of other specialized spaces include:

- Recreation and game rooms
- Bookstore, student store, convenience store, and other retail
- Student services
- Career and financial counseling
- Clubs and organizations
- Mail center
- Copy center
- ATM/banking
- Fitness facility
- Theater
- Art gallery
- Child care
- Offices, administrative and student government

SITE CONSIDERATIONS: LANDSCAPE AND PARKING

Building in the Landscape

The campus center site offers opportunities to create and activate outdoor spaces supporting student interaction. Entry sequences along pathways and stairways can become meaningful social spaces unto themselves. When integrated with the pedestrian circulation system of the campus, entrances for new buildings can serve to enhance the student experience by creating formal and informal "stopping places"—architectural and landscape features that allow students to intermingle, chat, and sit as part of arriving at the center.

Additional opportunities to activate the site can be found in the creation of outdoor spaces immediately adjacent to the campus center. These outdoor uses can serve as extensions of interior spaces and programs and can also reinforce the building's on-campus presence (see Figure 9.25).

Building orientation should take advantage of climatic conditions that will produce the most comfortable outdoor environment for the users, allowing those interaction spaces to flourish.

Looking beyond the immediate building footprint, the design team can also identify

◀ *Figure 9.25 Landscaped amphitheater and courtyard, Whittier College, Whittier, California.* Levin & Associates.

opportunities to create nearby programmed outdoor recreational spaces and general-use, unprogrammed landscape areas. It is the landscape, after all, that defines *campus*.

In this regard, "skyline" landscapes—composed of trees—can be planted to mark the campus center from a distance, and topography or elevation changes can be used to support notions of destination. Well-positioned lawns can become the campus "beach" where, on temperate days, either organized or casual gatherings occur near the campus center's amenities and programs.

Access: Public versus Service

Primary consideration should be given to pedestrian access to the building, whether single or multiple points of entry, and to strengthening the existing campus circulation. Public access points must be designed in accordance with campus security protocols. Where possible, service access should be separated from pedestrian access. When that is not possible, the design of the service access should be modified in order to be compatible with the pedestrian scale. Consider paving strategies, such as grass pavers and material and/or textural changes, to reduce the visual impact of vehicle lanes.

Parking and Transit

Parking at campus centers, if required, should be designed to minimize the presence of automobiles and thus reflect an institutional commitment to sustainability and the environment. Where parking is a part of the facility's program, preference must be given to spaces that meet the requirements of the Americans with Disabilities Act (ADA) and to short-term spaces, along with electric vehicle charging stations. Access to parking areas should be integrated with the campus circulation and formalized through planting, lighting, and paving.

Increasingly, the transportation focus must shift to bicycles and public transit. Ample accommodation for bicycle parking is key and may include docking stations for a campuswide bicycle-sharing program.

SYSTEMS AND INFRASTRUCTURE

Technology, Data, and Telecommunications

Distribution of power, telecommunications, and data access throughout all areas of the campus center, including many that have not traditionally been thought of as work spaces, is a central concern today, given the ubiquity of computer and wireless device use.

A technology master plan for the campus center can be used to identify key components to ensure that the facility remains relevant, including an adequate amount of high-speed cabling for data and telecommunications. As reliance on personal wireless devices increases, the quality of wireless coverage in campus centers will become even more important. These demands will drive a number of changes in the campus centers, including the requirement for in-building distributed antenna systems to amplify wireless signals of all types and service agreements with cellular carriers to place some of their own hardware in the building.

Electrical and Communication Systems

Electrical power distribution must be designed to meet the current and future demands of technology and have the ability to expand for future growth and, where appropriate, accept the integration of renewable energy sources. In addition, organizing the electrical distribution system allows a building to individually monitor and control the energy consumption of mechanical, receptacle power, and lighting systems. Real-time displays of energy usage are proving to be particularly compelling for today's environmentally conscious students and can be easily integrated as an interior feature of campus centers.

Power and data ports should be located throughout, but especially in food service areas, lounges, meeting spaces, and offices. Floor power and data outlets installed on a modular basis can eliminate the need for fixed wall locations. Easy access to power and data distribution cable trays will help to accommodate the rapid change in technology. Communication systems, including programmable audio systems and digital video boards for listing daily activities, are useful in providing background sound and public announcements. Within large auditoriums, meeting spaces, and food service areas, integrated audio-visual systems should be provided for ease of use. These general communication devices may also be part of the overall building safety/security program.

Structural System

In selecting a structural system for new construction, several factors should be considered:

- The range of open areas or clear-span requirements as dictated by the various program elements
- Fireproofing requirements generated by the building size, height, and configuration and local codes
- Flexibility for making modifications over time
- Preferences for interior finishes
- Cost analysis of alternative systems
- Availability, cost, and local construction market capabilities for production
- Aesthetics

For renovations and additions, several considerations should govern the decisions for adaptation or reuse:

- Expandability of the building from a spatial consideration
- Structural capacity and integrity of the existing building
- Constructability within the existing space, especially if portions are to remain occupied
- Cost factors—anticipating unforeseen conditions and phasing
- Schedule and material availability

Most new buildings are frame buildings, either concrete or steel braced or moment-frame systems, preferred for their flexibility and openness. Frame structures offer the greatest prospect for an open interior, where transparency across and between spaces is desired. While some spaces require clear spans, such as multipurpose rooms and auditoriums, most spaces can accommodate columns without compromising their use.

Most, but not all, campus centers are both large and open enough to require a fully fireproofed structure. Wood and steel structures do not have integral fireproofing and therefore require additional detailing and finish.

In the final analysis, structural steel construction allows for the greatest flexibility. Infill walls constructed of concrete or concrete masonry units (CMUs) can then provide acoustical separations while acting as shear walls for the lateral systems, thus achieving two goals—structural and acoustical—at once.

Mechanical Systems

The central issue in the selection of campus center heating, ventilation, and air conditioning (HVAC) systems is the wide diversity of uses within this building type. The types of systems selected depend on the types of spaces to be conditioned, ranging from large-scale assembly spaces, such as an auditorium or multipurpose hall, to meeting rooms, lounges, dining and kitchen, to many small-scale offices. In addition, every campus center has a food service program that requires specialized supply and exhaust systems for cooking and serving, including the now common open preparation areas. To make matters even more complex, some spaces are occupied almost continuously, whereas others are used only occasionally. Moreover, the building footprint is normally quite deep, so perimeter systems are capable of serving only a portion of the building volume.

As a result, no single system is appropriate for the entire structure. Increasingly, the focus is on energy efficiency in consideration of sustainable design goals. The appropriate system selection is often a composite or mix-mode system (air conditioning and natural ventilation) and is often dictated by local climate. Controls must be extensively zoned, as occupancy can vary over short time intervals from empty to several hundred people in an auditorium or multipurpose space.

Multistory atriums are often a design feature of the contemporary campus center and can affect various building systems, offering opportunities and challenges.[8] Atriums connecting more than 2 stories often require specialized smoke evacuation systems and provisions for large volumes of supply air in the event of an emergency (see Figure 9.26, Color Plate 17). However, the atrium is often a transition space where displacement ventilation and radiant floors for cooling and heating might be sufficient. Green roofs, those planted either partially or completely with vegetation, are increasingly popular to reduce both peak energy demand and the urban heat island effect and to assist in stormwater management.

8 Mark Richmond, "Atriums and Energy: Designing for Performance," *College Planning and Management*, July 2010, http://www.peterli.com/cpm/resources/articles/archive.php?article_id=2657.

Lighting Design

There is no single approach to campus center lighting that addresses the diverse needs of all spaces. Meeting space requires variable light levels, ranging from reading light to near total darkness for projection. Some food service areas, such as pubs or coffeehouses, require dimming at certain hours to create a proper atmosphere. Game rooms may be darkly lit, but lounges and offices must have reading-level lighting. When office spaces use flexible furnishing systems, ceiling lighting must be designed for a wide array of furniture configurations. Retail areas, as well as displays, often require spot-lighting. And, given the late evening hours of most campus centers, the quantity and location of exterior lighting and night safety and security require special attention. Because of the diversity of lighting types, the availability and storage of replacement lamps becomes an important factor in lighting selections. Long-lasting, energy-efficient lamps are now the standard. Compact fluorescent, LED (light-emitting diode), metal halide, and halogen fixtures offer the variety needed to accommodate the diversity of spaces in a campus center and, along with lighting control systems, are fundamental components of green building standards.

Acoustic Control

Acoustics permeate every aspect of campus center design, with objectives differing from area to area. The best separations are provided by a surrounding box of dense materials, such as concrete, CMUs, or multiple layers of drywall, but in many campus center spaces, partitions must be movable.

For meeting rooms, sound isolation is the central objective. Movable partitions are commonly used to provide variable-size meeting rooms; these require careful selection and detailing to ensure sound isolation. Reverberation in large meeting rooms can also be a concern. Sound-absorbing surfaces in sufficient quantity can normally lower reverberation to an acceptable level. In many program areas where hard durable finishes are required, such as food service areas, ease of maintenance can conflict with noise reduction. Where floors may be terrazzo, stone, or tile, sound-absorbing surfaces can be added to ceilings, walls, or built-in seating.

It would be helpful to establish early on the Noise Reduction Coefficient (NRC) requirements or Sound Transmission Class (STC) rating requirements for individual spaces in the campus center. These standards should be provided as part of the program document prepared for the building along with common effective practices already employed on campus.

Codes and the Americans with Disabilities Act

Building codes are adopted and amended by local jurisdictions, most now using the 2012 International Building Code as a starting point. It is therefore important to be aware of local and state amendments in the jurisdiction in which you are building. In addition to building codes, insurers of campus buildings may have more stringent requirements than the adopted building codes and standards.

Along with the accessibility requirements found in the adopted building code, every building must now comply with the federal Americans with Disabilities Act (ADA). Simply complying with the local building code may not assure compliance with ADA requirements.

The campus center is a building type that functions best with a single point of entry or multiple entries that bring students and visitors to a central area. Reconciling the requirement for a central lobby—a place of common experience—with the code-required multiple points of egress is often a design challenge.

Regardless of their size and configuration, campus centers almost always require a fire suppression system. Where fire suppression systems are not required, they may be used to allow a more transparent and open interior. Atriums more than 2 stories interconnected require additional fire and life safety protection systems such as smoke control and/or water curtains, which might affect the architecture.

SUSTAINABILITY AND ENVIRONMENTAL DESIGN

Sustainability is a means to maximize energy efficiency, maintain the well-being of occupants, and improve long-term performance. Strategies and features that promote sustainable design must be integrated at the earliest stages of a building's planning and must be considered not only from an initial cost perspective but also from a life-cycle perspective.

Fundamental to the green design strategy is a consideration of the building envelope to create passive systems, where possible, that will reduce energy demand, as well as the integration of low-energy active systems. These include:

- Orientation, solar control, and visibility
- Building shape and footprint
- Thermal mass and natural ventilation (climate dependent)
- Integrated renewable energy systems: photovoltaic, solar thermal, fuel cell, biomass
- Natural daylighting strategies
- Energy-efficient lighting systems

- Lighting control systems
- Mechanical system design

Additional green building strategies involve construction waste management; indoor air quality; recycling opportunities; landscaping; water conservation; wastewater control; and materials selection, including the use of recycled, renewable, and regional materials.

Extensive recycling programs for waste products are now common on college campuses, and providing spaces for recycling programs is important. In addition to central holding areas, collection stations must be conveniently located throughout the building to encourage participation. Food service is also a focal point for sustainable practices, with active recycling programs, composting and pulping, and use of "reusables."

Today's planners are familiar with Leadership in Energy and Environmental Design (LEED), promulgated by the U.S. Green Building Council, but also have the option of employing an alternative system to rate the success of their sustainability goals. The Association for the Advancement of Sustainability in Higher Education (AASHE) has released the Sustainability Tracking, Assessment and Rating System (STARS). Unlike LEED, which deals only with individual buildings, STARS is self-reporting and is a holistic approach to sustainability specifically for campuses.

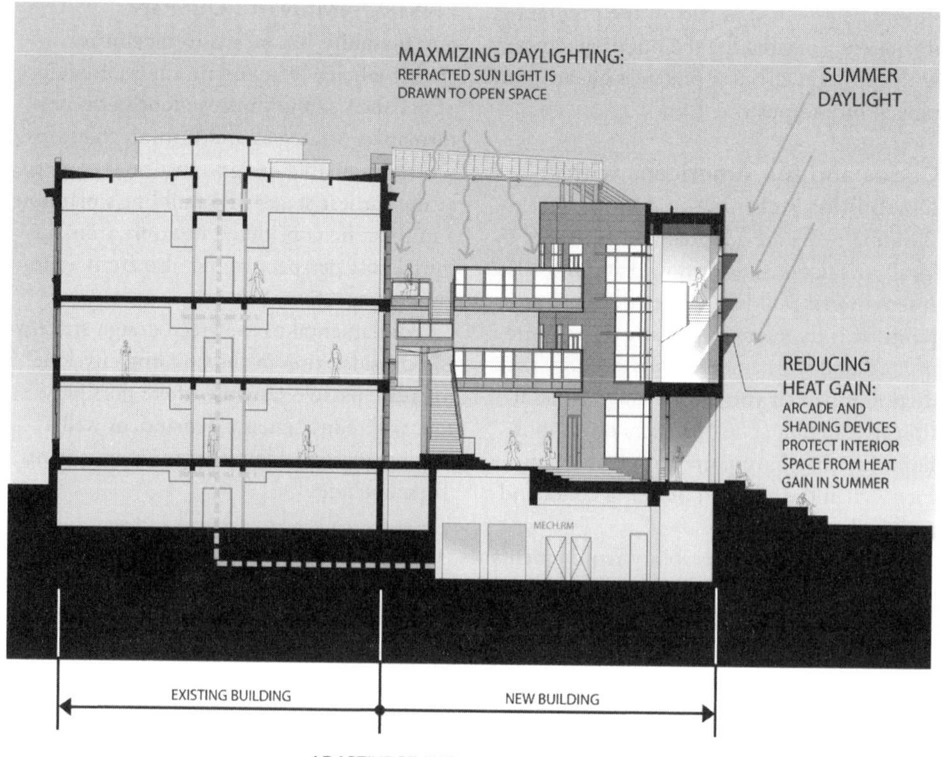

Figure 9.26 Passive strategies, such as providing operable windows to allow cross-ventilation and shaping the building to optimize daylighting, allow natural light to penetrate the building, reducing lighting loads during the day. Joseph A. Steger Student Center, University of Cincinnati, Cincinnati, Ohio. Moore Ruble Yudell, with Glaserworks. Moore Ruble Yudell

INTERIOR ISSUES

Warmth and comfort, coupled with durability, are often contradictory demands placed on both finishes and furnishings in the campus center. Unlike classroom buildings and dining halls, which largely have chairs for seating of a limited duration, the predominant image of the campus center is that of a lounge (see Figure 9.27). A campus center succeeds or fails based on the amount of time students use the building. Programs encourage use, but the design of the building and the quality of its interior amenities—furniture, materials, lighting, and color—play an important role in creating a welcoming environment.

Materials

Several observations about campus center use inform the selection of materials:

- *Long operating hours.* The typical campus center is open 7 days per week and 16–18 hours per day.
- *Intensity of use.* The campus center is the most visited facility on many campuses.
- *Security.* Because of the nature of the building, relatively few activities have continuous administrative or faculty supervision.
- *Food service.* Food service in a campus center can involve spills and waste, not always confined to the food service areas.
- *Flyers and postings.* Although most centers have management policies restricting the locations where flyers may be posted, these policies are difficult to enforce at all times.

These five aspects of campus center use, taken together, suggest a highly durable,

Figure 9.27 The predominant image of a campus center is that of a lounge, and its success or failure is measured by the amount of time students use the building. Wang Center, Wellesley College, Wellesley, Massachusetts. Mack Scogin Merrill Elam Architects. Image courtesy of Yazdani Studio of Cannon Design, photography by Timothy Hursley.

integrally finished materials palette that requires little maintenance. It is well worth the investment in high-grade materials to lengthen the life of finishes beyond the duration of most interior finishes (typically 5–15 years). Consideration for sustainable, "green" products must be factored into the selection criteria, in keeping with the overall sustainability goals of the facility as well as the institution.

As in most buildings, hierarchies of materials should be established, with the most public and permanent spaces receiving the most durable finishes. Conversely, the most private and flexible spaces (meeting and food service areas) will typically not be well served by long material life cycles that exceed their programmatic utility. Inevitably, food migrates into areas where it is not intended, such as study lounges. The resultant damage to carpet, furniture, and other less durable finishes can be rapid. Similarly, without high-grade wall finishes, unauthorized postings of flyers can swiftly damage the walls. Drywall should be impact-resistant or skim-coated with plaster to avoid surface damage from tape removal. Alternatively, digital messaging systems offer an attractive option to traditional paper postings.

The materials chosen must also convey warmth. As basic to the campus hearthstone concept, the interiors should have a distinctly noninstitutional presence. In conjunction with materials selection, a well-orchestrated color palette is encouraged to enliven and distinguish spaces.

In working with a client group to select the interior materials palette, first cost is always an issue. Life-cycle cost analysis is not often applied rigorously to building finishes, but it is a useful tool in selecting finishes that will maintain the character of the building for a longer time.

Furniture and Fixtures

Proper furniture selection can also encourage longer stays in the campus center. Movable, modular lounge furniture that may be readily combined, separated, and "flopped" on without damage is ideal and can reinforce the flexibility often desired in the use of spaces. For example, high-backed lounge chairs can be clustered together to create "pods"—an alternative to walled spaces.

A campus center may have more furniture types than any other campus building. In addition to flexible lounge furnishings, the following types of furniture are often required:

- Conference tables and chairs (readily moved and stored, yet solid and comfortable)
- Flexible office furniture (for student organizations)
- Individual or modular office furnishings (for student life administrators)
- Fixed seating (for auditoriums and theaters)
- Various types of dining furniture (tables of different shapes and sizes, chairs, booths, stools)

Although all these furniture types are specialized, each must also allow for various configurations and easy storage. Also look for furniture that allows compact storage, such as stackable seating and lounge furniture as well as tables that can be folded and stored flat.

Special Equipment

Special equipment in the campus center often includes the following:

- Audiovisual equipment—video, projection, flat-screen television, speakers (see Figure 9.28)

Figure 9.28 Liquid crystal display screens used as a room divider display the front page of daily newspapers from around the world. Claremont University Consortium, Claremont, California. Mary Beth Trama, Claremont University Consortium, Claremont, CA.

- Portable stages and lighting—for coffee-house or pub settings
- Game room equipment—billiard table, ping-pong table, video games
- Retail display systems—campus stores

Sufficient storage is critical. Without it, furnishings and equipment will be left in place, and flexibility and security will be compromised. Storage rooms should be large, with double doors, and readily accessed by freight elevators if they are not distributed throughout the building.

Signage and Wayfinding

The campus center is both a daily home for the campus and a visitors' center. Although it has many repeat users who come to know the building well, it also serves first-time visitors. Clear circulation and transparency of use are the best signs, but they must be supplemented by a graphics system for wayfinding, location identification, and safety (see Figure 9.29).

A good campus center graphics system has a hierarchy of three basic forms: building-wide directories, directional signage, and room indication. The ADA has very specific requirements for building signage with respect to the inclusion of raised letters and Braille.

The ability to easily change the graphics system at all levels is important. Few campus centers are static, particularly their student and administrative offices and support spaces.

In addition to wayfinding and directories, many campus centers are using display screens and other digital signage to notify users of events, news, and other time-sensitive information. These typically are located in areas of greatest foot traffic. Another consideration is donor signage in instances where buildings are funded in full or in part by philanthropic gifts. Development offices

▸ *Figure 9.29 In addition to wayfinding, directories, and room identification signage, wall graphics can be used to enliven a space and provide food for thought. Frist Center, Princeton University, Princeton, New Jersey. Venturi, Scott Brown and Associates.* Venturi, Scott Brown Collection, The Architectural Archives, University of Pennsylvania.

often are not involved in the evolution of a building design, but a thoughtful and integrated approach to all types of signage will produce a more coherent building.

INTERNATIONAL CHALLENGES

Although the culture of educational institutions varies greatly even within North America, the differences are even more striking abroad. In many urban universities outside North America, there is little tradition of centralized and extensive student services. The university is part of the city and vice versa, with the city seen as the central provider of student services such as housing, food, and places to meet for social and even intellectual purposes. The introduction of campus centers in these circumstances requires an understanding and acceptance of the real differences in the role of the university in the life of its students. The program for the campus center outside North America is likely to have a different mix of services and spaces.

Therefore, practical considerations in working abroad include a range of issues that impact design decisions—cultural issues relating to privacy, dining and food service, leisure and recreational preferences, and social and religious conventions, as well as regional factors such as climate and building materials. Moreover, the construction industry is organized differently abroad, affecting the design and construction process. For these reasons, it is wise to form alliances with local architects and construction professionals when working abroad.

OPERATION AND MAINTENANCE

Building operations and maintenance are directly affected by decisions made during the design process. Decisions that save money during construction may make a building more costly to operate. Materials and systems with long life spans generally make the building less expensive to operate. Critical issues in building operation and maintenance derive from the demands for flexible use inherent in the campus center program. The ability to swiftly move and store furniture and set up rooms and spaces for different purposes can be aided by the presence of a large freight elevator and ample storage. The closer storage is to the rooms and areas most likely to change, the easier it will be to reconfigure a space.

In food service areas, requirements for cleaning and maintenance between peak meal times, in both the dining and food preparation areas, necessitate convenient storage space for cleaning equipment. Ease of disposal and collection of trash and recyclables is another key consideration, along with the ability to move and reposition furniture for cleaning.

Direct digital control (DDC) mechanical systems are a good operational investment for a campus center. Room occupancies vary greatly during a single day. A large multipurpose hall may be empty much of the day and house an event with hundreds of people in the space during the evening. Light occupancy sensors will help mitigate unnecessary power consumption, and electronic controls can make the required mechanical system adjustments far easier to manage and monitor. Because a central purpose of the campus center is to provide meeting space, noise generated by mechanical systems is an important consideration. Low-velocity systems are preferred, along with acoustic treatments of floors, walls, and ceilings.

KEY COST FACTORS

There are no reliable rules of thumb for campus center construction costs that may be developed without detailed programs, code analyses, feasibility studies, and schematic designs. These documents can permit quantity-based cost estimating. The specific and highly variable circumstances involved in campus center design and construction make each project unique. Some have extensive food services, and others provide only supplementary snack operations. Some have large theaters and multipurpose rooms, and others only small meeting rooms. Some have retail stores, and some do not. In addition to wide variations in program, site circumstances are often difficult and can affect both site and building construction costs. Code upgrades triggered by partial renovations and additions can also increase costs substantially. Owing to their central locations, many campus center sites are difficult to access and involve additions and close adjacencies to existing structures. Contractor access, storage, and parking can also impact costs notably.

Additions ultimately have different and usually higher costs than freestanding new buildings. However, they are usually coupled with renovations that may cost somewhat less than new construction. Cost per square foot estimates without a specific design almost always prove inaccurate. The best approach is to develop project-specific estimates with locally based estimators early in the process, with subsequent phase-by-phase estimating and tracking. Developing and maintaining a realistic budget and schedule must take into consideration the retention of any existing operations, which will impact time and costs. Furnishing and equipment costs can be quite high as compared with those of other campus buildings, approximately 5–10 percent of the construction cost.

FINANCES, FEES, AND FEASIBILITY

The funding sources for the construction of campus centers, as well as their operation, are threefold: student activity fees, retail and rental operations, and donors. Many institutions use a combination of all three of these sources. Typically, for public institutions, student life facilities funding streams are mandated to be separate from academic and programmatic funding streams—hence, the reliance on the student activity fee.

For public university projects funded by these fees, the underlying finance mechanism is typically a bond issued by the institution for an associated student organization that is to be retired over a period of time by funds derived from the fees. These long-term obligations on behalf of future generations of students are entered into in a very deliberate way. The financial packaging of a fee-funded project requires attention to the details of student politics. If fees are to be increased, when is the increase to start? Are present students who are the decision makers for future generations to be assessed increased fees to support the project without their reaping the benefits of using the new facility prior to graduation? These and other questions must be dealt with to the satisfaction of students and administrators while the funding plan is formulated.

While food service and other retail operations are often viewed as a source of revenue to support the building and its activities, these funding streams are not considered reliable, as most food service operations strive simply to break even. Increasingly, however, large vendors bid for food service operations and often include some contribution toward the tenant improvement build-out. The same holds true for retail operations such as campus bookstores and reprographic operations that generate profits that may be used to support the facilities. During certain times of the year (e.g., summer session), some centers rent meeting facilities to outside groups.

Donors can be considered another source of support for campus center projects, more often in the case of private institutions. As a general rule, colleges like to use the building as a naming opportunity with the donor providing at least 50 percent of the total cost to name the building. Additional gifts may be raised for naming rooms, courtyards, and other interior spaces. Although the funding provided by donors may entail restrictions to a project, the funding process may be relatively simple as compared with that accompanying student activity fees.

Because of the way in which campus centers are often funded, the feasibility study assumes great importance. The feasibility study is the document that identifies what program elements are to be included. The depth and breadth of campus commitment to particular programs that are to be included may in the end determine the success of formal and informal student referendums. It is also the document that is used to convey the substance of the need and facts about the solution to prospective donors and students in a way that creates excitement about the building program. It must also include a pro forma of operating costs and maintenance costs over an extended period of 15–20 years.

The feasibility study must also clearly and accurately predict the construction and project budgets and present the phasing plan, and must project and manage the extent of disruption that will accompany a construction project. What facilities can be kept open during construction? Which can be relocated, and where and at what cost can they be relocated? What services may need to be temporarily eliminated, and for how long? How will campus circulation patterns be affected? Because of the central locations of many campus centers, these are questions that the campus community will want to evaluate at the project's inception.

In conclusion, a comprehensive feasibility study is the essential prerequisite for a successful project. Shaped by a well-orchestrated planning process, realized through rigorous project management, and bolstered by an institutional commitment to community building and architectural excellence, the campus center can become a beacon for the culture, values, and identity of a college or university.

CHAPTER 10

CULTURAL CENTERS: MUSIC, THEATER, DANCE, AND VISUAL ARTS FACILITIES

William L. Rawn, FAIA, LEED AP, and Clifford V. Gayley, AIA, LEED AP, William Rawn Associates, Architects, Inc.

INTRODUCTION

New buildings are connecting the arts to campuses in ways that have not been done before, reinforcing the crucial role that the performing and visual arts play in a broader liberal arts education. This is being done in two fundamental ways:

1. *Teaching innovation, creativity, and risk taking.* In academic settings, arts spaces are critical to fostering the spirit of innovation and risk taking that is at the core of the liberal arts.

   At Stanford University, the Arts Initiative acknowledges that "imagination, originality, and risk-taking should not be byproducts of a university education. They should be its core" (Jonathan Berger and Bryan Wolf, Faculty Leaders of the Arts Initiative).[1] Campus facilities for the performing and visual arts help develop "learners who are fearless and unafraid of new ideas and new concepts; learners who are unafraid of questioning 'conventional wisdom.'" (Barry Mills, President of Bowdoin College).[2]
2. *Engaging the broader community.* A center for the arts is an important platform for intellectual debate and innovation on a college or university campus—a venue not only for arts instruction but also for events that propel public discourse on campus and in the broader community.

   "A great university should both integrate the arts into its intellectual and social life and contribute to the artistic creativity in the broader world" (Lee C. Bollinger, President of Columbia University).[3] Campus arts facilities stand as prominent public symbols of an institution's commitment to the arts, "ensuring that the arts continue to play a preeminent role not only in student life, but also in shaping the cultural landscape in this country and internationally" (Richard C. Levin, President of Yale University).[4]

Many colleges and universities can point to a traditional core of moderately scaled academic and residential buildings that form the physical and symbolic heart of their institution. Over time, several types of campus buildings have developed a large size that poses a challenge to this traditional sense of campus: major libraries, science complexes, and athletic buildings. Following current trends, a fourth building type might be added: the performing and visual arts center. Sensitive design of these buildings is important not only to the success of the building but also to the character and function of the broader campus. The growing opportunities for arts buildings bring with them important challenges for the fabric of a campus, mainly the issues of size and scale.

1 J. Berger and B. Wolf, "The Arts Initiative: Engaging the Arts and Creativity," 2006, http://multi.stanford.edu/initiatives/arts.html.

2 B. Mills, "Sarah and James Bowdoin Day Remarks," October 31, 2008, http://www.bowdoin.edu/president/speeches/2010/sj-bowdoin-day-10.shtml.

3 L. C. Bollinger, "Appointments," *Columbia Magazine Online*, Spring 2004, http://www.columbia.edu/cu/alumni/Magazine/Spring2004/appointments.html.

4 R. C. Levin, "Yale University Has Newly Completed Arts Complex Designed by Charles Gwathmey," October 11, 2008, http://www.artdaily.com/index.asp?int_sec=2&int_new=26538.

Through an examination of key design issues and opportunities, this chapter explores how the design of arts centers can foster innovation and generate powerful community connections.

Three Scales: A Framework for Designing Centers for the Arts

With an eye on the growing importance and changing roles of arts facilities on campuses nationwide, this chapter explores fundamental ideas concerning the design of centers for music, theater, dance, and the visual arts at colleges and universities. These ideas are organized around a framework of three major scales that guide the design process: the *campus* scale; the *building* scale; and, finally, the *room* scale.

1. *Campus scale—creating connections.* As a building for both the campus community and the public, as well as a place for both education and performance, a center for the arts holds significant potential for creating campus connections. A focus on managing the size and scale of the building as it relates to its site and to the broader campus is key. Careful consideration should be given to the transparency and openness of the arts center, as well as to the location of entrances and landscaped spaces, in order to establish the building as a hub of activity. If it successfully connects to the broader campus in a way that fosters both prominence in the landscape and chance encounters, a center for the arts will expose students from all disciplines to the arts while fostering individual creativity and engaging the public.
2. *Building scale—interdisciplinary activity.* At the scale of building organization, the design focus turns to promoting interaction among the various activities taking place within the building. The layout of classrooms, rehearsal spaces, galleries, performance venues, and offices shapes how students, faculty, and visitors experience the arts. The building organization offers opportunities for creating community while encouraging individual study, generating a sense of openness and creative freedom that fosters risk taking. For example, connecting different types of spaces (such as front of house and back of house) can foster collaboration and add to the intensity of the creative spirit of the arts center.
3. *Room scale—flexibility and innovation.* Viewed at the room scale, the design of an arts center should consider the wide range of room types—from performance spaces and galleries, to rehearsal and practice spaces, to studios and laboratories. Each room type entails a different set of design priorities and challenges as well as technological issues. This chapter explores how these ideas apply to theaters, rooms for music, rooms for dance, and spaces for visual arts.

CAMPUS SCALE

Centers for the arts tend to be large, inwardly focused buildings. Program sizes are on the range of 60,000–200,000 sq ft, with many tall-volume spaces that amplify the bulk of the building's already-large floor area (see Figure 10.1).

Tall-volume spaces include 50–60 ft tall concert halls, theaters with 75–90 ft tall fly towers and 40–50 ft tall audience chambers, 40 ft high music rehearsal spaces, and a range of other double- or triple-height spaces such as dance studios, rehearsal spaces, art galleries, art studios, scene shops, and loading docks. Many of these spaces have traditionally not included windows, leading to

Figure 10.1 Large performing arts center—facing city along Eighth Street; facing campus at top of hill. Curtis R. Priem Experimental Media and Performing Arts Center, Rensselaer Polytechnic Institute, Troy, New York. Grimshaw Architects, 2008. © Peter Aaron/Esto.

significant amounts of tall, blank walls, which can create an uninviting sense of mass and overscaled structures.

To ensure that arts centers fully engage a campus as an epicenter of activity and not as an isolated outpost, several key campus planning issues must be addressed.

Managing Size/Scale

Manipulating the building massing to work with the scale of adjacent parts of the campus may involve several approaches:

- Narrowing the footprint of the building to fit within a more sensitive campus fabric (see Color Plate 19)
- Taming the "big box" by breaking down the mass into seemingly smaller objects, particularly at the perimeter, and by shielding the tallest mass (often the fly tower) from the street with shorter program elements
- Organizing entries to encourage campus movement patterns through the building rather than merely to and then around the building
- Utilizing creative landscape design to mitigate scale issues and to create connections with adjacent buildings

Celebrating Transparency

Introducing transparency can have two major benefits at the campus scale:

- Creating a greater sense of welcome and interior/exterior connection
- Breaking down the mass of otherwise large solid buildings

Lobbies are typically places where transparency can be celebrated, often connecting the building entry to a campus open space or a city street (see Figure 10.2). At night, this transparency can allow the building to

▸ *Figure 10.2 Transparent lobby, Richard B. Fisher Center for the Performing Arts, Bard College, Annandale-on-Hudson, New York. Gehry Partners, LLP, 2003.* © Peter Aaron/Esto.

serve as a glowing beacon. During the day, this transparency can signify a sense of accessibility and invitation. The value of transparency is greatest when the space is full of activity—a perennial challenge for performing arts lobbies, which tend to be oversized and underutilized.

Despite a tendency to place performing arts spaces in windowless volumes, it is worthwhile and timely, considering recent developments in glass technology and daylighting, to explore where transparency can be introduced beyond the lobby. Transparency can be emphasized by organizing program space with significant glazing at locations along the perimeter. Specifically, dance studios, music rehearsal and performance spaces, galleries, classrooms, auditoriums, art studios, cafés, and, more recently, theaters can all be carefully designed with significant glass.

Creating Multiple Front Doors

As very large campus buildings, arts centers require multiple front doors. In successful campuses, buildings work together to create a complex fabric of landscaped open spaces, including large quads, pedestrian promenades, and smaller courtyards. It is often said that campus buildings should not have "a front" and "a back," but rather multiple fronts. Typically, a single building plays an important role in at least two outdoor spaces and thus can have two or more front doors. For performing arts centers, which have a strong division between front of house and back of house, facing in two directions is uncommon—and yet highly valuable as a campus planning goal.

The importance of multiple entries is especially clear when centers for the arts are at a leading edge of a campus, with an opportunity to "front" outward toward the city or town and inward toward the campus, with neither side feeling like "the back."

Resolving Loading Imperatives

Performing and visual arts buildings have serious loading requirements that should be handled carefully to minimize disruption to the campus fabric. Depending on the program, a loading dock may be required to support up to three loading bays with access and turnaround space for 55 ft long trucks. Consequently, locating the loading dock and its requisite outdoor space is one of the earliest required decisions from the perspective of campus planning.

More than other arts programs, theaters place significant constraints on the location of the loading dock. Given the large size of the materials and stage sets that need to be loaded into theaters, the loading dock should be at the same elevation as the stage and have a direct path of travel to both the stage and the scene shop. If there is a second theater, direct access from the scene shop and loading dock to that second stage is also desirable. On campus sites with steep topography, these requirements can severely limit the options for organizing the program on the site.

Using elevators to move materials and sets from a loading dock to a stage is inefficient and costly (both in the initial cost of a freight elevator and in the incremental costs required each time large sets built off-site are disassembled and later reassembled in order to fit into the elevator). Direct loading to stage level is especially important for college and university facilities that present a program of touring shows, which typically require quick and efficient turnover between performances.

For arts centers, trucks may be in the loading dock for long periods of time; therefore, efforts to screen the loading area by building or landscape should account for the length of a parked truck.

Accommodation of Vehicular Access

A vehicular drop-off area near the front door is advantageous, especially with significant audiences coming from off campus. In some campus settings, this is difficult to achieve. Drop-off areas function best if there is parking nearby, but with adequate separation to avoid conflicts with postshow pickups, when egress for all patrons occurs simultaneously (see Figure 10.3).

Where there are significant off-campus audiences, parking adjacent to a performing arts center is highly desirable. How close, how many spaces, and whether this is surface parking or structured parking depends on the particular campus context. The parking load for general performing arts centers is typically calculated as one space for every three audience seats. For campus performing arts centers, the ideal number of spaces can be lowered to reflect the on-campus student audience arriving on foot, by bicycle, or by public transportation. In addition, ensuring

▾ *Figure 10.3 Multiuse theater, Blanche M. Touhill Performing Arts Center, University of Missouri, St. Louis. Pei Cobb Freed & Partners, 1993.* © Eric Schiller.

the daily use of this parking area (beyond the periodic peak load required for performances) is critical, as is the source of funding to construct and maintain the parking facility. Arts centers on campuses are rarely able to command their own parking resources.

BUILDING SCALE

Building organization establishes interconnections between the activities within a building and plays an important role in developing a sense of community. Through careful consideration of the layout of major venues, secondary spaces, and circulation, the design of a campus arts center can create both the sense of intensity, activity, and collaboration that is at the heart of an arts education and the environment that fosters innovation within and among disciplines.

Arts Centers: Revisiting the Public/Private Divide

One of the defining characteristics of arts centers is the distinction between the building's public side (the "front of house") and its private side (the "back of house").

Front of House

Front-of-house spaces are designed to serve large numbers of visitors or audience members whose visit is concentrated in a short period of time. These spaces include:

- Lobby
- Auditorium
- Gallery
- Café/gift shop
- Coatroom
- Restrooms
- Connecting circulation
- Donor lounge (as needed)

Between performances, many of these spaces are generally empty—an underused asset that presents a real challenge and opportunity for rethinking in college and university settings.

Back of House

Back-of-house spaces are designed to serve visiting artists, faculty, student actors, directors, choreographers, stagehands, and technicians before, during, and after a performance or exhibit. These spaces include:

- Stage
- Rehearsal spaces
- Directing and acting studios
- Scene shop
- Costume shop
- Faculty offices
- Curatorial and administrative offices
- Conservation facilities
- Art collection storage
- Practice rooms
- Makeup rooms
- Green room
- Dressing rooms
- Lighting labs
- Stage manager office
- Visiting artist studio (as needed)

In a college or university setting, back-of-house spaces serve as teaching spaces and centers of daily activity. Thus, it is a "double loss" when these spaces are too separated from the building's primary circulation: a loss of activity that could energize the public areas of the building and a loss for students spending significant time in areas that feel isolated. A more nuanced solution that allows back-of-house spaces to connect to public circulation can be pedagogically favorable.

Performing Arts: Building Organization Typology

The organization of performing arts buildings with multiple venues (whether theater, music, dance, or some combination) plus rehearsal space falls into one of three general categories: side-by-side type, front-to-front type, and linear path type (see Figure 10.4).

Side-by-Side Type

A common organization, this type places two or more venues side-by-side facing the same orientation, allowing for shared

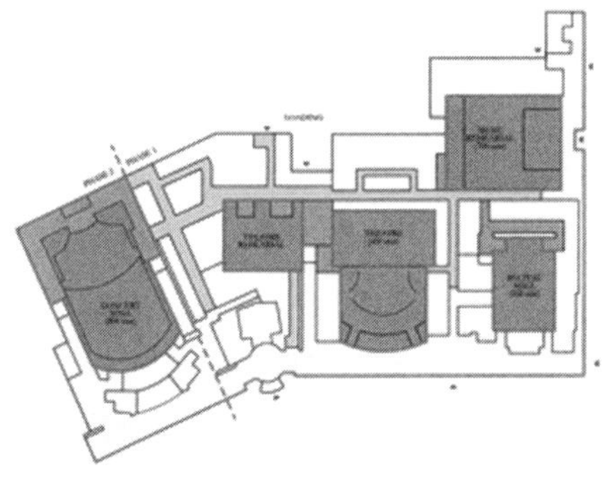

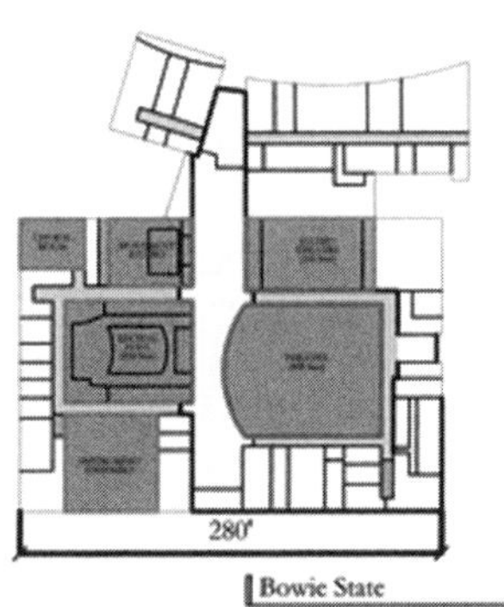

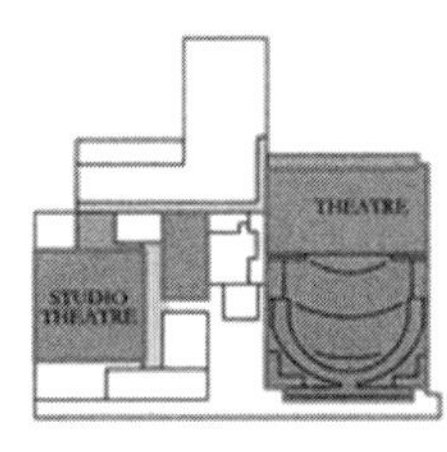

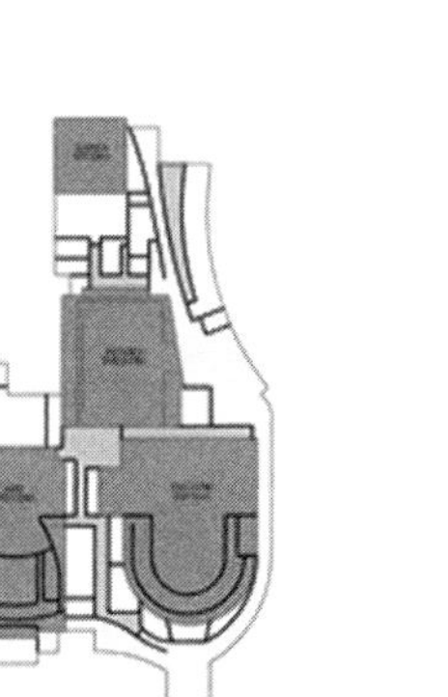

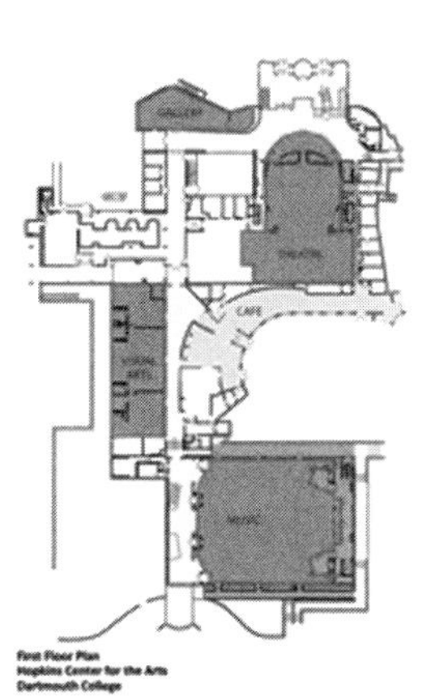

◀ *Figure 10.4 Performing arts building organizational typology. Plan diagrams of three organizational types: (a) University of Delaware; (b) Bowie State; (c) University of Maryland College Park; (d) Cornell; (e) Williams; (f) Dartmouth College, William Rawn Associates, Architects, Inc.* Drawing: William Rawn Associates, Architects, Inc.

front-of-house and shared back-of-house spaces to serve all performance venues.

The side-by-side organization creates a strong front with a shared single-loaded lobby, potentially quite open to the outside. The side-by-side layout also results in a strong division between the front of house and the back of house, separating the "anytime/all-the-time" activity of the back of house from the periodic use of front-of-house spaces, which are often left empty between performances. This organization results in a clear "back side" to the building, a challenge for many campus settings where buildings are expected to "front" in many directions.

Examples include the Roselle Center for the Arts, University of Delaware, Newark (see Figure 10.4d); RiverCenter for the Performing Arts, Columbus, Georgia; the Chan Centre for the Performing Arts, University of British Columbia, Vancouver; and the Schwartz Center for the Performing Arts, Cornell University, Ithaca, New York (see Figure 10.4b).

Front-to-Front Type

In the front-to-front type, venues face each other across a shared lobby, reducing the length of expensive lobby space and resulting in separate back-of-house areas.

This organization places the lobby at the center of the building, creating an opportunity for concentrating activity along a central spine. Back-of-house spaces are subsequently located along the perimeter. This peripheral location of teaching spaces heightens the separation between academic spaces in each back-of-house area.

Examples include the Clarice Smith Performing Arts Center, University of Maryland, College Park (see Figure 10.4e); the Fine and Performing Arts Center, Bowie State University, Prince George's County, Maryland (see Figure 10.4a); the DeBartolo Performing Arts Center, University of Notre Dame, Notre Dame, Indiana; and the Forbes Center for the Performing Arts, James Madison University, Harrisonburg, Virginia.

Front-to-front and side-by-side organizations often work well in commercial arts centers where clear front-of-house/back-of-house divisions are favored. In campus settings, however, where a breakdown of these front-of-house/back-of-house divisions may be desired to meet pedagogic goals and to help animate public circulation throughout the day, other building organization types can be explored.

Linear Path Type

This organization places venues along a primary interior path that weaves through the building, organizing back-of-house spaces and connecting multiple lobbies and building front doors. A linear path building organization begins to break down barriers between the front of house and the back of house, allowing some of the 18-hour activity of the teaching/rehearsal spaces to animate public circulation areas, which would otherwise be underused between performances.

The linear path type also makes departmental teaching activity more visible and accessible to other departments (whether in the building or not) for potential collaboration as well as to students of nonarts majors who may be inclined to explore an interest in the arts.

A notable example is the Hopkins Center for the Arts, Dartmouth College, Hanover, New Hampshire (Wallace K. Harrison, 1962; see Figure 10.4d), where an interior path connects two main building entrances. One lobby faces the Dartmouth Green and serves two theaters, while the other lobby faces active retail along Lebanon Street and serves a large auditorium. In between, the interior path connects two galleries, a café, visual arts studios and classrooms, and a range of performing arts rehearsal and production spaces.

A more recent example is the '62 Center for Theatre and Dance, Williams College, Williamstown, Massachusetts (William Rawn Associates, Architects, Inc., 2005; see Figure 10.4f), where a primary interior path links four main venues and two building entries, one facing the campus and one facing Main Street. This path is animated by numerous back-of-house spaces (e.g., costume shop, rehearsal and teaching studios, offices). Storefront glazing opens these back-of-house spaces onto the public circulation, and a large barn door opens one of the main theater venues to the lobby. During the school year, the building serves both the theater department and the dance department. During the summer, the building is home to the renowned Williamstown Theater Festival.

Additional examples of this type include the Performing Arts and Humanities Facility, University of Maryland, Baltimore County, Baltimore; the Curtis R. Priem Experimental Media and Performing Arts Center (EMPAC), Rensselaer Polytechnic Institute, Troy, New York; the College-Conservatory of Music, University of Cincinnati, Cincinnati, Ohio; and the Center for the Arts, Towson University, Towson, Maryland.

Reinventing the Lobby

Activating the Lobby

Innovative strategies for creating a sense of vibrant and constant activity in the lobby include:

- Designing the lobby to function as a multiuse space—a performance space in its own right with appropriate acoustic design and lighting (see Figure 10.5)

Figure 10.5 Lobby as performance space: site-specific dance. '62 Center for Theatre and Dance, Williams College, Williamstown, Massachusetts. William Rawn Associates, Architects, Inc., 2005. Image by Ben Rudick.

- Incorporating a café to encourage use throughout the day
- Organizing back-of-house and rehearsal spaces along the lobby
- Using large barn doors that can open venues to the lobby during rehearsal and tech work
- Incorporating transparent sound and light locks (with blackout shades) into rehearsal or performance spaces
- Deploying interior "storefront" windows to reveal support spaces (such as the costume shop, departmental office suites, and rehearsal and teaching studios) to the lobby
- Establishing a clear circulation diagram around the lobby—to avoid the "rabbit warren" effect that characterizes many arts buildings with endless corridors and breeds disconnection and creative isolation (see Figure 10.6)
- Opening gallery space(s) to the lobby by using glass storefront and/or movable walls and by displaying artwork in the lobby
- Designing the lobby with space for temporary pinup of student work (drawings, paintings, photographs), allowing the lobby to double as an informal "crit space" (where students pin up and present their work to fellow students, faculty, and guest critics)
- Organizing the lobby to engage with and extend the campus pathway system through the building

Lobby Size

Regardless of the building organization, lobby size is a critical design decision. Lobbies must accommodate the flow of audience during arrival, intermission, and departure. The metrics for lobby area require 4–8 sq ft

Figure 10.6 Continuous circulation. Gallery interior, Davis Museum and Cultural Center, Wellesley College, Wellesley, Massachusetts. Jose Rafael Moneo, 1993. Davis Museum and Cultural Center, Wellesley College, Wellesley, Massachusetts. Photo by Steve Briggs.

per person. A successful lobby for college and university projects is typically on the smaller end of this range. This scale encourages continuous use, whether enabling the "rubbing of shoulders" during peak periods or feeling intimate enough for a few people to gather informally when the lobby is not servicing a performance. Oversized lobbies typically suffer from the "dead-lobby syndrome," which tends to discourage informal use. Successful lobbies are also supported by ample restroom accommodations to minimize lines during short intermissions. For performing arts facilities, determining restroom count requires a more conservative standard than code minimums for the ratio of number of fixtures to total seats: a range of 1/40–1/60 for women (with the International Building Code [IBC] at 1/65) and a range of 1/60–1/80 for men (with the IBC at 1/125).

Visual Arts: Building Organization Typology

Facilities for the visual arts offer parallels to those for the performing arts in their combination of public, front-of-house spaces and private, back-of-house spaces, with galleries playing the role of front of house (and serving as the analogue to theaters and concert halls).

In regard to back-of-house spaces, an important distinction between performing and visual arts is the role of teaching studios and how they impact building organization. Rehearsal studios (theater rehearsal, music rehearsal, dance studios, acting/directing studios) serve as integral parts of performing arts buildings and play a vital role in shaping the work produced in a theater or concert hall. In comparison, visual arts studios (studios for drawing, painting, sculpture, pottery, photography) are independent of most campus galleries. Visual arts studios play little or no role in the production of work exhibited in campus galleries, which typically feature work by established artists (contemporary or historic) rather than student work.

At the broadest level, the organization of visual arts buildings can be defined by the size and location of their most public spaces: their galleries. Campus galleries, which are teaching spaces in their own right, fall into one of three scales: a stand-alone campus art museum (separate from studio spaces), a discrete wing of a larger building (visual arts building or other campus building), or a smaller-scale "retail" presence (often on the ground floor of a visual arts, performing arts, or other campus building).

Gallery as "Stand-Alone" Campus Art Museum

A "stand-alone" campus art museum is a common organizational strategy on campuses with significant permanent art collections. While its independence allows a campus museum to be prominently located, its design must work to open out to and engage students and faculty from a range of disciplines in other buildings (and perhaps in other precincts) in order to be a catalyst for innovation and not merely a repository (or mausoleum).

With this strategy, the location of a campus art museum is an important factor in shaping how galleries engage the intellectual culture of a campus as well as that of its host city or town. Campus art museums located in highly visible campus sites or at major campus gateways become accessible to both the campus community and the broader public. The proximity of a campus museum to other arts buildings (whether studio arts, art history, architecture, or the performing arts) is a natural way to strengthen the pedagogic role of the gallery and its integration into departmental curricula.

Another factor shaping how "stand-alone" galleries engage the campus community is the sense of openness of the building's interior organization. The lobby, whether linear or centralized, provides opportunities to strengthen connections to outdoor campus spaces, to create vertical connections to galleries on upper floors, and to bring significant controlled daylight deeper into the building. Ground-floor galleries for temporary exhibits should be designed to be quite permeable to the lobby, animating the ground floor and drawing visitors to and through the building. Permanent collections, commonly exhibited on upper floors, can take advantage of specialized skylights providing controlled, diffused, natural light.

An example of a stand-alone campus museum is the Blanton Museum of Art complex, University of Texas, Austin (Kallmann McKinnell & Wood Architects, 2006), where a campus museum is designed as one-half of a pair of buildings at the gateway to campus (see Figure 10.7). Together with its sibling building (the Smith Building, which includes academic spaces dedicated to both art history and general use), the Blanton Museum flanks an active outdoor space with arcades and defines a highly public sequence linking the pair of buildings—from interior atrium, to arcade, to outdoor green space, to arcade, to the other interior atrium.

Other examples of stand-alone campus art museums include the Yale University Art

Figure 10.7 Stand-alone campus museum, Jack S. Blanton Museum of Art, University of Texas, Austin. Kallmann McKinnell & Wood Architects, 2006. Photograph courtesy of, and copyright by, Emery Photography, Inc.–Columbus, OH.

Gallery and Yale British Art Center, New Haven, Connecticut; the Davis Museum of Art, Wellesley College, Wellesley, Massachusetts; the Fogg Museum, Harvard University, Cambridge, Massachusetts; the University of Virginia Art Museum, Charlottesville; the Weisman Art Museum, University of Minnesota, Minneapolis; and the Bowdoin College Museum of Art, Brunswick, Maine.

Gallery as Discrete Building Wing

This building organization incorporates significant gallery space as a discrete and legible wing of a larger building (whether a visual arts building or another type of campus building). For this hybrid building type, the key challenge is to find the right balance between maintaining the legibility of the gallery on campus and achieving an openness to the rest of the building's uses and users. Whether the gallery has its own front door and a secondary connection to the rest of the building, or is entered from a shared entry and lobby, is a critical decision for this building type. Equally important is how robustly each use opens to a shared lobby while addressing distinct requirements for humidity, acoustics, and security.

An example of a campus gallery as building wing is the Nerman Museum of Contemporary Art, Johnson County Community College, Overland Park, Kansas (Kyu Sung Woo Architects, 2007). The building wing features a double-height atrium that joins the museum to an adjacent technology center along a major campus pathway. By contrast, the Hood Museum, Dartmouth College, Hanover, New Hampshire (Charles Moore and Chad Floyd of Centerbook Architects, 1985), connects directly to the Hopkins Center for the Arts but has its own front door and forecourt. This forecourt, or outdoor lobby, is adjacent to the Hopkins Center lobby, and both face out to the Dartmouth Green. A secondary, yet decidedly public, connection exists between the two buildings as well: the indoor lobby of the Hood Museum is joined to the internal circulation of the Hopkins Center. An additional example of this type is the Smith College Museum of Art, a wing of the Brown Fine Arts Center, Northampton, Massachusetts.

Gallery as Ground-Floor "Retail"

A common type for smaller-scale galleries is the ground-floor "retail" configuration. These more intimate spaces capitalize on their proximity to building entrances and public spaces to connect directly to the life of the building.

Retail-scaled galleries are well suited for temporary exhibits, achieving visibility for a variety of exhibitions for a broad audience, including the campus community and campus visitors. These gallery spaces can be co-curated to resonate with academic projects or performances that are also occurring within the building, creating new disciplinary or interdisciplinary connections. Depending on the nature of the work displayed (and the requirements for security and humidity control), these galleries can connect to their lobbies in one of three ways: adjacent to the lobby, open to the lobby, or part of the lobby.

The Sam Fox School of Design and Visual Arts, Washington University, St. Louis, Missouri (Maki and Associates, 2006), has examples of all three levels of connection along its linear lobby. At the front door, the lobby acts as an open sculpture gallery. Immediately adjacent is a gallery space with a sliding wall that, when opened (with security guard present), expands the lobby to include the gallery.

This double-height lobby also opens to a separate, second-floor gallery with its own security and humidity and acoustic control.

Examples of the "retail" gallery typology include the Jaffe-Friede Gallery, Hopkins Center for the Arts (film and television studies, music, studio art, theater), Dartmouth College, Hanover, New Hampshire; the Faulconer Gallery, Bucksbaum Center for the Arts (visual and performing arts), Grinnell College, Grinnell, Iowa; the Dalton Gallery, Presser Hall (visual and performing arts), Agnes Scott College, Decatur, Georgia; the University Art Gallery (UAG), Claire Trevor School of the Arts, University of California, Irvine; and the Bakalar Gallery, South Building (admissions, studios, academic spaces), Massachusetts College of Art and Design, Boston.

Arts Precinct/Arts Village

Visual and performing arts buildings can be designed as places of innovation and creative collaboration and as places of openness and connection to campus and community, whether they are distributed across campus or located together in an "arts precinct."

On campuses where there is an opportunity to create a new or strengthen an existing arts precinct, a new arts building should be designed to reinforce two key precinct planning goals:

- Strengthening openness and interconnections between buildings (the precinct should not simply be a cluster of distinct and separate buildings)
- Strengthening pathways and thresholds linking the precinct with the rest of the campus

The term "arts village" has been used to describe an arts precinct with a greater degree of connection between buildings—achieved by a landscape with a carefully programmed network of active outdoor spaces or "outdoor rooms." These programmed landscapes are key places of creative interaction and art production, accommodating classes, art display, performance, outdoor theater, and a sculpture park as well as informal gathering. One example of an arts village is at the University of California, Irvine, where fine arts, music, theater and dance, and media arts buildings are organized around a landscaped mall with an outdoor gallery, performance space, learning space, and park. This concept, originated by William L. Pereira and refined subsequently, has become a vital campus lab.

Another example is at the University of Virginia, where the Arts Common (landscape by Olin) is programmed for collaborative use, drawing activity for architecture, studio arts, theater, and Smith Band rehearsal. The outdoor program includes an amphitheater, sculpture garden, outdoor classroom, and space for graduations and receptions. At the University of Virginia, the organization of arts spaces around the Arts Common applies lessons of Jefferson's Lawn to larger, more contemporary buildings.

CULTURAL CENTERS
CASE STUDY 1

JACK S. BLANTON MUSEUM OF ART

University of Texas, Austin

Architect: Kallmann McKinnell & Wood Architects
Associate architect: Booziotis & Company
Landscape architect: Peter Walker and Partners

Project Data

- The Blanton Museum of Art complex includes two buildings (totaling 180,000 sq ft) book-ending an outdoor campus plaza (see Figure 10.8)
- Mari and James A. Michener Gallery Building (124,000 sq ft)—permanent collection and traveling exhibit galleries
- Edgar A. Smith Building (56,000 sq ft)—café, museum shop, classrooms
- 300-seat auditorium, offices
- Collection includes more than 17,000 works

Figure 10.8 Meeting of the axes: view from university campus toward Texas State Capitol. Emery Photography, Inc.

Cultural Building as Campus Gateway

Marking a threshold where the city of Austin and the university campus meet (see Figures 10.8 and 10.9), the Blanton Museum welcomes the city onto the campus and invites the campus community to engage the city. Framing

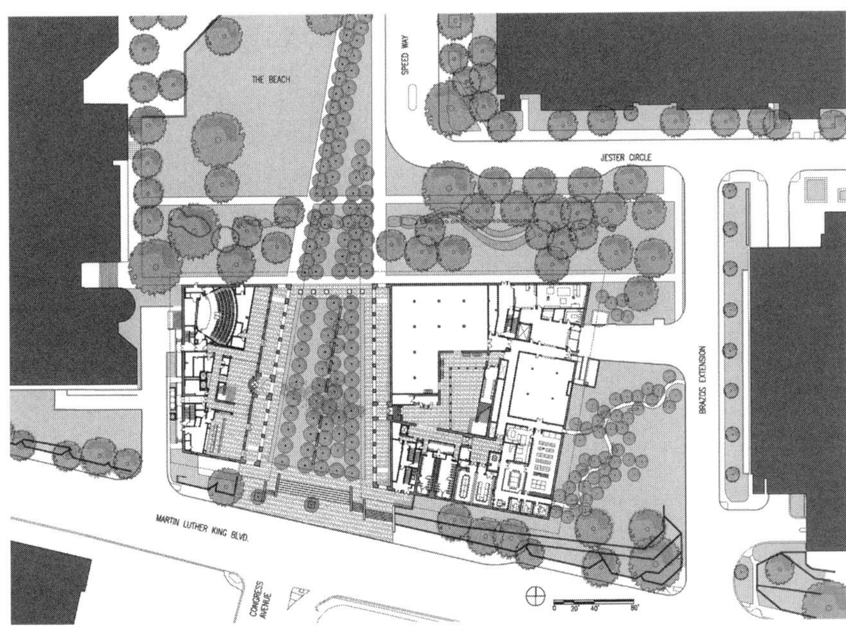

◄ *Figure 10.9 Site plan: the geometry of the plaza incorporates shift from campus grid to city grid.* Drawing: Kallmann McKinnell & Wood Architects.

views to the Texas State Capitol, the museum celebrates the arts as a significant connector between the two communities.

Gallery Typologies and Variation

- Temporary galleries on the ground floor are open, flexible spaces for traveling exhibits. Their connection to the lobby activates space, while reduced natural light ensures that the space can accommodate light-sensitive works.
- Permanent galleries on the second floor are designed specifically to house major university collections (including the Suida-Manning Collection and the Michener Collection).
- A series of intimate rooms with shaped ceilings capture the scale of these centuries-old works.
- Skylit spaces provide controlled daylight that recalls the environments in which the paintings would have originally been viewed (see Figure 10.10).
- Galleries are organized "enfilade" in two concentric rings around the atrium, with a cross connection that allows multiple possible circulation routes (see Figure 10.11).
- Outward-focused corner study rooms are embedded among the inward-focused gallery spaces.

Figure 10.10 Skylit permanent gallery (second floor). Emery Photography, Inc.

Figure 10.11 Michener Gallery Building entrance: double-height atrium with monumental stair beneath high glass ceiling. Emery Photography, Inc.

ROOM SCALE

The third scale for examining the design of a campus arts center—the room scale—focuses on flexibility and innovation as well as the specific needs of each different type of venue within an arts facility. This section reviews opportunities and issues at the room scale for theater, music, dance, and the visual arts with an eye on major design principles and current trends.

Theaters

Theaters are spaces that present movement and the spoken word in a scenic setting. They accommodate theater and dance productions and, with added features, can accommodate musical theater and opera.

There are four different theater types: proscenium theater, studio theater (i.e., the next generation of black box), thrust theater, and arena theater. These types relate to distinctly different relationships between actors and audience and between the stage, the scenery, and the auditorium.

Proscenium Theater

By far the most pervasive type is the proscenium theater, where the proscenium arch frames the audience's view of the stage and scenery and screens offstage areas where actors enter or exit (see Figure 10.12).

The proscenium arch creates a formal, frontal presentation of the work, which represents a predictable space for directors and choreographers. In this theater type, the auditorium and the stage are two distinct spaces, typically separated by a code-mandated fire curtain.

The height of the auditorium is determined by the number of balconies plus a catwalk level. The height of the fly tower (often 75–90 ft) is determined by the height of the proscenium arch (22–26 ft for theaters and up to 35 ft for multiuse theaters) plus an equivalent height for stage sets (a typical fly tower is approximately 2.4 times the arch height plus a 10 ft zone for the tech grid above). Driven by a visual intimacy and a desire to bring seats as close to the stage as possible, the shape of the auditorium for a proscenium theater is wider and squarer than the auditorium of a music hall, where a narrower space between side walls is better for developing appropriate sound.

Figure 10.12 Proscenium theater, '62 Center for Theatre and Dance, Williams College, Williamstown, Massachusetts. William Rawn Associates, Architects, Inc., 2005. © Robert Benson Photography.

Black Box/Studio Theaters

Black box and studio theaters are highly flexible. They have flat-floor spaces—with no separate stage house or fly tower—where seating risers can be reconfigured to create an end stage, wall stage, thrust stage, or arena stage (see Figure 10.13).

This flexibility is typically enabled by a continuous technical grid across the entire ceiling, where lighting positions can be adjusted for various configurations. The space enclosed is typically dark colored solid concrete or block walls. Continuous horizontal metal strut channels (e.g., Unistrut) attached at 4 ft on center up each wall can give additional flexibility, providing a demountable attachment system for theater components like lighting and backdrops.

A studio theater can be thought of as a black box with a "point of view," slightly larger and more rectangular than a black box. In addition, one wall can be created to act as a ready-made backdrop—a two-level architectural wall with a series of framed openings, easily used as doors, windows, and balconies, while the other three walls remain

▼ *Figure 10.13 Flexibility of studio theater layout: (a) end stage layout, (b) wall layout, (c) thrust layout, and (d) arena layout. William Rawn Associates, Architects, Inc.* Drawing: William Rawn Associates, Architects, Inc.

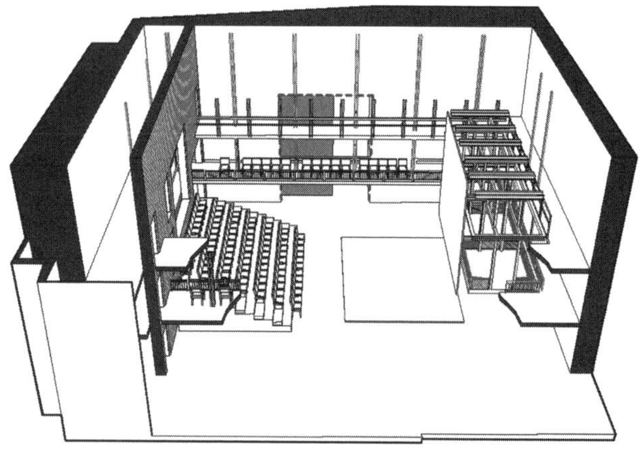

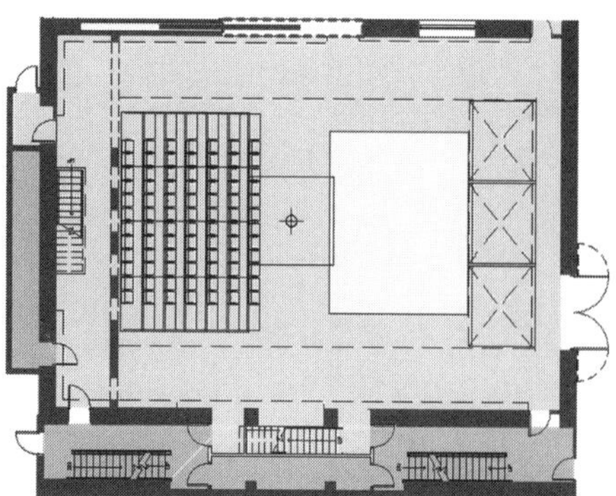

End Stage Layout

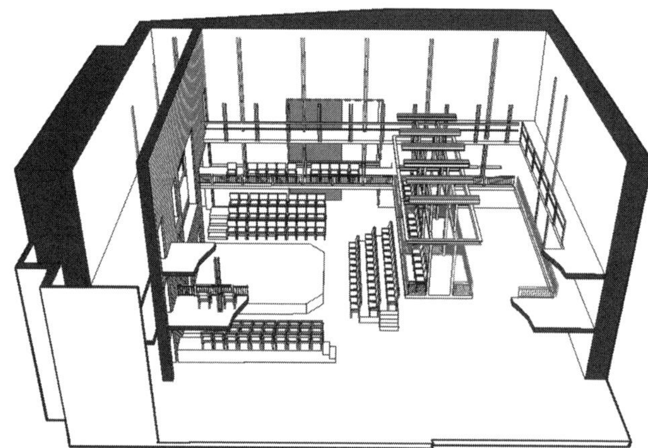

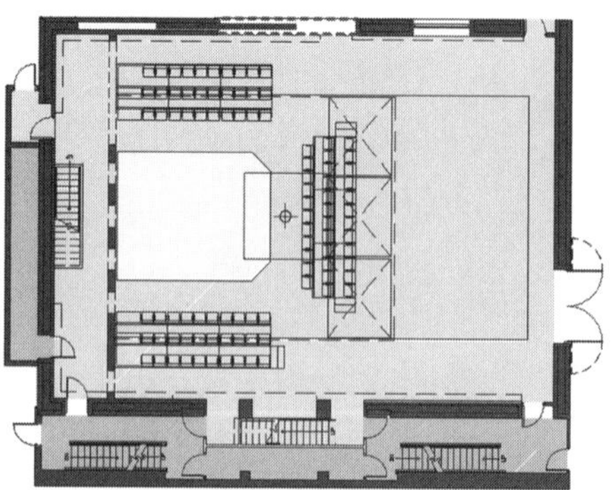

Wall Layout

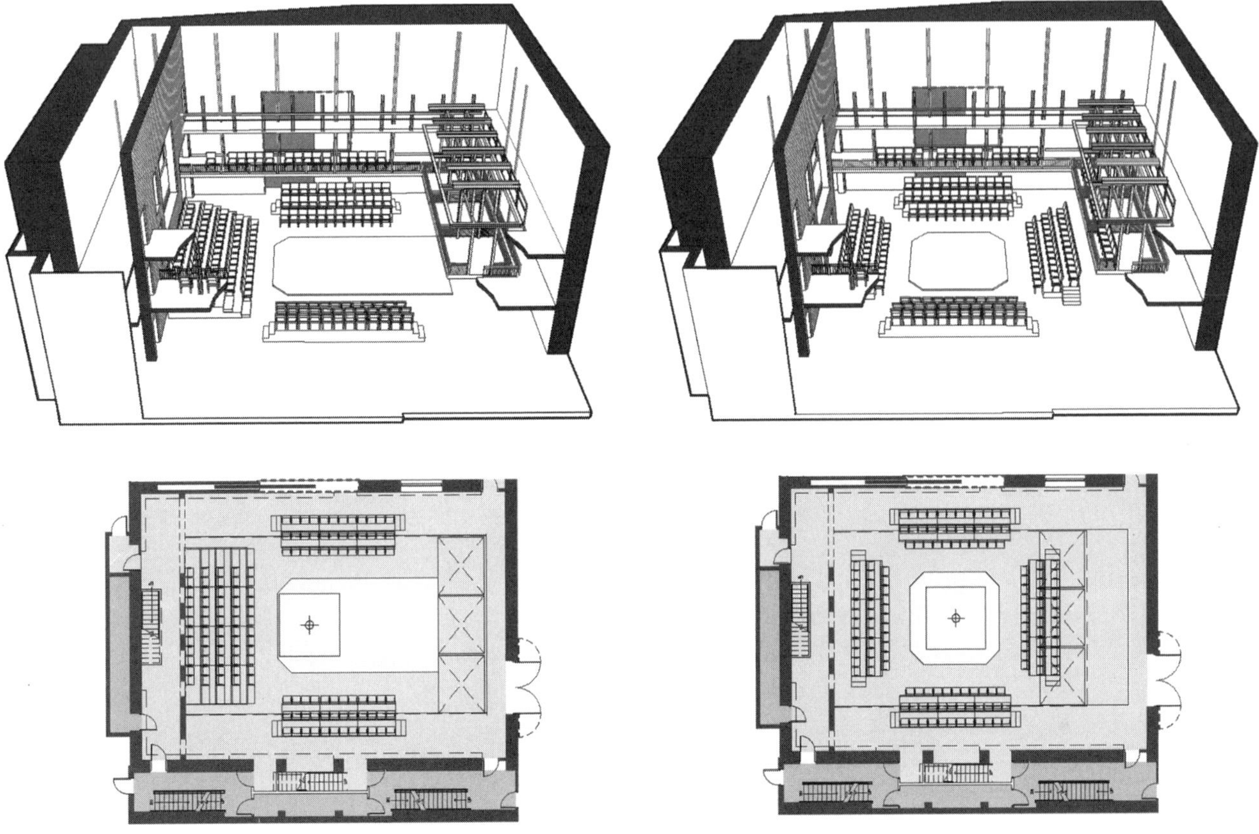

▲ *Figure 10.13 (continued)*

neutral (see Figure 10.14). This ready-made wall is useful in a college or university setting, where the students' limited time to rehearse can be further reduced if they are required to get control of the room to construct new backdrops and sets.

Thrust Theaters

A thrust theater pushes the stage and actors into the auditorium with a near-equivalent number of seats along all three sides of the stage. The fourth side of the stage remains connected to a proscenium and stage house.

Because most of the action occurs in front of the proscenium, the depth of the stage house can be less than that in a proscenium theater. Actors access the stage from all sides—from the proscenium edge, from audience aisles, and from vomitories ("voms") emerging from below the seating areas. Thrust theaters create an intense sense of intimacy and informality, breaking down the formal picture plane of the proscenium. With the stage merging into the auditorium, catwalks or lighting grids over the stage should be configured to support its size and location.

Figure 10.14 Studio theater with ready-made backdrop, '62 Center for Theatre and Dance, Williams College, Williamstown, Massachusetts. William Rawn Associates, Architects, Inc., 2005. © Robert Benson Photography.

Arena Stage

An arena stage places the stage in the center of the auditorium, creating a theater-in-the-round. Actors access the stage from aisles and voms. Scenic changes happen in front of the audience as there are no connections to offstage areas through a proscenium.

Multiuse Theater

There is another theater type that is becoming more common—the multipurpose or multiuse theater. Multipurpose theaters are proscenium theaters that are meant to accommodate music, music theater, opera as well as theater. To do this, these spaces are augmented with a movable shell that creates side walls and a ceiling over the stage that reflects the sound out into the auditorium. Typically, these shells are carefully designed with acousticians and theater consultants to be heavy enough to reflect low- and high-frequency sounds while being easily movable. Often, the side wall towers slide into a niche in the upstage wall while the ceiling is lifted up into the fly space, an approach used at the Main Theatre at the Mondavi Center at the University of California at Davis.

The downstage edge of the stage can be adjusted with a forestage lift, which can be positioned at orchestra level to accommodate the front rows of seats, lowered to create an orchestra pit, raised to create a forestage extension, or used as a lift to bring seating sections to and from basement storage areas.

The shaping of the multipurpose theater is similar to that of the proscenium theater except that the natural sound reinforcement of the side walls in the forestage area may become more parallel for the first 10–15 ft (like concert halls) before becoming more splayed to bring a greater number of audience members closer to the stage (like theaters).

All theatrical performance spaces utilize sound and light locks (vestibules) to protect both the audience space and the stage area from outside distraction. Any stage area can include a trap room with either mechanized platform lift(s) or manual trap door(s) with ladders to bring an actor or scenery from below. Like the orchestra pit, this space can be expensive and often becomes a storage space with relatively few production uses. Also, trap doors cut into the stage floor tend to make the stage surfaces less attractive to dancers as it interferes with the levelness and consistent sturdiness of the stage floor.

Transparency in Theaters

Although natural light has historically been absent from theaters, as it is usually unwanted during performance, theater designers have begun introducing natural light in varying degrees, all with the capability to black out light completely (see Figure 10.15). Transparency can also be accommodated in rehearsal spaces where windows have separate shades for room darkening and glare control. Improving the user experience, maximizing the flexibility of room character (for multiuse), and reducing energy consumption with daylighting are among the major benefits of incorporating natural light into theater spaces during nonperformance uses (such as lectures, rehearsals, technical preparation, scene construction, and seating changeover).

Figure 10.15 Transparency in theater, AT&T Performing Arts Center, Dee and Charles Wyly Theater, Dallas, Texas. REX/OMA, 2009. AT&T Performing Arts Center. Photo: Iwan Baan.

Other Innovations in Theater Design

Contemporary theater design continues to expand the opportunities for performing arts education through the integration of new technology and equipment:

- *Flexible floor area at orchestra level (mechanized or manual).* Raked seating at the orchestra level can become flat and the seats can be removed, allowing the space to be used for banquet events.
- *Seating.* The organization of seating into side balconies, parterres, and loge seating allows the house to feel full even when only partially occupied (which is especially important in a student facility).
- *Total room flexibility.* Arena theater, thrust theater, and flat-floor layouts may be combined in one venue through mechanized floor levels and multiple seating and stage configurations.
- *Barn door.* A large barn door can open a venue to the lobby or to the outdoors, increasing flexibility, improving accessibility to interior circulation, and enhancing a sense of openness and light.

CULTURAL CENTERS **CASE STUDY 2**

'62 CENTER FOR THEATRE AND DANCE

Williams College, Williamstown, Massachusetts

Architect: William Rawn Associates, Architects, Inc.
Theater consultant: Theatre Projects Consultants
Acoustician: Acoustic Dimensions

The '62 Center for Theatre and Dance at Williams College supports theater and dance students in their pursuit of artistic excellence and also serves as a world-class summer venue for the Williamstown Theatre Festival. Breaking down barriers between front-of-house and back-of-house activities is central to the design, enhancing the visibility of the performing arts programs among students of all disciplines. Campus pathways weave through the building, giving visitors and students a chance to see theater and dance activities as they walk about campus.

Project Data

- 106,000 GSF new construction
- 20,000 GSF renovation
- 8.21-acre site
- 970 seats in three theaters

> *Timelessness does not necessarily mean glancing backward. . . . While iconic buildings stand apart, the Williams theater and dance center is visually connected to its surroundings, contributing to a broader sense of place.*
>
> —Witold Rybczynski, "When Buildings Try Too Hard," *Wall Street Journal*, November 22, 2008

Connecting Audience and Performers

Each of the four major venues has a very different purpose and character, but in all cases, immediacy and intimacy are paramount:

1. *MainStage Theatre.* Marked by a warm wood interior, the encircling geometry of this 550-seat theater maximizes intimacy by allowing audience members to be aware of each other's presence.
2. *CenterStage Theatre.* Designed as a 200-seat "studio theater," this is a flexible space with a "point of view" (avoiding the pedagogic drawbacks of a totally neutral space). The venue has an industrial character and includes movable balconies, a flexible lift, and a giant steel sliding "barn door" that opens directly onto the CenterStage lobby (see Figure 10.16).

Figure 10.16 CenterStage Theatre. © Robert Benson Photography.

3. *Dance Studio.* The dance studio (50 × 65 ft) features three walls of glass, creating dramatic views to the Berkshire Hills. It serves as both a rehearsal space and a special performance space for small dance productions and music recitals (see Figure 10.17).

Figure 10.17 Transparent dance studio with extensive views and balanced natural light. © Robert Benson Photography.

4. *Renovated Adams Memorial Theatre.* This existing theater was converted to an intimate 250-seat thrust-type theater (a literal theater within a theater).

Breaking Down the Traditional Separation of Front-of-House and Back-of-House Activity

By organizing the building and its circulation pattern to enable students and the public to pass by and engage back-of-house activities (rehearsal spaces, breakout spaces, costume shops, faculty offices), the building celebrates the educational importance of these functions to the art and craft of theater and dance.

Performing Arts on a Liberal Arts Campus: An Emphasis on Connections

Featuring a 20 ft "barn door" that opens the CenterStage Theatre to the lobby, the building is designed to emphasize the importance of interdisciplinary connections on a

Figure 10.18 "Barn door": students walking from the dorms and dining complex encounter the theater activities through the CenterStage Theatre's 20 ft sliding barn door. © Robert Benson Photography.

liberal arts campus (see Figure 10.18). Multiple entrances are positioned to integrate with campus movement patterns, exposing theater and dance to students from all disciplines while maintaining highly active lobby and circulation spaces (see Figure 10.19).

Integrating a Large Building into a Delicate Campus Fabric

The form of the MainStage lobby allows this 126,000 GSF building to follow the consistent rhythm and scale of narrow facades along Main Street. The primacy of the lobby as a glass box helps conceal the scale of the fly tower beyond. The center is perpendicular to Main Street, ensuring the smaller side elevation presents itself to town.

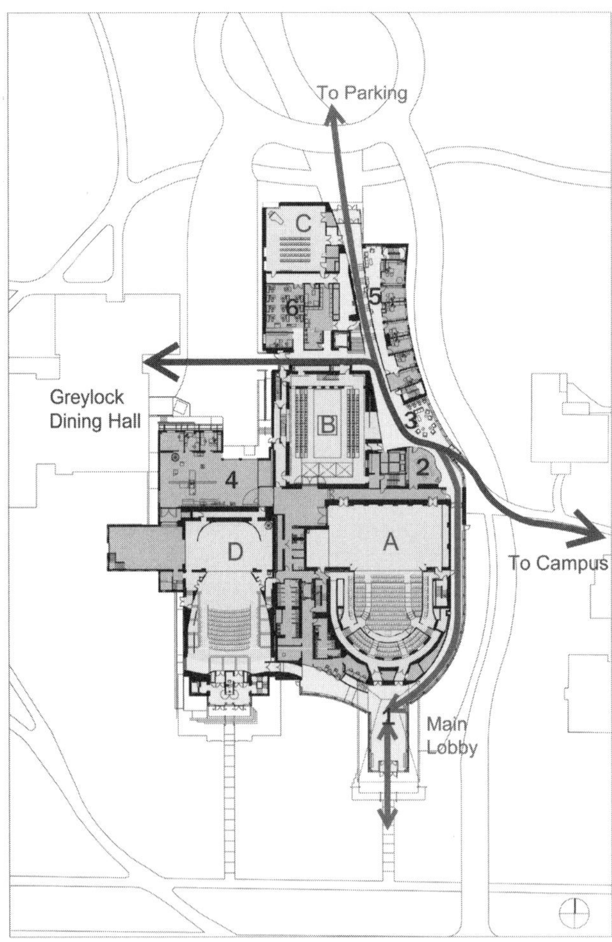

Figure 10.19 Direct cross paths through the building enable all students to be exposed to the excitement and inner workings of the theater and dance departments. Drawing: William Rawn Associates, Architects, Inc.

Rooms for Music

Concert and recital halls are first and foremost designed to provide acoustic excellence. By shaping the hall, defining the appropriate platform size, balancing materials of varying acoustic characteristics, and configuring precise audience-to-performer seating relationships, a room for music is "tuned" to maximize the listening experience (see Figure 10.20).

The mandate for acoustic clarity applies not only to the audience's experience but equally to the interactions between performers onstage. Designing the platform to allow musicians to hear one another playing can contribute as much to performance quality as does the room's broader acoustics. This is particularly true in academic settings with student performers.

The design of a music performance space starts with the development of an appropriately sized platform with strong (acoustically heavy) reflective rear and side walls that project the sound into the room. Defining the platform's size (width and depth) is a key design and program decision that correlates strongly with the overall width of the room as well as the quality of acoustics for various sizes of performer groups. Soloists, small ensembles, and chamber groups require a smaller platform than large orchestras. If the venue needs to accommodate less frequent use by larger orchestras (with choir accompaniment), mechanisms for stage expansion should be integrated into the stage design.

A narrowly proportioned room with tall acoustic volume (shoebox shape) has

Figure 10.20 Natural light and warm materials create intimacy, Seiji Ozawa Hall, Tanglewood Music Center, Lenox, Massachusetts. William Rawn Associates, Architects, Inc., 1994. © 1994 Steve Rosenthal.

historically served well in concert halls, like the Musikverein in Vienna, Austria (Theophil von Hansen, 1870); or the more recent Seiji Ozawa Hall at Tanglewood Music Center in Lenox, Massachusetts (William Rawn Associates, Architects, Inc., 1994), home of the Tanglewood Music Center Summer Fellowship Program for 160 leading young music students (see Figure 10.21). However, there are several notable examples, both old and new, that feature large proportions of seating around the stage. Among these are the Philharmonic Concert Hall in Berlin, Germany (Hans Sharoun, 1963); and the Walt Disney Concert Hall in Los Angeles (Frank Gehry and Partners, 2003).

In academic settings, a single hall is often designed for a variety of uses, ranging from small soloist recitals to larger end-of-year departmental productions to performances by visiting artists. The audience for each of these concert types may vary considerably in size. Organizing seating into discrete sections can allow the hall to feel full even when fewer seats are occupied.

By breaking down the proscenium, through the introduction of side parterres and loge boxes and the careful placement of aisles and balconies, multiple seating orientations are possible. This can allow for audience members in concert halls to be seated very close to performers, creating acoustic and spatial intimacy between performer and audience.

Audience seating around (or even on) the platform, as seen in Amsterdam's Concertgebouw (see Figure 10.22), can be particularly

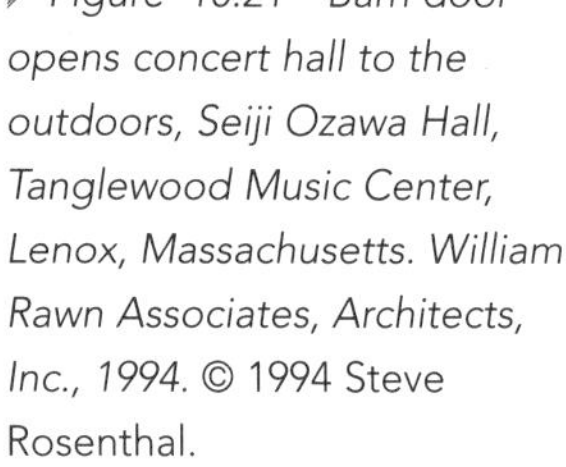

▸ *Figure 10.21 Barn door opens concert hall to the outdoors, Seiji Ozawa Hall, Tanglewood Music Center, Lenox, Massachusetts. William Rawn Associates, Architects, Inc., 1994.* © 1994 Steve Rosenthal.

◀ *Figure 10.22 Seating behind stage, Concertgebouw Concert Hall, Amsterdam, Netherlands. Adolf Leonard van Gendt, 1988.* William Rawn.

useful in an academic setting. These seats can be variably occupied by performers, choral members, or audience members, depending on the stage and audience configuration. Additionally, seats behind the stage can provide a good location for choral rehearsal, a use that is popular among both academic and extracurricular groups.

Variable acoustics are an important element in music rooms, as the deployment of absorptive drapes, particularly for lower frequencies and larger ensembles, dampens the room. Such variable acoustics (often in the form of large drapes and banners) can be exposed and manually operated at one end of the price scale or, alternatively, mechanically operated and concealed behind higher-grade acoustically transparent finish materials (such as grilles, meshes, or screens).

Other key design considerations and details that can contribute to the complexity and high cost per square foot of music spaces include:

- Careful detailing to avoid parallel wall surfaces and to avoid 90-degree corners, preventing unwanted acoustic flutter while still accounting for construction and design complexity
- Solid perimeter walls (and roofs) with significant acoustic mass (thick cast-in-place concrete or solid grouted concrete block) to keep low-frequency noise in while also isolating outside noise
- Thick and complex multilayer details to ensure absence of air spaces within wall assemblies, which can otherwise act as reverberation chambers
- Sound and light locks required at all doors into a hall to avoid outside disturbances
- Stringent penetration criteria and details to provide isolation from unwanted

vibrations for all penetrations of the room's exterior walls, including all wiring, conduit, ductwork, and structure
- Long-spanning structural elements to eliminate columns in large volumes
- Structural isolation to eliminate vibration through structure
- Slow-moving air in large ductwork to minimize duct noise
- Five-row limit in balcony overhangs to minimize trapped sound reflections, which can result in greater length of auditorium volume than is normal for theaters

Transparency in Music Spaces

Unlike in theaters, where natural light is unwanted during productions, natural light can be both welcome and desired in music spaces. This is true during both rehearsal and performance, as natural light and views to the exterior can provide a more pleasant environment (with adequate glare protection). These glazed music spaces can be located on any floor level, including at grade. Another value of transparency is that it enables active interior spaces to animate exterior campus spaces—a quality that is enhanced by the high utilization of music spaces.

Note that while many eighteenth- and nineteenth-century music performance halls incorporated natural light, twentieth-century halls tended not to. In 1994, Seiji Ozawa Hall, Tanglewood Music Center, Lenox, Massachusetts, opened with extensive windows on all four sides. Since then, others have followed, including the New World Symphony, Miami Beach, Florida (2011); the Emerson Concert Hall, Emory University, Atlanta, Georgia (2003); the Studzinski Recital Hall, Bowdoin College, Brunswick, Maine (2007); Mixon Hall, Cleveland Institute of Music (2007); and the Shalin Liu Performance Center, Rockport, Massachusetts (2010). Even Boston's Symphony Hall, which boarded its windows during World War II, reopened them in 2008.

To maintain acoustic integrity, music spaces typically use special laminated glass, often with large air spaces between multiple glass surfaces and often with a slightly angled interior glass surface to reflect sound toward the ceiling. Due to the high cost of this acoustic glazing, extremely large expanses of glass are not very common (except in locations with minimal external noise).

CULTURAL CENTERS
CASE STUDY 3

STUDZINSKI RECITAL HALL
Bowdoin College, Brunswick, Maine

Architect: William Rawn Associates, Architects, Inc.
Theater consultant: Theatre Projects Consultants, Inc.
Acoustician: Kirkegaard Associates

Project Data

- 19,000 GSF renovation
- 282-seat recital hall; rehearsal room; nine practice rooms
- Summer home for the prestigious Bowdoin International Music Festival
- Adjustable acoustical curtains accommodate a range of programs, including classical music, jazz, world music, electronic music, and lectures and projections (see Figure 10.23)

Located in the center of the campus just off the main quad, the 282-seat Studzinski Recital Hall is built within

Figure 10.23 Intimacy and natural light in a recital hall. © Robert Benson Photography.

the existing Curtis Pool, a historic McKim, Mead & White building that had been dormant for 20 years (see Figure 10.24). The transformation from Curtis Pool into Studzinski Recital Hall brings new life to this long-dormant campus landmark and preserves the college's extraordinary collection of McKim, Mead & White Buildings (over a dozen buildings). The pool's high-volume, column-free space and massive brick walls provide a natural home for this new performance space (see Figure 10.25).

Figure 10.24 Curtis pool circa 1928. Bowdoin College Archives.

Figure 10.25 Completed recital hall, 2007. © Robert Benson Photography.

Transforming a Campus Landmark

The decision to reuse the existing structure rather than finding a site for a new building on the periphery of the campus provides a prominent central location for the recital hall, appropriate to the central role of the arts in a liberal arts education.

Interior Renovation

The heavy base-supporting exterior walls of the existing building, along with its free span and lofty volume, were a perfect fit for a reinvention as a music building:

- All new interior partitions and finishes; state-of-the-art acoustic system, audiovisual system, theater equipment, and lighting
- New life safety systems; mechanical, electrical, and plumbing (MEP) systems; two-well geothermal system; full accessibility

Innovation: Brass Mesh Pylons

Ten perforated brass mesh pylons are central to the embracing spatial intimacy of the hall. The pylons cantilever 15 ft above the side aisles, supported by a bent steel moment frame. The two layers of brass mesh enclose an adjustable acoustical curtain, which helps to tune the high-frequency sound response of the hall. These acoustically transparent elements allow sound to penetrate to heavy base-supporting masonry walls and additional volume of catwalk space.

An Intimate, Nurturing Space for Student Performers

Central to the design was the vision of the hall as a warm, inviting space, defined by the insertion of two embracing curved forms along the north and south edges of the building. These curved edges introduce a strong, memorable geometry within the existing shell and are defined by crisply detailed natural birch paneling and a series of 10 freestanding pylons tautly clad in brass mesh. Audience seating extends all around the hall, including along this curved edge, creating at once a unified room with a strong sense of community between audience and performer and an exceedingly intimate shared experience among audience members as they see across to each other's facial expressions during a performance (see Figure 10.26).

Figure 10.26 In addition to its role as the college's principal music venue, the facility serves as a teaching and rehearsal space. © Robert Benson Photography.

Rooms for Dance

Dance programs on college campuses, which historically originated in athletics, are now commonly cultivated through theater departments and, increasingly, becoming popular as independent departments. For accredited dance programs, required spaces include performance venues, rehearsal studios (with specific minimum dimensions), changing areas directly adjacent to studios, and physical therapy facilities.

While flat-floor dance studios can be used for smaller performances in academic settings, the primary venue for larger-scale dance performances is often the campus's main proscenium theater. For this reason, dance-specific requirements (for floors, lighting, and dressing rooms) should be considered in planning a proscenium theater.

Floor area and room proportions are key components to the design of dance studios. Room width is often tied directly to the width of the proscenium in the main theater. Around the sides and rear of the dance area (typically 24 by 30 ft at minimum), wing space for dancer entry and circulation routes must be added.

If a dance studio needs to accommodate fixed or retractable risers, these must be added to the room length outside of the dance area. In this case, adequate setbacks are essential to ensure that the audience has clear sight lines to performers' feet—a critical feature of performance spaces for dance.

Other important components of a dance studio include one wall of 8 ft tall mirrors, sprung floors, dance barres, an elevated control booth, and pipe grids for lighting. Ease of circulation to elevated control booths is an early planning imperative (see Figure 10.27).

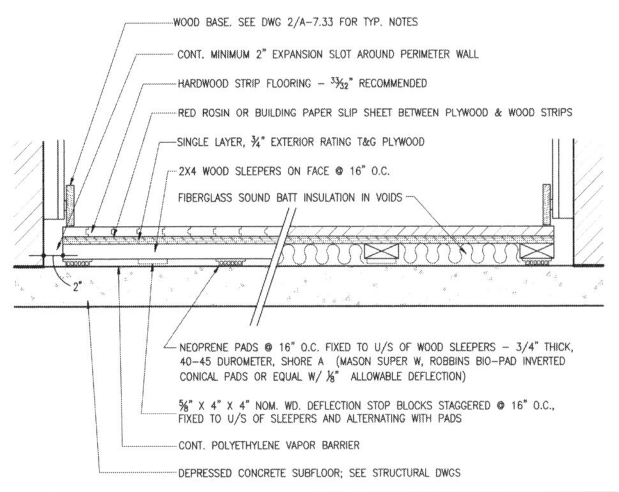

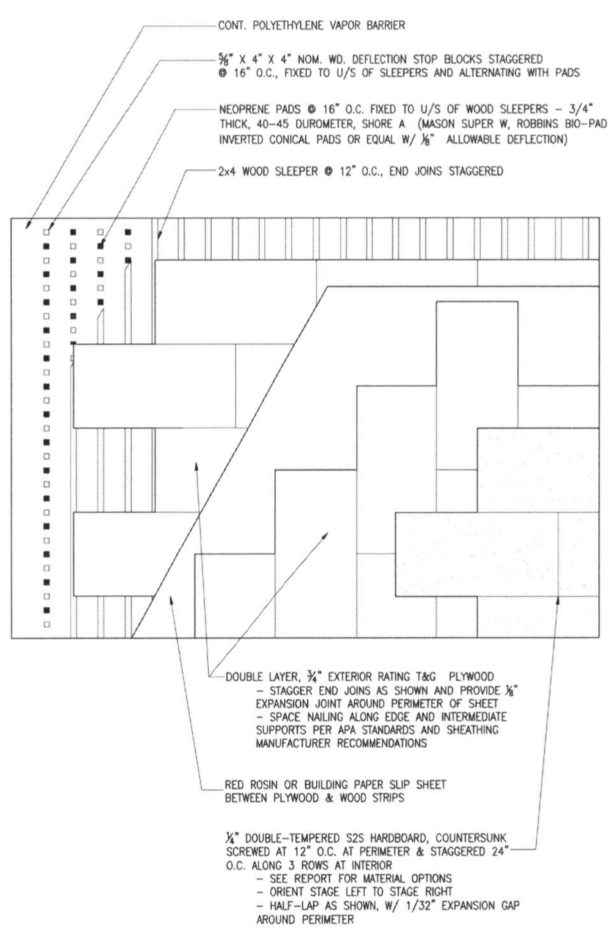

▲ *Figure 10.27 (a) Section detail of a sprung floor and (b) plan detail of a dance floor.* Drawing: William Rawn Associates, Architects, Inc.

Transparency in Dance Spaces

Abundant controlled natural light is desirable in dance studios, including floor-to-floor glazing. To achieve large amounts of glass, dance studios are best located on the second floor or above so that dancers can look out without people being able to look directly in. In addition, the glass should be designed to avoid glare and to minimize exposure with either north-facing glass or external shades. Motorized glare control and blackout curtains can provide additional flexibility. Moreover, provisions for cycloramas, backdrops, dance barres, and radiant heating should be incorporated at or near the perimeter walls.

Balanced daylight without glare can be achieved with significant glass on two sides of the studio, allowing the third wall to be used as a dance mirror surface and the fourth side for audience seating.

Large expanses of glass can animate the exterior of the building, providing a campus beacon at night and also offering the possibility for dance studios to serve as campuswide multipurpose spaces (see Figures 10.28 and 10.29). As tall, flat-floor spaces, dance studios are well suited (with adequate floor protection) for nondance functions.

Rooms for Visual Arts

Visual arts spaces fall into two main categories: galleries and studios. Galleries are secure, acoustically controlled environments for the display and viewing of artwork, while studios are teaching spaces that may accommodate a wide range of art production activities, classes, lectures, and critiques (see Figure 10.30).

▸ *Figure 10.28 Gallery as lobby and interior path connecting campus front door to the School of Architecture, Sam Fox School of Design and Visual Arts, Washington University, St. Louis, Missouri. Maki and Associates, 2006.* Maki and Associates.

▸ *Figure 10.29 Transparency in gallery space, Bowdoin College Museum of Art, Brunswick, Maine. Machado and Silvetti Associates, 2007.* Photo by Facundo de Zuviria.

◀ *Figure 10.30 Visual arts studio with robust daylight, Yale Sculpture Building, Yale University, New Haven, Connecticut. Kieran Timberlake, 2007.* © Peter Aaron/Esto.

Galleries

In a campus setting, a gallery can satisfy a range of purposes: a customized space to house a permanent collection, a flexible space for revolving exhibitions, or an informal space for student exhibits. For gallery space to be accredited as museum space, it must meet standards specified by the American Association of Museums.

For public exhibit space, circulation strategies shape how prescribed or self-directed the visitor experience is, thus framing the sequence in which an individual walks through the space. Museum and exhibition spaces typically follow one of three layouts:

Open-plan type. Defined by wide, open spaces and very few divisions, this type of organization provides little direction to visitors, instead encouraging visitors to determine their own path through the galleries. Examples include the Weisman Art Museum, University of Minnesota, Minneapolis; the Nerman Museum of Contemporary Art, Johnson County Community College, Overland Park, Kansas; and the Allen Memorial Art Museum, Oberlin College, Oberlin, Ohio.

Linear path type. Defined by a clear progression of gallery spaces from start to finish, this organization uses linear pathways to direct visitors through an exhibition. Examples include the Wexner Center for the Arts, Ohio State University, Columbus; and the Davis Museum, Wellesley College, Wellesley, Massachusetts.

Combination type. By mixing various sizes of rooms and hallways and reducing the sense of hierarchy of spaces, this type of exhibition space offers a varied experience. Examples include the British Art Center, Yale University, New Haven,

Connecticut; the List Visual Arts Center, Massachusetts Institute of Technology, Cambridge; and the Blanton Museum of Art, University of Texas, Austin.

Studios

Studio spaces provide teaching and work areas for a range of activities, including drawing, painting, sculpture, printmaking, ceramics, photography, and digital media. Studio spaces can be characterized as "clean" or "dirty" (depending on their function) and as more flexible or more fixed (due to heavy equipment or specific exhaust requirements). Maximizing the flexibility of studio spaces is favorable in the long term and requires reexamining levels of toxicity in specialized studios (as discussed later in the section on mechanical systems).

An artist-in-residence studio is a program element with interesting possibilities. When located among other studios, it embeds an outside perspective in the heart of day-to-day teaching. When located among gallery spaces, the artist-in-residence studio can create a dynamic connection between production space and exhibition space. Opening the studio to temporary gallery spaces allows the studio to expand into the gallery for exhibitions featuring the artist-in-residence and also provides extra gallery space when the studio is not in use by a resident artist.

The proliferation of digital studios is an increasing trend in visual arts buildings, where the quantity of digital studios and the intensity of their use day and night is on the rise. Digital studios are well placed to act as a bridge between disciplines, both within the visual arts and between the visual and performing arts. One such example is a computer dance studio planned for the University of Maryland, Baltimore County, which combines a digital classroom with a glass wall opening with a dance studio. The classroom can act as a control room for recording and streaming dance works or for orchestrating projected images with dance performance within the studio (designed by William Rawn Associates, Architects, Inc. with Grimm + Parker Architects).

"Crit space" (informal pinup areas where students can present their work and receive criticism from faculty, guest critics, and fellow students) is an important part of the visual arts pedagogy and can be included in studios as well as in more public areas. Strategically placing crit spaces to overlook public areas can enliven the sense of community in arts buildings and reinforce the important role of collective review and critique.

Transparency in Visual Arts Spaces

Indirect and balanced daylighting in visual arts spaces is desirable, particularly in fine arts studios (see Figure 10.31). Balanced daylight is created when daylight comes from more than one direction (thus avoiding glare caused by a single exposure). To avoid direct sunlight on horizontal working surfaces, glazing should take advantage of the northern exposure and use shading devices as required for other exposures. Other types of rooms within arts centers, such as galleries, film studios, and photography labs, may require extensive daylight control. In major exhibition areas, such as museum halls, a careful combination of indirect daylighting and artificial lighting is necessary to prevent light damage to displayed works of art and to maintain an even level of visibility throughout the day and evening (see Figure 10.34). While visual connections to the outdoors and to interior circulation are welcome in arts studios, privacy for spaces using live models should be accounted for.

◀ *Figure 10.31 Daylighting pottery studio, Bucksbaum Center for the Arts, Grinnell College, Grinnell, Iowa. Pelli Clarke Pelli Architects.* © Jeff Goldberg/Esto.

CULTURAL CENTERS
CASE STUDY 4

NERMAN MUSEUM OF CONTEMPORARY ART
Johnson County Community College, Overland Park, Kansas

Architect: Kyu Sung Woo Architects

Art, Architecture, and Everyday Life

Located in the suburbs of Kansas City, Kansas, the museum constitutes an important center for art and education. Its shape contrasts with the existing context, marking its presence on the campus and the adjoining landscape. The museum space is linked to the outdoors through expansive glazing on the ground-floor lobby and strategically placed windows on the upper level (see Figure 10.32).

Figure 10.32 Nerman Museum of Contemporary Art, exterior. Tim Hursley.

Gateway to Campus

The museum is a landmark for the college, distinguishing the campus entry from adjacent, well-traveled regional roads. This distinction is solidified by a 1.5-acre sculpture garden stretching from the museum to the knolls at the edge of the campus and to the bordering roads. A 22 ft cantilever off the main gallery space above the entrance is enhanced by a permanent light-emitting diode (LED) display, which extends the lantern-like effect of the glass facade (see Figure 10.33).

Figure 10.33 This connection to sunlight, and to the campus beyond, makes the new museum a building of the landscape—architecture that is always conscious of its place on the plains in Kansas. Tim Hursley.

Spaces for Art

The exhibition galleries are housed in a solid light-controlled volume that hovers above the open lobby function below. Gallery spaces are understated, focusing on the distribution of natural light from clerestories, and organized around circulation paths that provide a choice, views between galleries and connection to the sculpture garden and the campus beyond (see Figure 10.34).

Figure 10.34 Light-filled galleries. Tim Hursley.

The Changing Role of the Arts on Campus

In order to fully understand the imperatives of today's campus arts centers, it is important to reflect on current trends in the design and varied use of these facilities.

In their methods, media, and protocols of collective experience, the performing arts in the twentieth century remained faithful to their historical roots. The digital revolution of the twenty-first century, however, has introduced a technologically savvy generation to the arts with an entirely new understanding of production, authorship, and information sharing, a generation that is entirely comfortable with evolving new media (see Figure 10.35).

This "pro-amateur" generation of artists and audiences is rapidly influencing wider audience preferences. Patrons are voting

◀ *Figure 10.35 Twenty-first-century performance space, Le Poisson Rouge, New York, New York.* Anton Brookes.

with their feet (reflected perhaps in the increase in digital content and diminishing ticket sales for traditional modes of performance) and provoking important larger questions regarding the current and future direction of the performing and visual arts. (These concepts were broadly discussed at Dartmouth College's 2010 symposium, "The Arts Center of the 21st Century," at the Hopkins Center for the Arts.[5])

With the integration of new technologies, the explosion of artists/scholars with dual training, and the increasing commitment to cross-disciplinary collaboration within the arts, the very nature of the more traditional performing arts is evolving both across campuses and, more broadly, across society.

Twentieth-century performance can be defined by

- Venue as "high temple" for the arts
- Presentation or production modes
- Open to those who pay
- Passive audiences
- Specialized spaces

Twenty-first-century performance can be defined by

- Venue as flexible workshop
- Technological adeptness
- Accessibility to a broader audience; audience participation
- Collaboration and experimentation
- Transparency

For the planning of arts centers on campuses today, the most immediate expressions of this evolution appear to be a greater desire for transparency and a more participatory arts culture, where not all performance needs must be met by the stage (see Figure 10.36).

5 On June 23–24, 2010, the Hopkins Center for the Arts at Dartmouth College cohosted, with Major University Presenters (MUPS), a symposium on "The Arts Center of the 21st Century." The symposium's agenda had emerged as the result of planning by a working committee among several campuses which are members of MUPS—all with an eye toward future capital renovation or expansion projects on their campuses. The principal theme of the convening was to learn from artists and practitioners where their work and their interests are leading them, and how those directions might affect the physical manifestations of future arts centers. Details are available online at http://hop.dartmouth.edu/uncategorized/arts-of-the-21st-century.

▸ *Figure 10.36 Light-filled gallery space, Bucksbaum Center for the Arts, Grinnell College, Grinnell, Iowa. Pelli Clarke Pelli Architects, 1998. © Jeff Goldberg/Esto.*

The following planning and programmatic ideas for performance spaces are likely to see greater demand in the cultural context identified previously:

- Mechanized flexible spaces
- Interdisciplinary arts centers
- Transparency in the creative act
- Transparency in public space
- Experimental media
- Nondepartmentally specific spaces
- Expanded role of public space
- Building as performative object

Finally, it should be noted that evolving new structures of revenue sharing, funding, and venue types in the commercial performing arts realm may influence the future nature of the arts in academic settings. At performance venues such as Le Poisson Rouge (New York City) and the Orange Peel (Asheville, North Carolina), performances are provided in more informal and flexible settings. In some such venues, the performer receives the proceeds of ticket sales while the venue profits from the sale of alcohol in the event space.

The primary innovation here is that such venues are attracting not only musicians but also artists of all media who the night prior may have been performing in a traditional venue such as Carnegie Hall. The lesson from these commercially driven market trends is that the preferences of performers and audiences are changing and, with them, so is the exclusive desire for traditional venues for the arts.[6]

This recent evolution in the role of the arts is particularly relevant to college and university facilities, where young performers and artists cultivate the skills to continue driving the trend of rapid innovation and entrepreneurship. Centers for the arts on campuses must recognize, and indeed embrace, the ever-expanding opportunities found in new technology.

6 As derived from presentations at the June 2010 symposium on "The Arts Center of the 21st Century" at the Hopkins Center for the Arts at Dartmouth College, cohosted with Major University Presenters (MUPS).

INDEX

INDEX

INDEX

INDEX